English
ocabulary
in Use

Michael McCarthy
Felicity O'Dell

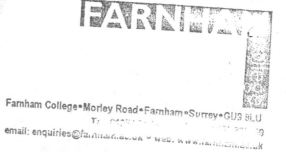

CAMBRIDGE
UNIVERSITY PRESS

PUBLISHED BY THE PRESS SYNDICATE OF THE UNIVERSITY OF CAMBRIDGE
The Pitt Building, Trumpington Street, Cambridge, United Kingdom

CAMBRIDGE UNIVERSITY PRESS
The Edinburgh Building, Cambridge CB2 2RU, UK
40 West 20th Street, New York, NY 10011–4211, USA
10 Stamford Road, Oakleigh, VIC 3166, Australia
Ruiz de Alarcón 13, 28014 Madrid, Spain
Dock House, The Waterfront, Cape Town 8001, South Africa

http://www.cambridge.org

First published 1994
Thirteenth printing 2001

Typeset in Sabon [CE]

Printed in the United Kingdom at the University Press, Cambridge

A catalogue record for this book is available from the British Library

ISBN 0 521 423961

Contents

Introduction

Word formation

Connecting and linking

Countables and uncountables

Topics

Notional concepts

Feelings and actions

Fixed expressions

Phrasal verbs and verb-based expressions

Varieties of English

Acknowledgements

We are particularly grateful to Jeanne McCarten and Geraldine Mark at Cambridge University Press who provided us with so much clear-sighted help and creative guidance at all stages during the writing of this book. We should also like to thank Stuart Redman for his thorough and invaluable report on the initial manuscript. We are grateful to students and staff at various institutions who assisted in piloting the materials: Jon Butt and Elaine Smith, International House, London; Nick Kenny, International Language Academy, Cambridge; Brigitte Marrec, Université Paris X, France; Suzanne Pilot, Lycée Blaise Pascal, Longuenesse, France; Tony Robinson, Eurocentre, Cambridge; Ian Scott, Centre for English Language Education, University of Nottingham; Karen Thompson, International House, Toulouse, France; Clare West, English Language Centre, Hove. Lastly, we thank Nóirín Burke at CUP who took over the management of the manuscript in its final stages.

The authors and publishers would like to thank the following for permission to reproduce copyright material in *English Vocabulary in Use*. While every effort has been made, it has not been possible to identify the sources of all the material used and in such cases the publishers would welcome information from the copyright holders.

p.2: extract from *The English Language* by David Crystal (Penguin Books, 1988), copyright © David Crystal, reproduced by permission of Penguin Books Ltd.; p.10: definition of 'malignant' from the *Oxford Advanced Learner's Dictionary of Current English*, edited by A. S. Hornby (fourth edition 1989), reproduced by permission of Oxford University Press; p.10: definition of 'hairy' and p.11: definition of 'casual' both from *Collins COBUILD English Language Dictionary* (1987), reproduced by permission of HarperCollins Publishers; p.90: extract from *Fodor's Ireland*, Fodor's Travel Publication (1989); p.92: extract from *The Cambridge Encyclopedia* by David Crystal (1991), Cambridge University Press.

Illustrations by Amanda MacPhail, Kathy Baxendale and Ken Brooks.

Using this book

Why was this book written?

It was written to help you to improve your English vocabulary. It will help you to learn not only the meanings of words but also how they are used. You can use this book either with a teacher or for self-study.

How is the book organised?

The book has 100 two-page units. In most units, the left-hand page explains the words and expressions to be studied in that unit. Where appropriate, it gives information about how the words are used as well as their meaning. The right-hand page checks that you have understood the information on the left-hand page by giving you a series of exercises practising what you have just learnt. Occasionally the right-hand page will also teach you some more new words.

There is a key at the back of the book. The key does not always simply give you one right answer. It sometimes also comments on the answers and will help you learn more about the words studied in the unit.

There is an index at the back of the book. This lists all the words and phrases covered in the book and refers you to the units where these words or phrases are discussed. The index also tells you how difficult and unusual words are pronounced. It uses the International Phonetic Alphabet to do this and the symbols you need to know are listed at the beginning of the index.

How should I use this book?

The book is divided into a number of sections. Complete the seven introductory units first. These units not only teach you some useful new vocabulary but they also help you with useful techniques for vocabulary learning in general. After completing those units, you might want to work straight through the book or you might prefer to do the units in any order that suits you.

What else do I need in order to work with this book?

You need some kind of vocabulary notebook or file where you can write down the new words you are learning. (See Unit 3 for advice on how to do this.)

You also need to have access to a couple of good dictionaries. This book selects the words that are most important for you to learn at your level and it gives you the most important information about those words but you will sometimes need to refer to a dictionary as well for extra information about meaning and usage. Firstly, you need an English-English dictionary for foreign learners. Good ones are The *Cambridge International Dictionary of English*, the *Longman Dictionary of Contemporary English*, the *Oxford Advanced Learner's Dictionary* and the *Collins Cobuild English Language Dictionary,* for example. Secondly, you will also find a good bilingual dictionary useful. Ask a teacher to recommend a good bilingual dictionary for you. (See Unit 5 for advice on using your dictionaries.)

1 Learning vocabulary – general advice

A What do you need to learn?

1 How many words are there in English? At least:
   a) 10,000   b) 100,000   c) 250,000   d) 500,000

2 Winston Churchill was famous for his particularly large vocabulary. How many words did he use in his writing?
   a) 10,000   b) 60,000   c) 100,000   d) 120,000

3 How many words does the average native English speaker use in his/her everyday speech?
   a) 2,500   b) 5,000   c) 7,500   d) 10,000

4 How many words make up 45% of everything written in English?
   a) 50   b) 250   c) 1,000   d) 2,500

To sum up, there are many words you don't need at all and there are other words that you simply need to understand when you read or hear them. Finally, there are words which you need to be able to use yourself. Clearly you need to spend most time learning this last group.

In the text below mark the words you'd like to be able to use.

> English vocabulary has a remarkable range, flexibility and adaptability. Thanks to the periods of contact with foreign languages and its readiness to coin new words out of old elements, English seems to have far more words in its core vocabulary than other languages. For example, alongside kingly (from Anglo-Saxon) we find royal (from French) and regal (from Latin). There are many such sets of words which add greatly to our opportunities to express subtle shades of meaning at various levels of style.

You probably marked many words that you would like to be able to use. Unless you are studying linguistics, however, you probably need only to understand, rather than to use, the verb 'coin' as used in the context above.

B What does knowing a new word mean?

- It is not enough just to know the meaning of a word. You also need to know:
  a) what words it is usually associated with
  b) whether it has any particular grammatical characteristics
  c) how it is pronounced
- Try to learn new words not in isolation but in phrases.
- Write down adjectives together with nouns they are often associated with and vice versa, e.g. royal family; rich vocabulary.
- Write down verbs with the structure and nouns associated with them, e.g. to add to our knowledge of the subject; to express an opinion.
- Write down nouns in phrases, e.g. in contact with; a train set; shades of opinion.
- Write down words with their prepositions, e.g. at a high level; thanks to your help.
- Note any grammatical characteristics of the words you are studying. For example, note when a verb is irregular and when a noun is uncountable or is only used in the plural.
- Make a note of any special pronunciation problems with the words you're learning.

1 How could you record the following?
   a) **chilly** b) **dissuade** c) **king** d) **up to the ears** e) **independent** f) **get married**
2 What would you record beside the following words?
   a) **scissors** b) **weather** c) **teach** d) **advice** e) **lose** f) **trousers**
3 What might you note beside the following words?
   a) **comb** b) **catastrophe** c) **photograph/photographer**

C

Can you learn just by reading or listening to English?

You will certainly help yourself to learn English vocabulary not only by studying with this book but also by reading and listening to English. Give each of the items on the lists below a mark from 0 to 4 describing how important this way of learning vocabulary could be for you personally. *Example*: newspapers 3

newspapers   TV (cable / subtitled)   cinema   magazines   video
radio (e.g. BBC World Service)   academic or professional literature   fiction
simplified readers (with or without cassettes)
music or other cassettes   talking to native speakers

D

What should you do when you come across new words?

When you are reading something in English, don't look up every new word or expression or you will soon get fed up. Only look up something that is really important for understanding the text. When you have finished reading, look back at what you have read and then perhaps look up some extra words and write down new expressions that interest you.

Similarly when you listen to English don't panic when you hear some words or expressions that you don't know. Keep listening and the overall meaning will often become clear.

When you read or listen to English it is sometimes possible to guess the meaning of a word you don't know before you look up or ask its meaning. Decide first what part of speech the word is and then look for clues in its context or form.

Before you read the text below, check whether you know what the underlined words mean.

> A tortoise is a <u>shelled</u> <u>reptile</u> <u>famed</u> for its slowness and <u>longevity</u>. The Giant Tortoise of the Galapagos may attain over 1.5 metres in length and have a <u>lifespan</u> of more than 150 years. Smaller tortoises from Southern Europe and North Africa make popular pets. They need to be <u>tended</u> carefully in cool climates and must have a warm place in which they can <u>hibernate</u>.

Which of the marked words can you perhaps guess from the context or from the way the word is formed? Guess and then check whether you were correct by using a dictionary. Some words are impossible to guess from context or the structure of the word. In such cases, ask someone or go to a dictionary for help.

E

How are you going to plan your vocabulary learning?

1 How many words and expressions do you intend to learn each week?
   a) 5   b) 10   c) 15   d) more than 15
2 Where and when are you going to learn them?
   a) on your way to school or work   b) before dinner   c) in bed   d) other
3 How often are you going to revise your work?
   a) once a week   b) once a month   c) before a test   d) once a year

2 Learning vocabulary – aids to learning

A Help yourself to learn by learning associated words together

Learn words with associated meanings together.

Learning words together that are associated in meaning is a popular and useful way of organising your vocabulary study.

1 Complete this network for the word CAT. Add as many other bubbles as you like.

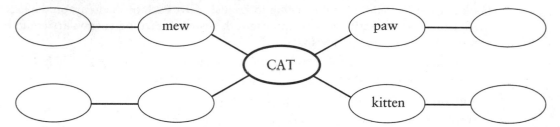

If possible, compare your network with those done by other students. Add any of their ideas that you like to your network.

Learn words with a grammatical association together.

2 Here are some groups of words, each of which has a grammatical connection. Can you see what the connection is? What other words could you add to these groups?

   a) **child tooth ox**   b) **cut split burst**   c) **information furniture food**

Learn together words based on the same root.

3 Can you add any words or expressions to these two groups?

   a) **price priceless overpriced**
   b) **handy single-handed give me a hand**

B Pictures and diagrams can help you learn

Here are some ways in which pictures might help you to remember vocabulary.

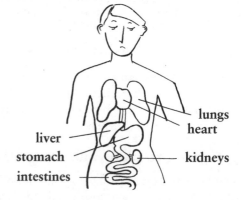

Can you draw any pictures that would help you remember the following vocabulary?

   a circle   to look a gift horse in the mouth   screwdriver

Word trees can be useful.

1 Look at the word tree for **holiday**. Now complete a tree for **school**.

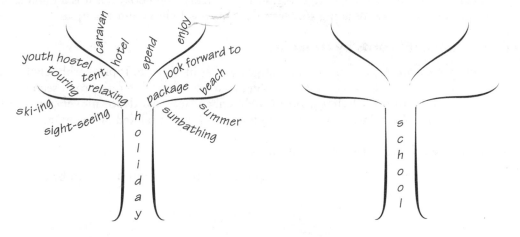

Word forks are good ways of learning adjectives and verbs.

2 Look at the complete word forks below. Finish the others.

original			shoot			magnificent			kick		
brilliant			edit			breathtaking			hit		
unusual	idea		direct	a film		superb	view		bounce	a ball
great			star in							
excellent			review							

Matrices can also clarify collocations.

This book will sometimes use matrices to help to clarify word associations. Look at the following example of a matrix:

	a car	a motorbike	a train	a horse	a plane
to fly					+
to drive	+		+		
to ride		+		+	

3 Now complete the following sentences.
   a) She has always wanted to have the chance to .... a train.
   b) Russian women are not allowed to .... passenger aircraft.
   c) .... a motorbike can be very dangerous.

You will do more practice with these and other ways of writing down vocabulary in Unit 3.

3 Organising a vocabulary notebook

There is no one correct way to organise a vocabulary notebook, but it is a good idea to think about possible ways of doing so. Here are some possibilities and examples.

A Organising words by meaning

This book divides vocabulary into a large number of different topics, probably far too many for a notebook, but you could try dividing your book into different broad sections, with sections for **words for feelings, words to describe places, words for movement, words for thinking**, etc. In this way you can build families of words related in meaning.

B Using various types of diagrams

Words that can be grouped under a heading or a more general word can be drawn as a tree-diagram. (See also Unit 2.)

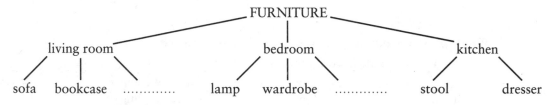

The dotted lines mean that you can add more words to the tree as you meet them.

A bubble-network is also useful, since you can make it grow in whatever direction you want it to. (See Unit 2.)

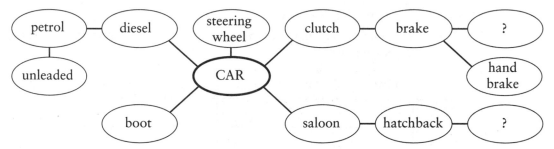

C Organising by word-class

A Spanish learner of English, Angeles, gave us an interview on how she marks word-class in her personal notebook. This is what she said:

'What I have just started doing is to write them depending on if they are verbs or nouns or adjectives or phrases. If they are phrases I write them in red and also the definition. If they are verbs, in black, and blue if they are nouns...And if I write the Spanish translation I write it in another colour, so it's easy to see...I draw some pictures too.'

D

When you meet a synonym or an antonym of a word you already have in your book, enter it next to that word with a few notes:

urban ≠ rural   stop = cease (more formal)

Exercises

3.1 Here is a list of words a Spanish learner of English has made in her vocabulary notebook. How could she improve them and organise them better?

> clock – reloj
> tell the time – decir la hora
> rush – darse prisa
> office – despacho
> beneath }
> under   }
> I must rush – tengo prisa/tengo que correr
> drowsy – the room was hot and I got drowsy
> wristwatch – reloj de pulsera
> What time do you make it?
> next to – junto a/al lado de
> hands – the minute-hand (minutero)
> wide-awake (fully awake)

3.2 Here is a word-map, a variation on the bubble-network. What word do you think should go in the middle of the diagram?

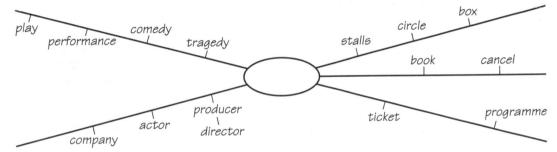

3.3 One learner we interviewed said he tested himself regularly with his notebook, covering up the word and trying to guess it from the translation he had written or from any other notes he had made. This was his system:

1 If the notes and/or translation were clear but he could not get the word, he made a small red mark in the margin. If any word got three red marks, then it needed extra attention and a special effort to learn it.

2 If the notes and/or translation could not help him guess what the word might be, then the word got a blue mark. A blue mark meant 'Write more information about this word!'

What is your testing system? Try to make one if you have not got one, or ask other people what they do. Try your system out and decide whether it needs improving.

3.4 Making tables for word-classes is a good idea, since you can fill in the gaps over time. What do you think this learner will put in the remaining gaps in the table?

noun	verb	adjective	person
production	produce	....	producer
industry	....	industrial	....
export	....	....	....

4 The names of English language words

A The names of basic parts of speech in English

article adjective noun verb adverb preposition conjunction pronoun gerund

A good student works hard at her books and she enjoys learning.

B Words relating to nouns

Look at the sentence *An artist loves beauty*; *artist* is **countable**, i.e. it has a plural form (artists), but *beauty* is **uncountable**; *artist* is the **subject** of the verb as it describes who does the verb; *beauty* is the **object**, i.e. what is affected by the verb.

C Words relating to verbs

infinitive (to go)   **-ing form** (going)   **past participle** (gone)

Go (go, gone, went) is an **irregular** verb whereas *live* (live, lived, lived) is **regular**. *Go* is also **intransitive** because it does not need an **object**, e.g. *Has Luis gone? Make* is **transitive** because it is followed by an **object** – you make something.

D Words relating to the construction of words

In the word, *irregularity*, *ir-* is a **prefix**, *regular* is a **root** and *-ity* is a **suffix**. *Fat* is the **opposite** or **antonym** of *thin* and *plump* is a **synonym** of *fat*. A **word family** is a set of words based on one **root**, e.g. *word, wordy, to reword*. A **phrase** does not include a **main verb** – 'in a word' is an example of a **phrase**. A **sentence** has a **main verb**; it begins with a **capital letter** and ends with a **full stop**.

E Words relating to pronunciation

A **syllable** is the minimum sound unit of a language consisting of one vowel and any consonants on either side. There are three **syllables** in the word 'minimum' (the first is *mi*, the second is *ni* and the third is *mum*) and the **stress** is on the first **syllable**. **Onomatopoeia** means forming words that sound like their meaning, e.g. **moo, buzz**.

F Words and their associations

Register means a style of speaking or writing appropriate to a particular social situation. Thus, **slang** is an extremely informal **register** and is only used by people who know each other very well. **Colloquial** is an adjective referring to language that is suitable mainly for conversation, e.g. *He's a nice guy.* **Pejorative** describes words which have a negative association. *Pig-headed* is **pejorative** whereas *determined*, which is very close in meaning, is not. **Collocation** refers to words which frequently occur together, e.g. *torrential rain, auburn hair*.

G Words describing punctuation

.	full stop	,	comma	;	semi-colon	'	apostrophe
-	hyphen	–	dash	!	exclamation mark	?	question mark
( )	brackets	" "	inverted commas	ANNE	block capitals		

Exercises

4.1 Look at the paragraph about register in F opposite. Find at least three examples of each of the following:

1 nouns ....
2 verbs ....
3 adjectives ....
4 adverbs ....
5 prepositions ....

4.2 Considering the words in their context in F opposite, mark the nouns you've written in 4.1 with a C (countable) or *UC* (uncountable). Mark the verbs *R* (regular) or *IR* (irregular) and *T* (transitive) or *IT* intransitive.

4.3 Complete the following table.

verb	infinitive	-ing form	past participle
define	to define	defining	defined
mean	to mean	meaning	meant
write	to write	writing	wrote

4.4 Think about the word *informal*.

1 What is its root, its prefix and its suffix?
2 What is its opposite or antonym?
3 Has it got any synonyms?
4 What words are included in its word family?
5 Use it in (a) a phrase and (b) a sentence.

4.5 Look at all the words in bold in sections E, F and G opposite. In each case mark which syllable is stressed.

4.6 Match the following colloquial words with their more formal equivalents below.

1 chat (verb)   2 loo   3 chap   4 put up with   5 fiddle (noun)

    man   violin   lavatory   converse   tolerate
       fiddle   loo   chat

4.7 The following pairs of words are close in meaning but one word in each case is pejorative. Which?

1 terrorist / freedom-fighter   3 fluent / wordy   5 cunning / shrewd
2 slim / skinny   4 mean / thrifty   6 generous / extravagant

4.8 Give examples of collocations based on the words *noun*, *word* and *colloquial*.

Example: uncountable noun

4.9 Cover the left-hand page and write the names of the following punctuation marks.

( ) ....   ? ....   ' ....
; ....   — ....   - ....
, ...   " " ....

5 Using your dictionary

Good dictionaries can tell you a lot more about a word than just its meaning, including (among other things):

- Synonyms and their differences, e.g. **mislay** and **lose**
- Antonyms (opposites), e.g. **friend** ≠ **enemy/foe**
- Collocations (how words go together), e.g. **auburn** combines only with **hair** (or connected words, e.g. **curls**)
- Pronunciation: this will mean learning some symbols which are different from the letters of the English alphabet.

θ	th in **thick**	ð	th in **then**	tʃ	ch in **church**
ʃ	sh in **she**	dʒ	j in **jam**	ʒ	s in **pleasure**
ŋ	ng in **ring**	æ	a in **bad**	ɒ	o in **top**
ɔː	o in **form**	ʊ	u in **put**	ə	a in **about**
ʌ	u in **up**	ɜː	i in **bird**		

Most other symbols look just like ordinary letters of the English alphabet and their pronunciation is not so hard to guess. But check the table given in the index.

- Word stress: often shown by a mark before the syllable to be stressed or by underlining, e.g. əd'ventʃə/, /<u>wes</u>tən/. Make sure you know how your dictionary marks stress.
- Usage: how a word is used and any special grammàtical pattern that goes with it, e.g. **suggest** + clause (not an infinitive) – I suggest you ring her right away.
- Whether a word is used for people and/or things. For example, look at this entry for **malignant**:

> **ma·lig·nant** /məˈlɪgnənt/ *adj* **1** (of people or their actions) feeling or showing great desire to harm others; malevolent: *a malignant slander, attack, thrust.* **2 (a)** (of a tumour) growing uncontrollably, and likely to prove fatal: *The growth is not malignant.* **(b)** (of diseases) harmful to life.
> ▷ **ma·lig·nancy** /-nənsɪ/ *n* **1** [U] state of being malignant. **2** [C] malignant tumour.
> **ma·lig·nantly** *adv.*

- Word-class (usually abbreviations **n**: noun, **adj**: adjective, etc.), whether a noun is countable or uncountable, and whether a verb is normally transitive (needs an object) or intransitive (doesn't need an object).

Don't forget that most words have more than one meaning. In this example, only the second meaning corresponds to the way **hairy** is used in this sentence:

It was a really **hairy** journey on the mountain road.

> **hairy** /ˈhɛərɪˈ/, **hairier, hairiest**. **1** Someone or something that is **hairy** is covered with hair. ᴇɢ ...*a plump child with hairy legs*... ...*a big, hairy man*... *The function of a mammal's hairy coat is to insulate the body.*   ADJ QUALIT
> **2** If you describe a situation as **hairy**, you mean that it is exciting, worrying, and rather frightening; a very informal use. ᴇɢ *It got a little hairy when we drove him to the station with less than two minutes to spare.*   ADJ QUALIT = nerve-racking, scary

Exercises

5.1 With a *bilingual* dictionary, try a double search: look up a word in your language; the dictionary may give several possibilities in English. Look up each of those possibilities in the English section of the dictionary to see how they translate back into your language. This may help you to separate synonyms.

If you own a dictionary, make a little mark in the margin each time you look a word up. If a word gets three or more marks, it is worth an extra effort to learn it. What other learning techniques are there for dictionaries?

5.2 Small, bilingual dictionaries often just give three or four translations for a word you look up, without any explanation. Here are some pictures with translations you might find in such a dictionary. Which ones fit in the sentences? You may need to use a monolingual dictionary.

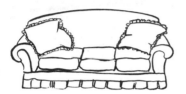

sofa   divan   boots   bootees   sailing boat   ketch
couch   settee   wellingtons   dinghy   yacht

1 Come and sit on the .... and relax a while.
2 She bought a huge, luxury .... and went off round the world.
3 If you're going to stand in the water you should take your ....
4 It's not a proper yacht; it's just a tiny little ....

5.3 Which definition of *casual* fits which sentence?

casual /ˈkæʒuʲəl/, **casuals. 1** Something that is **casual 1.1** happens or is done by chance or without planning. EG *Her casual remark caused a political storm... ...a casual meeting.* ◇ **casually.** EG *...a casually acquired object.* **1.2** is rather careless and done without much interest. EG *I had a casual glance at the papers... ...a casual friendship.* ◇ **casually.** **2** If you are **casual**, you are, or you pretend to be, calm and not very interested in what is happening or what you are doing. EG *He tried to appear casual as he asked her to dance... ...a casual wave.* ◇ **casually.** EG *I walked casually into his room.* ◇ **casualness.** EG *With studied casualness he mentioned it to Hilary.* **3 Casual** clothes are clothes that are suitable for when you are at home or doing things other than working, but are not suitable for work or formal occasions. EG *...a casual shirt.* ▸ used as a plural noun. EG *...smart casuals.* ◇ **casually.** EG *He was dressed casually.* **4 Casual** work is done for only a short time, and not on a permanent or regular basis. EG *They employ casual workers to pick the fruit... ...a casual job.*

ADJ CLASSIF ⇑ accidental
◇ ADV WITH VB
ADJ CLASSIF = superficial
◇ ADV WITH VB
ADJ QUALIT = nonchalant. unconcerned
◇ ADV WITH VB
◇ N UNCOUNT
ADJ CLASSIF: ATTRIB ⇑ informal
▸ N PLURAL
◇ ADV WITH VB
ADJ CLASSIF: ATTRIB = temporary

1 It was quite a casual outfit, just right for such an informal occasion. (definition no. ....)
2 I only said it casually, but it shocked her. (.........)
3 I don't get a salary; I'm just a casual. (.........)
4 It was just a casual encounter, but it changed my life. (.........)

5.4 Pronunciation. What English words are these?

1 /edʒuˈkeɪʃən/ *education*   4 /ˈlɪbəti/ *liberty*
2 /ˈpæspɔːt/ *passport*   5 /rəˈvɪʒən/
3 /ˈleŋθ/   6 /ˈbrʌðə/ *brother*

5.5 In the dictionary entry for *hairy* opposite how many synonyms can you see for the different meanings?

6 Revising vocabulary

Here is an extract from a psychology book on the importance of revising in an active way.

> Probably the commonest fault among students is failure to realise that learning is essentially an active process. Too many students sit for hours passively reading and re-reading notes and textbooks, without ever attempting actively to recall what they have read. The fallacy of this method has been amply shown by experiments.
>
> The same principles apply to more advanced forms of learning: for effective memory, some form of active expression is essential. The student, therefore, should read through the material he wants to master with close attention and should then reproduce the main points aloud or produce a written summary…An hour's concentrated work of this kind is more effective than three hours' passive reading.
>
> (From *A Modern Introduction to Psychology*, Rex and Margaret Knight)

B Revising with this book

When you revise a unit, first read it through. Then look at anything you wrote in your vocabulary notebook connected with the unit.

Then, and most importantly, try to do something different with the new words and expressions in that unit in order to help fix them in your memory.

Here are some suggestions:

- Highlight (or underline) any words and expressions that you had forgotten or were not sure about.

- Look at the unit and choose ten words and expressions that you particularly want or need to learn. Write them down.

- Look up any words that you selected in an English-English dictionary. Do these words have any other uses or associations that might help you learn them? Looking up the verb, **wish**, for example, might lead you to **wishbone** or **wishful thinking**. Write anything that appeals to you in an appropriate phrase or sentence.

- Perhaps the dictionary can also help you find some other words based on the same root. Looking up the noun, **employment**, will lead you to the verb, **employ**, to the nouns, **employer** and **employee**, and, perhaps, to the adjectives **employable**, **unemployed** and **self-employed**.

- Write down the words and expressions you wish to learn in phonetic script. Use a dictionary to help you.

- Write down the words and phrases from a unit in your notebook in a different way – put them into a network or a table, perhaps.

- The next day, ask yourself again: How much can I remember?

- Test yourself. Cover part of a word or phrase. Can you remember the complete word or phrase?

When you have done all the steps above that you feel will be useful to you, close your book and notebook and remind yourself of what you have been studying. How much can you remember?

C   Making the new words active

One of the great advantages of revising vocabulary is that it should help you to make the step from having something in your passive vocabulary to having it in your active vocabulary.

Encourage this process by:

- writing the words and expressions you are trying to learn in a sentence relating to your life and interests at the moment.
- making a point of using the new words and expressions in your next class or homework.
- keeping a learning diary in which you note down things that particularly interest you about the words you have learnt.
- watching out for the words and expressions you are trying to learn in your general reading of English. If you come across any of them in use, write them down in their context in your diary or notebook.
- writing a paragraph or story linking the words and expressions you want to learn.

D   What can you remember?

1   What do you remember now from the first six units in this book? Answer without looking back at the units.

2   Now read through the units again.

3   How much do you remember about the units now?

4   Choose at least one word and expression from each unit and work through all the suggestions made in B and C above. It may not always be appropriate in your future study to do all the steps in B but try them now for practice.

E   Some plans for your work with this book

1   How often are you going to revise what you have done? (Every week? Every five units?)

2   Which techniques are you going to use for revising?

3   Now write yourself some notes to remind yourself of when you are going to revise. You might like, for instance, to write *revise vocabulary* in your diary for the next eight Fridays, if you decided to revise every week. Alternatively you could write **REVISE** in capital letters after, say, every five units in the book.

7 Formal and informal words

Formality is all about your relationship with the person you're speaking or writing to. If you use formal language, it may be because you wish to show respect, politeness, or to put yourself at a distance (for example, 'official' language). Informal language can show friendliness, equality or a feeling of closeness and solidarity with someone. You should *never* use informal language just to sound fluent or clever.

A Scales of formality

Some groups of words can be put on a scale from (very) formal to (very) informal.

very formal	neutral	very informal
offspring	children	kids
abode/residence	house/flat	place
alcoholic beverages	drink	booze

B Short, monosyllabic informal words

Informal versions of words are often short and monosyllabic, as we can see in the right-hand column in the table in A. They include slang words. (Unit 95 has more examples.)

It cost me ten **quid**.　[pounds]
I'll help you peel the **spuds**.　[potatoes]
My **bike**'s been stolen.　[bicycle]
I always go by **tube**.　[word used for the London Underground]
Come and meet my **Mum** and **Dad**.　[mother and father]
Hi! Can't stop; see you, **bye**!　[hello; goodbye]
The milk's in the **fridge**.　[refrigerator]

C Clippings

Shortening a word tends to make it less formal, as in **fridge** and **bye** in B.

I'll meet you in the **lab**(oratory).　What's on **telly** tonight?　[television]
We should put an **ad**(vertisement) / an **advert**(isement) in the (news)**paper**.
Shall I (tele)**phone** them?
Her sister's a **vet**(erinary surgeon).

D Formality in notices, instructions, etc.

You will often see rather formal words in notices and suchlike. Make sure you know the meaning of the words used so that you could tell someone what the notice says using less formal words.

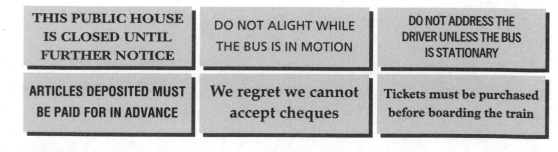

THIS PUBLIC HOUSE IS CLOSED UNTIL FURTHER NOTICE

DO NOT ALIGHT WHILE THE BUS IS IN MOTION

DO NOT ADDRESS THE DRIVER UNLESS THE BUS IS STATIONARY

ARTICLES DEPOSITED MUST BE PAID FOR IN ADVANCE

We regret we cannot accept cheques

Tickets must be purchased before boarding the train

Exercises

7.1 If you look up an informal word in a monolingual dictionary, you will often find a neutral equivalent as part of the definition or explanation. For example, the Collins COBUILD dictionary entry for *kid* says: A *kid* is a *child*; an informal use.

Use a monolingual dictionary to find neutral or more formal words for these:

1 kip   2 a pal   3 a chap   4 cheerio   5 swot   6 ta!   7 brainy

7.2 Make this conversation more *informal* by changing some of the words. Refer to the left-hand page if necessary.

JIM: Annie, can you lend me five pounds?

ANNIE: What for?

JIM: Well, I have to go and visit my mother and father, and my bicycle's not working, so I'll have to take a taxi.

ANNIE: Can't you telephone them and say you can't come?

JIM: Well, I could, except I want to go because they always have lots of food, and the refrigerator at our flat is empty, as usual.

ANNIE: Can't you go by Underground?

JIM: Erm…

ANNIE: Anyway, the answer's no.

7.3 Say whether you feel the following remarks/sentences are *okay, too formal* or *too informal* for each situation described. If the remark/sentence is unsuitable, suggest what the person might say instead.

1 (*Teenage boy to teenage girl at disco*): D'you fancy an appointment one night next week?

2 (*Parent to another parent at a school parents meeting*): How many offspring do you have at the school?

3 (*Dinner-guest to host/hostess*): No thanks, I never consume alcoholic beverages when I'm driving.

4 (*Student to University Professor*): Will there be lab demonstrations next week?

5 (*Business letter to a newspaper office*): Dear Sir/Madam,
I should like to enquire about the current charges for ads in your paper. My company is considering… etc.

7.4 Mini-quiz: Find words on the left-hand page for the following.

1 The opposite of **stationary**.
2 The opposite of **to board**.
3 a) to be sorry   b) to buy   c) to speak to
4 Informal versions of **Greetings!** and **Farewell!**

7.5 Express these notices in neutral or informal language.

1

> **Children are requested not to deposit litter in the play-area**

2

> Expenses can only be reimbursed upon production of dated receipts

(See also Units 95 and 96 for other informal and formal words and expressions.)

8 Suffixes

Suffixes can change the word-class and the meaning of the word.

A Common noun suffixes

-er /ə/ is used for the person who does an activity, e.g. **writer, worker, shopper, teacher.**
You can use -er with a wide range of verbs to make them into nouns.

Sometimes, the /ə/ suffix is written as -or instead of -er. It is worth making a special list of these as you meet them, e.g. **actor, operator, sailor, supervisor.**

-er/-or are also used for things which do a particular job, e.g. **pencil-sharpener, bottle-opener, grater, projector.**

-er and -ee can contrast with each other meaning 'person who does something.' (-er) and 'person who receives or experiences the action' (-ee), e.g. **employer/employee, sender/addressee, payee** (e.g. of a cheque).

-(t)ion /ʃ(ə)n/ is used to make nouns from verbs.

> complication   pollution   reduction   alteration   donation   admission

-ist [person] and -ism [activity or ideology]: used for people's politics, beliefs and ideologies, and sometimes their profession (compare with -er/-or professions above),
e.g. **Marxism, Buddhism, journalism, anarchist, physicist, terrorist.**

-ist is also often used for people who play musical instruments, e.g. **pianist, violinist, cellist.**

-ness is used to make nouns from adjectives. Note what happens to adjectives that end in -y: **goodness, readiness, forgetfulness, happiness, sadness, weakness.**

B Adjective suffix

-able/-ible /əbl/ with verbs, means 'can be done'.

> drinkable   washable   readable   recognizable   countable   forgivable

Examples with -ible: **edible** (can be eaten)   **flexible** (can be bent)

C Verbs

-ise (or -ize) makes verbs from adjectives, e.g. **modernise, commercialise, industrialise.**

D Other suffixes that can help you recognise the word class

> -**ment:** (nouns) excitement   enjoyment   replacement
> -**ity:** (nouns) flexibility   productivity   scarcity
> -**hood:** (abstract nouns especially family terms) childhood   motherhood
> -**ship:** (abstract nouns especially status) friendship   partnership   membership
> -**ive:** (adjectives) passive   productive   active
> -**al:** (adjectives) brutal   legal   (nouns) refusal   arrival
> -**ous:** (adjectives) delicious   outrageous   furious
> -**ful:** (adjectives) forgetful   hopeful   useful
> -**less:** (adjectives) useless   harmless   cloudless
> -**ify:** (verbs) beautify   purify   terrify

Note: the informal suffix -ish, which can be added to most common adjectives, ages and times to make them less precise, e.g. She's **thirtyish**. He has **reddish** hair. Come about **eightish.**

Exercises

8.1 The *-er/-or, -ee* and *-ist* suffixes. Use the suffixes to give the names of the following.

Example: A person who plays jazz on the piano. *a jazz pianist*

1 The thing that wipes rain off your car windscreen. *windscreen wiper*
2 A person who plays classical violin. *classical violinist*
3 A person who takes professional photographs. (**N.B.** pronunciation)
4 A person who acts in amateur theatre.
5 The person to whom a cheque is made out.
6 A machine for washing dishes.
7 A person who donates their kidneys upon their death. *donor*
8 The person to whom a letter is addressed.

8.2 Each picture is of an object ending in *-er*. Can you name them?

8.3 List six jobs you would like to have in order of preference. How many different suffixes are there in your list? Do any of the job names not have a suffix? (e.g. pilot, film star)

8.4 Do these words mean a thing, a person, or both?

| 1 a cooker | 3 a ticket-holder | 5 a cleaner | 7 a drinker |
| 2 a typewriter | 4 a record player | 6 a smoker | |

8.5 Spelling changes. Rewrite each sentence by changing the underlined words, using a suffix from the left-hand page. Make any spelling changes needed.

1 Most of his crimes can be <u>forgiven</u>.
  Most of his crimes are ...... *forgivable* ....
2 The Club refuses to <u>admit</u> anyone not wearing a tie.
  The Club refuses .... to anyone not wearing a tie.
3 Her only fault is that she is <u>lazy</u>.
  Her only fault is ... *laziness* ....
4 This firm has <u>produced</u> a lot in recent years.
  This firm has been very .... *productive* .... in recent years.
5 I found the book very <u>easy and pleasant to read</u>.
  I found the book very ....

8.6 Can you think of anything in your country which should be *nationalised* (e.g. banks, steel works), *standardised, modernised, computerised* or *centralised*?

8.7 Which word is the odd one out in each group and why?

1 brotherhood   neighbourhood   manhood   priesthood
2 hair-restorer   plant-holder   step-ladder   oven-cleaner
3 appointment   involvement   compliment   arrangement
4 tearful   spiteful   dreadful   handful
5 worship   kinship   friendship   partnership

9 Prefixes

Prefixes are often used to give adjectives a negative meaning. The opposite of 'comfortable' is 'uncomfortable', the opposite of 'convenient' is 'inconvenient' and the opposite of 'similar' is 'dissimilar'. Other examples are 'unjust', 'inedible', 'disloyal'. Unfortunately, there is no easy way of knowing which prefix any adjective will use to form its opposite. When you learn a new adjective note down whether it has an opposite formed with a prefix and, if so, what it is.

Note:

- in- becomes im- before a root beginning with 'm' or 'p', e.g. immature, impatient, impartial, improbable. Similarly in- becomes ir- before a word beginning with 'r', and il- before a word beginning with 'l', e.g. irreplaceable, irreversible, illegal, illegible, illiterate.

- The prefix in- does not always have a negative meaning – often it gives the idea of inside or into, e.g. internal, import, insert, income.

Although it is mainly adjectives which are made negative by prefixes, **un-** and **dis-** can also form the opposites of verbs too, e.g. appear **dis**appear. The prefix is used here to reverse the action of the verb. Here are some more examples: **dis**agree, **dis**approve, **dis**believe, **dis**connect, **dis**credit, **dis**like, **dis**mount, **dis**prove, **dis**qualify, **un**bend, **un**do, **un**dress, **un**fold, **un**load, **un**lock, **un**veil, **un**wrap, **un**zip.

Many other prefixes are used in English. Here is a list of prefixes which are useful in helping you to understand unfamiliar words. Some of these words are used with a hyphen. Check in a dictionary if you're not sure.

prefix	meaning	examples
anti	against	anti-war antisocial antibiotic
auto	of or by oneself	autograph auto-pilot autobiography
bi	two, twice	bicycle bi-monthly biannual bilingual
ex	former	ex-wife ex-student ex-president
ex	out of	extract exhale excommunicate
micro	small	micro-computer microwave microscopic
mis	badly/wrongly	misunderstand mistranslate misinform
mono	one/single	monotonous monologue monogamous
multi	many	multi-national multi-purpose multi-racial
over	too much	overdo overtired oversleep overeat
post	after	postwar postgraduate post-revolutionary
pro	in favour of	pro-government pro-revolutionary
pseudo	false	pseudo-scientific pseudo-intellectual
re	again or back	retype reread replace rewind
semi	half	semicircular semi-final semi-detached
sub	under	subway submarine subdivision
under	not enough	underworked underused undercooked

Exercises

9.1 Practise using words with negative prefixes. Contradict the following statements in the same way as the example. Not all the words you need are on the left-hand page.

Example: He's a very honest man. *I don't agree. I think he's dishonest.*

1 I'm sure she's discreet.
2 I always find him very sensitive.
3 It's a convincing argument.
4 That's a very relevant point.
5 She's always obedient.
6 He's very efficient.
7 I always find her responsible.
8 He seems grateful for our help.
9 I'm sure she's loyal to the firm.
10 He's a tolerant person.

9.2 Which negative adjective fits each of the following definitions?

1 *unmarried* means not having a husband or wife.
2 *inedible* means impossible to eat.
3 .... means unable to read or write.
4 *unemployed* means not having a job.
5 .... means fair in giving judgement, not favouring one side.
6 *irreplaceable* means unable to be replaced.

9.3 Choose a negative verb from B to fit each of the sentences below. Put it in the correct form.

Example: The runner was *disqualified* after a blood test.

1 Children (and adults) love *unwrapping* parcels at Christmas time.
2 I almost always find that I *disagree* with his opinion.
3 I'm sure he's lying but it's going to be hard to *disprove* his story.
4 After a brief speech the Queen .... the new statue.
5 It took the removal men an hour to *unload* our things from the van.
6 His phone was .... because he didn't pay his last bill.

9.4 Answer the following questions. The answers are all in the table opposite.

1 What kind of oven cooks things particularly fast?
2 What kind of drug can help somebody with an infection? *antibiotic*
3 What kind of company has branches in many countries?
4 How does a passenger aeroplane normally fly?
5 What is a student who is studying for a second degree?
6 What means 'underground railway' in the US and 'underground passage' in the UK?

9.5 Using the table opposite construct words or phrases to replace the underlined words.

Example: He's <u>in favour of the American approach</u>. *He's pro-American.*

1 The BBC tries to avoid <u>pronouncing</u> foreign words <u>incorrectly</u>.
2 Most people say they <u>have to work too hard but are paid too little</u>.
3 He <u>dated his cheque with a date that was later than the real date</u>.
4 She's still on good terms with <u>the man who used to be her husband</u>.
5 He made so many mistakes in the letter that he had to <u>write it again</u>.

9.6 Think of two more examples for each prefix in C opposite.

10 Roots

A Many words in English are formed from a set of Latin roots with different prefixes and suffixes. Knowing the roots of such words may help you to remember or guess their meaning when you see them in context. These words are usually fairly formal. In their formation, they can perhaps be seen as the Latinate, formal, equivalent of phrasal verbs.

B Here are some examples of the more common Latin roots, with some of the verbs derived from them. In each case an example sentence is given with the meaning of the verb in brackets at the end. You'll find some easier to understand than others.

spect: see, look
You should **respect** your parents / the laws of a country.   [look up to]
The police **suspected** he was guilty but they had no proof.   [had a feeling]
Many pioneers travelled west in America to **prospect** for gold.   [search]

vert: turn
I tried a word-processor but I soon **reverted** to my old typewriter.   [went back]
Missionaries went to Africa to **convert** people to Christianity.   [change beliefs]
The royal scandal **diverted** attention from the political crisis.   [took attention away]

port: carry, take
How are you going to **transport** your things to the States?   [send across]
Britain **imports** cotton and **exports** wool.   [buys in, sells out]
The roof is **supported** by the old beams.   [held up]

duc, duct: lead
She was **educated** abroad.   [went to school]
He **conducted** the orchestra with great vigour.   [led]
Japan **produces** a lot of electronic equipment.   [makes]

press: press, push
She was **impressed** by his presentation.   [full of admiration and respect]
This weather **depresses** me.   [makes me feel miserable]
She always **expresses** herself very articulately.   [puts her thoughts into words]

pose, pone: place, put
The meeting has been **postponed** until next week.   [changed to a later date]
The king was **deposed** by his own son.   [put off the throne]
I don't want to **impose** my views on you.   [force]

C Above you only have examples of verbs. Note that for all the verbs listed, there is usually at least one noun and at least one adjective as well. Here are some examples.

verb	person noun	adjective	abstract noun
inspect	inspector	inspecting	inspection
advertise	advertiser	advertising	advertisement
deport	deportee	deported	deportation
introduce	introducer	introductory	introduction
oppress	oppressor	oppressive	oppression
compose	composer	composite	composition

Exercises

10.1 Complete as much as possible of the table with other forms of some of the words presented in B. Use a dictionary to help you if necessary.

verb	person noun	adjective	abstract noun
convert			
produce	*producer*	*productive*	*production*
conduct	*conductor*	*conductive*	
impress		*impressive*	
support	*supporter*	*supportive*	
impose			

10.2 Fill in the gaps in the sentences below using words from the table in C.

1 We stayed in a town surrounded by high mountains. I found it very ...*oppressive*....... .
2 He ...*was deported*........ from the USA for having a forged passport.
3 The magazine seems to have nothing in it but ...*advertisement*....... for cosmetics.
4 May I ....*introduce*........... you to my boss?
5 The tax ...*inspector*......... decided I owed a lot of money.
6 The new take-away pizza service has a very good .... offer.
7 Business people always say that it pays ....
8 Tchaikovsky ......*composed*............ some wonderful ballet music.

10.3 Can you work out the meanings of the underlined words in the sentences below?
To help you, here are the meanings of the main Latin prefixes:

    intro: within, inward   **o, ob**: against   **in, im**: in, into   **re**: again, back

    de: down, from   **ex**: out   **sub**: under   **trans**: across

1 She's a very <u>introspective</u> person and he's also very <u>introverted</u>.
2 He always seems to <u>oppose</u> everything I suggest.
3 They have a very good <u>induction</u> programme for new staff in that company.
4 I don't think it is healthy to <u>repress</u> one's emotions too much.
5 Perhaps you can <u>deduce</u> what the word means from the way it is formed.
6 The documentary <u>exposed</u> corruption in high places.
7 She tried hard to <u>suppress</u> a laugh.
8 She <u>transposed</u> the music for the flute.

10.4 Think of three other words based on each of the roots listed in B opposite. Put each into an appropriate phrase.

10.5 Pair the formal verbs below with their phrasal verb equivalents.

    support ¹put off ³oppose ⁴look at ²cut down deposit hold up
    ¹postpone turn away ⁴inspect ³go against divert ²reduce put down

11 Abstract nouns

A An abstract noun is one which is used to mean an idea, experience or quality rather than an object. Thus **happiness**, **intention** and **shock** are abstract nouns whereas, for example, pen, bed and trousers are not.

B There are a number of suffixes which are used particularly frequently in the formation of abstract nouns. Some of the most common are **-ment**, **-ion**, **-ness** and **-ity**.

Note: **-ment** and **-ion** are usually used to make verbs into abstract nouns whereas **-ness** and **-ity** are added to adjectives; **-ion** sometimes becomes **-tion**, **-sion**, **-ation** or **-ition**.

Here are some examples of abstract nouns using those suffixes.

achievement	action	aggressiveness	absurdity
adjustment	collection	attractiveness	anonymity
amazement	combination	bitterness	complexity
discouragement	illusion	carelessness	curiosity
improvement	imagination	consciousness	generosity
investment	production	permissiveness	hostility
replacement	recognition	tenderness	prosperity
retirement	reduction	ugliness	sensitivity

C Less common suffixes associated with abstract nouns are **-ship**, **-dom**, **-th** and **-hood**.

Note: **-ship** and **-hood** are usually used in combination with other nouns whereas **-th** combines with an adjective to form an abstract noun and **-dom** can combine with either a noun or an adjective.

Here are some examples of abstract nouns using those suffixes.

apprenticeship	boredom	breadth	adulthood
companionship	freedom	depth	brotherhood
membership	kingdom	length	childhood
ownership	martyrdom	strength	motherhood
partnership	stardom	warmth	neighbourhood
relationship	wisdom	width	(wo)manhood

D There are also a large number of abstract nouns which do not use any suffix at all. Here are some examples of these.

anger	belief	calm	chance
faith	fear	humour	idea
luck	principle	rage	reason
sense	sight	speed	thought

You will find more examples of the use of suffixes in Units 8 and 10 and of abstract nouns in Units 68 and 69.

Exercises

11.1 What is the abstract noun related to each of the following adjectives? All the nouns are formed in ways described on the opposite page although not all are listed opposite.

Example: affectionate *affection*

1 affectionate	5 amused	9 attentive	13 equal
2 excited	6 graceful	10 happy	14 hopeful
3 kind	7 original	11 popular	15 resentful
4 secure	8 stupid	12 weak	16 wise

11.2 Find at least one more noun using each of the suffixes in B and C.

11.3 Which abstract noun on the opposite page is a synonym of each of the following?

Example: animosity *hostility* or *aggressiveness*

1 animosity	5 substitution	9 vision
2 astonishment	6 fame	10 liberty
3 inquisitiveness	7 decrease	11 fury
4 fraternity	8 area	12 wealth

11.4 Complete the following table.

abstract noun	adjective	verb	adverb
contentment	content(ed)	to content	contentedly
argument	....	argue	arguably
emptiness	empty	to empty	emptily
intensity	....	....	....
satisfaction	satisfied	to satisfy	....
sentiment	....	....	....
strength	....	....	....

11.5 Which of the words in the list below is being described in the following quotations?

love   permanence   hope   jealousy   happiness   beauty

1 '.............................. is no more than feeling alone among smiling enemies.'
2 '.............................. is like coke; something you get as the by-product of making something else.'
3 '.............................. is the power of being cheerful in circumstances which we know to be desperate.'
4 '.............................. is a universal migraine.'
5 'The British love .... more than they love..............................'

11.6 Write your own quotations to describe the following abstract nouns.

1 freedom   2 friendship   3 life   4 curiosity   5 imagination

12 Compound adjectives

A compound adjective is an adjective which is made up of two parts and is usually written with a hyphen, e.g. **well-dressed, never-ending** and **shocking-pink**. Its meaning is usually clear from the words it combines. The second part of the compound adjective is frequently a present or past participle.

B

A large number of compound adjectives describe personal appearance.
Here is a rather **far-fetched** description of a person starting from the head down.

*Tom was a **curly-haired**, **sun-tanned**, **blue-eyed**, **rosy-cheeked**, **thin lipped**, **broad-shouldered**, **left-handed**, **slim-hipped**, **long-legged**, **flat-footed** young man, wearing an **open-necked** shirt, **brand-new**, **tight-fitting** jeans and **open-toed** sandals.*

C

Another set of compound adjectives describes a person's character. Here is a rather **light-hearted** description of a girl. The meanings are explained in brackets.

Melissa was **absent-minded** [forgetful], **easy-going** [relaxed], **good-tempered** [cheerful], **warm-hearted** [kind] and **quick-witted** [intelligent] if perhaps a little **big-headed** [proud of herself], **two-faced** [hypocritical], **self-centred** [egotistical] and **stuck-up** [snobbish (colloquial)] at times.

D

Another special group of compound adjectives are those where the second part is a preposition. Some of these adjectives are listed below with a typical noun.

an **all-out** strike [total]   a **burnt-out** car [nothing left in it after a fire]
a **broken-down** bus [it won't work]   a **built-up** area [lots of buildings in it]
a **hard-up** student [poor]   **cast-off** clothes [no longer wanted by the owner]
worn-out shoes [can't be worn any more; of people – exhausted]
a **drive-in** movie [you watch from your car]   **well-off** bankers [wealthy]
a **run-down** area [in poor condition]

E

Here are some other useful compound adjectives.

air-conditioned	bullet-proof	cut-price	drip-dry
duty-free	hand-made	interest-free	last-minute
long-distance	long-standing	off-peak	part-time
record-breaking	remote-controlled	second-class	so-called
sugar-free	time-consuming	top-secret	world-famous

F

You can vary the compound adjectives listed by changing one part of the adjective. For example, **curly-haired, long-haired, red-haired** and **straight-haired; first-hand** (knowledge), **first-class** (ticket) and **first-born** (child).

Exercises

12.1 Fill each of the blanks to form a new compound adjective. Use a dictionary if necessary.

1 .... - eyed   5 .... - made
....
....

2 .... - proof   6 .... - free
....
....

3 .... - minded   7 .... - headed
....
....

4 .... - necked   8 .... - hearted
....
....

12.2 Put the words in E opposite into any categories which will help you learn them.

12.3 List as many compound adjectives beginning with *self*, as you can. Mark them *P* or *N for* positive or negative characteristics, or write *neutral*.

12.4 Answer the questions by using a compound adjective which is opposite in meaning to the adjective in the question. Note that the answer may or may not have the same second element as the adjective in the question.

Example: Is he working full-time? *No, part-time.*

1 Isn't she rather short-sighted?   4 Are her shoes high-heeled?
2 Is your brother well-off?   5 Is this vase mass-produced?
3 Would you say the boy's well-behaved?   6 Do they live in south-east England?

12.5 Think of two nouns that would frequently be associated with any ten of the compound adjectives listed in E opposite.

12.6 Add a preposition from the list below to complete appropriate compound adjectives.

back   up   out   off   on   of

1 She's been doing the same low-paid job for so long that she's really fed-
.....up........ with it now.
2 The two cars were involved in a head-....on........ collision.
3 He has a very casual, laid-....back..... approach to life in general.
4 It'll never happen again. It's definitely a one-....off....... situation.
5 He's a smash hit here but he's unheard-.....of....... in my country.
6 She bought a cut-....out........ paper pattern and made her own dress.

12.7 Which of the adjectives from this unit could you use to describe yourself and other students in your class or members of your family?

13 Compound nouns – combinations of two nouns

A A compound noun is a fixed expression which is made up of more than one word and functions as a noun. Such expressions are frequently combinations of two nouns, e.g. **address book, human being, science fiction.** A number of compound nouns are related to phrasal verbs and these are dealt with in Unit 14.

B Compound nouns may be written as two words, e.g. **tin opener, bank account,** or they may be written with a hyphen instead of a space between the words, e.g. **pen-name, baby-sitter.** Some expressions are occasionally written with a hyphen and occasionally as two separate words. For instance, both **letter box** and **letter-box** are correct. Sometimes they may be written as one word, e.g. **earring.**

C Compound nouns may be countable, uncountable or only used in either the singular or the plural. There are examples of each of these types below. Check that you understand the meanings of each of the expressions listed. If you understand both elements of the expression, the meaning will usually be clear. If the meaning is not fairly obvious, then it is provided below.

D Usually the main stress is on the first part of the compound but sometimes it is on the second part. The word which contains the main stress is underlined in the compound nouns below.

Here are some examples of common countable compound nouns.

<u>alarm</u> clock	<u>assembly</u> line	<u>blood</u> donor	<u>book</u> token
<u>burglar</u> alarm	<u>contact</u> lens	<u>credit</u> card	<u>handcuffs</u>
<u>heart</u> attack	<u>package</u> holiday	<u>pedestrian</u> crossing	<u>shoe</u> horn
<u>tea</u>-bag	<u>windscreen</u>	<u>windscreen</u> wiper	<u>youth</u> hostel

Here are some examples of common uncountable compound nouns. These are never used with an article.

air-<u>traffic</u> control	<u>birth</u> control	<u>blood</u> pressure	cotton <u>wool</u>
data-<u>processing</u>	family <u>planning</u>	<u>food</u> poisoning	<u>pocket</u> money
<u>income</u> tax	<u>junk</u> food	<u>mail</u> order	<u>hay</u> fever (allergy to pollen)

Here are some examples of common compound nouns used only in the singular.

<u>arms</u> race (countries wanting most powerful weapons) <u>death</u> penalty
<u>generation</u> gap <u>labour</u> force
<u>mother</u>-tongue <u>sound</u> barrier
<u>greenhouse</u> effect <u>welfare</u> state
<u>brain</u> drain (highly educated people leaving country to work abroad)

Here are some examples of common compound nouns used only in the plural.

grass <u>roots</u>	luxury <u>goods</u>	human <u>rights</u>	kitchen <u>scissors</u>
<u>race</u> relations	<u>roadworks</u>	<u>sunglasses</u>	<u>traffic</u> lights

Exercises

13.1 Complete these networks with any appropriate expressions from the opposite page. Add extra bubbles if you need them.

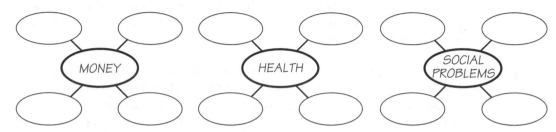

13.2 In some cases more than one compound noun can be formed from one particular element. What, for example, are the two expressions listed opposite with *blood* as an element and what are the two based on *control*? Complete the following compound nouns with a noun other than the one suggested opposite.

1 .... token
2 junk.....................
3 sound.....................
4 blood.....................

5 tea.........................
6 mother.....................
7 ....tax
8 ....processing

9 ....crossing
10 ....lights
11 food.........................
12 ....race

13.3 What are they talking about? In each case the answer is a compound noun opposite.

Example: 'I had it taken at the doctor's this morning and he said it was a little high for my age.' *blood pressure*

1 'You really shouldn't cross the road at any other place.'
2 'It's partly caused by such things as hair sprays and old fridges.'
3 'She always has terrible sneezing fits in the early summer.'
4 'I can't understand why they spend so much money on something so destructive.'
5 'Working there is supposed to be much more stressful than being a pilot.'
6 'The worst time was when I dropped one at the theatre and spent the interval scrabbling around on the floor.'
7 'I don't think it should ever be used under any circumstances.'
8 'It's much easier not to have to make your own arrangements.'
9 'He can't possibly run away from the policeman with those on!'

13.4 Now make up some sentences like those in exercise 13.3 relating to some of the new expressions you made in exercise 13.2.

13.5 Choose any article in a magazine or newspaper and write down all the compound nouns which you find.

13.6 Look at all the compound expressions you have worked with in this unit. Mark all those that you feel you need to be able to use yourself rather than just to understand when others use them.

14 Compound nouns – verb + preposition

A A large number of compound nouns (see Unit 13) are based on phrasal verbs. In Sections B to E you will see a number of examples of such nouns in context. The meaning of the compound noun is indicated in brackets at the end of the sentence. To form the plural, 's' is added to the end, e.g. **pin-ups**.

B Nouns based on phrasal verbs often have an informal feel to them and they are particularly common in newspaper reporting. Here are examples of such nouns in use.

In response to the pay offer, there was a **walk-out** at the factory.   [strike]
There is going to be a **crack-down** on public spending.   [action against]
There has been a **break-out** from the local prison.   [escape]
Last month saw a tremendous **shake-up** in personnel.   [change]
I never expected the **break-up** of the USSR.   [collapse]

C A number of these nouns have economic associations.

The **takeover** of one of our leading hotel chains has just been announced.   [purchase by another company]
We're trying to find some new **outlets** for our products.   [places to sell]
Take your things to the **check-out** to pay for them.   [cash-desk]
Cutbacks will be essential until the recession is over.   [reductions]
We made a profit of £1000 on a **turnover** of £10,000.   [money passing through a company]

D Some of these nouns are associated with technology and other aspects of contemporary life.

What the computer produces depends on the quality of the **input**.   [information that is put in]
Output has increased thanks to new technology.   [production]
We have a rather rapid staff **turnover**.   [change]
Just after leaving school he went through the stage of being a **dropout**.   [person who rejects society]
It will be a long time before the consequences of **fallout** from Chernobyl are no longer felt.   [radio-active dust in the atmosphere]
I can easily get you a **printout** of the latest figures.   [paper on which computer information has been printed]
A **breakthrough** has been made in AIDS research.   [important discovery]

E Some of the words can be used in more general circumstances.

Many of the problems were caused by a **breakdown** in communications.   [failure]
The **outlook** for tomorrow is good – sunny in most places.   [prospect]
There are **drawbacks** as well as advantages to every situation.   [negative aspects]
The **outcome** of the situation was not very satisfactory.   [conclusion]
TV companies always welcome **feedback** from viewers.   [comments]
It was clear from the **outset** that the **set-up** would cause problems.   [start; situation]
We parked in a **lay-by** on the **by-pass**.   [parking space at the side of a road; road avoiding the centre of a town]
The **outbreak** of war surprised them.   [start of something unpleasant, e.g. disease, violence]

Exercises

14.1   Here are some more compound nouns based on phrasal verbs. Guess the meaning of the underlined word from its context.

1   Because of the accident there was a three-mile <u>tailback</u> along the motorway.
2   Police are warning of an increased number of <u>break-ins</u> in this area.
3   The papers are claiming the Prime Minister organised a <u>cover-up</u>.
4   Unfortunately, our plans soon suffered a <u>setback</u>.
5   I'm sorry I'm late. There was a terrible <u>hold-up</u> on the bridge.
6   The robbers made their <u>getaway</u> in a stolen car.

14.2   Which of the words studied on the opposite page would be most likely to follow the adjectives given below?

1   radioactive............................   5   final................................
2   nervous................................   6   sales...............................
3   computer..............................   7   positive............................
4   annual.................................   8   drastic.............................

14.3   Fill in the blanks with an appropriate word from those opposite.

1   A and C Ltd. have made a .... bid for S and M plc.
2   The Prime Minister yesterday announced a .... in the Cabinet.
3   The negotiations aim to end the 10-day-old ....
4   She provided some very valuable .... to the discussion.
5   CIRCUS LION IN HORROR ....
6   There's a terrible queue at this .... Let's find another one.
7   There has been a disturbing .... of violence in prisons recently.
8   The office wall was covered in ....

14.4   Here are some more words of this type. In each case the preposition element of the noun is given but the other part is missing. Choose from the list of possibilities.

work   hand   hold   clear   write   lie   turn   press

1   Their car was a ....-off after the accident.
2   The lecturer distributed ....-outs before she started speaking.
3   Jack does a daily ....-out at the gym, starting with 20 .... -ups.
4   There is an interesting ....-up of the match in today's paper.
5   I'm giving my office a major ....-out this week.
6   Did you read about the........................-up at our bank?
7   There was a surprisingly large ....-out at the concert.
8   I love having a ....-in on Sundays.

14.5   Can you explain the difference between these pairs? Use a dictionary if necessary.

1   outlook/look-out   2   set-up/upset   3   outlet/let-out   4   outlay/layout

14.6   Choose eight of the words in this unit which you particularly want to learn and write your own sentences using them.

15 Words with interesting origins – people and places

A

A number of words in English have originated from the names of people.

biro: [ball-point pen] named after Laszlo Biro, its Hungarian inventor

boycott: [refuse to deal with or a refusal to deal with] after a landlord in Ireland who made himself unpopular by his treatment of his tenants and was socially isolated

braille: [name of a raised writing system used by blind people] from the name of its French inventor, Louis Braille

chauvinist: [strong belief that your country or race is superior to others] after the Frenchman, Nicolas Chauvin, who was fanatically devoted to Napoleon

hooligan: [a rough, lawless youth] from the Irish family name, Hooligan

machiavellian: [cunning, deceitful, unscrupulous in the pursuit of a goal] from Niccolo Machiavelli, the Italian statesman who died in 1527

mentor: [loyal and wise adviser] from Mentor, friend to Odysseus

pamphlet: [a small leaflet] from a character Pamphilus, in a 12th century love poem

to pander: [to indulge someone's desires] from Pandaros, a procurer or pimp in Ancient Greek mythology

saxophone: [musical instrument] invented by the Belgian, Adolphe Sax

tawdry: [cheap and tasteless] from St Audrey, at whose annual fair in the town of Ely, near Cambridge, cheap gaudy scarves were sold

watt: [unit of power] from the 18th century Scottish inventor, James Watt

Quite a few names of types of clothing, particularly hats, originate from the people who invented them or made them popular.

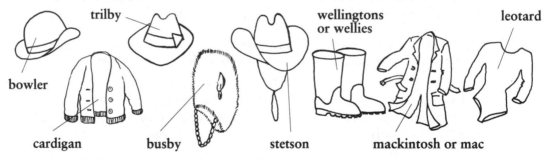

B

A number of other words in English come from place names.

bedlam: [chaos] from the name of a famous London mental hospital once situated where Liverpool Street Station now stands

spartan: [severely simple] from the ancient Greek city of Sparta, famed for its austerity

canter: [movement of a horse, faster than a trot but slower than a gallop] a shortening of Canterbury, a town in south-east England

gypsy: [member of a particular group of travelling people] These people were once thought to have come from Egypt, hence the name.

A number of names of different kinds of cloth originate from place names. The place of origin is shown in brackets ( ).

angora (Ankara)	**cashmere** (Kashmir)	**damask** (Damascus)
denim (Nimes, France)	**gauze** (Gaza)	**muslin** (Mosul, Iraq)
satin (Qingjiang, China)	**suede** (Sweden)	**tweed** (River Tweed, Scotland)

Exercises

15.1 Which (if any) of the words listed on the opposite page are familiar to you because there are similar words in your own language?

15.2 Complete the networks below with as many other words as you can from the words listed on the opposite page.

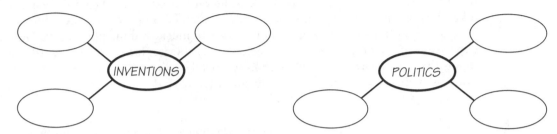

15.3 Complete the sentences with appropriate words.

1 It looks like rain. Don't forget your .... and your ....
2 I wish I could play the ....
3 It's .... in here. Let's go somewhere quieter.
4 The anarchist speaker urged all citizens to .... the elections.
5 What a beautiful .... sweater! Where did you get it?

15.4 Choose two adjectives to use with the following words.

Example: wellington *red, muddy*

1 hooligan   3 stetson   5 leotard
2 pamphlet   4 gypsy   6 biro

15.5 Now give two nouns that you might expect to follow each of these adjectives.

Example: denim *jeans, jacket*

1 suede   2 machiavellian   3 spartan   4 tawdry

15.6 And now suggest how the following sentences could end.

1 I can't stand the way he panders...
2 She buttoned up her cardigan because...
3 The horse cantered...
4 It has been agreed to boycott...
5 A busby must be...

15.7 Here are some more words of this type in English. Can you explain (a) their meaning and (b) their origin?

1 **herculean** effort   4 **jersey**   7 bottle of **champagne**
2 **platonic** friendship   5 **Caesarean** section 8 **atlas**
3 **teddy** bear   6 **July**   9 **magnolia**

16 Words with interesting origins – from other languages

A English has taken over words from most of the other languages with which it has had contact. It has taken many expressions from the ancient languages, Latin and Greek, and these borrowings usually have academic or literary associations. From French, English has taken lots of words to do with cooking, the arts, and a more sophisticated lifestyle in general. From Italian come words connected with music and the plastic arts. German expressions in English have been coined either by tourists bringing back words for new things they saw or by philosophers or historians describing German concepts or experiences. The borrowings from other languages usually relate to things which English speakers experienced for the first time abroad.

B There are borrowings from a wide range of languages. For example, from Japanese, **tycoon, karate, origami, judo, futon** and **bonsai**. From Arabic, **mattress, cipher, alcove, carafe, algebra, harem, mufti** and **yashmak**. From Turkish, **yoghurt, jackal, kiosk, bosh** [nonsense (colloquial)], **tulip** and **caftan**; from Farsi, **caravan, shawl, taffeta, bazaar** and **sherbet,** and from Eskimo, **kayak, igloo** and **anorak**.

C The map of Europe below shows the places of origin of some English words and expressions borrowed from some other European languages. Use a dictionary to check the meanings of any words you are not sure about.

Norway
fjord
floe
ski
slalom
lemming

Holland
yacht
easel
tattoo
cruise

France
cuisine
gateau
chauffeur
boutique
crèche
duvet
coup
elite
sauté
avant garde
cul de sac
aubergine
bidet

Spain
embargo
junta
siesta
guerrilla
macho
mosquito
bonanza
lasso
patio

Portugal
marmalade
palaver
dodo
cobra

Finland
sauna

Sweden
ombudsman
tungsten

Germany
kindergarten
dachshund
rottweiler
hamburger
frankfurter
delicatessen
blitz
waltz
poodle
snorkel
Wanderlust
seminar

Italy
ghetto
piano
soprano
ballerina
confetti
fiasco
spaghetti
bandit
casino
vendetta

Russia
bistro
sputnik
cosmonaut
perestroika
steppe
tundra
tsar
balalaika
mammoth

Greece
dogma
drama
psychology
hippopotamus
theory
pseudonym
synonym

Exercises

16.1 Which of the words listed opposite are also used in your language?

16.2 Is your own language represented on the opposite page? If so, can you add any words to the lists opposite? If not, do you know of any words English has borrowed from your language? (There are almost sure to be some.) Do the words mean exactly the same in English as in your language? Are they pronounced in the same way?

16.3 Look at all the words opposite and complete the following networks.

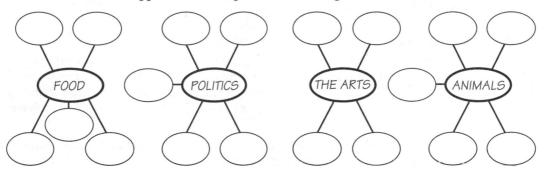

16.4 Make two or three other networks to help you to learn the words on the opposite page.

16.5 Match the adjectives on the left with the noun they are most likely to be associated with, on the right.

1 right-wing	kindergarten
2 prima	casino
3 strawberry	duvet
4 ice	vendetta
5 Chinese	ballerina
6 long-sleeved	embargo
7 total	cuisine
8 long-standing	floe
9 noisy	yoghurt
10 cosy	coup
11 all-night	caftan

16.6 What verbs collocate, in other words, are frequently used with the following nouns?

Example: *study* algebra

1 karate	4 embargo	7 coup	10 cruise
2 kayak	5 guerrilla	8 confetti	11 sauna
3 mufti	6 cul de sac	9 siesta	12 seminar

16.7 Give three nouns likely to follow *macho* and *avant-garde*.

16.8 Have some words or expressions been borrowed from English into your own language? Give some examples. Have they kept exactly the same meaning as they have in English?

17 Onomatopoeic words

A Onomatopoeic words are those which seem to sound like their meaning. The most obvious examples are verbs relating to the noises which animals make, e.g. cows **moo** and cats **mew** or **meow**. See Unit 73 for more about animal noises.

B If the vowel sound in a word is short, an onomatopoeic word usually signifies a short, sharp sound. If it is long (indicated in the International Phonetic Alphabet by ː) then the word usually signifies a longer, slower sound. Compare **pip** /pɪp/ which is a short sound with **peep** /piːp/ which is a long sound.

C Particular combinations of letters have particular sound associations in English.

gr- at the beginning of a word can suggest something unpleasant or miserable, e.g. **groan** [make a deep sound forced out by pain or despair], **grumble** [complain in a bad-tempered way], **grumpy** [bad-tempered], **grunt** [make a low, rough sound like pigs do, or people expressing disagreement or boredom], **growl** [make a low, threatening sound].

cl- at the beginning of a word can suggest something sharp and/or metallic, e.g. **click** [make a short sharp sound], **clang** [make a loud ringing noise], **clank** [make a dull metallic noise, not as loud as a clang], **clash** [make a loud, broken, confused noise as when metal objects strike together], **clink** [make the sound of small bits of metal or glass knocking together]. Horses go **clip-clop** on the road.

sp- at the beginning of a word can have an association with water or other liquids or powders, e.g. **splash** [cause a liquid to fly about in drops], **spit** [send liquid out from the mouth], **splutter** [make a series of spitting sounds], **spray** [liquid sent through the air in tiny drops either by the wind or some instrument], **sprinkle** [throw a shower of something onto a surface], **spurt** [come out in a sudden burst].

ash- at the end of a word can suggest something fast and violent, e.g. **smash** [break violently into small pieces], **dash** [move or be moved violently], **crash** [strike suddenly violently and noisily], **bash** [strike heavily so as to break or injure], **gash** [a long deep cut or wound].

wh- at the beginning of a word often suggests the movement of air, e.g. **whistle** [a high pitched noise made by forcing air or steam through a small opening], **whirr** [sound like a bird's wings moving rapidly], **whizz** [make the sound of something rushing through air], **wheeze** [breathe noisily especially with a whistling sound in the chest], **whip** [one of these or to hit with one of these].

-ckle, -ggle, or **-zzle** at the end of a word can suggest something light and repeated, e.g. **trickle** [to flow in a thin stream], **crackle** [make a series of short cracking sounds], **tinkle** [make a succession of light ringing sounds], **giggle** [laugh lightly in a nervous or silly way], **wriggle** [move with quick short twistings], **sizzle** [make a hissing sound like something cooking in fat], **drizzle** [small, fine rain].

Exercises

17.1 Which of the consonant combinations listed in C opposite exist in your language? Do they ever have similar associations?

17.2 Look in your dictionary. Can you find any other examples of words beginning with *gr-*, *cl-*, *sp-* or *wh-* with the associations described opposite?

17.3 Which of the words from C opposite fit best in the sentences below.

1 She heard his key .... as it turned in the lock.
2 The blades of the propeller .... noisily.
3 I love to hear sausages .... in the pan!
4 They .... glasses and drank to each other's health.
5 There was a terrible car .... on the motorway today.
6 Everyone .... with disappointment at the news.
7 The baby loves .... in its bath.
8 I can feel raindrops .... down the back of my neck.

17.4 Almost all the words in C opposite can be both nouns and regular verbs. There is, however, one irregular verb, one word which is only an adjective, one word which is both verb and noun but the noun has a rather different meaning from the verb. What are these words? Choose from the alternatives offered below.

1 The irregular verb: whip, grunt, spurt, spit or wriggle?
2 The word which is only an adjective: gash, grumpy, clip-clop, or whirr?
3 The word which is both a verb and a noun but the noun has a different meaning: trickle, spray, growl, splutter, spit, splash or crash?

17.5 Can you guess the meanings of the underlined words from their sounds?

1 The child <u>sploshed</u> through the puddles.
2 If you have a sore throat, try <u>gargling</u> with some salt water.
3 I couldn't concentrate on the play because of the <u>rustle</u> of sweet papers behind me.
4 Speak up. Don't <u>mumble</u>.
5 That step always <u>creaks</u>.
6 He <u>whacked</u> the ball into the air.

17.6 What words on the page opposite do these pictures represent?

17.7 Pair the words below so that in each case there is a noun and a matching verb.

schoolchildren   crackles   tinkles   a bad-tempered person or dog
the bell on a cat's collar   a bored child   clanks   whistles   a fire   giggle
growls   a churchbell   a steam train   clangs   wheezes   a prisoner's chain
wriggles   someone with asthma

18 Words commonly mispronounced

English spelling is notoriously unphonetic. This page looks at some of the words which cause most pronunciation difficulties for learners of English. The phonetic transcription is provided for some of the words below. If you are not sure of the pronunciation of any of the other words, check in the index at the back of the book.

A

To master English pronunciation you need to learn the 20 phonetic symbols for English vowel sounds. It is not really necessary to learn the consonant symbols as it is usually not difficult to know how consonants should be pronounced. Vowels are important because the vowel letters can be pronounced in many different ways.

a	about /ə/ wander /ɒ/ last /ɑː/ late /eɪ/
i	alive /aɪ/ give /ɪ/
u	put /ʊ/ cut /ʌ/ cupid /juː/
ie	fiend /iː/ friend /e/ science /aɪə/
ei	rein /eɪ/ receive /iː/ reinforce /iːɪ/
e	met /e/ meter /iː/ /ə/
o	sorry /ɒ/ go /əʊ/ love /ʌ/ to /uː/
ea	head /e/ team /iː/ react /iːæ/
ou	our /aʊ/ route /uː/ would /ʊ/
oo	cool /uː/ cook /ʊ/ coopt /əʊɒ/

B

Silent letters can be a problem. The letters below in **bold** are silent in the following words:

p **p**sychic /saɪkɪk/ **p**sychiatry **p**neumatic recei**p**t **p**seudonym **p**sychology
b com**b** /kəʊm/ dum**b** num**b** tom**b** clim**b** wom**b** lam**b**
b dou**b**t /daʊt/ su**b**tle de**b**t de**b**tor
l cou**l**d /kʊd/ shou**l**d ca**l**m ha**l**f ta**l**k pa**l**m wa**l**k sa**l**mon cha**l**k
h **h**onour /ɒnə/ **h**onourable **h**onest **h**our **h**ourly **h**eir **h**eiress
t whis**t**le /wɪsəl/ cas**t**le lis**t**en fas**t**en sof**t**en Chris**t**mas
k **k**nee /niː/ **k**nife **k**now **k**nob **k**nowledge **k**not **k**nit
r ca**r**d /kɑːd/ pa**r**k fa**r**m bu**r**n wo**r**k sto**r**m ta**r**t
r (unless followed by a vowel) mothe**r** /mʌðə/ siste**r** teache**r** wate**r**

C

In a number of two-syllable words in English, the stress is on the first syllable of the word when it is a noun and the second syllable if it is a verb, e.g. 'Wool is a major Scottish <u>ex</u>port.' 'Scotland ex<u>ports</u> a lot of wool.' Here are some other words like this.

conduct	conflict	contest	decrease	suspect
desert	import	increase	insult	transfer
permit	present	progress	protest	transport
record	reject	reprint	subject	upset

D

Here are a number of other words which are often mispronounced.

apostrophe /əˈpɒstrəfi/	catastrophe /kəˈtæstrəfi/	cupboard /ˈkʌbəd/
recipe /ˈresɪpi/	hiccough /ˈhɪkʌp/	sword /sɔːd/
plough /plaʊ/	muscle /ˈmʌsəl/	interesting /ˈɪntrəstɪŋ/

Exercises

18.1 Mark all the silent letters in each of the following sentences.

1 They sang a psalm to honour the memory of the world-famous psychologist as she was laid to rest in the family tomb.
2 The psychiatrist was knifed in the knee as he was walking home.
3 He should have whistled as he fastened his sword to his belt.
4 You should have left me half the Christmas cake on Wednesday.

18.2 Which word is the odd one out in each of these groups?

1	worry	sorry	lorry	5	doubt	could	shout
2	sword	cord	word	6	plough	rough	tough
3	come	some	dome	7	land	wand	sand
4	head	plead	tread	8	soot	root	foot

18.3 What word could a poet use to rhyme with each of the words below?

1 hiccough *cup*......................... 4 through ....
2 bough .... 5 cough ....
3 plough .... 6 though ....

18.4 Underline or highlight the stressed syllable in each of the words in bold.

1 They paid a £1 million **transfer** fee for **transferring** the player to their team.
2 Although they **suspected** several people were partly involved, the police decided to concentrate on Jo as the main **suspect**.
3 There are **conflicting** views as to the cause of the **conflict**.
4 All this **upset** over the wedding has really **upset** them.
5 The cost of living has **increased** while there has been a **decrease** in wages.
6 A work **permit permits** you to work for a period of six months.
7 I wish I could **record** a hit **record**!
8 Despite the disgraceful **conduct** of the audience, James went on **conducting** the orchestra.

18.5 Write out the words below using the normal English alphabet.

1 /'mʌsəl/   3 /'hæŋkətʃiːf/   5 /'sʌtəl/   7 /haɪt/
2 /kə'tæstrəfi/   4 /'kemɪkəl/   6 /rə'siːt/   8 /'resɪpi/

18.6 Underline the stressed syllable in each of the words below.

1 photograph photography photographer photographically
2 telephone telephonist
3 zoology zoologist zoological
4 arithmetic arithmetical arithmetician
5 psychology psychologist psychological
6 psychiatry psychiatric psychiatrist

18.7 Are there other words which you know you have particular problems pronouncing? You might like to ask a teacher to help you answer this question. Note any such words down with their phonetic transcription beside them.

19 Homonyms

Homonyms can be subdivided into **homographs** and **homophones**. **Homographs** are words which are written in the same way but have different meanings. Compare **bow** in 'He took a **bow** /baʊ/ at the end of the concert' and 'He was wearing a **bow** /bəʊ/ tie'. **Homophones** are words which are pronounced in the same way but are spelt differently, e.g. **bow** as in 'He took a **bow**' and **bough**, 'the **bough** of a tree'.

Here are some more examples of homographs.

I **live** in the north of England.   /lɪv/
Your favourite pop star is singing **live** on TV tonight.   /laɪv/

I **read** in bed each night.   /riːd/
I **read** War and Peace last year.   /red/

The **lead** singer in the group is great.   /liːd/
Lead pipes are dangerous.   /led/

The **wind** blew the tree down.   /wɪnd/
Don't forget to **wind** your watch.   /waɪnd/

I **wound** my watch last night.   /waʊnd/
He suffered a terrible **wound** in the war.   /wuːnd/

Some students at Oxford spend more time learning to **row** well than studying.   /rəʊ/
They shared a flat for ages until they had a **row** over money and split up.   /raʊ/

This book is called *English Vocabulary in Use*.   /juːs/
You must know how to **use** words as well as their meaning.   /juːz/

They lived in a large old **house**.   /haʊs/
The buildings **house** a library and two concert halls as well as a theatre.   /haʊz/

The **sow** has five piglets.   /saʊ/
The farmers **sow** the seeds in the spring.   /səʊ/

I **bathed** the baby this morning.   /baːθt/
We **bathed** in the sea every day when we were on holiday.   /beɪðd/

Here are some of the many examples of homophones in English.

air/heir	aloud/allowed	dough/doe	fare/fair
faze/phase	floe/flow	flu/flew	grate/great
groan/grown	hoarse/horse	its/it's	lays/laze
might/mite	mown/moan	our/hour	pale/pail
pane/pain	peal/peel	place/plaice	practise/practice
pray/prey	raise/rays	read/reed	rein/rain
right/rite/write	rough/ruff	sale/sail	scene/seen
sent/scent	sight/site	sole/soul	sought/sort
steak/stake	tea/tee	there/their/they're	through/threw
tire/tyre	toe/tow	waist/waste	wait/weight
weather/whether	whine/wine		

Exercises

19.1 How would you pronounce each of the underlined words in the sentences below? Choose a word with a similar sound from the brackets.

1 The girl I <u>live</u> with knows a good pub with <u>live</u> music. (dive/give)
2 The main <u>house</u> <u>houses</u> a collection of rare stamps. (mouse/rouse)
3 They <u>bathed</u> the children after they had <u>bathed</u> in the sea. (lathe/path)
4 You <u>sow</u> the seeds while I feed the <u>sow</u>. (cow/glow)
5 The violinist in the <u>bow</u> tie took a <u>bow</u>. (allow/flow)
6 He's the <u>lead</u> singer in the group 'Lead piping'. (head/deed)
7 What a <u>row</u> from the last house in the <u>row</u>! (plough/though)
8 Does he still suffer from his war <u>wound</u>? (found/mooned)
9 I <u>wound</u> the rope around the tree to strengthen it against the gale. (round/tuned)
10 It's quite hard to <u>wind</u> in the sails in this <u>wind</u>. (find/tinned)

19.2 Write the word in phonetic script in the correct spelling for the context.

Example: I really must do some more exercise or I'll never lose /weɪt/ *weight*.

1 Watching sport on TV is such a /weɪst/ of time.
2 There is a hole in the /səʊl/ of my shoe.
3 He broke a /peɪn/ of glass in the kitchen window.
4 The eldest son of the monarch is the /eə/ to the throne.
5 You are not /əˈlaʊd/ to talk during the test.
6 Let's /ˈpræktɪs/ our swimming together this evening?
7 He's going /θruː/ a rather difficult /feɪz/ at the moment.
8 Don't throw away that orange /piːl/. I need it for a recipe.

19.3 Write one sentence using both of the words corresponding to the phonetic script.

Example: /peɪl/ *She was quite pale after the exertion of carrying such a heavy pail of water.*

1 /ðeə/   3 /ˈpræktɪs/   5 /waɪn/   7 /saɪt/   9 /hɔːs/
2 /ɪts/   4 /greɪt/   6 /sɔːt/   8 /preɪ/   10 /reɪz/

19.4 Homophones and homographs are at the root of many jokes in English. Match the first part of each of these children's jokes with the second part and then explain the play on words involved in each.

1 What did the big chimney say to the little chimney?	Because it's got a tender behind.
2 What did one lift say to the other lift?	A drum takes a lot of beating.
3 What did the south wind say to the north wind?	I think I'm going down with something.
4 Why did the man take his pencil to bed?	A nervous wreck.
5 Why is history the sweetest lesson?	He wanted to draw the curtains.
6 What's the best birthday present?	Because it's full of dates.
7 Why can't a steam engine sit down?	Let's play draughts.
8 What's pale and trembles at the bottom of the sea?	You're too young to smoke.

20 Time

A One thing before another

Before I went to work I fed the cat.   [or, more commonly in written English: **Before** going to work...]

I had written to her **prior to** meeting the committee.   [formal/written style]

It was nice to be in Venice. **Previously** I'd only been to Rome.   [fairly formal, more informal would be **before that**, I...]

I was in the office from 2.30. I was out **earlier on**.   [**before then**, fairly informal]

The city is now called Thatcherville. **Formerly** it was Grabtown.   [used when something has changed its name, state, etc.]

B Things happening at the same time

While I waited, I read the newspaper.   [or, more formal: **While waiting**, I read...; the waiting and reading happen together.]

As I was driving to work, I saw an accident.   [**As** describes the background when something *happens* in the foreground.]

I saw her **just as** she was turning the corner.   [precise moment]

During the war, I lived in Dublin.   [does not specify how *long*]

Throughout the war, food was rationed.   [from beginning to end]

She was entering **at the very time/the very moment** I was leaving.   [These two are stronger and more precise than **as** or **just as**.]

C One thing after another

After I'd locked up, I went to bed.   [or, more formal: **After** locking up... ; we do not usually say 'After **having** locked up...'.]

We went to the castle. **Then** we caught a bus to the beach.

First we went to the theatre. **After that**, we had a meal.

He fell ill and was admitted to hospital. He died soon **afterwards**.   [In these two examples, **after that** and **afterwards** are interchangeable.]

Following my visit to Peking, I bought lots of books about China.   [fairly formal]

D Time when

When I'm rich and famous, I'll buy a yacht.   [*Note*: not 'When I will be rich...']

As soon as we've packed we can leave.   [immediately after]

Once we've finished we can go and have a coffee.   [less specific]

The moment/the minute I saw his face I knew I'd met him before.

I stayed in that hospital **the time (that)** I broke my leg.

I met Polly at Ken's wedding. **On that occasion** she was with a different man.

E Connecting two periods or events

The meal will take about an hour. **In the meantime**, relax and have a drink.   [between now and the meal]

The new whiteboards are arriving soon. **Till then**, we'll have to use the old ones.

I last met him in 1985. **Since then** I haven't set eyes on him.

By the time I retire, I will have worked here 26 years.

Exercises

20.1 Look at these pages from the personal diary of Laura, a businesswoman who travels a lot, then do the exercise.

Mon 12	Paris – day 5 Pompidou Centre then theatre	Up early. Said goodbye to Nick and left. Saw bad accident on motorway.	**Fri** 16
Tue 13	Been away 6 days! Paris OK, but miss home.	Answered all the mail, then felt I could watch TV!	**Sat** 17
Wed 14	Left Paris 10 am. Huge pile of mail waiting! Manchester, then	Lots of phone calls! Sandra, Joyce – and Dougy all in a row! Lazy day!	**Sun** 18
Thu 15	Glasgow. Met Maura at Nick's.	book tickets for Dublin – 24th!	**Notes**

Fill in the blanks with connectors. An example is given.

1 *Prior.* to going to Manchester, Laura was in Paris.
2 Her next trip after Glasgow is on 24th. .... she can have a quiet time at home.
3 She was in Paris for over a week. .... she got home there was a big pile of mail waiting for her.
4 ....she was at Nick's place on the 16th, she met Maura.
5 She went to the theatre in Paris on Monday. ...., she had been to the Pompidou Centre.
6 .... she had said goodbye to Nick, she left.
7 .... she had answered all her letters, she felt she could watch TV for a while.
8 .... she put the phone down it rang again. This time it was Dougy.

Make more sentences with connectors you haven't used, based on the diary information.

20.2 Think of things that are true for you in these situations and complete the sentences. Add more sentences if you can. An example has been done.

1 While I'm asleep, *I usually dream a lot.*
2 After I've eaten too much,...
3 The moment I wake up, I...
4 Throughout my childhood I...
5 I'm doing vocabulary right now. Earlier on, I was...
6 Once I've finished my language course, I'll...
7 Before I go on holiday, I always...
8 Following an argument with someone, I always feel

Follow-up: If you can, get hold of a news report in English. Underline all the time connectors and see if there are any which you can add to those on the left-hand page. If there are, write a whole sentence in your notebook showing how the connector is used.

21 Condition

A As well as **if**, there are a number of other words and phrases for expressing condition.

1 You can't come in **unless** you have a ticket.

2 You can borrow the bike **on condition that** you return it by five o'clock.

3 **In case of** fire, dial 999. [usually seen on notices (see Unit 96); it means 'when there is a fire'; don't confuse with 'take your mac **in case** it rains'; *not* it might rain.]

4 You can stay, **as long as** you don't mind sleeping on the sofa. [less formal than **so long as** and less formal and not so strong as **on condition that**]

Providing (that) or **provided (that)** can also be used in examples 2 and 4. They are less formal and not so strong as **on condition that** but stronger and more restricting than **as long as**, e.g. **Provided/Providing** you don't mind cats, you can stay with us. Note the use of **supposing** and **what if** (usually in spoken language) for possible situations in the future. **What if** is more direct, e.g. **Supposing/What if** he doesn't turn up; what shall we do then?

B Conditions with -ever

However you do it, it will cost a lot of money.
You'll get to the railway station, **whichever** bus you take.
Whoever wins the General Election, nothing will really change.
That box is so big it will be in the way **wherever** you leave it.

These four sentences can also be expressed using **no matter**.

No matter how you do it, it will cost a lot of money.
You'll get to the railway station, **no matter** which bus you take.

C Some nouns which express condition

Certain **conditions** must be **met** before the Peace Talks can begin.
A good standard of English is a **prerequisite** for studying at a British University. [absolutely necessary; very formal word]
What are the entry **requirements** for doing a diploma in Management at your college? [official conditions]
I would not move to London **under any circumstances**. It's awful!

> Notice in the examples in A and B how the present tense is used in the clause with the conditional word or phrase. Don't say: Take your umbrella in case it will rain.

Exercises

21.1 Fill the gaps with a suitable word from A opposite.

1 You can come to the party .... you don't bring that ghastly friend of yours.

2 .... emergency in the machine-room, sound the alarm and notify the supervisor at once.

3 .... I hear from you, I'll assume you are coming.

4 A person may take the driving test again .... they have not already taken a test within the previous fourteen days.

5 .... I lent you my car, would that help?

21.2 The pictures show conditions that must be met to do certain things. Make different sentences using words and phrases from the opposite page.

Example: You can have a passenger on a motorbike provided they wear a helmet.
or *Unless you wear a helmet, you can't ride on a motorbike.*

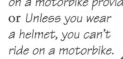

1   2   3   4

21.3 Change the sentences with *-ever* to *no matter*, and vice-versa.

1 Wherever she goes, she always takes that dog of hers.

2 If anyone rings, I don't want to speak to them, no matter who it is.

3 No matter what I do, I always seem to do the wrong thing.

4 It'll probably have meat in it, whichever dish you choose. They don't cater for non-meat eaters here.

5 No matter how I do it, that recipe never seems to work.

21.4 What would your answers be to these questions?

1 Are there any prerequisites for the job you do or would like to do in the future?

2 Under what circumstances would you move from where you're living at the moment?

3 What are the normal entry requirements for university in your country?

4 On what condition would you lend a friend your house/flat?

22 Cause, reason, purpose and result

A Cause and reason

You probably know how to use words like **because, since** and **as** to refer to the **cause** of or **reason** for something. Here are some other ways of connecting clauses to express causes and reasons. Note how verbs and nouns can do the same job as conjunctions.

Look at the picture of an accident, on the right. Here are several ways of talking about it.

Owing to the icy conditions, the two lorries collided.
The collision **was due to** the icy conditions.
The collision **was caused by** ice on the road.
The cause of the collision was ice on the road.

Here are some other 'cause' words and typical contexts they are used in.

The rise in prices **sparked off** a lot of political protest.   [often used for very strong, perhaps violent, reactions to events]
The President's statement **gave rise to / provoked / generated** a lot of criticism.   [slightly less strong than **spark off**]
The new law has **brought about / led to** great changes in education.   [often used for political/social change]
This problem **stems from** the inflation of recent years.   [explaining the direct origins of events and states]
The court-case **arose out of** allegations made in a newspaper.   [the allegations started the process that led to the court-case]

B Reasons for and purposes of doing things

Her **reason for** not going with us was that she had no money. *or* **The reason** she didn't go with us was that...   [less formal]
I wonder what his **motives** were **in** sending that letter?   [purpose]
I wonder what **prompted** him to send that letter?   [reason/cause]
She wrote to the press **with the aim of** exposing the scandal.   [purpose]
I've invited you here **with a view to** resolving our differences.   [sounds a bit more indirect than **with the aim of**]
He refused to answer **on the grounds that** his lawyer wasn't there.   [reason]
The purpose of her visit was to inspect the equipment.

C Results

He did no work. **As a result / As a consequence / Consequently,** he failed his exams.
The result/consequence of all these changes is that no-one is happy any more.   [The examples with **consequence/consequently** sound more formal than **result**]
His remarks **resulted in** everyone getting angry.   [as a verb + **in**]
The events had an **outcome** that no-one could have predicted.   [result of a process or events, or of meetings, discussions, etc.]
The **upshot** of all these problems was that we had to start again.   [less formal than **outcome**]
When the election results were announced, chaos **ensued**.   [formal]

Exercises

22.1 Make full sentences using 'cause' words from A opposite.

Example: closure of 20 mines → strikes in coal industry *The closure of 20 mines sparked off a lot of strikes in the coal industry.*

1 announcement ⟶ strong attack from opposition
2 new Act of Parliament ⟶ great changes in industry
3 signalling fault ⟶ train crash
4 violent storm ⟶ wall collapsed
5 food shortages ⟶ riots in several cities
6 food shortages ⟶ poor management of the economy

22.2 Make two sentences into one, using the 'reason and purpose' words in brackets. Look at B opposite if you aren't sure.

Example: **There was a controversial decision. She wrote to the local newspaper to protest. (prompt)** *The controversial decision prompted her to write to the local newspaper to protest.*

1 I didn't contact you. I'd lost your phone number. (reason)
2 I will not sign. This contract is illegal. (grounds)
3 The government passed a new law. It was in order to control prices. (aim)
4 She sent everyone flowers. I wonder why? (motives)
5 The salary was high. She applied for the job. (prompt)

22.3 The pictures show the *results* of events. Imagine what the *causes* might be and describe the events in different ways.

1 The road was blocked.

2 Everyone got a refund.

3 The customers got angry.

4 We had to walk home.

22.4 Fill in the missing words.

1 My reasons .... not joining the club are personal.
2 The purpose .... this pedal is to control the speed.
3 I came here .... the aim .... resolving our dispute.
4 His stupidity has resulted .... us having to do more work.
5 All this arose .... one small mistake we made.
6 It was done .... a view .... lowering inflation.
7 That press article has .... rise .... a lot of criticism.

23 Concession and contrast

Concession means accepting one part of a state of affairs but putting another argument or fact against it.

> **Although** they were poor, they were independent.
> He is a bit stupid. He's very kind, **nevertheless**.

A Verbs of concession

example

I **acknowledge/accept** that he has worked hard but it isn't enough.

I **admit** I was wrong, but I still think we were right to doubt her.

I **concede** that you are right about the goal, but not the method.

paraphrase and comments

→ I agree but...
[**accept** is less formal than **acknowledge**]

→ I accept I'm guilty of what I'm accused of.

→ You have won this point in our argument.   [formal]

B Adverbs and other phrases for concession

OK, you're sorry. **That's all well and good**, but how are you going to pay us back?
You shouldn't seem so surprised. **After all,** I did warn you.
It's all very well saying you love dogs, but who'll take it for walks if we *do* get one?
He *is* boring, and he *is* rather cold and unfriendly, but, **for all that**, he *is* your uncle and we should invite him.
Admittedly, she put a lot of effort in, but it was all wasted.

C Contrast

I expected Mr Widebody to be fat. **The reverse was true.**

We're not almost there at all; **quite the opposite.** We've got five miles to go yet.

Everywhere in Europe they use metric measures. **In contrast,** Britain still uses non-metric.
It's not actually raining now. **On the other hand,** it may rain later, so take the umbrella.

Remember: **On the other hand** means 'that is true *and* this is true'; **On the contrary** means 'that is *not* true, but this *is* true', e.g. John, quiet? On the contrary, he's the noisiest person I know *or* John is rather arrogant. On the other hand, he can be very kind.

Note also these collocating phrases for contrast.

> When it comes to politics, Jim and Ann are **poles apart**.
> There's a **world of difference** between being a friend and a lover.
> There's a **great divide** between left and right wing in general.
> A **yawning gap** divides rich and poor in many countries.
> There's a **huge discrepancy** between his ideals and his actions.

Exercises

23.1 Rewrite these sentences using the most likely verb from A opposite (there is usually more than one possibility).

1 I know that you weren't solely to blame, but you must take *some* responsibility.
2 Okay, I was wrong, you were right; he *is* a nice guy.
3 The company is prepared to say that you have suffered some delay, but we do not accept liability.
4 She didn't deny that we had done all we could, but she was still not content.

23.2 Write a *beginning* for these sentences, as in the example.

1 *I expected Mary to be tall and dark.* The reverse was true; she was short, with fair hair.
2 .... On the other hand, it does have a big garden, so I think we should rent it.
3 *Jim:* ....? *Mary:* On the contrary, it's one of the cheapest hotels in town.
4 .... In contrast, the traffic in Britain drives on the left.
5 ....; quite the opposite. I feel quite full. I had a huge breakfast.

23.3 Try to do this word puzzle from memory.
If you can't, look at C opposite.

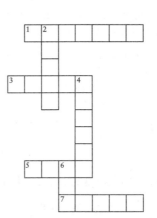

Across

1 a .... gap
3 a .... of difference
5 a .... discrepancy
7 .... apart

Down

2 poles ....
4 a great ....
6 a yawning ....

Now use the phrases from the word puzzle to make comments on these statements.

1 Some people believe in the nuclear deterrent, some in world disarmament.
2 She says one thing. She does quite the opposite.
3 Jim believes in God. Sandra's a total atheist.
4 Being a student's one thing; being a teacher's quite another.

23.4 Complete the sentences with phrases from B opposite.

1 Okay, you've cleaned the kitchen, ..., but what about the mess in the dining-room.
2 No need to panic. ...., it doesn't start till six.
3 She's bossy and sly, but ...., she *is* a friend.
4 .... saying you'll pay me back soon; *when* is what *I* want to know!

23.5 Choose between *on the other hand* and *on the contrary*.

1 I'm not worried; ...., I feel quite calm.
2 It's expensive, but ...., we do need it.

24 Addition

There are a number of ways of adding one idea to another in English. You probably already know words like **and, also** and **too**.

Words for linking sentences/clauses

sentence/clause 1	*and*	*sentence/clause 2*
For this job you need a degree.	**In addition**	you need some experience.
Video cameras are becoming easier to use.	**Furthermore** **Moreover** **What's more*** }	they're becoming cheaper.
It'll take ages to get there and it'll cost a fortune.	**Besides****	we'll have to change trains three times at least.
Children should respect their parents.	**Equally** **Likewise** }	they should respect their teachers.
We'll have all the stress of going to court and giving evidence.	**On top of** **(all) that*****	we'll have to pay the lawyers' bills.

*   **furthermore** and **moreover** are normally interchangeable; **what's more** is informal; **what is more** is more formal.
**   a more emphatic way of adding; similar in meaning to **anyway**.
*** even more emphatic; used mostly in informal spoken English.

Note also: To keep fit you need a good diet **plus** regular exercise.   [normally used to connect noun phrases, but can connect clauses in informal speech]

Adding words at the end of clauses/sentences

They sell chairs, tables, beds, **and so on / etc.** /et'setrə/
It'll go to the committee, then to the board, then to another committee, **and so on and so forth.**   [suggests a long continuation]
He was a good sportsman and an excellent musician **into the bargain / to boot.**   [emphasises the combination of items]

Adding words that begin or come in the middle of clauses/sentences

Further to my letter of 18/9/92, I am writing to...   [formal opening for a letter]
In addition to his BA in History he has a Ph.D. in Sociology.
He's on the school board, **as well as** being a local councillor.
Besides / Apart from having a salary, he also has a private income.
Alongside her many other hobbies she restores old racing cars.
Jo Evans was there, **along with** a few other people who I didn't know.

Note: This last group are followed by nouns or by -ing. Do *not* say: As well as she speaks French, she also speaks Japanese. (You can say: As well as **speaking** French, she...)

Exercises

24.1 Fill the gaps in this letter with suitable adding words and phrases. Try to do it without looking at the opposite page.

> Dear Mr Stoneheart
>
> .... (1) my letter of 16.3.94, I should like to give you more information concerning my qualifications and experience. .... (2) holding a Diploma in Catering, I also have an Advanced Certificate in Hotel Management. The course covered the usual areas: finance, front services, publicity, space allocation, ... (3) I also wish to point out that, ... (4) holding these qualifications, I have now been working in the hotel trade for five years. .... (5), my experience prior to that was also connected with tourism and hospitality.
>
> I hope you will give my application due consideration.
>
> Yours sincerely
>
> *Nora Hope*
>
> Nora Hope

24.2 Rewrite the sentences using the word or phrase in brackets at the end.

1 Physical labour can exhaust the body very quickly. Excessive study can rapidly reduce mental powers too. (equally)
2 My cousin turned up and some schoolmates of his came with him. (along with)
3 He owns a big chemical factory and he runs a massive oil business in the USA. (as well as)
4 She was my teacher and she was a good friend. (into the bargain)
5 I'm their scientific adviser and act as consultant to the Managing Director. (in addition to)

24.3 Correct the mistakes in the use of addition words and phrases in these sentences.

1 I work part-time as well as I am a student, so I have a busy life.
2 Besides to have a good job, my ambition is to meet someone nice to share my life with.
3 Alongside I have many other responsibilities, I now have to be in charge of staff training.
4 In addition has a degree, she also has a diploma.
5 Likewise my father won't agree, my mother's sure to find something to object to.
6 To boot she is a good footballer, she's a good athlete.
7 He said he'd have to first consider the organisation, then the system, then the finance and so forth so on.

24.4 What adding words/phrases can you associate with these pictures?

1   2   3   4

25 Text-referring words

A

Text-referring words are ones that pick up their content from the surrounding text. This sentence in isolation does not mean much:

> We decided to look at the problem again and try to find a solution.

What problem? We need to refer to some other sentence or to the context to find out. **Problem** and **solution** help organise the argument of the text, but they do not tell us the topic of the text. They refer to something somewhere else.

Here are some examples. What the word in bold refers to is underlined.

> <u>Pollution is increasing</u>. The **problem** is getting worse each day.
>
> <u>Should taxes be raised or lowered</u>? This was the biggest **issue** in the election.   [topic causing great argument and controversy]
>
> <u>Whether the war could have been avoided</u> is a **question** that continues to interest historians.
>
> Let's discuss <u>crime</u>. It's always an interesting **topic**.   [subject to argue about or discuss, e.g. in a debate or in an essay]
>
> <u>Punishment</u> is only one **aspect** of crime.   [part of the topic]

B

Problem-solution words

Text-referring words are often associated with common patterns in text, such as the 'problem-solution' type of text. Note the words in bold connected with problems and solutions here and try to learn them as a family.

> The **situation** in our cities with regard to traffic is going from bad to worse. Congestion is a daily feature of urban life. The **problem** is now beginning to affect our national economies. Unless a new **approach** is found to controlling the number of cars, we will never find a **solution** to the **dilemma**.

In this dialogue, two politicians are arguing on the radio. Note how the words in bold refer to parts of the argument.

A: **Your claim** that we are doing nothing to invest in industry is false. We invested £10 billion last year. You have ignored **this fact**.

B: But the investment has all gone to service industries. **The real point** is that we need to invest in manufacturing.

A: **That argument** is out of date in a modern technological society. **Our position** has always been that we should encourage technology.

B: But **that view** will not help to reduce unemployment.

A: Rubbish. Utter rubbish.

Here are some more words associated with problem-solution texts. They are grouped in families associated with the key-words in bold. The prepositions which are normally used with these words are given in brackets.

situation: state of affairs   position (with regard to)
problem: difficulty [more formal]   crisis   matter
response: reaction (to)   attitude (to)
solution: answer (to)   resolution (to)   key (to)   way out (of)
evaluation [of the solution]: assessment   judgement

Exercises

25.1 Draw lines from the left-hand column to the right-hand column joining each sentence with a suitable label, as in the example.

1 The earth is in orbit around the sun.   problem
2 World poverty and overpopulation.   evaluation
3 God exists and loves everybody.   fact
4 I've run out of cash.   belief
5 It has proved to be most efficient.   view
6 They should get married, to my mind.   issue

25.2 Fill the gaps with an appropriate word to refer to the underlined parts of the sentences.

1 So you were talking about <u>animal rights</u>? That's quite a big .... in Britain nowadays.
2 We are <u>running short of funds</u>. How do you propose we should deal with the .... ?
3 <u>Is there life on other planets</u>? This is a .... nobody has yet been able to answer.
4 (Teacher to the class) You can write your essay on '<u>My best holiday ever</u>'. If you don't like that ...., I'll give you another one.
5 She thinks we should all <u>fly around in tiny little helicopters</u>. This .... to the traffic problem in cities is rather new and unusual. I wonder if it is viable?

25.3 These newspaper headlines have got separated from their texts. Put each one with a suitable text.

NEW APPROACH TO CANCER TREATMENT

NEW ARGUMENT OVER ECONOMIC RECESSION

SCIENTIST REJECTS CLAIMS OVER FAST FOOD

PRIME MINISTER SETS OUT VIEWS ON EUROPEAN UNION

SOLUTION TO AGE-OLD MYSTERY IN KENYA

SITUATION IN SAHEL WORSENING DAILY

1 she said if the world community failed to respond, thousands of children could die and

2 there was no proof at all that such things were harmful, and in

3 also said that he believed that most people had a similar vision of

4 tests were being carried out to see if the new drug really did

5 the bones proved beyond doubt that human beings had inhabited the region during

6 Mr Wallis denied that this was true and said instead that all the evidence pointed to

25.4 Answer these questions with regard to yourself.

1 What's your approach to learning vocabulary?
2 What aspect of your work/studies do you find most interesting?
3 Which topics in this book are most useful?

26 Uncountable words

Uncountable nouns are not normally used with a(n) or the plural, e.g. **information**, *not* an information, or some informations. It is a good idea to learn uncountable nouns in groups associated with the same subject or area. Here are some possible headings.

A Travel

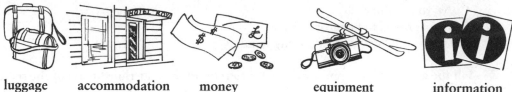

luggage   accommodation   money   equipment   information
baggage (Am. Eng.)   currency   (e.g. for skiing)

Travel is also an uncountable noun, e.g. Travel broadens the mind.

B Day-to-day household items

soap   toothpaste   washing powder   washing-up liquid   polish   paper

C Food

The word **food** is uncountable. Try adding more uncountable words to this list.

    sugar rice spaghetti butter flour   *soup*..

D Some rather abstract words are uncountable

    She gave me some **advice** on how to study for the exam.
    I picked up some interesting **knowledge** on that course.
    She's made a lot of **progress** in a very short time.
    She has done some **research** on marine life.
    They've done a lot of **work** on the project.

E Materials and resources

For making clothes, etc.: cloth (e.g. cotton, silk) leather wool
For buildings: stone brick plastic wood/timber concrete
For energy: coal oil petrol gas

F Typical mistakes

Don't say: What a terrible weather!   She has long hairs.   I have a news for you.
We bought some new furnitures.   *Say*: What terrible weather!   She has long hair.   I have
some news for you.   We bought some new furniture. (See also Unit 27.)

> *Tip*: always mark an uncountable noun with (U) in your vocabulary notebook, or write
> 'some...' or 'a lot of...' before it.

Exercises

26.1 Say whether these sentences need *a(n)* or not. Some of the nouns are not on the left-hand page. Use a dictionary that tells you whether the nouns are uncountable.

1 He gave us all .... advice on what to take with us.
2 I'm sorry. I can't come. I have .... homework to do.
3 She's doing .... investigation of teenage slang in English for her university project.
4 You'll need .... rice if you want to make a Chinese meal.
5 Paula getting divorced? That's .... interesting news!
6 I have to buy .... film for the holiday. I think I'll get about five rolls.
7 We saw .... beautiful silk and .... cotton in Thailand.

26.2 Sort these words into two columns side by side, one for *uncountables* and one for *countables*. Then join the words which have similar meaning.

tip   clothing   case   information   job   advice   travel   garment
trip   work   baggage   fact

26.3 Imagine you are going away for a week's holiday and you pack a suitcase with a number of things. Make a list of what you would pack and consider how many of the items on your list are *uncountable* nouns in English.

26.4 Correct the mistakes in these sentences.

1 We had such a terrible weather that we left the camp-site a~~~~ ~~~~ ccommodation in town instead.
2 In the North of England, most houses are made of stones, ~~~~ ~~~~ ie South, bricks are more common.
3 I love antique furnitures, but I would need an advice from a specialist before I bought any. My knowledges in that area are very poor.
4 Her researches are definitely making great progresses these days. She has done a lot of original works recently.

26.5 Another area that has a number of uncountable words is personal qualities and skills. For example, we might say that a secretary should have *intelligence, reliability, charm* and *enthusiasm*. These are all uncountable nouns. Choose from the list and say what qualities these people should have. Say whether they need *some, a lot* or *a bit* of the quality. Use a dictionary for any difficult words.

Jobs: soldier   nurse   teacher   explorer   actor   athlete   writer
surgeon   receptionist

Qualities: patience   courage   determination   goodwill   charm
stamina   reliability   loyalty   energy   experience   commitment
talent   creativity   intelligence   training

26.6 Could I have...? Practise asking for these everyday items and decide whether you must say *a* or *some*.

vinegar   duster   needle   thread   sellotape   tea-bag   polish

27 Words that only occur in the plural

A Tools, instruments, pieces of equipment

Some of these are always plural.

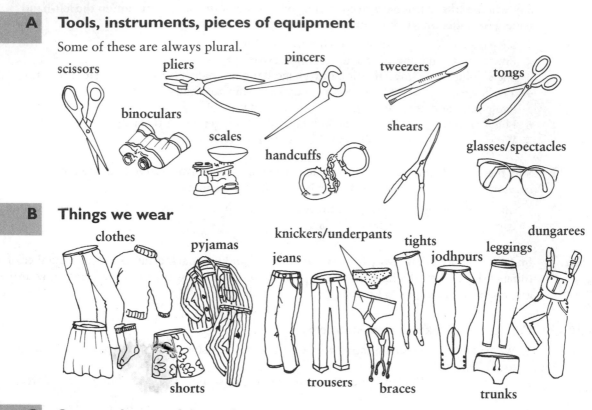

scissors pliers pincers tweezers tongs binoculars scales handcuffs shears glasses/spectacles

B Things we wear

clothes pyjamas knickers/underpants tights dungarees jeans jodhpurs leggings shorts trousers braces trunks

C Some other useful words

When I move to London, I'll have to find **lodgings**. [e.g. a room]
When will the **goods** be delivered? [articles/items]
The architect inspected the **foundations** before declaring that the **premises** were safe.
The military **authorities** have established their **headquarters** in the old Town Hall.
The **acoustics** in the new opera-house are near-perfect.
The **contents** of the house were sold after her death.
Looks are less important than personality in a partner.
As you come to the **outskirts** of the village, there are **traffic-lights**. Turn left there.
The **stairs** are a bit dangerous; be careful.
The **proceeds** of the concert are going to the children's fund.
A terrorist has escaped from prison. Her **whereabouts** are unknown.

D Words with plural form but used mostly with singular verbs

Names of some games: billiards dominoes draughts darts bowls
Names of subjects/activities: physics economics classics gymnastics aerobics
  athletics maths

Note: some words look plural but are not, e.g. series, means, news, spaghetti

There was a **series** of programmes on TV about Japan.
Is there a cheap **means** of transport I could use to get there?

Exercises

27.1 Make a list of (a) subjects you studied at school or elsewhere, and (b) your leisure interests. How many of the words are plural? Check the left-hand page or in a dictionary.

27.2 What things which are always plural can be used to:
1 cut a hedge? *shears*
2 weigh something?
3 cut paper?
4 hold your trousers up?
5 get a splinter out of your skin?
6 look at distant objects?
7 get a nail out of a piece of wood?
8 keep a prisoner's hands together?

27.3 How many articles on the clothes line are plural nouns?

27.4 Fill the gaps with an appropriate plural-form noun.
1 (To a child) Come on! Get your .... on! It's time to go to bed.
2 The .... of the rock concert are going to the international 'Save the Children fund'.
3 The .... in the new concert hall are superb. I've never heard such clear sound.
4 The escaped prisoner is tall, dark and has a beard. His .... are unknown, but the search is continuing.
5 You don't have to wear .... to ride, but it's much more comfortable.
6 The .... have forbidden the import of all foreign ....

27.5 Odd one out. In each of these groups, one of the nouns is always used in the plural. Which one?
1 wellington   trouser   slipper
2 billiard   squash   archery
3 knife   scissor   razor
4 tracksuit   costume   dungaree

27.6 In this little story, there are some nouns that should be plural but are not. Change the text where appropriate.

I decided that if I wanted to be a pop star I'd have to leave home and get lodging in London. I finally got a room, but it was on the outskirt of the city. The owner didn't live on the premise, so I could make as much noise as I liked. The acoustic in the bathroom was fantastic, so I practised there. I made so much noise I almost shook the foundation! I went to the headquarter of the Musicians' Union, but a guy there said I just didn't have a good enough look to be famous. Oh well, never mind!

28 Countable and uncountable with different meanings

A When we use a noun countably we are thinking of specific **things**; when we use it uncountably we are thinking of **stuff** or **material** or the **idea of a thing in general**.

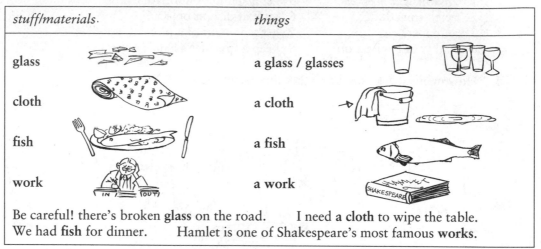

stuff/materials	things
glass	a glass / glasses
cloth	a cloth
fish	a fish
work	a work

Be careful! there's broken **glass** on the road.   I need **a cloth** to wipe the table.
We had **fish** for dinner.   Hamlet is one of Shakespeare's most famous **works**.

Here are some more nouns used in both ways. Make sure you know the difference between the uncountable and the countable meaning.

> drink / a drink   hair / a hair   paper / a paper   land / a land
> people / a people   home / a home   policy / a policy   trade /a trade

Drink was the cause of all his problems.   [alcohol]
There's **a hair** in my sandwich, a dark one; it must be yours.
Did you buy **a paper** this morning?   [a newspaper]
I love meeting **people** from different countries.   [individuals]
The different **peoples** of Asia.   [races / national groups]
Her grandmother lives in **a home**.   [an institution]
I've lost my car **insurance policy**.   [a document]
Trade with China has increased.   [imports and exports]

B The names of food items often have a different shade of meaning when used countably and uncountably (see **fish** above).

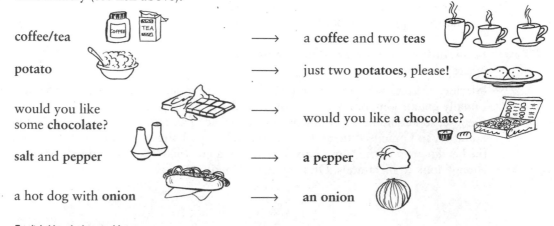

coffee/tea	⟶	a **coffee** and two **teas**
potato	⟶	just two **potatoes**, please!
would you like some **chocolate**?	⟶	would you like **a chocolate**?
salt and pepper	⟶	a **pepper**
a hot dog with **onion**	⟶	an **onion**

Exercises

28.1 Would you normally expect to find the following things in most people's houses/flats or garages/gardens? Where in those places would you expect to find them?

Example: an iron *Yes, most people have an iron to iron their clothes; they might keep it in the kitchen somewhere.*

1 a cloth	3 iron	5 pepper	7 paper	9 drink
2 a wood	4 a fish	6 glass	8 a tape	10 a rubber

28.2 Which question would you ask? *Can I have/borrow a...?* or *Can I have/borrow some...?*

Example: cake *Can I have some cake?*

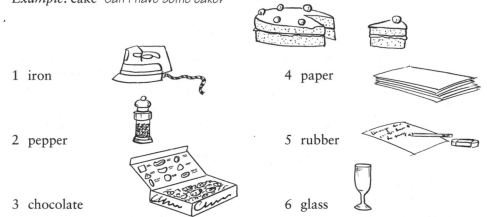

1 iron

2 pepper

3 chocolate

4 paper

5 rubber

6 glass

28.3 Answer these remarks using the word in brackets, as in the example. Use *a(n)* if the meaning is countable.

Example: Oh dear! I've spilt water on the floor! (cloth) *Never mind. Here's a cloth; just wipe it up.*

1 How did you get that puncture in your tyre? (glass)
2 I was surprised to hear that old Mrs Jones doesn't live with her family any more. (home)
3 What do you think my son should do? He's just left school and he's not really academic. He needs a job. (trade)
4 Why did you choose this house in the end? (land)
5 Mum, what's the *Mona Lisa*? (work)
6 How can I find out what the restrictions are on this car insurance? (policy)

28.4 What is the difference between (a) and (b) in each pair?

1 a) Have some sauce with your hot dog.
   b) Shall I make a sauce with the fish?

2 a) PLANT AND HEAVY MACHINERY CROSSING (road sign)
   b) I've bought you a house plant.

3 a) Can I have some light?
   b) Can I have a light?

29 Collective nouns

Collective nouns are used to describe a **group** of the same things.

A People

a **group** of people
(small group)

a **crowd** of people
(large number)

a **gang** of football fans
(rather negative)

B Words associated with certain animals

A **flock** of sheep or birds, e.g. geese/pigeons; a **herd** of cows, deer, goats; a **shoal** of fish (or any particular fish, e.g. a **shoal** of herring/mackerel – note the use of singular here); a **swarm** of insects (or any particular insect, most typically flying ones, e.g. a **swarm** of bees/gnats)

Note: a **pack** of... can be used for dogs or hyenas, wolves, etc. as well as for (playing) cards.

C People involved in the same job/activity

A **team** of surgeons/doctors/experts/reporters/scientists/rescue-workers/detectives arrived
    at the scene of the disaster.
The **crew** were all saved when the ship sank.   [workers on a ship]
The **company** are rehearsing a new production.   [group of actors]
The **cast** were all amateurs.   [actors in a particular production]
The **staff** are on strike.   [general word for groups who share a place of work,
    e.g. teachers in a school, people in an office]

D Physical features of landscapes

In the picture we can see a **row** of cottages near a clump of trees with a **range** of hills in the background. Out on the lake there is a small **group** of islands.

E Things in general

a **pile/heap** of
papers (or clothes,
dishes, toys, etc.)

a **bunch** of flowers
(or grapes, bananas,
berries, etc.)

a **stack** of chairs
(or tables, boxes,
logs, etc.)

a **set** of tools
(or pots and pans,
etc.)

Exercises

29.1 Fill each gap with a suitable collective noun.

1 There are .... of mosquitoes in the forests in Scandinavia in the summer.
2 As we looked over the side of the boat, we saw a .... of brightly coloured fish swimming just below the surface.
3 There was a .... of youths standing on the corner; they didn't look at all friendly.
4 You'll see a .... of cards on the bookshelf. Will you fetch them for me, please?
5 The government has appointed a .... of biologists to look into the problem.

29.2 In each case, one of the examples is wrong. Which one?

1 <u>Company</u> is often used for: actors   opera singers   swimmers
2 <u>Cast</u> is often used for people in: a play   a book   a film
3 <u>Crew</u> is often used for the staff of: an ambulance   a plane   a hospital
4 <u>Pack</u> is often used for: cats   hyenas   wolves
5 <u>Flock</u> is often used for: sheep   starlings   pigs

29.3 Draw a line from the left-hand column to the right-hand column joining collective words with appropriate nouns, as in the example.

1 a clump of   houses
2 a range of   midges
3 a gang of   fir-trees
4 a swarm of   elephants
5 a row of   bed-linen
6 a heap of   mountains
7 a herd of   schoolkids

29.4 Rewrite these sentences using collective words. Don't forget to make the verb singular where necessary.

1 There are <u>some tables on top of one another</u> in the next room.
2 There are <u>a large number of people</u> waiting outside.
3 <u>The people who work there</u> are very well-paid.
4 <u>A large number of sheep</u> had escaped from a field.
5 She gave me <u>six identical sherry glasses</u>.
6 She gave me <u>five or six beautiful roses</u>.

29.5 Some collective nouns are associated with words about using language. Underline any you can see in this news text and make a note of them in your vocabulary notebook.

THE JOURNALISTS raised a whole host of questions about the actions of the police during the demonstration. There had been a barrage of complaints about police violence. The Chief of Police replied that he was not prepared to listen to a string of wild allegations without any evidence. In the end, he just gave a series of short answers that left everyone dissatisfied.

30 Making uncountable words countable

You can make many uncountable nouns singular by adding **a bit of** or **a piece of**. Similarly you can make such nouns plural with **bits of** or **pieces of**. (**Bit** is less formal than **piece**.)

> She bought an attractive old **piece of** furniture at the auction sale.
> How many **pieces of** luggage have you got with you?
> I heard a really useful **bit of** information yesterday.
> Chopin wrote some wonderful **pieces of** music.
> Before you go to England I should give you two **bits of** advice...
> He spends all his money buying new **bits of** computer equipment.

B

Although **bit** and **piece** can be used with the majority of uncountable nouns there are also a number of other words which can be used with specific uncountable nouns.

Weather

> We have certainly had a good **spell of** summer weather this year.
> Did you hear that **rumble of** thunder?
> Yes, I did. It came almost immediately after the **flash of** lightning.
> I heard a sharp **clap of** thunder, then a few rumbles in the distance.
> A sudden **gust of** wind turned my umbrella inside out.
> There was a sudden **shower of** rain this morning.
> Did you feel a **spot of** rain?

Groceries

'Can I have a **loaf of** bread, a **slice of** cake*, two **bars of** chocolate, a **tube of** toothpaste, two **cartons of** milk and three **bars of** soap?'

*Slice can also be used with toast, bread, meat and cheese.

Nature

> Look at the ladybird on that **blade of** grass!
> What's happened? Look at that **cloud of** smoke hanging over the town!
> She blew little **puffs of** smoke out of her cigarette straight into my face.
> Let's go out and get a **breath of** fresh air.
> Put another **lump of** coal on the fire, please.   [lump can also be used with 'sugar']

Other

> I had an amazing **stroke of** luck this morning.
> I've never seen him do a **stroke of** work.   [only in negative sentences]
> I've never seen him in such a **fit of** temper before.
> The donkey is the basic **means of** transport on the island.
> Tights must be the most useful **article/item of** clothing ever invented.
> There was an interesting **item of** news about France on TV last night.

C

The phrase **a state of** can serve to make uncountable nouns singular. The nouns used with **state** are usually abstract and include chaos, emergency, tension, confusion, health, disorder, uncertainty, poverty, agitation, disrepair and flux, e.g. **a state of** emergency.

Exercises

30.1 Match the words in the list on the left with their partner on the right.

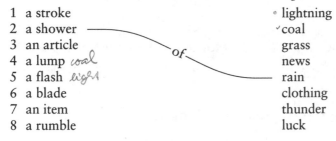

1 a stroke   lightning
2 a shower   coal
3 an article   grass
4 a lump *coal*   news
5 a flash *light*   rain
6 a blade   clothing
7 an item   thunder
8 a rumble   luck

30.2 Change the uncountable nouns to countable nouns in the following sentences by using either a *bit/piece of* or one of the more specific words listed in B opposite.

Example: Could you buy me some bread, please? *Could you buy me a loaf of bread, please?*

1 My mother gave me some advice which I have always remembered.
2 Suddenly the wind almost blew him off his feet.
3 We had some terribly windy weather last winter.
4 Would you like some more toast?
5 He never does any work at all in the house.
6 Let's go into the garden – I need some fresh air.
7 I can give you some important information about that.
8 We could see smoke hovering over the city from a long way away.
9 There is some interesting new equipment in that catalogue.
10 I need to get some furniture for my flat.

30.3 Use words from C opposite to fit the clues for the puzzle below.

1 The government announced a state of .... after the earthquake.
2 My granny wouldn't be in such a bad state of .... now if she hadn't smoked all her life.
3 We fell in love with the house although it was in a dreadful state of ....
4 We are still in a state of .... as to who has won the election.
5 Although this is supposed to be an affluent society, more people are living in a state of .... here now than for the last 50 years.

30.4 Make up a puzzle of your own like the one above using the language practised in this unit. If possible, test a friend.

30.5 Now decide who or what might be in the following states and write your own sentences using these expressions.

1 chaos   2 flux   3 confusion   4 tension

(See also Unit 32 for more weather words.)

3 I Countries, nationalities and languages

A Using 'the'

Most names of countries are used without 'the', but some countries and other names have 'the' before them, e.g. **The USA, The United Kingdom / UK, The Commonwealth.**

Some countries may be referred to with or without 'the' (the) **Lebanon,** (the) **Gambia,** (the) **Ukraine,** (the) **Sudan.**

B Adjectives referring to countries and languages

With **-ish:** British Irish Flemish Danish Turkish Spanish
With **-(i)an:** Canadian Brazilian American Russian Australian
With **-ese:** Japanese Chinese Guyanese Burmese Maltese Taiwanese
With **-i:** Israeli Iraqi Kuwaiti Pakistani Yemeni Bangladeshi
With **-ic:** Icelandic Arabic

Some, adjectives are worth learning separately e.g. **Swiss, Thai, Greek, Dutch, Cypriot.**

C Nationalities

Some nationalities have nouns for referring to people, e.g. a Finn, a Swede, a Turk, a Spaniard, a Dane, a Briton, an Arab. For most nationalities we can use the adjective as a noun, e.g. a German, an Italian, a Belgian, a Catalan, a Greek, an African. Some need woman/man/person added to them (you can't say 'a Dutch'), so if in doubt, use them, e.g. a Dutch man, a French woman, an Irish person, an Icelandic man.

D World regions

E Peoples and races

People belong to **ethnic groups** and **regional groups** such as **Afro-Caribbeans, Asians** and **Orientals** and **Latin Americans.** What are you? (e.g. **North African, Southern African, European, Melanesian**)

They speak **dialects** as well as languages. Everyone has a **mother tongue** or **first language;** many have **second** and **third languages.** Some people are perfect in more than one language and are **bilingual** or **multilingual.**

name: Wanija Krishnamurthan
nationality: Malaysian
mother tongue: Tamil (S. India)

second/third languages: English, Malay
type or dialect of English: Malaysian
ethnic group: Asian (Tamil Indian)

Exercises

31.1 Ways of learning nationality and language adjectives. Some adjectives can form regional groups, e.g. Latin American countries are almost all described by *-(i)an* adjectives.

1 Complete this list of Latin American adjectives. Look at a world map if you have to!
Brazilian, Chilean,...

2 The same applies to former European socialist countries and parts of the former Soviet Union. Complete the list. Hungarian, Armenian,...

3 What other regional groupings can you see on the left-hand page? (e.g. many *-ish* adjectives are European)

31.2 Famous names. Can you name a famous...

Example: Argentinian sportsman or woman? *Diego Maradonna*

1 Chinese politician?
2 Black Southern African political figure?
3 Polish person who became a world religious leader?
4 Italian opera singer?
5 Irish rock-music group?

31.3 All these nationality adjectives have a change in stress and/or pronunciation from the name of the country. Make sure you can pronounce them. Use a dictionary for any you don't know. Use phonetic script if possible (see Unit 5).

Example: Iran → Iranian /ɪˈreɪnɪən/ (US = /ɪˈrænɪən/)

1 Panama	→ Panamanian		4 Jordan	→	Jordanian
2 Cyprus	→ Cypriot		5 Egypt	→	Egyptian
3 Ghana	→ Ghanaian		6 Fiji	→	Fijian

31.4 Correct the mistakes in these newspaper headlines.

1 **Madonna to marry a French? Hollywood sensation!**

2 **Britains have highest tax rate in EC**

3 **Vietnamian refugees leave Hong Kong camps**

4 **POLICE ARREST DANISH ON SMUGGLING CHARGE**

5 **Iraqian delegation meets Pakistanian President**

31.5 World quiz

1 What are the main ethnic groups in Malaysia?
2 Which countries, strictly speaking, are in Scandinavia?
3 What are the five countries with the highest population?
4 How many languages are there in the world?
5 Where is Kiribati?
6 Where do people speak Inuit?
7 What are the five most widely spoken languages?

Follow-up: Make sure you can describe your nationality, country, region, ethnic group, language(s), etc. in English.

32 The weather

Cold weather

In Scandinavia, the **chilly** (1) days of autumn soon change to the cold days of winter. The first **frosts** (2) arrive and the roads become icy. Rain becomes **sleet** (3) and then snow, at first turning to **slush** (4) in the streets, but soon **settling** (5), with severe **blizzards** (6) and **snowdrifts** (7) in the far north. Freezing weather often continues in the far north until May or even June, when the ground starts to **thaw** (8) and the ice **melts** (9) again.

(1) cold, but not very   (2) thin white coat of ice on everything   (3) rain and snow mixed   (4) dirty, brownish, half-snow, half-water   (5) staying as a white covering   (6) snow blown by high winds   (7) deep banks of snow against walls, etc.   (8) change from hard, frozen state to normal   (9) change from solid to liquid under heat

B ## Warm/hot weather

close /kləʊs/ [warm and uncomfortable]   **stifling** [hot, uncomfortable, you can hardly breathe]   **humid** [hot and damp, makes you sweat a lot]   **scorching** [very hot, often used in positive contexts]   **boiling** [very hot, often used in negative contexts]   **mild** [warm at a time when it is normally cold]   *Note also*: We had a **heatwave** last month. [very hot, dry period]

C ## Wet weather

This wet weather scale gets stronger from left to right.

damp → drizzle → pour down / downpour → torrential rain → flood

Autumn in London is usually **chilly** and **damp** with **rain** and **drizzle**.
It was absolutely **pouring down**. *or* There was a real **downpour**.
In the Tropics there is usually **torrential rain** most days, and the roads often get **flooded**.
   or There are **floods** on the roads.

This rain won't last long; it's only a **shower**.   [short duration]
The **storm** damaged several houses.   [high winds and rain together]
We got very wet in the **thunderstorm**.   [thunder and heavy rain]
Hailstones were battering the roof of our car.   [small balls of ice falling from the sky].
   Note also **hail** (uncountable).
The sky's a bit **overcast**; I think it's going to rain.   [very cloudy]
We had a **drought** /draʊt/ last summer. It didn't rain for six weeks.

D ## Mist and fog

Nouns and adjectives: **haze/hazy** [light mist, usually caused by heat]   **mist/misty** [light fog, often on the sea, or caused by drizzle]   **fog/foggy** [quite thick, associated with cold weather]   **smog** [mixture of fog and pollution (smoke + fog)]

E ## Wind

There was a gentle **breeze** on the beach, just enough to cool us.
There's a good **wind** today; fancy going sailing?
It's a very **blustery** day; the umbrella will just blow away.
There's been a **gale** warning; it would be crazy to go sailing.
People boarded up their windows when they heard there was a **hurricane** on the way.

Exercises

32.1 Match each word with a word from the box.

1 thunder   2 torrential   3 down   4 heat   5 hail   6 snow   7 gale

stones   drift   storm   warning   rain   wave   pour

32.2 Fill the gaps with words from the left-hand page.

My first experience of real winter weather was when I went to Northern Canada. I was used to the sort of snow that falls in London, which quickly turns into brown .... (1) with all the people walking on it. In fact, most of the time I was in London, it didn't really snow properly, it was mostly .... (2). Apart from that, British winters meant a bit of white .... (3) on my garden and occasionally having to drive very carefully on icy roads early in the morning. I had never experienced the .... (4) and .... (5) that can paralyse a whole city in less than an hour and close roads completely. However, when the earth finally .... (6) and all the snow .... (7) away in spring, everything comes to life again and looks more beautiful than ever.

32.3 What kinds of weather do you think caused the following to happen? Write a sentence which could go *before* each of these.

1 We had to sit in the shade every afternoon.
2 The sweat was pouring out of us.
3 I can hardly breathe; I wish it would rain to cool us down.
4 Cars were skidding out of control.
5 Even the postman had to use a boat to get around.
6 They had to close the airport; the snow was a metre deep.
7 We were able to sit in the garden in the middle of winter.
8 The earth became rock-hard and a lot of plants died.
9 It blew the newspaper clean out of my hands.
10 A row of big trees had been uprooted like matchsticks.
11 I could hardly see my hand in front of my face.

32.4 What types of weather are bad and good for doing these things?

Example: Skiing *bad: mild weather which makes the snow melt; good: cold, clear days*

1 Planting flowers in a garden
2 Having an evening barbecue
3 Going out in a small sailing boat
4 A day of sightseeing in a big city
5 Camping out in a tent
6 Looking at ships through binoculars

32.5 This chart shows anyone who wants to visit the West of Ireland what weather to expect at different times of the year. Make a similar chart for your country or home region.

Dec–Mar	April–June	July–Aug	Sep–Nov
coldest months; usually quite wet; snow on high ground	generally cool, often wet and windy but improving	warmest months; bright with showers; cool sea breezes	often mild becoming cold; mist and fog

Describing people – appearance

A Hair, face, skin and complexion

straight hair
and **thin-faced**

wavy hair
and **round-faced**

curly hair
and **dark-skinned**

a **crew-cut**

bald
with **freckles**

beard and **moustache**
with a **chubby** face

receding hair
and a few **wrinkles**

He used to have **black** hair but now it's gone **grey**, almost **white**.
What sort of person would you like to go out with? **Blonde, fair, dark** or **ginger-haired /
red-haired**?
She has such beautiful **auburn** hair.   [red-brown]

Fair and **dark** can be used for hair, complexion or skin.

B Height and build

a rather **plump** or
stout man

a **slim** woman
[positive]

an **obese** person
[negative, very fat]

Fat may sound impolite. Instead we often say **a bit overweight**. If someone is broad and
solid, we can say they are **stocky**. A person with good muscles can be **well-built** or **muscular**.
If someone is terribly thin and refuses to eat, they may be **anorexic**.

C General appearance

She's a very **smart** and **elegant** woman, always **well-dressed**; her husband is quite the
opposite, very **scruffy** and **untidy-looking**.
He's very **good-looking**, but his friend's rather **unattractive**.
Do you think **beautiful** women are always attracted to **handsome** men? I don't. I think
first impressions matter most.

> *Tip*: The suffix **-ish** is useful for describing people: (see Unit 8)
> She's **tallish**.   He has **brownish** hair.   He must be **thirtyish**.

Exercises

33.1 Answer these remarks with the *opposite* description.

Example: A: I thought you said he was the short, chubby one.
            B: No, quite the opposite, *he's the tall, thin-faced one*

1 A: Was that his brother, the dark-skinned, wavy-haired one?
   B: No, quite the opposite, his brother's…
2 A: She's always quite well-dressed, so I've heard.
   B: What! Who told you that? Every time I see her, she's…
3 A: So Charlene's that rather plump fair-haired woman, is she?
   B: No, you're looking at the wrong one. Charlene's…
4 A: So, tell us about the new boss; good looking?
   B: No, I'm afraid not; rather…
5 A: I don't know why, but I expected the tour-guide to be middle-aged or elderly.
   B: No, apparently she's only…

33.2 Write one sentence to describe each of these people, giving information about their hair and face, their height and build and general appearance.

1 you yourself   3 a neighbour
2 your best friend   4 your ideal of a handsome man/a beautiful woman

Now, in the same way, describe somebody very famous, give some extra clues about them, e.g. *pop star/politician*, and see if someone else can guess who you are describing.

33.3 From these jumbled words, find combinations for describing people, as in the example. Not all of the words are on the left-hand page. Some of the combinations are hyphenated. Use a dictionary if necessary. *Example*: *good-looking*

looking   long   haired   good   aged   dressed   legged
stocky   round   faced   complexion   build   race
middle   over-   well   mixed   red   weight   tanned

33.4 WANTED! MISSING! Complete the gaps in these police posters.

33.5 Make a collection of descriptions of people from newspapers and magazines. Court/crime reports, celebrity and gossip pages of magazines, and the 'personal' columns where people are seeking partners are good places to start.

34 Describing people – character

A Intellectual ability

Ability: intelligent bright clever smart shrewd able gifted talented brainy (colloquial)

Lacking ability: stupid foolish half-witted simple silly brainless daft dumb dim (the last four are predominantly colloquial words)

Clever, in a negative way, using brains to trick or deceive: cunning crafty sly

B Attitudes towards life

Looking on either the bright or the black side of things: optimistic pessimistic

Outward-looking or inward-looking (i.e. to the world around one or to one's own inner world): extroverted introverted

Calm or not calm with regard to attitude to life: relaxed tense

Practical, not dreamy in approach to life: sensible down-to-earth

Feeling things very intensely: sensitive

C Attitudes towards other people

Enjoying others' company: sociable gregarious

Disagreeing with others: quarrelsome argumentative

Taking pleasure in others' pain: cruel sadistic

Relaxed in attitude to self and others: easy-going even-tempered

Not polite to others: impolite rude ill-mannered discourteous

Telling the truth to others: honest trustworthy reliable sincere

Unhappy if others have what one does not have oneself: jealous envious

D One person's meat is another person's poison

Some characteristics can be either positive or negative depending on your point of view. The words in the right-hand column mean roughly the same as the words in the left-hand column except that they have negative rather than positive connotations.

determined	⟶	obstinate stubborn pig-headed
thrifty/economical	⟶	miserly mean tight-fisted
self-assured	⟶	self-important arrogant full of oneself (colloquial)
assertive	⟶	aggressive bossy (colloquial)
original	⟶	peculiar weird eccentric odd
frank/direct/open	⟶	blunt abrupt brusque curt
broad-minded	⟶	unprincipled permissive
inquiring	⟶	inquisitive nosy (colloquial)
generous	⟶	extravagant
innocent	⟶	naive
ambitious	⟶	pushy (colloquial)

(See also Units 12, 73 and 78.)

Exercises

34.1 Match these words with their opposites.

1	clever	introverted
2	extroverted	tight-fisted
3	rude	courteous
4	cruel	gregarious
5	generous	kind-hearted
6	unsociable	half-witted

34.2 Do you think that the speaker likes or dislikes the people s/he is talking about?

1 Di's very thrifty.
2 Molly's usually frank.
3 Liz's quite broad-minded
4 Sam can be aggressive.
5 Dick's quite bossy.
6 I find Dave self-important.
7 Don't you think Jim's nosy?
8 Jill is very original.

34.3 Reword the sentences above to give the opposite impression. *Example*: Di's very stingy.

34.4 Magazines often publish questionnaires which are supposed to analyse your character for you. Look at the words below and then match them to the question which aims to decide whether a person is like that.

Example: If you arrange to meet at 7 p.m., do you arrive at 7 p.m.? *Reliable*

pessimistic   argumentative   sensitive   sociable
extravagant   assertive   inquisitive

1 Do you prefer to be in the company of other people?
2 Look at the picture. Do you think 'my glass is half empty'?
3 Do you find it easy to tell your boss if you feel he or she has treated you badly?
4 Do you always look out of the window if you hear a car draw up?
5 Do you often buy your friends presents for no particular reason?
6 Do you frequently disagree with what other people say?
7 Do you lie awake at night if someone has said something unkind to you?

34.5 What questions like those in 34.4 could you ask to try to find out whether a person is the following:

1 thrifty   3 sensible   5 even-tempered   7 obstinate
2 blunt   4 intelligent   6 original

34.6 Can you complete each of these word forks?

1 self- ……………   2 ……………… -tempered   3 ……………… -minded

Write a sentence to illustrate the meanings of each of your words.

34.7 Choose five or six adjectives from the opposite page which you think best describe either your own or a friend's character. How do you or your friend demonstrate these characteristics? *Example*: Sociable – I am sociable because I love being with other people.

35 Relationships

Types of relationships

Here is a scale showing **closeness** and **distance** in relationships in different contexts.

	CLOSER ←	→ MORE DISTANT
friendship:	best friend good friend	friend acquaintance
work:	close colleague	colleague/workmate
love/romance:	lover steady boy/girlfriend	ex-*
marriage:	wife/husband/partner	ex-*

* ex- can be used with or without (informally) another word: She's my **ex**. (girlfriend, etc.)

Mate is a colloquial word for a good friend. It can also be used in compounds to describe a person you share something with, e.g. **classmate, shipmate, workmate, flatmate**.

Workmate is usual in non-professional contexts; **colleague** is more common among professional people.

Fiancé/ée can still be used for someone you are engaged to, but a lot of people feel it is dated nowadays. You will sometimes see **husband-/wife-to-be** in journalistic style.

English has no universally accepted word for 'person I live with but am not married to', but **partner** is probably the commonest.

Liking and not liking someone

core verb	positive	negative
like	love adore worship idolise	dislike hate can't stand loathe
respect	look up to admire	look down on despise
attract	turn s.b. on	repel turn s.b. off
be attracted to	fancy	

She doesn't just like Bob she **idolises** him! I **can't stand** him.
I really **fancy** Lisa, but her friend just **turns me off**.

Fancy and **turn off** are informal. **Repel** is very strong and rather formal.

Phrases and idioms for relationships

Jo and I **get on well with each other**.   [have a good relationship]
Adrian and Liz **don't see eye to eye**.   [often argue/disagree]
I've **fallen out with** my parents again.   [had arguments]
Tony and Jane have **broken up / split up**.   [ended their relationship]
George is **having an affair** with his boss.   [a sexual relationship, usually secret]
Children should respect **their elders**.   [adults/parents, etc.]
Let's try and **make it up**.   [be friends again after a row]
She's **my junior** / I'm **her senior** / **I'm senior to her**, so she does what she's told.   [refers to position/length of service at work]

(See Unit 69 for more words relating to likes and dislikes.)

Exercises

35.1 Use words with the suffix *-mate* to resay or rewrite these sentences.

1 This is Jack. He and I share a flat.
2 My grandad still writes to his old friends he was at sea with.
3 We were in the same class together in 1978, weren't we?
4 She's not really a friend, she's just someone I work with.

35.2 How many relationships can you find between the people in column A and column B, using words from the left-hand page?

Example: *John Silver and Lorna Fitt were once colleagues.*

A

John Silver: owns a language school for business people in Bath. Worked at the Sun School, Oxford, 1984–5.

Josh Yates: politician, was married to Eve Cobb 1973–1980. Met Bill Nash a couple of times.

Ada Brigg: was married to Bill Nash 1981–4. Swam for Britain in 1982 Olympics.

Ana Wood: has lived as a couple (unmarried) with Bill Nash·for the last five years.

B

Nora Costa: was in UK Olympic swimming team in 1982. Was in same class at school as Ada Brigg.

Bill Nash: works every day with John Silver. Shared a flat years ago with Eve Cobb.

Fred Parks: politician. Knew Ada Brigg years ago, but not very well.

Lorna Fitt: taught at Sun School Oxford 1980–7. Lives with Josh Yates. ·

35.3 Liking and disliking. Using the verbs, phrases and idioms opposite, what sort of relations do you think the people on the left might have with the people on the right?

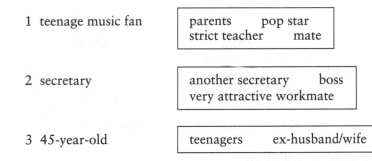

1 teenage music fan

| parents | pop star |
| strict teacher | mate |

2 secretary

| another secretary | boss |
| very attractive workmate |

3 45-year-old

| teenagers | ex-husband/wife |

35.4 The person who typed this book has got some of the phrases and idioms opposite mixed up with one another. Correct them.

1 Jo and Phil don't get on eye to eye with each other.
2 I fell up with my parents last night. It wasn't my fault.
3 We had a quarrel but now we've made it well.
4 Do you think Jim and Nora are making an affair? I do.
5 I see very well with all my colleagues at work.
6 She should learn to respect her olders.
7 Jo's attractive, but her mate just turns me up completely.

36 At home

A Places in the home

You probably already know the names of most rooms and locations in a typical home. Here are some less common ones and what they are for.

utility room: usually just for washing machine, freezer, etc.
shed: small building separated from the house usually for storing garden tools
attic: room in the roof space of a house (could be lived in)
loft: space in the roof of a house usually used only for storage
cellar: room below ground level, no windows, used for storage
basement: room below ground level, windows, for living/working
landing: flat area at the top of a staircase
hall: open area as you come into a house
porch: covered area before an entrance-door
pantry or **larder:** large cupboard (usually big enough to walk into) for storing food
terrace or **patio:** paved area between house and garden for sitting and eating, etc.
study: a room for reading/writing/studying in

B Small objects about the home

Ordinary, everyday objects are often difficult to name and are often not listed in dictionaries. Here is just a sample of such words.

remote control

power-point and plug

table-mat

coaster

corkscrew

tea-towel

washing-up liquid

grater

ironing-board

dust-pan and brush

bin-liners

mop

C Types of house/places people live

detached house: not joined to any other house
semi-detached house (informal: **semi-**): joined to one other house
terraced house: joined to several houses to form a row
cottage: small house in the country or in a village
bungalow: house with only one storey (no upstairs)
bedsit: bedroom and living room all in one
villa: large house with big gardens or a rented house in a holiday resort/tourist area
time-share: holiday flat or house where you have the right to live one or two weeks a year

Tip: If you visit an English-speaking country, go to a supermarket and look at the names of ordinary, everyday things for the home. This is often a good way of getting vocabulary that just does not appear in dictionaries.

Exercises

36.1 Where in a typical house would you look for the following things?

1 a rake   5 suitcases   9 a grater
2 cutlery   6 a tumble-dryer   10 old empty boxes
3 dental floss   7 a power point
4 a coat-hanger   8 a porch

36.2 Fill in the room and place labels on the plan of the house.

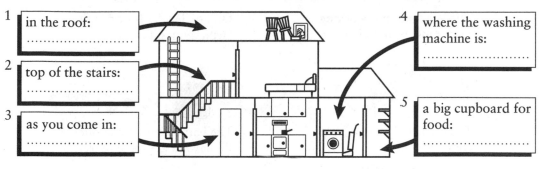

1 in the roof:
....

2 top of the stairs:
....

3 as you come in:
....

4 where the washing machine is:
....

5 a big cupboard for food:
....

36.3 Fill the gaps with a suitable word.

1 I've got a darkroom in the .... where I develop films. It's perfect because there are no windows down there.
2 Is there a .... where I can plug in this radio?
3 You'd better have a .... under your drink in case you mark that side-table. It's an antique.
4 The waste-bin's full again. I'll empty it. Are there any more ....? Where are they?
5 We keep our skis up in the .... during the summer. They're out of the way up there.
6 You'll find the garden-chairs in the .... at the bottom of the garden. Bring them up and we'll have a drink on the .... and watch the sunset.
7 The light-switch for the stairs is on the .... as you come out of your bedroom.
8 I've moved to a .... now as I found I couldn't manage the stairs any more at my age.

36.4 Answer these questions about yourself and, if possible, find out how someone else would answer them.

1 Is your house detached? What sort is it if not?
2 Are time-shares common in any part of your country?
3 Do houses still have pantries in your country?
4 Is it common to rent bedsits in your country? If so, what sorts of people do so?

36.5 Everyday objects.

1 How can you make very small pieces of cheese to sprinkle on a dish?
2 What might you fetch if someone dropped a saucer and it broke into small pieces on the floor?
3 What could you put under a dinner plate to prevent it marking the table?
4 How can you switch off the TV without leaving your chair?

37 Everyday problems

A Things that go wrong in houses and flats

The lights are not **working** there must be a **power-cut.**

Oh no! The bathroom's **flooded!** Get a mop, quick!

The kitchen door-handle's **come off.**

The batteries have **run out.** I'll have to get some more.

The washing machine **broke down** the other day. I'll have to wash by hand.

Oh dear! This chair's **broken.** I wonder how that happened?

This pipe's **leaking.**

I'm sorry, your cup's **chipped.**

B Everyday minor injuries

Sharon **fell down** and **cut** her knee this morning.

I **bumped/banged** my head against the cupboard door and got a **bruise.**

She **twisted her ankle** coming down the stairs.

C Other everyday problems

I've **mislaid** Bob's letter. Have you seen it anywhere?   [put it somewhere and can't find it]
She **spilt** some coffee on the carpet. I hope it doesn't **stain.**   [leave a permanent mark]
I **overslept** this morning and was half an hour late for work.
I've **locked myself out.** Can I use your phone to ring my wife?
The car **won't start.** I hope it's nothing serious.
The kitchen clock's **slow/fast/stopped.** What time d'you make it?

Exercises

37.1 What do you think happened to make these people do/say what they did?

Example: We had to send for a plumber. *Maybe a pipe was leaking/the lavatory was flooded.*

1 I had to call out our local mechanic.
2 Our neighbours let us use their washing machine.
3 Don't worry, it often does that; I'll screw it back on.
4 Come here and I'll put a plaster on it.
5 How many batteries does it take? I'll get some for you.
6 I don't know where you've put them. Try the bedside table.

37.2 Odd one out. Which of the three words is the odd one out in each case?

Example: spill   flood   chip   *chip – the other two involve liquids.*

1 break down   smash   break   3 leak   come off   chip
2 run out   stain   stop   4 cut   bruise   flood

37.3 What would you do if...

1 you mislaid your credit card?   4 your TV set broke down?
2 you noticed your guest's glass was chipped?   5 you bruised your forehead?
3 one of your coat-buttons came off?   6 your watch was slow?

37.4 Here is a matrix. There are the names of things and things that can go wrong with them. Not all of the words are on the left-hand page. Use a dictionary for any you are not sure of. Put just one tick (✓) along each horizontal line, for things that most typically go together, as in the example.

	cake-tin	vase	elbow	clock	moped	sink
banged						
cracked						
broken down						
dented						
stopped				✓		
blocked						

37.5 Complete these sentences using words and phrases from the opposite page.

Example: There was a power-cut so we... *had to sit in the dark / light candles.*

1 I was so tired when I finally went to bed that next morning I...
2 The wind blew the door shut and I realised I'd...
3 I would ring her but I'm afraid I've...
4 I can't take a photo, my camera's...
5 I tried to run over the rocks but I...

38 Global problems

A Disasters/tragedies

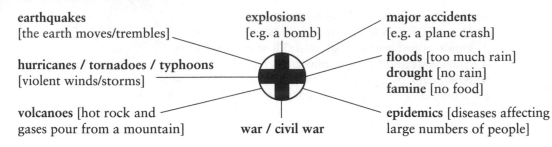

earthquakes
[the earth moves/trembles]

explosions
[e.g. a bomb]

major accidents
[e.g. a plane crash]

hurricanes / tornadoes / typhoons
[violent winds/storms]

floods [too much rain]
drought [no rain]
famine [no food]

volcanoes [hot rock and
gases pour from a mountain]

war / civil war

epidemics [diseases affecting
large numbers of people]

Verbs connected with these words

A volcano has **erupted** in Indonesia. Hundreds are feared dead.
The flu epidemic **spread** rapidly throughout the country.
Millions are **starving** as a result of the famine.
A big earthquake **shook** the city at noon today.
The area is **suffering** its worst drought for many years.
Civil war has **broken out** in the north of the country.
A tornado **swept** through the islands yesterday.
Remember: **injure** [people], **damage** [things]:
200 people were **injured** and dozens of buildings were **damaged** in the hurricane.

B Words for people involved in disasters/tragedies

The explosion resulted in 300 **casualties**.   [dead and injured people]
The real **victims** of the civil war are the children left without parents.   [those who suffer
the results of the disaster]
There were only three **survivors**. All the other passengers died instantly.   [people who
live through a disaster]
Thousands of **refugees** have crossed the border looking for food and shelter.
During the battle, the **dead** and **wounded** were flown out in helicopters.   [**wounded**:
injured in a battle/by a weapon]

C Headlines

Here are some headlines from newspapers all connected with diseases and epidemics.
Explanations are given.

disease can be
caused by bite
from a dog, fox,
etc.; very serious

Rabies out of
control in many
parts of Asia

tropical disease;
skin goes yellow

yellow fever
figures drop

New **malaria**
drug tested

usually caught
because of
mosquito bites

diseases causing sickness, diarrhoea etc.;
caused often by infected food and water

terrible skin
disease; leaves
the skin deformed

Minister says fight
against **leprosy** goes on

Cholera and **typhoid** injections
not needed says Tourism Minister

Exercises

38.1 What type of disaster from the list at A opposite are these sentences about? Why?

Example: The lava flow destroyed three villages. *volcano; lava is the hot rocks and metal*

1 The earth is cracked and vegetation has withered.
2 The tremor struck at 3.35 p.m. local time.
3 People had boarded up shops and houses during the day before, and stayed indoors.
4 Shelling and mortar fire could be heard all over the town.
5 Witnesses said they saw a fire-ball fall out of the sky.
6 People were stranded in the upper floors and sometimes on the roofs of their homes, unable to move about.

38.2 Complete the missing items in this word-class table, using a dictionary if necessary. Where there is a dash (–), you do not need to write anything.

verb	noun: thing or idea	noun: person
....	explosion	–
....	....	survivor
injure	....	....
starve	....	....
erupt	....	–

38.3 In these headlines, say whether the situation seems to be getting *worse* or *better*, or whether a disaster has *happened* or has been *avoided/prevented*.

1 Poison gas cloud spreads
2 AIDS time-bomb ticking away
3 POLICE DEFUSE TERRORIST BOMB
4 All survive jumbo crash-landing
5 Oil slick recedes
6 Flood warnings not heeded in time

38.4 Fill the gaps with a suitable word from B opposite. Try to work from memory.

1 Another 50 people died today, yet more .... of this terrible famine.
2 The government has agreed to allow 3,000 .... trying to escape the civil war to enter the country.
3 It was the worst road accident the country has ever seen, with over 120 ....
4 A: Were there any .... when the ship sank? B: I'm afraid not.
5 The .... and .... were simply left lying on the battlefield; it was a disgrace.

38.5 Which diseases are we talking about? Try to do this from memory.

1 One that can be caused by a mosquito bite.
2 One that leaves the skin badly deformed.
3 One you can get by drinking infected water.
4 One you can get from an animal bite.
5 One that makes the skin go yellow.

39 Education

A Stages in a person's education

Here are some names that are used to describe the different types of education in Britain.

play-school nursery school	pre-school (2–5 years old)	mostly play with some early learning
infant school junior school	primary (5/6–12/13)	basic reading, writing arithmetic, art, etc.
comprehensive school or grammar school	secondary (12/13–16/18)	wide range of subjects in arts and sciences and technical areas
college or polytechnic or university	further/higher (18+)	degrees/diplomas in specialised academic areas

Note: **Comprehensive schools** in the UK are for all abilities, but **grammar schools** are usually by competitive entry. **Public schools** in the UK are very famous private schools. **Polytechnics** are similar to **universities**, but the courses tend to be more practically-oriented. **Colleges** include **teacher-training colleges**, **technical colleges** and general **colleges of further education**.

B Exams and qualifications

take/do/sit/resit an exam   **pass / do well in** an exam   **fail / do badly in** an exam

Before an exam it's a good idea to **revise** for it.
If you **skip classes/lectures**, you'll probably do badly in the exam.   [informal; miss deliberately]

Some schools give pupils **tests** every week or month to see if they are making progress. The **school-leaving exams** are held in May/June. In some schools, colleges and universities, instead of tests and exams there is **continuous assessment**, with **marks**, e.g. 65%, or **grades**, e.g. A, B+, for essays and projects during the term. If you pass your university exams, you **graduate** /ˈgrædjʊeɪt/ (get a degree), then you're a **graduate** /ˈgrædjʊət/.

C Talking about education

Asking somebody about their country's education system.

> What age do children start school at?
> What's the **school-leaving age**?
> Are there **evening classes** for adults?
> Do you have **state** and **private universities**?
> Do students get **grants** for **further education**?

Note: A **professor** is a senior university academic, not an ordinary teacher. University and college teachers are usually called **lecturers** or **tutors**.

Exercises

39.1 Make a table for the various stages and types of education in your country, like the table at A opposite. How does it compare with the UK system and with the system in other countries represented in your class or that you know of? Is it possible to find satisfactory English translations for all the different aspects of education in your country?

39.2 Fill the gaps in this life story of a British woman.

At 5, Nelly Dawes went straight to ....(1) school, because there were very few ....(2) schools for younger children in those days. When she was ready to go on to secondary school, she passed an exam and so got into her local ....(3) school. Nowadays her own children don't do that exam, since most children go to a ....(4) school. She left school at 16 and did not go on to ....(5) education, but she goes to ....
.................................(6) once a week to learn French. She would like to take up her education again more seriously, if she could get a ....(7) or scholarship from the government. Her ambition is to go to a ....
.................................(8) and become a school-teacher.

39.3 Correct the mis-collocations in these sentences.

1 I can't come out. I'm studying. I'm passing an examination tomorrow.
2 Congratulations! I hear you succeeded your examination!
3 You can study a lot of different careers at this university.
4 I got some good notes in my continuous assessment this term.
5 She's a professor in a primary school.
6 He gave an interesting 45-minute conference on Goethe.
7 She got a degree in personnel management from a private college.

39.4 What questions could you ask to get these answers?

1 No, they have to finance their own studies.
2 There isn't much difference; it's just that the courses are more practical in a polytechnic instead of being very academic.
3 Well, they learn one or two things, like recognising a few numbers, but most of the time they play around.
4 Because I wanted to be a teacher, no other reason.
5 It's sixteen, but a lot of kids stay on until eighteen.
6 Well, I've been up all night revising for an exam.
7 No, ours are given in grades, you know, B+, A, that sort of thing.
8 No, I was ill. I didn't miss it deliberately.

Follow-up: The education system in the USA is a bit different from in the UK. How could you find out what the following terms mean in the US education system?

high-school   college   sophomore   graduate school

40 Work

A

It is impossible to give the names of every job or profession here, and you probably already know many of them. However, some job-titles are found in a wide range of different work places. Check the general meanings in a dictionary. The right-hand page exercises will help you work out the more precise meanings.

> boss   director   manager   executive   administrator   secretary   clerk   skilled worker
> unskilled worker   labourer   receptionist   public relations officer
> safety officer   security officer   union official   economist   personnel officer
> sales assistant   adviser   education officer   research-worker   supervisor

B

Here are some **professions** (jobs that require considerable training and/or qualifications) and **trades** (skilled manual jobs requiring on-the-job and other training).

> lawyer   dentist   hairdresser   mechanic   architect   priest   farmer   vet   librarian
> physiotherapist   child-minder   police officer   accountant   engineer   scientist   chef
> firefighter   civil servant   tailor/dressmaker   designer   builder   carpenter   plumber

C

Collocations of words connected with work

It's not easy to **get/find work** round these parts.
I'd love to **do** that kind of work.

What d'you **do for a living**?
It's difficult to **make a living** as a freelance writer.
[earn enough money to live comfortably]

I've been **offered a job** in Paris. She's not prepared to **take on that** job.
[includes the idea of 'having personal responsibility']

D

Expressions connected with work

to work shift-work   [nights one week, days next]
to be on flexi-time   [flexible working hours]
to work nine-to-five   [regular day work]
⎫ hours of work

to go/be on strike   [industrial dispute]
to get the sack   [thrown out of your job]
to be fired   [more formal than 'get the sack'; often used as a direct address: 'You're fired!']
to be dismissed   [more formal than 'be fired']
to be made redundant   [thrown out, no longer needed]
to be laid off   [more informal than 'made redundant']
to give up work   [e.g. in order to study]
to be on / take maternity leave   [expecting a baby]
to be on / take sick leave   [illness]
to take early retirement   [retire at 55]
⎫ reasons for *not* working

to be a workaholic   [love work too much]
to be promoted   [get a higher position]
to apply for a job   [fill in forms, etc.]
⎫ other useful verbs

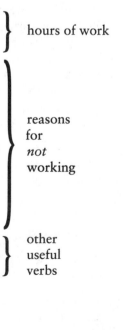

Exercises

40.1 Which of the job-titles at A opposite would best describe the following?

1 The person who represents the workers' interests in disputes with the management in a factory.
2 A person who has a high (but not the highest) position in a company and whose job it is to make important decisions.
3 An important person in a company who sits on the Board.
4 A worker whose job requires no special training.
5 A person generally in charge of the day-to-day administration in a company.
6 The person who makes sure there are no risks of accidents from machinery, etc.
7 A person whose job it is to keep an eye on the day-to-day work of other workers.
8 A person who does hard physical work.
9 The person who handles applications for vacant posts.
10 The person who gives out information to the press for a company.

40.2 Think of five people you know who work for a living. Can you name their jobs in English? If you cannot, look them up in a good bilingual dictionary, or in a thesaurus.

40.3 Using the expressions in E opposite, say what you think has happened / is happening.

Example: I'm not working now; the baby's due in 3 weeks. *She's on maternity leave.*

1 I lost my job. They had to make cutbacks.
2 He's enjoying life on a pension, although he's only 58.
3 One week it's six-to-two, the next it's nights.
4 They've made her General Manager as from next month!
5 I was late so often, I lost my job.
6 I get in at nine o'clock and go home at five.
7 Your trouble is you are obsessed with work!

Now make a sentence for each of the verbs you have not used.

40.4 Whose job do these things belong to?

Example: bucket   ladder   leather   *window-cleaner*

1 board overhead projector chalk	4 make-up script microphone
2 scalpel mask forceps	5 tractor plough barn
3 tippex filing cabinet stapler	6 sewing machine scissors needle

40.5 Would you call the following a *trade*, a *profession* or an *unskilled job*?

1 vet	3 plumber	5 electrician	7 cleaner	9 refuse collector
2 chef	4 architect	6 dressmaker	8 tailor	10 lawyer

40.6 Fill in the collocations.

I'd love to .... (1) a job in journalism, but it's not easy without qualifications. Since I have to earn a .... (2) somehow, I'll have to get .... (3) wherever I can find it. I've been .... (4) some part-time work editing a typescript for a book, but I'm not sure I want to .... it .... (5).

41 Sport

A Common sports

hang-gliding   windsurfing   bowls   darts

riding   snooker/pool/billiards   motor-racing

B Equipment – what you hold in your hand

golf – **club**   squash/tennis/badminton – **racket**   darts – **dart**   archery – **bow**
cricket/table-tennis/baseball – **bat**   hockey – **stick**   snooker/pool/billiards – **cue**
canoeing – **paddle**   rowing – **oar**   fishing – **rod/line**

C Athletics – some field events

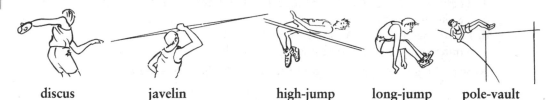

discus   javelin   high-jump   long-jump   pole-vault

She's a good **sprinter**.   [fast over short distances]
He's a great **long-distance** runner.   [e.g. 5000 metres, marathon]
Jogging round the park every Saturday's enough for me.

D Verbs and their collocations in the context of sport

Our team **won/lost by** three **goals/points**.
She **broke the** Olympic **record** last year.
He **holds the record** for the 100 metres breast-stroke.
Liverpool **beat** Hamburg 4–2 yesterday.
The team have never been **defeated**.   [more formal than **beat**]
How many **goals/points** have you **scored** this season?
I think I'll **take up** bowls next spring and **give up** golf.

E People who do particular sports

-er can be used for many sports, e.g. footballer, swimmer, windsurfer, high-jumper,
cricketer, golfer, etc. **Player** is often necessary, e.g. tennis-player, snooker-player, darts-
player; we can also say football-player, cricket-player. Some names must be learnt separately,
e.g. canoeist, cyclist, mountaineer, jockey, archer (**not** archerer), gymnast.

Exercises

41.1 Which of the sports opposite are these people probably talking about?

1 'The ball has a natural curve on it so it doesn't go in a straight line on the grass.'
2 'Provided it's not too windy at the top, there's no problem.'
3 'It is incredibly noisy, fast and dangerous, but it's really exciting to watch.'
4 'You get sore at first and can hardly sit down, but you get used to it after a while.'
5 'It's all a matter of balance really.'
6 'You need a good eye and a lot of concentration.'

41.2 Look at the sports page of one or two newspapers (either in English or in your own language). Are there any sports mentioned not listed at A opposite? If so, what are their English names? Use a bilingual dictionary if necessary.

41.3 Name one *other* piece of equipment necessary to play these sports apart from the item given, as in the example. What special *clothing*, if any, is worn for each sport?

Example: golf: clubs, *balls*

1 archery: bow, ...
2 badminton: racket, ...
3 hockey: stick, ...
4 baseball: bat, ...
5 darts: darts, ...

41.4 Collocations. Fill the gaps with suitable verbs.

1 Were many records .... at the Olympics?
2 We've been .... so many times we deserve to be bottom of the league!
3 Congratulations! How many points did you .... by?
4 You should .... jogging. That would help you lose weight.
5 Who .... the world record for the 1000 metres? Is it a Russian?
6 I only ever once .... a goal, and that was sheer luck.

41.5 What do you call a person who...?

1 does the long-jump? *a long-jumper*
2 rides horses in races?
3 drives cars in races?
4 throws the discus/javelin?
5 does gymnastics?
6 plays hockey?
7 plays football?
8 does the pole-vault?

41.6 Make sure you know which sports these places are associated with, as in the example. Use a dictionary if necessary.

1 court *tennis, squash, etc.*
2 course
3 ring
4 pitch
5 rink
6 alley
7 piste

42 The arts

Things which generally come under the heading of 'the arts'

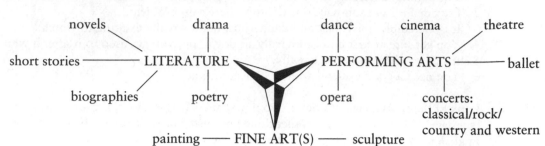

We often also include **architecture** and **ceramics** within the arts.

The arts (plural) covers everything in the network. **Art** (singular, uncountable) usually means **fine art**, but can also refer to technique and creativity.

> Have you read the **arts page** in *The Times* today?   [that part of the paper that deals with all the things in the network]
> She's a great **art lover**.   [loves painting and sculpture]
> Shakespeare was skilled in **the art of poetry**.   [creative ability]

Dance usually refers to modern artistic dance forms; **ballet** usually has a more traditional feel, unless we say **modern ballet**. *Remember*: a **novel** is a long story, e.g. 200–300 pages; a short prose fiction, e.g. 10 pages, is a **short story**.

Use of the definite article

When we refer to a performing art in general, we can leave out the article.

> Are you interested in (the) **cinema/ballet/opera/theatre**?
> Would you like to come to **the cinema/ballet/opera/theatre** with us next week.
>   [particular performance]

B Describing a performance

> We went to see a new production of *Hamlet* last night. The **sets** (1) were incredibly realistic and the **costumes** (2) were wonderful. It was a good **cast** (3) and I thought the **direction** (4) was excellent. Anthony O'Donnell **gave** a marvellous **performance** (5). **It got rave reviews** (6) in the papers today.

(1) scenery, buildings, furniture on the stage or in a studio
(2) clothes the actors wear on stage
(3) all the actors in it
(4) the way the director had organised the performance
(5) and (6) note these typical collocations; (6) means 'got very enthusiastic comments'

C Words connected with events in the arts

> There's an **exhibition** (Am. Eng.: **exhibit**) of paintings by Manet on in London.
> They're going to **publish** a new **edition** of the **works** of Cervantes next year.
> The Opera Society are doing a **performance** of *Don Giovanni*.
> Our local cinema's **showing** Bergman's *Persona* next week.

Note: What's **on** at the cinema/theatre, etc. next week?

Exercises

42.1   **Which branch of the arts do you think these people are talking about?**

Example: 'It was a strong cast but the play itself is weak.' *Theatre*

1   'It's called *Peace*. It stands in the main square.'
2   'Animation doesn't have to be just *Disney*, you know.'
3   'It was just pure movement, with very exciting rhythms.'
4   'It doesn't have to rhyme to be good.'
5   'Oils to me don't have the delicacy of water-colours.'
6   'Her design for the new shopping centre won an award.'
7   'I read them and imagine what they'd be like on stage.'
8   'The first chapter was boring but it got better later.'
9   'I was falling asleep by the second act.'

42.2   **Definite article or not? Fill the gap with *the* if necessary.**

1   The government doesn't give enough money to .... arts.
2   She's got a diploma in .... dance from the Performing Arts Academy.
3   I've got some tickets for .... ballet. Interested?
4   .... art of writing a short story is to interest the reader from the very first line.
5   I can't stand .... modern poetry; it's so pretentious.
6   I was no good at .... art at school. What about you?

42.3   **Each one of these sentences contains a mistake of usage of words connected with the arts. Find the mistake and correct it. You may need a dictionary.**

Example: The scene at this theatre projects right out into the audience.
not 'scene' but 'stage' (the place where the actors perform)

1   What's the name of the editorial of that book you recommended? Was it Cambridge University Press?
2   'I wandered lonely as a cloud' is my favourite verse of English poetry.
3   He's a very famous sculpture; he did that statue in the park, you know, the one with the soldiers.
4   Most of the novels in this collection are only five or six pages long. They're great for reading on short journeys.
5   There's an exposition of ceramic at the museum next week.
6   The sceneries are excellent in that new production of *Macbeth*, so dark and mysterious.
7   What's in the Opera House next week? Anything interesting?

42.4   **Ask *questions* for which these remarks would be suitable answers.**

Example: It's an oil on canvas. *What sort of painting is it?*

1   Yes, it got rave reviews.
2   No, I'm not really a concert-goer, but thanks anyway.
3   Oh, some beautiful old buildings and some ugly new ones.
4   The cast were fine, but the direction was weak.
5   A new Hungarian film; fancy going to see it?

Follow-up: **Make sure you can name all the parts of a typical theatre in English. A picture-dictionary might help you.**

43 Food

A

vegetables: cabbage   cauliflower   broccoli   spinach   cucumber   courgettes
(Am. Eng: zucchini)   aubergines (Am. Eng: egg plants)   leeks
meat: venison   liver   kidneys   veal
fish: cod   hake   plaice   whiting   mackerel   herring   sardine   trout   salmon /ˈsæmən/
seafood: prawns   shrimps   crab   lobster   crayfish   squid   cockles   mussels   oysters
herbs: parsley   rosemary   thyme   chives   oregano   tarragon   sage
spices: curry   cinnamon   ginger   nutmeg

B

Flavours and tastes – adjectives and some opposites (≠)

sweet ≠ **bitter** [sharp/unpleasant]   **sour** [e.g. unripe fruit]
hot, spicy [e.g. curry] ≠ **mild**   **bland** [rather negative]
salty [a lot of salt]   **sugary** [a lot of sugar]   **sickly** [too much sugar]
savoury [pleasant, slightly salty or with herbs]
tasty [has a good taste/flavour] ≠ **tasteless** [no flavour at all]

C

General appearance, presentation and quality

These chips are terribly **greasy.**   [too much oil/fat]
This meat is **over-cooked/overdone / under-cooked/underdone.**
British cooking can be very **stodgy.**   [heavy, hard to digest]
Mm, this chicken's **done to a turn.**   [just perfect, not overdone]
These pistachio nuts are terribly **more-ish.**   [informal; you want to eat more]

D

Ways of cooking food – verbs

boil   fry   bake   roast   grill

Shall I **stew** the beef?   [boiled with vegetables in the same pot], or would you prefer it as
a **casserole?**   [similar, but in the *oven*]
These lamb chops would be nice **barbecued.**   [done over hot coals, usually outdoors]
Have you **seasoned** the stew?   [added herbs/spices/salt/pepper]

E

Courses and dishes – a typical menu

86   *English Vocabulary in Use*

Exercises

43.1 To learn long lists of words, it is sometimes helpful to divide them up into groups. Try dividing these vegetable names into groups, in any way you like, e.g. 'vegetables which grow underground' (potatoes, carrots etc.). If possible, compare your answers with someone else's. There are some words not given opposite.

aubergine	leek	cucumber	spinach	carrot	potato	cauliflower
green/red pepper		courgette	sweetcorn	lettuce	onion	rice	pea
cabbage	garlic	radish	bean	shallot	turnip	asparagus
beetroot	celery					

43.2 Use the taste and flavour words opposite to describe the following.

1 Indian curry
2 pizza
3 sea water
4 an unripe apple
5 a cup of tea with five spoonfuls of sugar
6 strong black coffee with no sugar
7 factory-made white bread

43.3 Sort these dishes out under the headings *starters, main courses* or *desserts*.

chicken casserole   coffee gateau   fresh fruit salad   sorbet   Irish stew
paté and toast   prawn cocktail   rump steak   chocolate fudge cake
grilled trout   shrimps in garlic

43.4 What might you say to the person/people with you in a restaurant if...

1 your chips had too much oil/fat on them?
2 your dish had obviously been cooked too much/too long?
3 your piece of meat was absolutely perfectly cooked?
4 your dish seemed to have no flavour at all?

43.5 How do you like the following foods prepared? Use words from D opposite and look up others if necessary. What do you like to put on the foods from the list in the box?

a leg of chicken   eggs   potatoes   cheese   sausages
a fillet of cod   prawns   mushrooms

---

salt   pepper   vinegar   mustard   brown sauce   ketchup
salad-dressing   oil   mayonnaise   lemon juice

43.6 1 Which are *fish* and which are usually called *seafood*?

prawns   sardines   squid   oysters   mackerel   mussels   hake   crab
plaice   trout   lobster   cod   sole   whiting

2 What do we call the *meat* of these animals?

calf   deer   sheep (two names)   pig (three names)

3 Which of these fruit grow in your country/region? Are there others not listed here?

peach   plum   grapefruit   grape   nectarine   star-fruit   blackcurrant
raspberry   melon   lime   kiwi-fruit   mango

44 The environment

A There are many different words referring to features of the environment. Here are some arranged on small to large scales.

brook → stream → river   hillock → hill → mountain   cove → bay → gulf
copse → wood → forest   puddle → pond → lake   footpath → lane → road

B You have to be careful about the use of 'the' with features of the environment.

	use with the?	example
countries	no	France
countries which are in a plural form	yes	The USA
countries when limited by time	yes	The Spain of today
individual mountains	no	Mount Everest
mountains in the Bernese Oberland	yes	The Jungfrau
mountain chains	yes	The Rockies
islands	no	Sicily
groups of islands	yes	The West Indies
rivers	yes	The Volga
oceans	yes	The Pacific
seas	yes	The Mediterranean
gulfs, bays and straits	yes	The Gulf of Mexico
		The Bay of Biscay
lakes	no	Lake Erie
current	yes	The Gulf Stream

C Look at this encyclopaedia entry about Iceland and note any words that refer to particular features of the environment.

> **Iceland** An island republic in the North Atlantic. The landscape consists largely of barren plains and mountains, with large ice fields particularly in the south west. The island has active volcanoes and is known for its thermal springs and geysers. With less than 1% of the land suitable for growing crops, the nation's economy is based on fishing, and fish products account for 80% of the exports. Area: 103,000 km². Population: 227,000. Capital: Reykjavik.

D Here are some other nouns which are useful when talking about the environment. Check their meanings with a dictionary if necessary.

Where land meets sea: coast shore beach estuary cliff cape peninsula
Words connected with rivers: source tributary waterfall mouth valley gorge
Words connected with mountains: foot ridge peak summit glacier

E There are many environmental problems in the world today. Check with a dictionary if you do not know any of the terms below.

air, river and sea pollution   overfishing   the greenhouse effect
the destruction of the ozone layer   destruction of the rainforests
battery farming   waste disposal   overpopulation

Exercises

44.1 Label the pictures below.

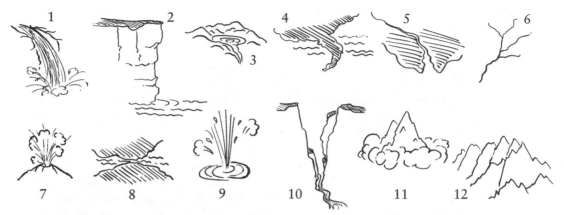

44.2 In the paragraph below all the instances of *the* have been omitted. Insert them wherever they are necessary.

> Brazil is fifth largest country in world. In north densely forested basin of River Amazon covers half country. In east country is washed by Atlantic. Highest mountain chain in South America, Andes, does not lie in Brazil. Brazil's most famous city is Rio de Janeiro, former capital. Capital of Brazil today is Brasilia.

44.3 Can you answer the following general knowledge questions about the environment?

1 What is the highest mountain in Africa?
2 What is the longest river in Europe?
3 Where is the highest waterfall in the world?
4 Name another country, apart from Iceland, which has geysers and hot springs.
5 What is a delta and which famous river has one?
6 Where are the Straits of Gibraltar and the Cape of Good Hope?

44.4 Complete the paragraph below about your own country, or any other country that interests you. Remember to use 'the' whenever it is necessary.

.... (1) is a .... (2) in .... (3). The countryside is .... (4) in the north and .... (5) in the south. The country's economy is based on .... (6). The best-known river in .... (7) is .... (8). The most famous chain of mountains is .... (9) and the highest mountain in that chain is .... (10). .... (11) is a major environmental problem in .... (12) today.

44.5 Give two nouns from the opposite page to go with the adjectives below. Try not to repeat any of the nouns you choose.

Example: sandy beach/shore

1 sandy   2 steep   3 shallow   4 rocky   5 turbulent   6 dangerous

44.6 Why do environmentalists say we should avoid spray cans, practise organic farming and use unleaded petrol, recycled paper and bottle banks? What else are they in favour of?

45 Towns

A Look at this description of Cork, one of Ireland's main towns. Underline any words or phrases that might be useful for describing your own or any other town.

> Cork city is the major metropolis of the south; indeed with a population of about 135,000 it is the second largest city in the Republic. The main business and shopping centre of the town lies on the island created by two channels of the River Lee, with most places within walking distance of the centre. (The buses tend to be overcrowded and the one-way traffic system is fiendishly complicated.) In the hilly area of the city is the famous Shandon Steeple, the bell-tower of St Anne's Church, built on the site of a church destroyed when the city was besieged by the Duke of Marlborough. Back across the River Lee lies the city's cathedral, an imposing 19th century building in the French Gothic style. Cork has two markets. Neither caters specifically for tourists but those who enjoy the atmosphere of a real working market will appreciate their charm. The Crawford Art Gallery is well worth a visit. It regularly mounts adventurous exhibitions by contemporary artists. The fashionable residential districts of Cork city overlook the harbour. There are other residential areas on the outskirts.

B Towns can be convenient places to live in because they have many facilities. Check with a teacher or a dictionary if you are not sure what anything means.

Sports: swimming pool   sports centre   golf course   tennis courts   football pitch
skating rink
Cultural: theatre   opera house   concert hall   radio station   art gallery
Educational: school   college   university   library   evening classes   museum
Catering and night-life: restaurant   cafe   nightclub   take-away   hotel
B and B (bed and breakfast)   youth hostel   dance-hall   disco
Transport: bus service   taxi rank   car hire agency   car park   parking meters
Other: health centre   law courts   registry office   citizens' advice bureau
job centre   bottle bank   department store   chemist's   estate agent
garden centre   police station   Town or City Hall   suburbs   housing estate
industrial estate   pedestrian precinct

C Towns also have their own special problems. Here are some to be found in London now.

Traffic jams: every day, particularly in the rush-hour, the streets get so packed with traffic that travel is very slow or even comes to a standstill. This is particularly stressful for commuters, people who travel to work in the town
Slums: certain parts of the city which are poor and in a very bad condition
Vandalism: pointless destruction of other people's property
Overcrowding: too many people live in too small a place
Pollution: the air and the water are no longer as pure as they were
Crime: see Unit 55

D Here are some useful adjectives for describing towns.

picturesque   historic   spacious   elegant   magnificent   atmospheric
quaint   lively   hectic   deserted (e.g. at night)   bustling   crowded
packed   filthy   run-down   shabby

Exercises

45.1 Check that you understand the text about Cork by answering the following questions.

1 Where is Cork?
2 Where is the shopping and business centre of Cork?
3 What is Cork's traffic system like?
4 What is special about the site of St Anne's Church?
5 In what style is the architecture of Cork Cathedral?
6 Can you buy souvenirs at the markets?
7 Is the Crawford Gallery worth visiting and why?
8 Where do Cork people live?

45.2 The description of Cork comes from a guidebook for tourists. Write sentences about a town of your choice, using the following expressions from the text.

the second/third/fourth ...est
within walking distance of
built on the site
cater for
to overlook
well worth a visit / visiting
a working market/museum/steam
    railway/model

the main ... area of the town lies
in the Victorian/Georgian/Classical/
    Baroque/French Gothic style
tend to be
whether or not it merits
those who enjoy
on the outskirts
to mount an exhibition
to appreciate the charm

45.3 Look at the list of facilities listed in B opposite. Tick all those which your town, or any town you know well, has.

45.4 Suggest three words which would collocate well with each of the nouns below, as in the examples.

1 *art* ....
.... museum
....

3 ....
.... college
....

5 *night* ....
golf .... club
....

2 *leisure* ....
.... centre
....

4 ....
.... court
....

6 ....
.... agency
....

45.5 What facilities would your ideal town have? Name the three most important facilities for you in each of the categories listed in B opposite. You may choose facilities other than those listed opposite if you wish.

45.6 Are any of the problems mentioned in C opposite to be found in your city or a city you know well? Could you suggest a solution for these problems?

45.7 Write sentences about any towns you know, using each of the adjectives in D.

Example: The most picturesque part of my town is the old market-place.

46 The natural world

A Animals

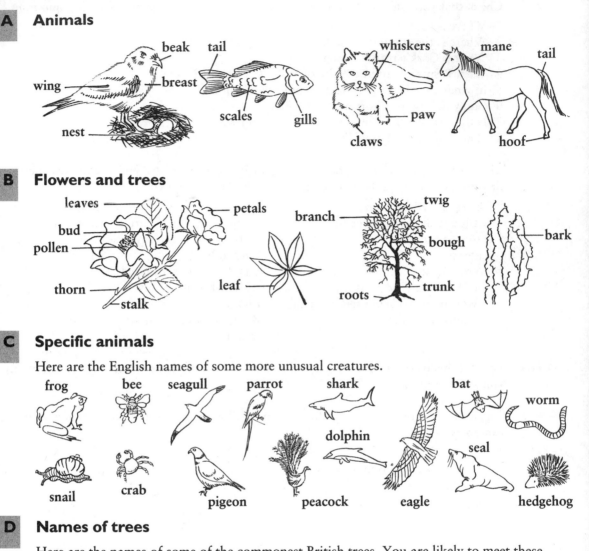

wing · beak · tail · breast · nest · scales · gills · whiskers · claws · paw · mane · tail · hoof

B Flowers and trees

leaves · petals · twig · branch · bud · pollen · bough · bark · thorn · leaf · roots · trunk · stalk

C Specific animals

Here are the English names of some more unusual creatures.

frog · bee · seagull · parrot · shark · bat · worm · dolphin · seal · snail · crab · pigeon · peacock · eagle · hedgehog

D Names of trees

Here are the names of some of the commonest British trees. You are likely to meet these words if you read fiction or poetry in English.

oak · willow · elm · fir · pine

E Some verbs for talking about the natural world

Our apple tree **flowers/blossoms** in April. Our garden **is thriving** after the rain. Let's **pick** some flowers (*not* pick up). Farmers **plant, fertilise** and **harvest** their crops.

Exercises

46.1 Can you answer the following general knowledge questions about the natural world?

1 Is the whale a fish or a mammal?
2 Which reptile alive today is a descendant of the dinosaurs?
3 Are the following trees deciduous or evergreen – poplar, yew, birch?
4 What does the bee take from flowers to make honey?
5 Name three animals that hibernate in winter.
6 What does a British boy or girl traditionally say while pulling the petals off a daisy one by one?
7 Which is the fastest of all land animals?
8 Which bird symbolises peace?
9 What plants or animals are the symbols of England, Scotland, Canada and New Zealand?
10 What do fish use their gills for?
11 Can you name an endangered species of plant or animal?
12 Which of these creatures is extinct – emu, dinosaur, phoenix?
13 Name three white flowers and three birds of any colour.
14 What plant or animal is the symbol of your country?

46.2 Write an appropriate adjective to go with each of the following nouns:

hedgehog   mane   petals   eagle   oak   willow   worm   bark

46.3 Fill in the blanks in the sentences below using words from the opposite page.

1 A tree's .... go a long way under ground.
2 A cat sharpens its .... against the .... of a tree.
3 Most fruit trees .... in spring.
4 Plants will not .... unless they get enough water and light.
5 The horse is limping. It must have hurt its ....
6 Flowers last longer in a vase if you crush the end of their ....
7 A flower that is just about to open is called a ....
8 Take care not to prick yourself. That plant has sharp ....
9 If we pick up those ...., we can use them to start the fire.
10 Jim's as blind as a ....
11 Anne's as busy as a .... while Jo works at a ....'s pace.
12 Most crops in the UK are .... in the autumn.

46.4 Look at this description of a camel from an encyclopaedia. Underline any words which you think would frequently be found in such descriptions of animals.

> **camel** A mammal of the family Camelidae, (2 species): the **Bactrian**, from cold deserts in Central Asia and domesticated elsewhere, and the **dromedary**; eats any vegetation; drinks salt water if necessary; closes slit-like nostrils to exclude sand; humps are stores of energy-rich fats. The two species may interbreed; the offspring has one hump; the males are usually sterile while the females are fertile.

46.5 Write a similar description for an encyclopaedia of an elephant, or any other animal of your own choice. Use reference books to help you if necessary.

47 Clothes

A At this level you probably already know most of the everyday words for clothes. Here are some items of clothing or parts of them which are perhaps less familiar.

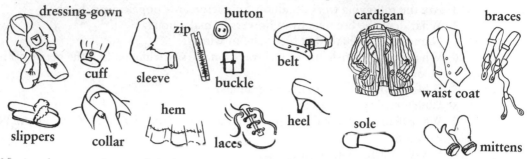

B Notice that most items of clothing covering the legs are plural words only and, if you wish to count them, you need to say, e.g. 'Six pairs of trousers'. (See Unit 24.)

C Here are some words used to describe materials which clothes are often made of. These words can be either nouns or adjectives.

silk   cotton   velvet   corduroy   denim   leather   wool/woollen   suede

D Here are some adjectives used to describe the patterns on materials.

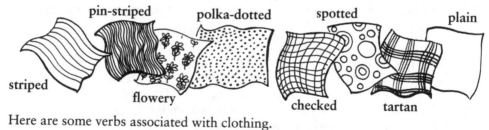

E Here are some verbs associated with clothing.

He **undressed / got undressed**, throwing all his clothes on the floor.
She quickly **dressed** the child.
I love **dressing up** for parties as I normally wear jeans.
Can I **try on** those grey shoes in the window?
The skirt is too tight and too short – it needs **letting out** and **letting down**.
The dress is too loose and too long – it needs **taking in** and **taking up**.
She **took off** her shoes and **put on** her slippers.
He **changed out of** his weekend clothes **into** his uniform.
Red usually doesn't **suit** people with ginger hair.
Her black bag **matches** her shoes.
Those shoes don't **fit** the boy any more. He's **grown out** of them.

F Here are some adjectives for describing people's clothing.

How things fit: baggy   loose   tight   close-fitting
Style: long-sleeved   V-neck   round-neck
General: elegant   smart   scruffy   chic   trendy   with-it
Appearance: well-dressed   badly-dressed   old-fashioned   fashionable

See Unit 33 for more useful vocabulary for describing someone's appearance.

Exercises

47.1 Which of the words illustrated in A fit best in the following sentences?

1 I must get my black shoes repaired. One .... is broken and both the .... have holes in them.
2 Do up your .... or you'll fall over.
3 There's someone at the door. You'd better put your .... on before you open it.
4 Put your .... on – this floor is very cold.
5 I've eaten too much – I'll have to loosen my ....
6 I've almost finished making my dress for the party but I've still got to sew up the .... and sew on some ....

47.2 Complete these sentences with any appropriate word. Use 'pair' where it is necessary.

1 Many women wear nighties in bed whereas most men and children wear
....
2 Blue .... are a kind of international uniform for young people.
3 People with ugly knees shouldn't wear ....
4 I need some new underwear. I'm going to buy three new .... today.
5 Bother! I've got a hole in my tights. I'll have to get a new ....
6 Bother! I've got a hole in my tights. I'll have to get some new ....

47.3 Match the following materials with the item which they are most likely to be associated with from the box.

Example: velvet ribbon

1 silk   2 cashmere   3 leather   4 corduroy   5 velvet   6 cotton

sweater   trousers   T-shirt   ribbon   evening blouse   boots

47.4 Describe in as much detail as possible what the people in the pictures are wearing.

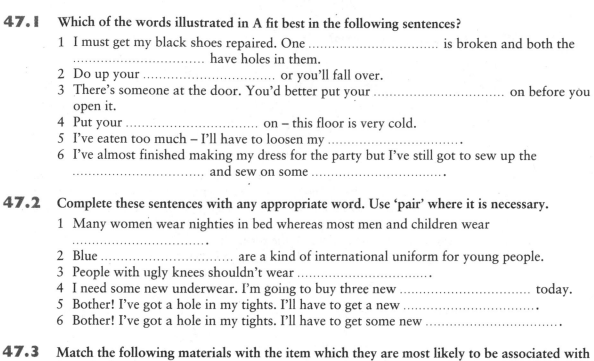

47.5 Put the right verb, *match*, *suit* or *fit*, into each of these sentences.

1 The blue dress .... her properly now she's lost some weight.
2 The blue of her dress .... the blue of her eyes.
3 That blue dress .... the girl with the blonde hair.

47.6 Describe in as much detail as you can how (a) you and (b) someone else you can see are dressed.

48 Health and medicine

Health and medicine

A What are your symptoms?

rash   bruise   lump   spots   a black eye

I've got a cold / a cough / a sore throat / a temperature / a stomach ache / chest pains / earache / a pain in my side / a rash on my chest / spots / a bruise on my leg / a black eye / a lump on my arm / indigestion / diarrhoea / painful joints / blisters / sunburn.
I feel sick / dizzy / breathless / shivery / faint / particularly bad at night.
I am depressed / constipated / tired all the time.
I've lost my appetite / voice; I can't sleep, my nose itches and my leg hurts.

B What do doctors do?

They take your temperature, listen to your chest, look in your ears, examine you, take your blood pressure, ask you some questions and weigh and measure you before sending you to the hospital for further tests.

C What's the diagnosis?

You've got flu / chickenpox / mumps / pneumonia / rheumatism / an ulcer / a virus / a bug something that's going round.
You've broken your wrist and sprained / dislocated your ankle.
You're pregnant / a hypochondriac.
He died of lung cancer / a heart attack / a brain haemorrhage / AIDS.

D What does the doctor prescribe?

a) Take one three times a day after meals.
b) Take a teaspoonful last thing at night.
c) Rub a little on before going to bed each night.
d) We'll get the nurse to put a bandage on.
e) You'll need to have some injections before you go.
f) I'll ask the surgeon when he can fit you in for an operation.
g) You'll have to have your leg put in plaster.
h) I think you should have total bed rest for a week.

E What might the doctor ask you?

What would you say if the doctor asked you the following questions?

Do you have health insurance?   Have you ever had any operations?

Are you taking any medication?   Are you allergic to anything?

Exercises

48.1 Match the diseases with their symptoms.

1 flu   swollen glands in front of ear, earache or pain on eating
2 pneumonia   burning pain in abdomen, pain or nausea after eating
3 rheumatism   rash starting on body, slightly raised temperature
4 chickenpox   dry cough, high fever, chest pain, rapid breathing
5 mumps   headache, aching muscles, fever, cough, sneezing
6 an ulcer   swollen, painful joints, stiffness, limited movement

48.2 What does the doctor or nurse use the following things for?

Example: stethoscope *For listening to a patient's chest.*

1 thermometer   2 scales   3 tape measure   4 scalpel

48.3 Look at statements (a) to (g) in D opposite. Which do you think the doctor said to each of the following patients?

1 Anne with bad sunburn.   5 Liz with a bad cough.
2 Jo who's broken her leg.   6 Sam who needs his appendix out.
3 John who's off to the Tropics.   7 Rose suffering from exhaustion.
4 Paul with flu.   8 Alf who's sprained his wrist.

48.4 Complete the following table.

noun	adjective	verb
....	breathless	....
....	faint	....
....	shivery	....
....	dislocated	....
ache	....	....
treatment	–	....
....	swollen	....

48.5 What medical problems might you have if...

1 you wear shoes that rub?   7 you eat food you're allergic to?
2 you eat too fast?   8 you run unusually fast for a bus?
3 you smoke a lot?   9 you eat food that is bad?
4 you play football?   10 a mosquito bites you?
5 you go ski-ing?   11 you get wet on a cold day?
6 you stay too long in the sun?   12 you think you're ill all the time?

48.6 Think of some of the illnesses you (or members of your family or friends) have had. What were the symptoms and what did the doctor prescribe?

Follow-up: Look at the health page of a magazine or newspaper. Make a note of any new vocabulary on the theme that you find there. Look in your medicine cabinet at home, at school or work. Can you name everything that you find there?

49 Travel

Look at the table of some basic travel vocabulary. Highlight any of the words that you are not sure about and look them up in your dictionary.

transport type	different kinds of vehicle	parts of vehicle	people working with it	associated facilities
road	sports car, estate car, bus, coach, tram, van, lorry	boot, engine, gears, steering-wheel, brakes, tyres	driver, mechanic, chauffeur, bus-conductor	petrol station, garage, service station
rail	passenger train, freight train, local train, express	sleeping-car, buffet, restaurant-car, compartment	engine-driver, ticket collector, guard, porter	waiting-room, ticket office, signal-box
sea	yacht, rowing-boat, fishing-boat, liner, ferry, trawler	engine-room, deck, bridge, gangplank, companionway	captain, skipper, purser, docker, steward(ess)	port, buoy, quay, customs shed, light-house, docks
air	aeroplane, jet, helicopter, supersonic aircraft	cockpit, nose, tail, wings, fuselage, joystick	pilot, ground staff, steward, air traffic controller	duty-free shop, departure lounge, hangar, runway

B Words at sea

Traditionally sailors use different words at sea – a bedroom is a **cabin**, a bed is a **bunk**, the kitchen on a ship is a **galley**, right is **starboard** and left is **port** and the group of people who work on the ship is called the **crew**. These terms are also now used in the context of an aircraft. Sailors also refer to their vessels as 'she' rather than 'it'.

C Some international road signs

There's a hump bridge ahead.

There's going to be a steep hill downwards.

There may be cattle on the road ahead.

There's a cycle route ahead.

D Some words connected with travel

Last week he **flew** to New York. It was an early-morning **flight**. The **plane** was to **take off** at 6 a.m. and **land** at 7 a.m. **local time**. He was **stranded** at the **airport** overnight. The **plane** was **delayed** by fog. Air **passengers** often suffer such delays.

Trains always **run on time** here. You have to **change** trains at Crewe.

We are **sailing** on the QE2. It **sets sail** at noon. It will **dock** in New York at 6 p.m. and we shall **disembark** as soon as we can.

The **ship** was **wrecked**. The passengers were **marooned** on a desert island.

Our **car does 10 km to the litre**. It **goes** quite **fast**. We can usually **overtake** other cars.

The car **swerved** into the middle of the **road** to avoid the **cyclist**.

He **backed** the car into the **drive** and **parked** in front of the house.

Exercises

49.1 Label the diagrams below. Use a dictionary to help you if necessary.

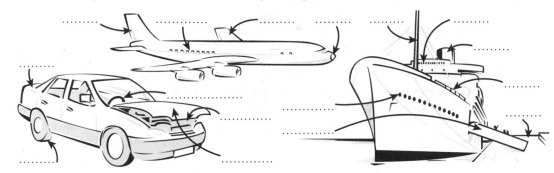

49.2 Here are some more words which could have been included in the table in A opposite. Where would they fit into the table?

bonnet	balloon	deck-chair	guard's van
mast	petrol pump	bus driver	anchor
glider	oar	rudder	left luggage lockers
check-in desk	control tower	canoe	dual carriageway

49.3 Here are some more road signs. Write an explanation of their meaning similar to the explanations given in C opposite.

1   2   3   4   5

49.4 Fill in the blanks. Most of the words you need can be found opposite.

Yesterday John was supposed to take a ......*flight*...........(1) from London to Paris. He got up very early, put his luggage in the ....*boot / trunk*......(2) of his car and tried to start the engine. It wouldn't start. John lifted the ...*bonnet*...............(3) but he couldn't see what the matter could be. He immediately called his local ....(4) to ask them to send a ....(5) at once. Fortunately, the garage had a man free and he was with John within ten minutes. He quickly saw what the matter was. 'You've *run out*...........(6) of petrol', he said. John felt very foolish. 'Why didn't I *...che...*.....................(7) everything last night?' he wondered. Despite all this, he got to the airport, checked in quite early and then went straight through to the ....(8) to read a newspaper while he waited. Soon he heard an announcement. 'Passengers on flight BA 282 to Paris are informed that all flights to and from Paris are ...*delayed*...............(9) because of a heavy snowfall last night.' 'If only I had decided to go by ....*train*.........(10)', John thought. 'It would probably have been quicker in the end and even if I sometimes feel sick on the ....(11) across the Channel, it can be quite pleasant sitting in a ....(12) on the deck, watching the seagulls and the other ....(13). The .*galley*.............(14) on a ship seem to produce much better food than those on an aircraft too.'

49.5 Write two advantages and two disadvantages for each of the four forms of travel opposite.

50 Holidays

A Here are a number of different places where you can spend a holiday.

camp site: a place where you can pitch a tent or park a caravan
self-catering flat: flat which you rent, you cook for yourself
guesthouse: accommodation like a hotel but cheaper and with fewer services
youth hostel: cheap accommodation, mainly for young people, with, perhaps, ten or more people sleeping in bunk beds in one room
holiday camp: a place providing holiday accommodation in little chalets or flats, with restaurants, bars, swimming pools and lots of other facilities and entertainment
time-share apartment: accommodation which one owns, say, a 26th part of and so has the right to stay there for 2 weeks every year

B Here are a number of different things which people like to do on holiday.

sunbathe

swim *or* go swimming

do some *or* go sightseeing

ski *or* go skiing

go for a drive

hike *or* go hiking

tour *or* go touring

go on an excursion

climb *or* go climbing/mountaineering

camp *or* go camping

Note: You usually ask 'Have you ever been skiing/hang-gliding?' rather than 'Have you ever gone...?' 'He's been wind-surfing' means that at some point in his life he has done this.

C Here is some useful language for when you are staying in a hotel.

I'd like to book a single/double room with a cot.
I'd like a room with a shower, a colour TV, and a view of the sea.
What time do you serve breakfast?
Am I too late for dinner/to get something to eat?
Is service included?
Could I have a call at 7.30, please?
Could we have dinner in our room, please?
The teasmade [tea-making machine] in my room isn't working.
I'd like an extra pillow, please.
I'd like to make a call to New Zealand, please.
What time do you like rooms to be vacated by?
Sorry to bother you, but...
I'm afraid there's something wrong with the..., could you have a look at it?

Exercises

50.1 Which of the holiday places in A have you or any of your friends stayed at? What are the advantages and disadvantages of each? Try and note down at least one advantage and one disadvantage for each even if you have no direct personal experience of them.

50.2 List the ten activities shown in B opposite according to your personal preferences.

50.3 Look at B opposite again. Note the way you can say either 'We *camped* in Spain this year' or 'We *went camping* in Spain this year'. Write the sentences below in an alternative form, either with or without *go* or *be*.

1 They went canoeing in the Dordogne last year.
2 Have you ever been windsurfing?
3 I love going sailing.
4 He spends too much time fishing.
5 It's quite expensive to shop in Rome.
6 I enjoy cycling at weekends.

50.4 What would you say in a hotel when...

1 you want to reserve a room for a couple with a small baby?
2 you have to wake up early for an important meeting?
3 your TV screen suddenly goes blank?
4 it's midnight, you've just arrived and you're very hungry?
5 you'd rather not go to the dining-room for breakfast?
6 you are not sure whether to leave a tip or not?

50.5 There are six typical language mistakes in the paragraph below. Underline them and then write the corrections.

> camp-site
>
> The Smiths stayed at a camping last summer because all other kinds of holiday
>
> accommodations are too expensive for them. Every day Mrs Smith had a sunbath, Mr
>
> Smith made a sight-seeing and the children made a travel around the island. One day
>
> they made an excursion to a local castle.

50.6 To find more useful language relating to holidays, get some holiday brochures or other tourist information written in English. You could either try the embassies of those countries or a travel agency. Remember to make it clear that you want the information in English. When you receive the information, make a point of noting down any useful new words and expressions that you learn.

50.7 Find a tourist brochure in your own language about your own town or region. Try to translate it for English-speaking visitors.

50.8 Where would you spend your ideal holiday? What kind of accommodation would you stay in? How would you spend your time? Write a paragraph.

51 Numbers and shapes

Anyone who works with any branch of science or technology needs to be able to talk about figures. Notice how the following are said in English.

28%	twenty-eight per cent	10 m × 12 m	ten metres by twelve metres
10.3	ten point three	1⅔	one and two thirds
4/9	four ninths	9/13	nine thirteenths or nine over thirteen
4^2	four squared	7^3	seven cubed
8^4	eight to the power of four		

32° C or F   thirty-two degrees centigrade/celsius or fahrenheit

1,623,457 one million, six hundred and twenty-three thousand, four hundred and fifty-seven

B

All scientists and technologists also need to be able to talk about shapes. Note the names of the shapes below.

Two-dimensional shapes

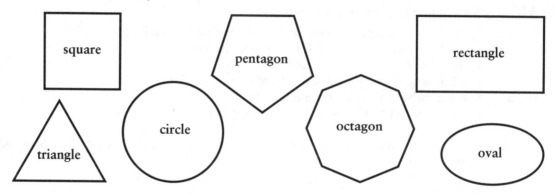

A **rectangle** has four **right angles**.
A **circle** is cut in half by its **diameter**. Its two halves can be called **semi-circles**.
The **radius** of a circle is the distance from its centre to the **circumference**.

Three-dimensional shapes

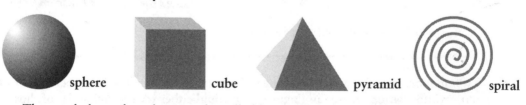

The two halves of a sphere can be called **hemispheres**.

C

Here are the four basic processes of arithmetic.

+ **addition**   − **subtraction**   × **multiplication**   ÷ **division**

Notice how these formulae would be read aloud.

$2x + 3y - z = \dfrac{3z}{4x}$ Two x plus three y minus z equals three z divided by four x. *or* Three z over four x.

$6 \times 7 = 42$ Six times seven is forty two. *or* Six sevens are forty two.

Exercises

51.1 How numerate are you? Try this numbers quiz.

1 Name the first four odd numbers.
2 Name the first four even numbers.
3 Name the first four prime numbers.
4 Give an example of a decimal fraction.
5 Give an example of a vulgar fraction.
6 How do you read this formula and what does it represent: $e=mc^2$?
7 How do you read this and what does it represent: $2\pi r$?

51.2 Write the following in words rather than in figures or symbols.

1 2% of the British population owned 90% of the country's wealth in 1992.
2 0° C = 32° F
3 62.3% of adults have false teeth.
4 ⅔ + ¼ × 4^2 = 14⅔.
5 2,769,425 people live here.

51.3 Look at the figures in B opposite. What is the adjective relating to each of the shapes illustrated? Use a dictionary if necessary.

51.4 Read the following records aloud.

1 Oxygen accounts for 46.6% of the earth's crust.
2 The nearest star to earth is Proxima Centauri. It is 33,923,310,000,000 km from earth.
3 The highest waterfall in the world is Angel Falls in Venezuela with a drop of 979 m.
4 The top coffee-drinking country in the world is Finland where 1,892 cups per annum are consumed per head of the population.
5 The tallest church in the world is the Chicago Methodist Temple which is 173 m or 568 ft high.
6 The commonest item of lost property on London transport is the umbrella. 23,250 umbrellas were handed in to London transport lost property offices in 1987/8.
7 The country with the most telephones in the world is Monaco. It has 733 telephones per 1,000 population.
8 The smallest country in the world is the Vatican City with an area of 0.4 sq km.

51.5 Draw the following figures.

1 A right-angled triangle with two equal sides of about two centimetres in length. Draw a small circle at the centre of the triangle and then draw lines from the centre of the circle to each of the angles of the triangle.
2 A rectangle with diagonal lines joining opposite angles.
3 An octagon with equal sides. Draw an oval in the middle of the octagon.
4 A three-dimensional rectangular shape of roughly 6 cm by 3 cm by 2 cm.

52 Science and technology

A You are probably familiar with the traditional branches of science e.g. chemistry, physics, botany and zoology. But what about these newer fields?

genetic engineering: the study of the artificial manipulation of the make-up of living things

molecular biology: the study of the structure and function of the organic molecules associated with living organisms

cybernetics: the study of the way information is moved and controlled by the brain or by machinery

information technology: the study of technology related to the transfer of information (computers, digital electronics, telecommunications)

bioclimatology: the study of climate as it affects humans

geopolitics: study of the way geographical factors help to explain the basis of the power of nation states

nuclear engineering: the study of the way nuclear power can be made useful

cryogenics: the study of physical systems at temperatures less than 183° C

astrophysics: the application of physical laws and theories to stars and galaxies

B Here are some of the modern inventions which we are now becoming quite used to.

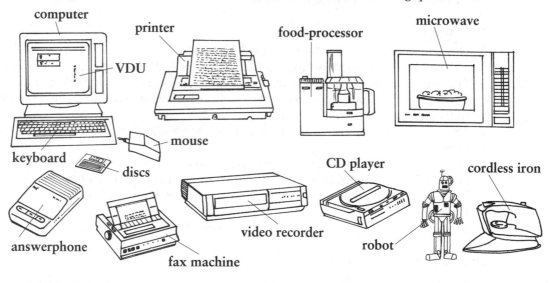

computer, printer, VDU, food-processor, microwave, keyboard, mouse, discs, answerphone, fax machine, video recorder, CD player, robot, cordless iron

C The verbs in the sentences below are all useful in scientific contexts.

He **experimented** with a number of different materials before **finding** the right one.

The technician **pressed** a button and lights started **flashing**.

When she **pulled** a lever, the wheel began to **rotate**.

The zoologist **dissected** the animal.

When they were **combined**, the two chemicals **reacted** violently with each other.

After **analysing** the problem, the physicist **concluded** that there was a flaw in his initial hypothesis.

James Watt **invented** the steam engine and Alexander Fleming, another Scot, **discovered** penicillin.

After **switching on** the computer, **insert** a floppy disc into the disc drive.

You must **patent** your invention as quickly as possible.

Exercises

52.1 Complete the following list with the name of the specialists in the particular fields.

science   *scientist*

chemistry   ....

physics   ....

zoology   ....

genetics   ....

information technology   ....

cybernetics   ....

civil engineering   ....

52.2 Below you have some of the amazing achievements of modern technology. Match the names on the left with the definitions on the right.

1 video recorder   a kind of sophisticated typewriter using a computer
2 photocopier   a machine which records and plays back sound
3 fax machine   a machine which records and plays back sound and pictures
4 tape recorder   a camera which records moving pictures and sound
5 modem   a machine for chopping up, slicing, mashing, blending etc.
6 camcorder   a machine which makes copies of documents
7 robot   a machine which makes copies of documents and sends them
                          down telephone lines to another place
8 word-processor   a machine which acts like a person
9 food-processor   a piece of equipment allowing you to send information from one
                          computer down telephone lines to another computer

52.3 Write descriptions like those in exercise 52.2, for the following objects.

    1   2   3   4   5

52.4 What are the nouns connected with the following verbs?

1 discover   3 rotate   5 patent   7 dissect   9 combine
2 invent   4 conclude   6 analyse   8 experiment

52.5 Give each of the sciences in A opposite a number from 0 to 5 depending on whether it doesn't interest you at all (0) or interests you enormously (5). Similarly mark each of the inventions in B, 0 to 5, depending on how important they are to you in your life.

Follow-up: Increase your knowledge of scientific vocabulary by reading articles of general scientific interest in English language newspapers or magazines. If possible, get a textbook in English for schoolchildren studying a branch of science that you have studied. Choose a book where the science is relatively easy for you so that you can concentrate on the English used.

53 The press and media

A
The term the **mass media** in English refers basically to TV, radio and newspapers: means of communication which reach very large numbers of people. This page looks at some useful words for talking about the **mass media** and about **publishing** in general.

B
Radio and television

Types of TV programmes: documentaries news broadcasts current affairs programmes soap operas quizzes sitcoms drama chat shows detective stories sports programmes weather forecasts music programmes game shows variety shows commercials

A **serial** is a story that continues from one **programme** or **episode** to the next. A **series** is about the same **characters** or has the same format each week but each programme is complete in itself.

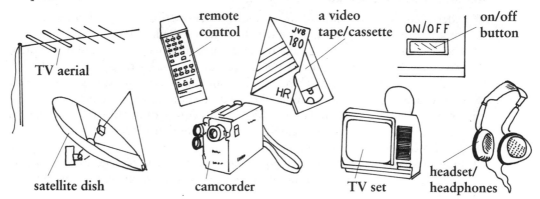

TV aerial
remote control
a video tape/cassette
ON/OFF
on/off button
satellite dish
camcorder
TV set
headset/ headphones

C
Newspapers and publishing

Parts of the newspaper: headlines news reports the editorial feature articles, e.g. about fashion or social trends horoscope cartoons crossword small ads business news sports reports scandal the letters page

A **popular** or **tabloid newspaper** focuses more on sensation than real news whereas a **quality newspaper** professes to be more interested in real news than in sensation. A **tabloid** usually has a smaller format than a **quality paper**, it has larger **headlines** and shorter stories and, in Britain, it prefers stories about film stars, violent crimes and the royal family.

A **journal** is the name usually given to an academic **magazine**. A **colour supplement** is a **magazine** which comes out once a week (often on Sundays) as an addition to a newspaper: A **comic** is a **magazine**, usually for children or teenagers, with lots of picture stories and/or cartoons.

D
Make sure you know the verbs in these sentences.

The BBC World Service **broadcasts** throughout the world.
I can **receive / pick up** broadcasts from Moscow on my radio.
They're **showing** a good film on TV tonight.
This book was **published** by CUP but it was **printed** in Hong Kong.
The film was **shot / made on location** in Spain.
They **cut / censored** the film before showing it on TV.
This article / programme has been badly **edited**.

See Unit 92 for the language of newspaper headlines.

Exercises

53.1 What sort of TV programmes do you think these would be?

1 Murder at the Match
2 The Amazing Underwater World
3 World Cup Special
4 The $10,000 Question
5 Last Week in Parliament
6 Hamlet from Stratford

53.2 Give the name of one programme you know in your country of each type listed in B.

53.3 Write definitions explaining what jobs each of these people involved in the media do?

Example: A make-up artist makes up the faces of people who are to appear on TV.

1 a foreign correspondent
2 a sub-editor
3 a continuity person
4 an editor
5 a librarian
6 a bookseller
7 a publisher
8 a columnist
9 a camera operator
10 a critic

53.4 Fill in the gaps in the sentences below with the most appropriate word from the opposite page.

1 He doesn't even get up from the sofa to change channels; he just presses the
.... on the ....
2 You can hear BBC news .... all over the world.
3 A short wave or a VHF radio can .... many interesting stations.
4 Although our .... was expensive, we've taken some priceless film of our children.
5 Children often prefer looking at .... to reading books.

53.5 Choose any newspaper (it could be in your own language if you can't find an English one) and complete the following sentences.

1 The main story today is about ....
2 The editorial is about ....
3 There are readers' letters on page .... and they deal with the following topics:
....
4 The most interesting feature is about ....
5 There is some scandal on page ...., a crossword on page ...., a cartoon on page .... and some small ads on page ....
6 The most interesting business story is about .... and the largest sports article is about ....
7 The most striking photograph shows ....
8 There are advertisements for ....,
.... and ....
9 An article about .... on page .... made me feel
....

53.6 Look at the TV page of an English language paper and/or listen to the News on the BBC World Service. Make a note of any other useful vocabulary on this theme.

54 Politics and public institutions

Look at the definitions below taken from a dictionary of politics. Make sure you understand not only the words listed but the words used in the definitions too.

A Types of government

republic: a state governed by representatives and, usually, a president
monarchy: a state ruled by a king or queen
democracy: government of, by and for the people
dictatorship: system of government run by a dictator
independence: freedom from outside control; self-governing

The British Isles

::: The United Kingdom
/// The Republic of Ireland

B People and bodies involved in politics

Member of Parliament (MP): a representative of the people in Parliament
politician: someone for whom politics is a career
statesman/woman: someone who uses an important political position wisely and well
Prime Minister: the head of government or leading minister in many countries
chamber: hall used by a group of legislators; many countries have two chambers
cabinet: a committee of the most important ministers in the government
President and Vice-President: the head of state in many modern states
Mayor: head of a town or city council
ambassador: top diplomat representing his/her country abroad
embassy: the building where an ambassador and his/her staff are based
ministry: a department of state headed by a minister.

C Elections

constituency: a political area whose inhabitants are represented by one MP
candidate: someone who stands in an election
policy: the programme of action of a particular party or government
majority: the number of votes by which a person wins an election
referendum: a direct vote by the population on some important public issue
by(e)-election: an election in one constituency in contrast to a General Election
marginal seat: a parliamentary seat held by a very small majority of votes
the opposition: members of parliament who do not belong to the party in power
stand/run for Parliament: to be a candidate in an election
vote: to choose in a formal way, e.g. by marking a ballot paper
elect: to choose someone or something by voting

You will find words dealing with types of political belief in Unit 67.

Exercises

54.1 Choose the correct word from the choices offered.

1 India gained republic/independence/democracy from the UK in 1948.
2 Our MP's just died and so we'll soon need to have a vote/referendum/bye-election.
3 She's running/sitting/walking for Parliament in the next election.
4 His father was voted/stood/elected MP for Cambridge City.
5 What is your country's economic politics/policy/politician?
6 Do you think Bush deserved to be referred to as a politician/statesman/President?

54.2 Look at this text about politics in the UK. Fill in the missing words.

Parliament in the UK consists of two ....(1): the House of Commons and the House of Lords. In the House of Commons there are 650 ....(2), each representing one ....(3). The ruling party in the Commons is the one which gains a ....(4) of seats. The main figure in that party is called the ....(5). The Commons is elected for a maximum period of 5 years although the Prime Minister may call a general ....(6) at any time within that period.

54.3 Make some more words based on those you studied opposite.

abstract noun	person noun	verb	adjective
revolution	revolutionary	revolutionise	revolutionary
representation	....	....	....
election	....	....	....
dictatorship	....	....	....
presidency	....	....	....

54.4 Try this political quiz.

1 Name three monarchies.
2 Which is the oldest parliament in the world?
3 Name the President and the Vice-President of the USA.
4 Who is the Mayor of the place where you live?
5 What politicians represent you in local and national government?
6 What are the main political parties in the country where you now are?
7 What are the main political issues in that country and what are the policies of the different parties on those issues?
8 What do these political abbreviations stand for – MP, PM, UN, EU, NATO, OPEC?

54.5 Write a paragraph about the political system in your country, using as much of the vocabulary on the opposite page as you can.

55 Crime

A Make sure you know the difference between the verbs: **steal** and **rob**. The object of the verb 'steal' is the thing which is taken away, e.g. they stole my bike, whereas the object of the verb 'rob' is the person or place from which things are stolen, e.g. I was robbed last night. A masked man robbed the bank. 'Steal' is irregular: steal, stole, stolen.

B The table below gives the names of some other types of crimes together with their associated verbs and the name of the person who commits the crimes.

crime	definition	criminal	verb
murder	killing someone	murderer	murder
shoplifting	stealing something from a shop	shoplifter	shoplift
burglary	stealing from someone's home	burglar	burgle
smuggling	taking something illegally into another country	smuggler	smuggle
arson	setting fire to something in a criminal way	arsonist	to set fire to
kidnapping	taking a person hostage in exchange for money or other favours, etc.	kidnapper	kidnap

All the verbs in the table above on the right are regular apart from set (set, set, set).

C Here are some more useful verbs connected with crime and law. Note that many of them have particular prepositions associated with them.

to **commit** a crime or an offence: to do something illegal
to **accuse** someone **of** a crime: to say someone is guilty
to **charge** someone **with** (murder): to bring someone to court
to **plead guilty** or **not guilty**: to swear in court that one is guilty or otherwise.
to **defend/prosecute** someone in court: to argue for or against someone in a trial
to **pass verdict on** an accused person: to decide whether they are guilty or not
to **sentence** someone **to** a punishment: what the judge does after a verdict of guilty
to **acquit** an accused person **of** a charge: to decide in court that someone is not guilty
   (the opposite of to **convict** someone)
to **fine** someone a sum of money: to punish someone by making them pay
to **send** someone **to prison**: to punish someone by putting them in prison
to **release** someone **from prison/jail**: to set someone free after a prison sentence
to **be tried**: to have a case judged in court.

D Here are some useful nouns.

trial: the legal process in court whereby an accused person is investigated, or tried, and then found guilty or not guilty
case: a crime that is being investigated
evidence: information used in a court of law to decide whether the accused is guilty or not
proof: evidence that shows conclusively whether something is a fact or not
verdict: the decision: guilty or not guilty
judge: the person who leads a trial and decides on the sentence
jury: group of twelve citizens who decide whether the accused is guilty or not

Exercises

55.1 Put the right form of either rob or steal in the sentences below.

1 Last night an armed gang .... the post office. They .... £2000.
2 My handbag .... at the theatre yesterday.
3 Every year large numbers of banks ....
4 Jane .... of the opportunity to stand for president.

55.2 Here are some more crimes. Complete a table like the one in B opposite.

crime	criminal	verb	definition
terrorism	....	....	....
blackmail	....	....	....
drug-trafficking	....	....	....
forgery	....	....	....
assault	....	assault	....
pickpocketing	....	....	....
mugging	....	....	....

55.3 Fill the blanks in the paragraph below with one of the verbs from C opposite.

One of the two accused men .... (1) at yesterday's trial. Although his lawyer .... (2) him very well, he was still found guilty by the jury. The judge .... (3) him to two years in prison. He'll probably .... (4) after eighteen months. The other accused man was luckier. He .... (5) and left the courtroom smiling broadly.

55.4 Here are some words connected with law and crime. If necessary, use a dictionary to help you check that you understand what they all mean. Then divide them into three groups, in what seems to you to be the most logical way.

theft	member of a jury	judge	smuggling
witness	prison	fine	bribery
detective	hi-jacking	flogging	community service
probation	traffic warden	death penalty	rape
drunken driving	lawyer		

55.5 Look at all the crimes named in this unit. Look both at the left-hand page and at exercises 55.2 and 55.4. Which do you think are the three most serious and the three least serious?

55.6 Write a paragraph to fit this newspaper headline. Give some details about the crime and the court case, using as many words from this unit as is appropriate.

> ## Local girl's evidence gets mugger two years prison

Follow up: If possible look at an English language newspaper. List all the words connected with crime and the law which you can find in it.

56 Money – buying, selling and paying

A Personal finance

Sometimes in a shop they ask you: 'How do you want to pay?'
You can answer: '**Cash / By cheque / By credit card.**'

In a **bank** you usually have a **current account**, which is one where you **pay in your salary** and then **withdraw** money to **pay your everyday bills**. The bank sends you a regular **bank statement** telling you how much money is in your account. You may also have a **savings account** where you **deposit** any extra money that you have and only **take money out** when you want to **spend** it **on** something special. You usually try to avoid having an **overdraft** or you end up paying a lot of **interest**. If your account is **overdrawn**, you can be said to be **in the red** (as opposed to **in the black** or **in credit**).

Sometimes the bank may **lend** you money – this is called a **bank loan**. If the bank (or **building society**) lends you money to buy a house, that money is called a **mortgage**.

When you **buy** (or, more formally, **purchase**) something in a shop, you usually **pay** for it **outright** but sometimes you buy **on credit**. Sometimes you may be offered a **discount** or a **reduction** on something you buy at a shop. This means that you **get**, say, £10 off perhaps because you are a student. You are often offered a discount if you buy **in bulk**. It is not usual to **haggle** about prices in a British shop, as it is in, say, a Turkish market. If you want to return something which you have bought to a shop, you may be given a **refund**, i.e. your money will be returned, provided you have a **receipt**.

The money that you pay for services, e.g. to a school or a lawyer, is usually called a **fee** or **fees**; the money paid for a journey is a **fare**.

If you buy something that you feel was very **good value**, it's a **bargain**. If you feel that it is definitely **not worth** what you paid for it, then you can call it a **rip-off** (very colloquial).

B Public finance

The government collects money from citizens through **taxes. Income tax** is the tax collected on **wages** and **salaries. Inheritance tax** is collected on what people inherit from others. **Customs** or **excise duties** have to be paid on goods imported from other countries. **VAT** or **value added tax** is a tax paid on most goods and services when they are bought or purchased. Companies pay **corporation tax** on their profits. If you pay too much tax, you should be given some money back, a **tax rebate**.

The government also sometimes pays out money to people in need, e.g. **unemployment benefit** (also known informally as **the dole**) **disability allowances** and **student grants** (to help pay for studying). Recipients **draw a pension / unemployment benefit** or are **on the dole** or **on social security**.

Every country has its own special **currency**. Every day the **rates of exchange** are published and you can discover, for example, how many dollars there are currently to the pound sterling.

A company may sell **shares** to members of the public who are then said to have **invested** in that company. They should be paid a regular **dividend** on their **investment**, depending on the **profit** or **loss** made by the company.

Exercises

56.1 Answer the following money quiz.

1 What currencies are used in Japan, Australia, India and Russia?
2 What does the expression, 'hard currency', mean?
3 Name two credit cards which are usable world-wide.
4 Give two examples of imports that most countries impose customs duties on.
5 Give three examples of kinds of income that would be classed as unearned.
6 What is the Dow Jones index and what are its equivalents in London and Japan?
7 Give an example of something that is priceless and something that is valueless.
8 Name the coins and banknotes used in your country and one other country.

56.2 Match the words on the left with their definitions on the right.

1 interest   3 a bank account with minus money in it
2 mortgage   8 money paid towards the cost of raising a family
3 an overdrawn account   9 money given by the government for education, welfare, etc.
4 savings account   4 an account that is used mainly for keeping money
5 current account   6 money paid to people after a certain age
6 pension   5 an account that cheques are drawn on for day-to-day use
7 disability allowance   money chargeable on a loan
8 child benefit   7 money paid to people with a handicap
9 grant   2 a loan to purchase property

56.3 Is the ordinary 'person-in-the-street' pleased to see these newspaper headlines or not?

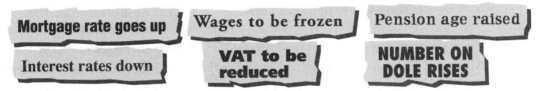

Mortgage rate goes up   **Wages to be frozen**   **Pension age raised**

Interest rates down   **VAT to be reduced**   **NUMBER ON DOLE RISES**

56.4 Complete the sentences with words from the opposite page.

1 Money which has to be paid on what you inherit is known as ....
2 If the bank lends you money, you have a bank ....
3 If you have some money in your account you are in the ....
4 I paid too much tax last year so I should get a .... soon.
5 If it's no good, take it back to the shop and ask for a ....

56.5 Fill in the table below for your own, or any other, country.

Rate of inflation	....
Exchange rate (against the US dollar)	....
Interest rate	....
Basic level of income tax	....
Rate of VAT	....
Monthly state pension	....

Follow-up: To improve your financial vocabulary, read articles on business in any English magazine or newspaper. Write down any new words or expressions that you come across.

57 Number, quantity, degree and intensity

A Number and quantity

Number is used for countable nouns, **amount** for uncountables.

Scale of adjectives useful for expressing number and quantity:

tiny   small   average   large/considerable   huge/vast

> Add just a **tiny amount** of chilli pepper, or else it may get too hot.
> A **considerable number** of people failed to get tickets.　[formal]
> **Vast amounts** of money have been wasted on this project.
> Were there many people at the airport? Oh, about **average**, I'd say.　[fairly informal]

Much/many, a lot, lots, plenty, a good/great deal

example	comments
Is there **much** work to do? No, not **much**.	mostly used in questions and negatives with uncountable nouns
There are **lots of** nice shops in this street.	mostly for affirmatives; has a rather positive feeling; informal
Don't worry, there's **plenty of** time.	mostly affirmatives, used in positive contexts
You were making **a lot of** noise last night.	used in all structures; neutral, better than **lots** in negative contexts
There's **a great deal of** hard work still to do.	+ uncountables, more formal

Much and **many** do occur in affirmatives, but they sound formal and are probably best kept for formal written contexts.

> **Much** criticism has been levelled at the government's policy.
> **Many** people are afraid of investing in stocks and shares.

B Informal and colloquial words for number/quantity

> I've got **dozens of** nails in my tool-box. Why buy more?　[especially good for countables]
> There's **heaps/bags/loads of** time yet, slow down!　[countable or uncountable and informal]
> There was absolutely **tons of** food at the party; far too much.　[especially good for things, not so good for abstract nouns]
> There are **tons of** apples on this tree this year; last year there were hardly any.　[note how the verb here is plural because of 'apples', but singular in the example before with 'food' – number depends on the *noun* following, not on **tons/lots/loads**]
> Just **a drop of** wine for me, please.　[tiny amount of any liquid]

C Degree and intensity

Typical collocations of adverbs: a bit/quite/rather/fairly/very/really/awfully/extremely combine with 'scale' adjectives such as tired, worried, weak, hot.

Totally/absolutely/completely/utterly combine with 'limit' adjectives such as ruined, exhausted, destroyed, wrong.

Exercises

57.1 Comment on the following numbers and quantities using adjective-noun combinations from A opposite.

Example: The Government will only give us a grant of £20.
But that's a tiny sum of money. How mean!

1 £5 billion was wasted on developing the new rocket.
2 Over 50 people came to Sally's lecture yesterday. We were pleasantly surprised.
3 We have 120 students most years, and we'll probably have about that this year, too.
4 There was only five pounds in my purse when it was stolen.
5 We've wasted over 100 hours in meetings and got nowhere.

57.2 Here are some more adjectives which can combine with *amount*. Divide them into two groups, *small* and *large* and fill in the bubbles. Use a dictionary if necessary.

miniscule   gigantic   overwhelming   minute /maɪˈnjuːt/   meagre
excessive   insignificant   sizeable

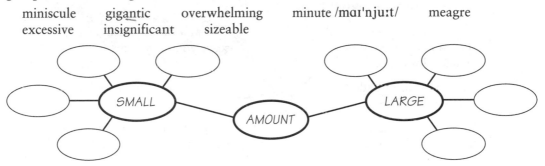

Now try using them to fill in the gaps below. More than one answer may be possible.

1 Even a .... amount of sand can jam a camera.
2 I've had an absolutely .... amount of work lately.
3 Oh, you've given me a .... amount of food here!
4 It takes a .... amount of money to start a business.
5 An .... amount of fat in your diet is dangerous.

57.3 Fill in the gaps with *much/many, a lot/lots of, plenty of, a good/great deal of.*

1 There's .... dust on these books. Fetch me a duster.
2 Please eat up; there's .... food.
3 There wasn't .... we could do, so we went home.
4 We've put .... energy into this plan. I hope it works.
5 .... people seem unable to cope with computers.

57.4 Using intensifiers from C opposite, say how you might feel if the following happened.

1 You heard that a friend was in trouble with the police.
2 A close friend coming to stay did not turn up and sent no message to say why.
3 Three people gave you different directions to get to the same place.
4 You passed an exam you expected to fail.
5 Your best friend was going abroad for two years.
6 You had been working non-stop for 18 hours.

57.5 Make four sentences of your own using the informal words from B opposite. Write about yourself / where you live, etc.

58 Time

A Periods of time – words and typical contexts

The **Ice Age**   The **Stone Age**   The **Middle Ages**   The **age** of the computer.
[major historical/geological periods]
After the war, a new **era** of peace began.   [long period, perhaps several decades]
The doctor said I needed a **period** of rest and relaxation, so I'm taking three months'
unpaid leave.   [very general word]
A **spell** of hot weather. He's had a couple of **spells** in hospital in the last two or three
years.   [indefinite but short]
During the 1950s I lived in Cork for a **time**.   [vague, indefinite]
D'you want to borrow this book for a **while**?   [indefinite but not too long]

B Useful phrases with time

The doctor says you should
stay in bed **for the time
being**.   [not specific]

He can get a bit bad-
tempered **at times**.

By the time we get home
this pizza will be cold!

TIME

One **at a time**, please! I can't
serve you all together.

We got there **just in time** for
dinner.

I expected you to be late, the
trains are never **on time**.

I've told you **time and time again**
not to ring me at the office!

C Verbs associated with time passing

1980 ⟶ 1990   Ten years have **passed/elapsed** since I last heard from her.

Elapse is more formal and is normally used in the perfect or past, without adverbs. **Pass** can
be used in any tense and with adverbs.
Don't worry. The time will **pass** quickly. Time **passes** very slowly when you're lonely.

London ⟶ ✈ ⟶ Singapore   It **takes** 12 hours to fly to Singapore.

The batteries in this radio usually **last** about three or four months.

This videotape **lasts/runs** for three hours.

The meeting **went on** for two hours.
[suggests longer than expected or desired]

Note also: **Take your time**, you don't need to hurry.

D Adjectives describing duration (how long something lasts)

He's a **temporary** lecturer; the **permanent** one's on leave.
Could we make a **provisional** booking now and confirm it later?
Venice has a **timeless** beauty.
Christians believe in **eternal** life after death.

Exercises

58.1 Age, era, period, spell, time. Fill the gaps as appropriate.

1 The Minister said that before the new law came into force there would be a
.... of six months when people could hand in firearms without being
prosecuted.

2 The twentieth century will be seen by historians as the .... of the
motor car.

3 These factories mark the beginning of a new .... of industrial
development for the country.

4 For a .... I thought I would never find a job, but then I was lucky.

5 We had a very cold .... in February when all the pipes froze up.

58.2 Which phrases from B opposite could you use in the following situations? Write exactly
what you might say, as in the example.

1 To a child who repeatedly leaves the fridge door open despite being told off often.
'I've told you time and time again not to leave that fridge door open!'

2 To someone you're happy to see who arrives just as you are serving tea/coffee.

3 On a postcard you expect will arrive at someone's house after you do.

4 A large group of people want to talk to you but you'd prefer to see them individually.

5 Ask someone to use an old photocopier while the new one is being repaired.

6 Explain to someone that the weather occasionally gets very cold in your country.

7 Tell someone you'll do your best to arrive punctually at a meeting.

58.3 Complete the sentences using verbs from C opposite.

1 The ferry crossing…
2 Use this cassette to record, it will…
3 These shoes have been great, they've…
4 Everyone got bored because the speeches…
5 The disaster occurred in 1932. Many years…
6 I'll miss you terribly. I only hope the weeks…
7 There's no hurry at all, just…

58.4 Match the queries with suitable responses.

1 So, she's been promoted?	Well, provisionally.
2 A lovely, quiet place?	Yes, she's permanent now.
3 So she's agreed to do it?	It's a temporary measure.
4 So, after death, life goes on?	Yes, absolutely timeless.
5 Language classes in the gym?	Yes, I believe it's eternal.

59 Distances and dimensions

You probably know all the common words for distances and dimensions. In this unit we shall concentrate on derived words and compounds and other connected words/phrases you may not know or be unsure of how to use accurately.

A Broad and wide and tall and high

Wide is more common than **broad**, e.g. It's a very **wide** road/garden/room.

Make a note of typical collocations for **broad** as you meet them, e.g. Economics is a very broad subject; We came to a broad expanse of grassland. [big area]

Note the word order for talking about dimensions, e.g. The room's **five metres long** and **four wide**.

Don't forget that **tall** is for people but can be used for things such as buildings and trees when they are **high** and **thin** in some way. Otherwise, use **high** for things.

> She's very **tall** for a five-year-old.
> Her office is in that **tall** building in the square.
> There are some **high** mountains in the North.

B Deep ≠ shallow

The **deep** and **shallow** ends of a swimming pool.

C Derived words, phrases and compounds

long: Let's measure the **length** of this rope.
I swam 20 **lengths** (of the swimming pool).
I've **lengthened** her skirt for her.   [**shorten**, see below]
Getting a visa's a **lengthy** process.   [usually refers to time; rather negative]
Can I make a **long-distance** phone call?

short: The new road will **shorten** our journey by ten minutes.
There's a **short-cut** to the station.   [quick way]

wide: Let's measure the **width** of the room.
They're **widening** the road.

broad: I want to **broaden** my experience.   [usually more abstract contexts]

high: The **height** of the wall is two metres.
The fog **heightened** the feeling of mystery.   [usually used only for feelings and emotions]

low: You can **lower** that table if it is too high.

far: He loves travelling to **faraway** places.

deep: the **depth** of the river here is about 3 metres.
His death so soon after hers **deepened** our sadness even further.   [often with feelings]

E

Other verbs for dimensions and for changing them.

> Our garden **stretches** all the way to the river, so we have plenty of room to **extend** the house if we want to.
> The cities are **spreading** and the countryside is **shrinking**.

Exercises

59.1 Complete B's replies using a suitable form of the dimension/distance words opposite.

1 A: These trousers I've bought are too long.
 B: Well, why not get.. *them shortened?*

2 A: He's a big boy, isn't he? 1.90 metres!
 B: Yes, he's...

3 A: Why are we going across the field?
 B: Just to get there that bit quicker; it's...

4 A: We'll have to measure how high the room is.
 B: That's not necessary; we already know the... *height*

5 A: The traffic seems to move far quicker on this road since I was last here.
 B: Yes, well, they...

6 A: Why do they have to have music on TV news programmes? It seems totally unnecessary!
 B: Well, I think they want to create a feeling of drama, and the music is supposed to...

59.2 Give opposites for:

1 a length of the pool   3 a very broad range of goods   5 deep water
2 to shorten   4 a local call   6 nearby places

59.3 Match the left- and right-hand columns.

1 The city's spread a lot;   for miles along the river.
2 It takes ten weeks;   you should broaden it.
3 We extended the house   it's much bigger now.
4 You can choose;   there's a wide range.
5 Your experience is too narrow;   it's a lengthy business
6 The forest stretches   to give us more room.

59.4 Prepositions with distance. Fill in the prepositions. If you are unsure, try looking up the word *distance* in a good dictionary.

1 The car was parked .... a distance .... about 150 metres from the scene of the robbery.

2 I saw you .... the distance yesterday but I didn't call out as I could see you were with someone.

3 She's a great shot. She can hit an empty can .... a distance of about 100 feet, which I can't.

4 What's the total distance .... here .... Paris?

59.5 Use these verbs to fill the gaps. Check their usage in a dictionary if necessary.

expand   extend   spread   shrink   grow   contract

1 AIDS .... rapidly during the 1980s.

2 The steel industry .... when the economy was strong, but now it has .... and only employs 8,000 people.

3 This sweater of mine has ... *spread on* ... in the wash!

4 Our land .... as far as those trees there.

5 Our problems have .... since that new boss came.

A Obligation

Must is an instruction or command; that is why we see it on notices, e.g. Dogs **must** be kept on a lead. Cars **must** not be parked here.

Have (got) to says that circumstances oblige you to do something. Often, the two meanings overlap and there will be a choice of how to express the obligation, but not always.

I **must** get my hair cut!
[command to yourself]

I've **got to** get my hair
cut. I've got an interview
tomorrow. [circumstances]

There's no bus service, so I **have
to** walk to work. [circumstances]

I really **must** get a bicycle.
[instruction to yourself]

The company **is obliged to** give a refund if the tour is cancelled.
You will **be liable** to pay tax if you work.   [formal/legalistic]
The bank robbers **forced** him at gunpoint to open the safe.
We **had no choice/alternative but** to sell our house; we owed the bank £100,000.
The death sentence is **mandatory** for drug-smuggling in some countries.   [automatic;
   there is no alternative]
Was sport **compulsory/obligatory** at your school? No, it was **optional** at mine.
   [**optional**: you can choose]
I am **exempt** from tax as I'm a student.   [free from obligation]

The negative of **must** and **have (got) to** are formed with **need** and **have to**, when we mean something is not necessary/not obligatory.

You **don't need to/don't have to/needn't** wash up; we've got a dishwasher.

B Need

The grass **needs** cutting (badly).
[or '**wants** cutting' – informal]

This plant is **in need of** water.
[more formal than 'needs/wants']

The miners died through a **lack of** oxygen.   [there was none]
There is a **shortage of** doctors.   [there are not enough]
There's a **need for** more discussion on the matter.   [we feel a need]

C Scale of probability: 'cannot happen' to 'has to happen'

impossible → unlikely → possible → probable → certain → inevitable

Note: I've been given **an opportunity** to go to Bonn. [a real chance] *but,* Is there any
chance/possibility you'll be free next week?   [**chance** is less formal than **possibility**]

Exercises

60.1 Continue the sentences using 'obligation' words and phrases from A opposite, and using the words in brackets.

1 They were losing £1 million a year, so the company... (close down)
2 You don't have to buy travel insurance... (optional)
3 You can hire a video camera, but you... (pay a deposit)
4 We'll have to sell the house, I'm afraid we have... (otherwise, bankrupt)
5 This jacket's got curry stains on it; I really... (the cleaners)
6 He didn't want to give them the money, but they had guns; they... (hand it over)
7 No, he couldn't choose to pay a fine; the prison sentence is... (for dangerous driving)
8 I didn't want to do maths, but I had to. It's... (in all secondary schools)
9 How kind of you! You really... (buy us a present)
10 If you're over 50, you're... (military service)

60.2 List something in your world which...

1 regularly needs cutting. *my hair, the lawn*
2 there is a lack of.
3 is obligatory once a year.
4 you are in need of.
5 is inevitable.
6 you no longer have to do.
7 was compulsory when you were at school.

60.3 Collocations with 'possibility/probability' words. Use a dictionary to try to fill in the rest of this matrix. One line has already been done for you. If you cannot find out the collocations at all, use the key to this unit.

✔ = typical collocation   ✗ = not a typical collocation

	highly	*quite*	*very*	*absolutely*
possible	✗	✔	✔	✗
impossible		✓		✓
probable	✓	✓	✓	
(un)likely				
inevitable				
certain				

60.4 Use the collocations in 60.3 to say how probable/possible these are.

1 Most people will have a videophone in their homes by 2025.
2 There will be rain in the Amazon forest within the next 8 days.
3 A human being will live to be 250.
4 We will all be dead by the year 2250.
5 A flying saucer will land in Hong Kong.
6 You'll be given an opportunity to meet the US President.
7 There will be a third world war.

61 Sound and light

A General words to describe sound

I could hear the **sound** of voices/music coming from the next room.   [neutral]

Our neighbours had a party last night. The **noise** went on till 3 a.m.   [loud, unpleasant sounds]

I tried hard to hear what she was saying above the **din** of the traffic.   [very loud, irritating noise]

The children are making a terrible **racket** upstairs. Could you go and tell them to be quiet?   [very loud, unbearable noise, often of human activity]

Racket and **din** are quite informal words. **Noise** can be countable or uncountable. When it means sounds of short duration, it is countable, when it means a lot of continual or continuous sounds, it is uncountable.

Their lawnmower makes **a lot of noise**, doesn't it?   [uncountable]

I heard **some** strange **noises** in the night.   [countable]

B Sound words and things that typically make them

The words can be used as nouns or verbs

I could hear the rain **pattering** on the roof.   We heard the **patter** of a little child's feet.

verb/noun	example of what makes the sound
bang	a door closing in the wind, someone bursting a balloon
rustle	opening a paper/plastic bag, dry leaves underfoot
thud	a heavy object falling on to a carpeted floor
crash	a big, solid, heavy object falling on to a hard floor
clang	a big bell ringing, a hollow metal object being struck
clatter	a metal pan falling on to a concrete floor
hiss	gas/steam escaping through a small hole
rumble	distant noise of thunder, noise of traffic far away
roar	noise of heavy traffic, noise of a huge waterfall

C Darkness

Some adjectives for **dark** conditions. (For adjectives describing brightness, see Unit 64.)

These brown walls are a bit **gloomy**. We should paint them white.

This torch gives a **dim** light. I think it needs new batteries.

It was a **sombre** room, with dark, heavy curtains.   [serious, imposing]

D Types of light

The sun **shines** and gives out **rays** of light.
A torch gives out a **beam** of light.
A camera gives a **flash** of light.
Stars **twinkle**.
A candle-flame **flickers** in the breeze.
White-hot coal on a fire **glows**.
A diamond necklace **sparkles**.
A gold object **glitters**.

Exercises

61.1 Choose *sound, noise(s), din* or *racket* to fill the gaps.

1 There was a terrible .... outside the pub last night; it was a fight involving about six people.
2 I could sit and listen to the .... of the river all day.
3 My car's making some strange .... I'll have to get it looked at.
4 Gosh! What an awful ....! I think you should take up a different instrument; the violin's just not for you!
5 I can't sleep if there's .... of any kind, so I use these ear-plugs.

61.2 Using the table opposite at B, what sound do you think each of these might make?

1 A bottle of fizzy mineral water being opened.
2 A typewriter being dropped down an iron staircase.
3 A mouse or a hedgehog moving among dead grass and leaves.
4 A rather overweight person falling on to a wooden floor.
5 A starting-pistol for a sporting event.
6 A train passing at high speed a few feet away from you.
7 A slow train passing, heard through the walls of a house.

61.3 As in the table at B opposite, make a note of something that might make the sound.

verb/noun	typical source(s) of the sound
hum	....
rattle	....
bleep	....
screech	....
chime	....

61.4 Join up the left-hand sentences with the right-hand ones so that they make sense.

1 I saw a beam of light coming towards me.   Then it died, leaving us in complete darkness.
2 It sparkled in the morning sunlight.   It was a police officer holding a flashlamp.
3 It began to flicker uncertainly.   It was clearly time to get up and move out.
4 The first rays shone into the room.   I'd never seen such a beautiful bracelet.

61.5 What do you think the *figurative* meanings of the underlined words are? Choose from the alternatives.

1 She beamed at him.
  a) smiled   b) shouted   c) attacked
2 After the day's skiing, our faces glowed.
  a) were frozen   b) were dried up   c) were full of colour
3 He has a twinkle in his eyes.
  a) a piece of grit   b) a sign of humour/enjoyment   c) a sign of anger

62 Possession, giving and lending

A Possession

All his **possessions** were destroyed in the terrible fire.   [everything he owned; always
    plural in this meaning]
Don't leave any of your **belongings** here; we've had a few thefts recently.   [smaller
    things, e.g. bag, camera, coat; always plural]
Estate in the singular can mean a big area of private land and the buildings on it, or all of
someone's wealth upon death.
She owns a huge **estate** in Scotland.   [land, etc.]
After his death, his **estate** was calculated at £3 million.   [all his wealth]
Property (uncountable) is used in a general sense for houses, land, etc.
He's only fourteen; he's too young to own **property**.
A **property** (countable) is a building, e.g. house, office-block.
She's just bought a very nice **property** near the town-centre.

B Words for people connected with ownership

The **proprietor** of this restaurant is a friend of mine.   [used for shops, businesses etc. The
    owner would be less formal]
The **landlord/lady's** put the rent up.   [owner of rented property]
Do you own this house? No we're just **tenants**.   [we rent it]

C Giving

The river **provides** the village **with** water / **provides** water **for** the village. (or **supplies**)

Would you like to **contribute** / **donate** something to the children's hospital fund?

Jakes Ltd. **supplies** our school **with** paper and other items.   [often for 'selling' contexts]
It gives me pleasure to **present** you **with** this clock from us all.
The school restaurant **caters for** 500 people every day.
That uncle of mine that died **left** £3,000 to a dogs' home.
When she died she **donated** all her books to the library.   [for large gifts to institutions]
You've been **allocated** room 24. Here's your key.

D Lending, etc.

We've decided to **hire/rent** a car. Can you recommend a good **car-hire/car-rental** firm?
    [**rent** and **hire** are both commonly used]
We'd like to **rent** a flat in Oxford for six months.   [not hire]
We've **hired** the lecture-room for a day.   [not **rent**; short, temporary arrangements]

Remember: when you **lend,** you give, when you **borrow,** you receive.

That step-ladder you **lent** me last week, could I **borrow** it again?
I'm trying to get a **loan** from the bank to buy a boat.

Exercises

62.1 What questions do you think were asked to get these answers?

1 Oh no, we own it. Most houses here are owner-occupied.
2 Well, sorry, no; I need it to take photos myself.
3 You will be in Room 44B. It's quite a big office.
4 No, you have to buy exercise books and pens yourself.
5 Actually, I've already given something. Sorry.
6 Oh, just a small house with a garden, you know, typical.
7 Yes, the charge is £50 for one that seats 30 people.

62.2 The verbs in the middle column have been jumbled. Put them in their right sentences.

1 A millionaire	provided	a swimming pool to the school.
2 The Director was	presented	the best parking-place.
3 My mother's cousin	donated	me £5,000 in her will.
4 A farmer nearby	catered	us with logs for the fire.
5 When I retired they	left	me with a camcorder.
6 The restaurant	allocated	for vegetarians.

62.3 Some phrasal verbs connected with 'giving'. Check their meaning in a dictionary and then fill the gaps below.

hand over   give out   let go of   give away   hand down

1 That bed has been .... in the family. It was my great-grandmother's originally.
2 Would you help us .... some leaflets in the shopping-centre?
3 I don't want to .... that old painting. It might be valuable one day.
4 When Tim's bike got too small for him we .... it ....; it wasn't worth trying to sell it, too much bother.
5 The landlord will .... the keys as soon as you pay the deposit and the first month's rent.

62.4 Think of something that...

1 you would hand over to a mugger if threatened.
2 has been handed down in your family.
3 you have given away at some time in your life.
4 is often given out in classrooms.
5 you value and would not want to let go of.

62.5 The rise and fall of Mr Fatcatt – a sad story. Fill the gaps with suitable words.

Horace Fatcatt began his career by buying up old .... (1) in London when prices were low. He got .... (2) from several banks to finance his deals, and soon he was one of the biggest private .... (3) in the city, with some 3,000 .... (4) renting houses and flats from him. He was also the .... (5) of many shops and businesses. He became very rich and bought himself a huge .... (6) in Scotland, but he .... (7) more and more money from the banks and soon the bubble burst. Recession came and he had to sell all his .... (8) and .... (9), everything. He was left with just a few personal .... (10) and finally died penniless.

63 Movement and speed

A

Move is the basic verb for all movement, but do not forget it also means 'to move to a new house/flat', e.g. We've **moved**. Do you want our new address?

Particular types of movement

Cars, lorries, etc. **travel/drive** along roads.
Trains **travel** along rails.
Boats/ships **sail** on rivers / across the sea.
Rivers/streams **flow/run** through towns/villages.

Things often have particular verbs associated with their types of movement. You should learn these as collocations as you meet them, and record them with a phrase or sentence.

White clouds **drifted** across the sky.
The flag **fluttered** in the wind.
The leaves **stirred** in the light breeze.
The trees **swayed** back and forth as the gale grew fiercer.
The car **swerved** to avoid a dog which had run into the road.

B ## Useful verbs to describe fast and slow movement

The traffic was **crawling along** because of the roadworks.

We'll be late! Stop **dawdling!**

Suddenly a car came round the bend and **tore** along the road at high speed. Seconds later, a police car **shot past** after it.

Everyone was **hurrying/rushing** to get their shopping done before closing time.
The train was just **trundling/plodding** along at about 30 miles per hour. I knew we'd be late.

C ## Nouns describing speed and their typical contexts

speed	general word: used for vehicles, developments, changes, etc., e.g. We were travelling at high **speed**.
rate	often used in statistical contexts; the rate of increase/decrease, e.g. The birth **rate** is going down.
pace	how you experience something as happening fast or slow, e.g. The lesson was going at a very slow **pace**.
velocity	for technical/scientific contexts, e.g. The **velocity** of a bullet.

Exercises

63.1 Write sentences which could come immediately *before* each of these sentences so that they make sense together.

1 It was moving so much I thought it would break altogether.
2 It sails at dawn.
3 It flows through the capital city.
4 I had to swerve hard and nearly ended up in the river.
5 It was travelling at 80 miles per hour when it happened.

63.2 What other things do you think could be described by each verb apart from the contexts given on the left-hand page. Use a dictionary if necessary.

1 **sway**: a tree, *a person dancing / someone drunk / a boat* ....
2 **crawl**: traffic, ...
3 **shoot**: a car, ...
4 **flutter**: a flag, ...
5 **drift**: a cloud, ...

63.3 Fill the gap with *speed, rate, pace* or *velocity*. Use the guidelines on the left-hand page to help you.

1 The .... of decline in this species is alarming.
2 I just couldn't stand the .... of life in the city, so I moved to a small village.
3 The police scientist said the bullet had come from a high- .... rifle.
4 A: What .... were you doing at the time?   B: Oh, about 60, I'd say.

63.4 Use a dictionary to make notes to help you learn the difference between these near-synonyms. Make notes under the headings *usage* and *grammar*, as in the example.

	usage	grammar
fast	e.g. fast car/fast train – refers to speed	adjective and adverb – 'she drove fast'
quick		
rapid		
swift		

63.5 In what situations might you...

1 tear out of the house?
2 deliberately dawdle?
3 plod along at a steady pace?
4 not even dare to stir?
5 shoot past somebody's office/room?

63.6 People and verbs of motion. What sorts of people do you think these are? Use a dictionary if necessary.

1 a slowcoach   2 a streaker   3 a plodder   4 a stirrer

64 Texture, brightness, weight and density

A Texture – how something feels when you touch it

adjective	typical examples
smooth	the paper in this book
polished	varnished wood / a shiny metal surface
silky	silk itself / fine, expensive tights or stockings
sleek	highly polished, streamlined new car bodywork
downy	new-born baby's hair
slippery	a fish just out of the water
furry	a thick sheepskin rug
rough	new, unwashed denim jeans / bark of a tree
coarse	sand
jagged	sharp, irregular edges of broken glass or metal
prickly	a thistle, a hedgehog, thorns on a rose
gnarled	twisted, dead wood from an old tree

Your hair has a silky **feel**.   This cotton is very smooth **to the touch**.
The table had a beautiful polished **surface**.   The ground was rough **underfoot**.

B Brightness – some adjectives

A **shiny** object lying in the sand

a carnival full of **vivid** colours

a **dazzling** light

a **shady** corner of the garden

You wear such **dull** colours: why not get some **brighter** clothes?
This torch is getting a bit **dim**; it needs new batteries.
I wear sun-glasses because of the **glare** of the sun on the sand.

C Density and weight

A **solid** ≠ **hollow** object   She has **thick** ≠ **thin/fine** hair
An area with **dense** ≠ **sparse** vegetation.
These boxes are rather **weighty**.   [heavier than expected]
Your bag's **as light as a feather**! Have you brought enough?
Your bag's **as heavy as lead**! What's in it, bricks?
This suitcase is very **cumbersome**.   [difficult, big and heavy]

Exercises

64.1 How would you personally expect the following things to feel?

1 The cover of a well-produced brochure.
2 The feathers in a pillow or duvet.
3 A wet bar of soap.
4 The branches of a rose-bush.
5 A gravel pathway.
6 The inside of a pair of sheepskin gloves.
7 The edge of a piece of broken, rusty metal.
8 Heavy, stone-ground wholemeal flour.
9 The surface of a mirror.
10 An old, dead log on the forest floor.

Look round your own house/flat and find:

1 something sleek to the touch
2 something rough underfoot
3 something with a polished surface
4 something furry
5 something smooth

64.2 Here are the commonest British weights with their metric equivalents. Try and answer the questions that follow.

weight	written as	approximate metric equivalent	
ounce	oz	28 grams	} used for goods in shops, etc.
pounds	lb	454 grams	
stone	st	6.3 kilos	} used for personal weight

1 A friend tells you her new baby weighed seven pounds at birth. Is this a huge, tiny or more or less average baby?
2 Someone tells you their cousin weighs 20 stone. What would you expect the cousin to look like?
3 You ask someone to get you a piece of cheese at the market, enough for you personally for a week. They ask if 8 ounces will do. What would you say?
4 Make a note (a private one if you wish!) of your approximate weight in British terms.

64.3 Quiz. Name the following.

1 A creature with a sleek coat.
2 A slippery creature.
3 A prickly creature.
4 A creature with a furry coat.
5 A creature with a downy coat.

64.4 Pair-puzzles. Each word has a letter in it that is part of a *related* word from the left-hand page. Fill in the letters, as in the example.

```
                                              C          D
   P                    D        S            O          A
   O        SHADY       E        H            A          Z
OUNCE       U           N        VI _ _     RO _ _ _      Z
   N            _    S _ _ _SE    N           S         GL _ _ _
   D            _        E        Y           E           E
```

Can you make pair-puzzles with *cumbersome, lead* and *feather*?

A Succeeding

I **managed** to contact him just before he left his office.

I don't think I can **manage** the whole walk. I think I'll turn back.   [**manage**, but not **succeed**, may have a direct object in this meaning]

We **succeeded in** persuading a lot of people to join our protest.   [**in** + **-ing**]

We've **achieved/accomplished** a great deal in the last three years.   [both are used with quantity phrases such as 'a lot'/'a little']

The company has **achieved** all its **goals/aims/targets** for this year   [**achieve** is more common than **accomplish** with nouns expressing **goals** and **ambitions**]

D'you think his plan will **come off**?   [succeed; informal]

Matrix for some typical collocations with 'succeeding' verbs

	reach	*attain*	*secure*	*realise*	*fulfil*	*achieve*
an ambition		✔		✔	✔	✔
a dream				✔		✔
an agreement	✔		✔			
an obligation					✔	
a target	✔	✔				✔
a compromise	✔					✔

B Failing

Plans and projects often go wrong or **misfire**.   [don't turn out as intended]

Companies, clubs and societies often **fold** through lack of success.   [close down]

A plan or project may **falter**, even if it finally succeeds.   [go through ups and downs]

All your plans and hard work/efforts may **come to nothing**.

C Difficulty

I have great **difficulty in** getting up in the morning. I **find it difficult** to remember the names of everybody in the class. [hard can be used here; it is more informal]

It's **hard/difficult** to hear what she's saying.

I often **have trouble** starting the car on cold mornings.

We've **had a lot of bother with** the neighbours lately.

Can you **cope with** three more students? They've just arrived.

I've no money, my girl-friend's left me; I need help; I just can't **cope** any more.

D Word-classes

verb	*noun*	*adjective*	*adverb*
succeed	success	successful	successfully
accomplish	accomplishment	accomplished	–
achieve	achievement	achievable	–
attain	attainment	attainable	–
fulfil	fulfilment	fulfilling	–
–	–	hard	hard

Exercises

65.1 Using the collocation matrix opposite, choose a suitable verb to fill the gap. If the exact word in the sentence is not in the vertical column of the matrix, look for something that is close in meaning.

1 The management have .... an agreement with the union which will guarantee no strikes for the next three years.
2 Now that I've .... all my responsibilities to my family, I feel I can retire and go round the world.
3 The church building-fund has failed to .... its target of £250,000.
4 I never thought I would .... my ambition, but now I have.
5 Very few people .... all their hopes and dreams in life, very few indeed, I can tell you.
6 We hope the two sides .... a compromise and avoid war.
7 I'm afraid that little scheme of mine didn't .... off.

65.2 Fill in the missing word forms where they exist.

verb	noun	adjective	adverb
realise	....	....	....
....	difficulty	....	....
....	target	....	....
....	ambition	....	....
fail	....	....	....
....	trouble	....	....

65.3 Correct the mistakes in these sentences.

1 I find very difficult to understand English idioms.
2 She succeeded to rise to the top in her profession.
3 Do you ever have any trouble to use this photocopier? I always seem to.
4 I've accomplished to work quite hard this last month.
5 I'm amazed that you can cope all the work they give you.

65.4 What might happen if... / What would you do if...

1 a plan misfired? *Abandon it. / Look for an alternative.*
2 you were having a lot of bother with your car?
3 a club had only two members left out of fifty?
4 a student faltered in one exam out of six, but did well in all the rest?
5 you started a small business but it came to nothing?
6 you couldn't cope with your English studies?

65.5 In what sorts of situations would you hear the following remarks? Check any new words/phrases if you are not sure.

1 We'll have to get an au pair. I just can't cope.
2 £5,000 and I've got nothing to show for it!
3 It collapsed, I'm afraid, and he's bankrupt now.
4 Yes, she pulled it off despite the competition.

66 Containers and contents

A There are a number of special words in English which are used to describe different kinds of containers. Look at the following pictures.

bag   barrel   basin   basket   bottle   bowl   box   bucket

can   carton   case (e.g. for spectacles)   crate   glass   jar   jug   mug

pack   packet   pan   pot   sack   tin   tub   tube

B Here is some additional information about each of these types of containers.

container	usually made of	typical contents
bag	cloth, paper, plastic	sweets, shopping, letters
barrel	wood and metal	wine, beer
basin	pottery, metal	ingredients for making a cake
basket	canes, rushes	shopping, clothes, waste paper
bottle	glass, plastic	milk, lemonade, wine
bowl	china, glass, wood	fruit, soup, sugar
box	cardboard, wood	matches, tools, toys, chocolates
bucket	metal, plastic	sand, water
can	tin	coca cola, beer
carton	card	milk, yoghurt, 20 packets of cigarettes
case	leather, wood	jewellery, spectacles
crate	wood, plastic	bottles
glass	glass	milk, lemonade, wine
jar	glass, pottery	jam, honey, olives, instant coffee
jug	pottery	milk, cream, water
mug	pottery	tea, coffee, cocoa
pack	card	cards, eight cans of coca cola
packet	card, paper	cigarettes, tea, biscuits, juice, cereal
pan	metal	food that is being cooked
pot	metal, pottery	food, plant
sack	cloth, plastic	coal, rubbish
tin	tin	peas, baked beans, fruit
tub	wood, zinc, card	flowers, rainwater, ice-cream
tube	soft metal, plastic	toothpaste, paint, ointment

Exercises

66.1 Try to complete the blanks in the shopping list without looking at the opposite page.

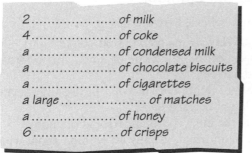

2 .... of milk
4 .... of coke
a .... of condensed milk
a .... of chocolate biscuits
a .... of cigarettes
a large .... of matches
a .... of honey
6 .... of crisps

66.2 Try the following quiz about the words on the opposite page.

1 Which two of the containers listed would you be most likely to find holding flowers in a garden?
2 Which three are you most likely to find in a cellar?
3 Which six would you be likely to find in an off-licence (a shop which sells drink)?
4 Which five would you be most likely to see on the breakfast table?
5 Which ones does a postman carry with him?
6 Which two are often used for carrying shopping?
7 How many cigarettes would you expect to find in (a) a carton   (b) a packet?

66.3 Name the containers and their contents.

66.4 Think of three words which are often used with the following containers.

Example: shopping, wastepaper, linen basket

1 .... box   4 .... jug
2 .... bottle   5 .... glass
3 .... bag   6 .... pot

66.5 Look in a kitchen cupboard or a supermarket. Can you name everything that you see there? You will find more useful vocabulary for this exercise in Unit 43.

67 Belief and opinion

A Verbs connected with beliefs and opinions

You probably already know **think** and **believe**; here are more.

I'm **convinced** we've met before.   [very strong feeling that you're right]

I've always **held** that compulsory education is a waste of time.   [used for very firm beliefs; **maintain** could be used here]

She **maintains** that we're related, but I'm not convinced.   [insist on believing, often against the evidence; **hold** could not be used here]

I **feel** she shouldn't be forced to do the job.   [strong personal opinion]

I **reckon** they'll get married soon.   [informal, usually an opinion about what is likely to happen / to be true]

I **doubt** we'll ever see total world peace.   [don't believe]

I **suspect** a lot of people never even think about pollution when they're driving their own car.   [have a strong feeling about something negative]

B Phrases for expressing opinion

In my view / in my opinion, we haven't made any progress.

She's made a big mistake, **to my mind**.   [fairly informal]

If you ask me, he ought to change his job.   [informal]

Note how **point of view**, is used in English:

From a teacher's **point of view**, the new examinations are a disaster.   [how teachers see things, or are affected]

C Prepositions used with belief and opinion words

Do you **believe in** God?   What are your **views on** divorce?

What do you **think of** the new boss?   I'm **in favour of** long prison sentences.

Are you **for** or **against** long prison sentences?   I **have my doubts about** this plan.

D Beliefs, ideologies, philosophies, convictions

If you would rather organise this word tree differently or can add more examples, do so; it will probably help you to remember the words better.

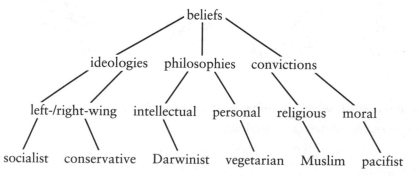

E

Some adjectives for describing people's beliefs and views, in pairs of similar, but not the same, meaning.

fanatical/obsessive   eccentric/odd   conservative/traditional
middle-of-the-road/moderate   dedicated/committed   firm/strong

Exercises

67.1 Draw lines connecting the left and right, as in the example, adding the appropriate preposition.

1 I have strong views   my opinion.
2 Most people believe   the proposed changes.
3 I was in favour   marriage.
4 What does she think ——— *of*   my mind.
5 This is absurd   life after death.
6 He's quite wrong   the new teacher?
7 Well, that's just silly   our point of view.

67.2 Use adjectives from E opposite which fit the phrases describing the beliefs and views of these people, as in the example.

1 A person who insists that the earth is flat. (An *eccentric* belief.)
2 A person who believes absolutely in the power of love to solve world problems. (A .... believer in the power of love.)
3 A socialist neither on the left or the right of the party. (A .... socialist.)
4 A vegetarian who refuses even to be in the same room as people who like meat. (A(n) .... vegetarian.)
5 Someone who is always suspicious of change. (A rather .... view of the world.)

67.3 Rewrite these sentences using the verbs in brackets.

1 I've always suspected that ghosts don't really exist. (doubt)
2 My view has always been that people should rely on themselves more. (hold)
3 Claudia is convinced that the teacher has been unfair to her. (maintain)
4 I felt a very strong feeling that I had been in that room before. (convince)
5 In his view, we should have tried again. (feel)

67.4 Are you...? Consider how many of these words apply to you, and in what situations. Some ideas for situations are given in the box, but you can add your own. Look up any words you don't know in a dictionary.

a perfectionist   left-wing   a moralist   an intellectual   a traditionalist
a philosopher   middle-of-the-road   a radical thinker   narrow-minded
open-minded   dedicated   dogmatic

food preferences	politics	learning English	sport
sexual relations	life and existence	religion	work

68 Pleasant and unpleasant feelings

A Happiness and unhappiness

You feel:

ecstatic when you are madly in love or are spiritually uplifted for some reason.
content(ed) when you are peaceful and satisfied with what you have. Notice that **content** is not used before a noun. You can say 'She is content' or 'She is contented' but only 'a contented person'.
cheerful when life is looking quite bright and positive.
grateful when someone has done you a favour.
delighted when something has happened that gives you great pleasure, when you hear news of someone's good fortune, for instance.
miserable when everything seems wrong in your life.
discontented when your life is not giving you satisfaction.
fed-up / sick and tired when you have had enough of something disagreeable. You could **be fed up with** someone's rudeness, for instance, or **sick and tired** of someone's behaviour.
depressed when you are miserable over a long period of time. Depression is considered an illness in some severe cases.
frustrated when you are unable to do something that you want to do.
confused / mixed up when you cannot make sense of different conflicting feelings or ideas; **mixed up** is more colloquial.

B Excitement, anger and anxiety

You feel:

excited when you are expecting something special to happen, e.g. before a party or before a meeting with someone special.
inspired when you are stimulated to creative deeds or words. You might feel **inspired** after listening to some very powerful music, perhaps, or you might be **inspired** to action by a friend.
enthusiastic when you have very positive feelings about something, e.g. a new project.
thrilled when something extremely exciting and pleasing happens – quite a colloquial word. She was **thrilled** when the film star kissed her.
cross when you are angry or bad-tempered. It is ofen, though not exclusively, used about small children; quite a colloquial word.
furious/livid/seething when you are extremely angry; **livid** and **seething** are more informal; **in a rage/fury** are other ways of saying furious or violently angry.
anxious when you are afraid and uncertain about the future. I am so **anxious** about the results of my exams that I can't sleep.
nervous when you are afraid or anxious about something that is about to or may be about to happen. I always feel nervous when I have to go to the dentist. Feeling nervous is a little bit like feeling excited but it is a negative feeling whereas excitement is positive.
apprehensive when you are slightly nervous or anxious about something in the future.
worried when anxious thoughts are constantly going through your head.
upset when something unpleasant has happened to disturb you. It often combines feelings of both sadness and anger.

Exercises

68.1 Complete the following table.

adjective	abstract noun	adjective	abstract noun
furious	....	frustrated	....
....	anxiety	....	cheerfulness
grateful	....	enthusiastic	....
....	ecstasy	....	apprehension
inspired	....	excited	....

68.2 Choose the best word from those given to complete each of the sentences which follow.

enthusiastic   confused   cross   thrilled   depressed
upset   fed-up   frustrated   discontented

1 I didn't know who was telling the truth. I felt totally ....
2 Some mothers are .... for several months after the birth of a baby.
3 I think she is bad-tempered because she is .... She wanted to be an actress and not a school-teacher.
4 Although he seems to have everything anyone could possibly want, he is still ....
5 He went skiing for the first time last month, but now he is so .... about it that he can talk of little else.
6 My baby brother gets very .... by the evening if he doesn't have an afternoon sleep.
7 This rainy weather has gone on for so long. I feel really .... with it.
8 He was terribly .... when he heard the news of his friend's accident.
9 She was .... when she learnt that she had won the first prize.

68.3 Write sentences about when you have experienced the following feelings.

Example: anxious *I felt anxious until we heard the results of my mother's medical tests.*

1 anxious   3 grateful   5 miserable   7 enthusiastic
2 apprehensive   4 in a rage   6 inspired

68.4 The words opposite ending in -ed (apart from contented and delighted) also have -ing forms e.g. interested/interesting and bored/boring. Add the correct ending -ed or -ing.

Example: She was thrill*ed* by her present.

1 I found the film very excit............... .
2 The poet was inspir............... by the sunset.
3 This weather is terribly depress............... .
4 It is very frustrat............... when the phones aren't working.
5 She was confus............... by the ambiguous remarks he made to her.

68.5 You, of course, know the basic expressions: 'I'm hungry/thirsty/hot/cold/tired/cross'. Colloquially, we often say the same things using a much stronger expression. What do you think people mean when they say:

1 I'm boiling   3 I'm seething   5 I'm starving
2 I'm dying for a drink 4 I'm freezing   6 I'm worn out

69 Like, dislike and desire

Words and expressions relating to liking

I **quite liked** Tom when we first met. However, although lots of my friends said they found him attractive, I didn't **fancy** him at all. He invited me out and I must admit that I was more **tempted** by his sports car than by him at first. However, I really **enjoyed** spending time with him. He **fascinated** me with his stories of his travels around the world and something mysterious about his past also **attracted** me. Moreover, we were both very **keen on** sailing. Soon I realised I had **fallen in love** with him. His sense of humour really **appealed to** me and I was also **captivated by** his gift for poetry. Now, three years later I absolutely **adore** him and I cannot understand why I didn't **fall for** him the moment we first set eyes on each other. He is a very **caring** person, **fond of** animals and small children. He is always **affectionate** and **loving** towards me and **passionate about** the causes he believes in and the people he **cares for**. I hope we shall always **worship** each other as much and be as **devoted to** our life together as we are now.

B Words and expressions relating to desiring

Desire is used either as a formal verb to express a sexual wish for someone or else it is quite a formal word for wish.
He **desired** her the moment he saw her.
I have a strong **desire** to see the Himalayas before I die.

Looking forward to means thinking about something in the future with pleasant anticipation. The opposite of **look forward to** is **dread**.
I am **looking forward to** going to Fiji but I'm **dreading** the flight.
Note: 'to' is a preposition here and not part of the infinitive and is followed by a noun or an -ing form.

Long for means to wish for something very much.
As soon as I get back from one holiday, I'm **longing for** the next.
Yearn for is a more poetic way of saying **long for**.
He will never stop **yearning for** his country although he knows he can never return.

C Words and expressions relating to disliking.

Loathe, detest, hate, cannot stand and **cannot bear** are all stronger ways of saying dislike and they are all followed by a noun or an -ing form.
I **loathe / detest / hate / cannot stand / cannot bear** bad-mannered people.

Repel, revolt and **disgust** are all strong words used to describe the effect which something detested has on the person affected.
His paintings **disgust** me. I was **revolted** by the way he spoke. His behaviour **repels** me.

D Ways of addressing loved ones

dearest   sweetheart   darling   love   dear   pet

Pet is used mainly to children. Note that the last three words in the list are not confined to use with people who are really loved. It is not uncommon for a London bus conductor, for example, to address any girl or woman as '**love**'. (His Glasgow equivalent calls his female passengers '**hen**'.) It's best for you, however, to keep such words for people you have a close relationship with!

Exercises

69.1 Complete the following table.

verb	noun	adjective	adverb
–	passion	....	....
tempt	*Temptation*	....	....
attract	....	....	....
appeal	....	....	....
disgust	....	....	....
hate	....	....	....
repel	....	....	....
–	affection	....	....
adore	....	....	....

69.2 Complete the following sentences.

1 Misogynists hate ....
2 Ornithologists are fascinated by ....
3 People who suffer from arachnophobia find .... repulsive.
4 Kleptomaniacs are constantly tempted to ....
5 Masochists enjoy ....
6 Optimists look forward to ....

69.3 Reword the sentences without changing the meaning. Use the word in brackets.

Example: I very much enjoy his novels. (love) *I love his novels.*

1 I strongly dislike jazz. (stand)
2 Beer makes me feel sick. (revolt)
3 I don't really care for tea. (keen)
4 His art attracts me. (appeal)
5 She has totally charmed him. (captivate)
6 Do you fancy a pizza tonight? (like)
7 She likes rowing and golf. (keen)
8 I'm dreading the exam. (look)

69.4 In each pair of sentences which person probably feels more strongly?

1 a Dear Louise, How are things?
2 a He's devoted to his sister.
3 a I dislike his poetry.
4 a She's yearning to see him.
5 a He worships her.

b Darling Louise, How are things?
b He's very fond of his sister.
b I loathe his poetry.
b She's longing to see him.
b He loves her very much.

69.5 Complete the sentences or answer the questions in any way that is true for you.

1 What kind of food do you like? I like .... and I adore
.... but I can't stand ....
2 I'm longing for ....
3 I'm fascinated by ....
4 What attracts you most in a person of the opposite sex?
5 What do you enjoy most about your job?
6 If you were on a diet, what food or drink would tempt you most to break the diet?
7 What characteristics in people do you most detest?
8 What do you dread most about getting old?
9 What do you fancy doing this evening?

70 Speaking

A The verbs in the table below describe how loudly or quietly a person is speaking and also, often, indicate mood. These verbs are all followed by clauses beginning with 'that'.

verb	loudness	most likely mood
whisper	soft	–
murmur	soft	romantic *or* complaining
mumble	soft (and unclear)	nervous *or* insecure
mutter	soft	irritated
shout	loud	angry *or* excited
scream	loud (usually without words)	frightened *or* excited
shriek	loud (and shrill)	frightened *or* amused
stutter, stammer	neutral	nervous *or* excited

B The following verbs all indicate something about how the speaker feels. What they usually indicate is given in the *feeling* column. (*Note*: s.b. = somebody s.t. = something)

verb	patterns	feeling	verb	patterns	feeling
boast	to s.b. about s.t. / that...	proud of oneself	complain	to s.b. about s.t. / that...	displeased
insist	on s.t. / that...	determined	maintain	that...	confident
object	that... / to + ing	unhappy	confess	that... / to + ing	repentant
threaten	that... / to do s.t.	aggressive	urge	s.b. to do s.t.	encouraging
argue	with s.b. about s.t. / that...	not in agreement	beg	s.b. to do s.t./ for s.t.	desperate
groan	that...	despair, pain	grumble	about s.t/	displeased

C It is also possible to give an idea of the way someone speaks by using a speaking verb, plus an adverb. For example, 'He said **proudly**'. 'She spoke **angrily**'. This is most common in written style.

Some useful adverbs describing the way someone is feeling while they are speaking.

If someone feels angry: angrily   crossly   furiously   bitterly
If someone feels unhappy: unhappily   gloomily   miserably   uneasily   sadly
If someone feels happy: happily   cheerfully   gladly   hopefully   eagerly
If someone feels worried: anxiously   nervously   desperately   hopelessly

Other useful adverbs are boldly, excitedly, gratefully, impatiently, passionately, reluctantly, shyly, sincerely.

Exercises

70.1 Choose the verb which best fits the meaning of the sentences.

Example: 'I love you,' he *murmured*.

1 'It was I who broke the vase,' he ....
2 'I am the cleverest person in the class,' the little boy ....
3 'Look, there's a mouse over there!' he ....
4 'I'll stop your pocket money if you don't behave,' she ....
5 'I d-d-d-did it,' he ....
6 'Please, please, help me,' he ....
7 'This hotel is filthy,' she ....
8 'Go on, Jim, try harder,' he ....

70.2 Change the sentences above into reported speech using the same verbs.

Example: He murmured that he loved her.

70.3 Add the appropriate adjectives and nouns to the table below.

adverb	adjective	noun
angrily	....	....
furiously	....	....
bitterly	....	....
miserably	....	....
cheerfully	....	....
gratefully	....	....
anxiously	....	....

70.4 The answers to the following questions are all words which are from the same root as the verbs on the page opposite.

Example: How do you describe a person who boasts a lot? *boastful*

What do you call:
1 what you make when you threaten?
2 what you make when you complain?
3 what you make when you object?
4 a person who asks for money on the streets?

How do you describe:
5 someone who insists a lot?
6 someone who argues a lot?

70.5 Look at the verbs in the table in B and answer the following quiz.

1 Which verbs could replace <u>ask</u> in the sentence 'She asked me to dance with her' without changing the grammar of the sentence?
2 Which prepositions usually follow a) object b) insist c) complain?
3 Which verb could grammatically replace <u>promise</u> in 'He promised to do it'?
4 Which of the verbs can be followed by 'that' and a clause?
5 Find a synonym for each of the six verbs in the fourth column of the table.

70.6 Write a sentence to match each of the eight adverbs listed at the end of C.

Example: Excitedly. 'Let's go at once,' she said excitedly.

71 The six senses

A Our basic five senses are **sight, hearing, taste, touch** and **smell**. What is sometimes referred to as a 'sixth sense' is a power to be aware of things independently of the five physical senses, a kind of supernatural sense. The five basic verbs referring to the senses are modified by an adjective rather than an adverb.

He **looks** dreadful.   The trip **sounds** marvellous.   The cake **tastes** good.

It **felt** strange.   The soup **smelt** delicious.

B ## Sight

Look at the verbs of seeing in the text below.

Yesterday I **glanced** out of the window and **noticed** a man **observing** a house opposite through a telescope. I thought I **glimpsed** a woman inside the house. Then I **saw** someone else **peering** into the window of the same house. I **gazed** at them wondering what they were doing. Suddenly the first man stopped **staring** through his telescope. He went and hit the other one on the head with the telescope and I realised that I had **witnessed** a crime.

C ## Hearing

The following scale relates to the sense of hearing and how loud things are.

noiseless → silent → quiet → noisy → loud → deafening

D ## Taste

Some different tastes with an example of a typical food. (See also Unit 43.)

sweet (honey)   **salty** (crisps)   **bitter** (strong coffee)   **sour** (vinegar)   **spicy** (Indian food)

If you say something tastes **hot** it may mean **spicy** rather than **not cold**. Food can be **tasty**, but **tasteful** is used to refer to furnishings, architecture or a style of dressing or behaviour. The opposite of both is **tasteless**.

E ## Touch

Some good verbs for describing different ways of touching.

She nervously **fingered** her collar.   He **stroked** the cat and **patted** the dog.
She **tapped** him on the shoulder.   He **grasped** my hand and we ran.
She **grabbed** her bag and ran.   It's rude to **snatch**.   **Press** the button.
Please **handle** the goods with great care.
The secretaries complained that their boss was always **pawing** them.

F ## Smell

These adjectives describe how something smells.

stinking   evil-smelling   smelly   aromatic   scented
fragrant   sweet-smelling   perfumed

G ## Sixth sense

Different phenomena which a person with sixth sense may experience:

telepathy   ghosts   UFOs   premonitions   intuition   déjà vu

Exercises

71.1 Make a sentence using any of these verbs, *look, sound, taste, touch* and *smell,* plus an adjective about the situations.

Example: You see a film about the Rocky Mountains. *They look magnificent.*

1 You come downstairs in the morning and smell fresh coffee.
2 A friend has just had her hair cut.
3 You hear the record that is top of the pops.
4 A friend, an excellent cook, tries a new soup recipe.
5 A friend asks how you feel today.
6 A little boy asks you to listen to his first attempts at the piano.
7 You see a friend of yours with a very worried look on her face.
8 Someone you are working with smells strongly of cigarettes.

71.2 Which of the verbs in the text in B suggests looking:

1 on as a crime or accident occurs?   4 quickly?
2 closely, finding it hard to make things out?   5 fixedly?
3 in a scientific kind of way?

71.3 Replace the underlined words with a more interesting and precise verb from the opposite page.

1 I <u>saw</u> a crime.
2 He <u>looked fixedly</u> at me.
3 She <u>took</u> my hand <u>firmly</u>.
4 <u>Touch</u> the button to start.
5 He <u>touched</u> the cat affectionately.
6 The zoologist <u>looked at</u> the lion's behaviour.
7 The robber <u>took</u> the money and ran.
8 I <u>quickly looked</u> at my watch.

71.4 Are the following best described as *sweet, salty, bitter, sour, spicy* or *hot*?

1 unsweetened coffee   3 chilli   5 Chinese cooking
2 pineapple   4 lime   6 sea water

71.5 Match the verbs used in E with these definitions.

1 to take something very quickly   3 to touch with the hands
2 to move between the fingers   4 to touch in an offensive way

71.6 Which of the adjectives in F describes best for you the smell of the following?

1 herbs in a kitchen   3 rotten eggs   5 a baby's bottom
2 old socks   4 roses   6 a hairdresser's

71.7 Which of the phenomena mentioned in G have you experienced if you:

1 see a flying saucer?
2 suddenly think of someone two minutes before they phone you?
3 see someone in white disappearing into a wall?
4 feel certain someone cannot be trusted although you have no real reason to believe so?
5 walk into a strange room and feel you have been there before?
6 refuse to travel on a plane because you feel something bad is going to happen?

71.8 Write a sentence about the most remarkable experience each of your six senses has had.

72 What your body does

This unit deals with some interesting words used to describe things your body does.

Note: All the verbs on this page (except **shake** and **bite**) are regular verbs; almost all the words have an identical noun form: **to yawn/a yawn, to cough/a cough** etc. (except for **breathe** and **perspire**; the nouns are **breath** and **perspiration**).

A Verbs connected with the mouth and breathing

breathe: A nurse gave the old man the kiss of life and he started **breathing** again.
yawn: If one person **yawns** everyone else seems to start too.
cough: It was so smoky in the room that he couldn't stop **coughing**.
sneeze: Dust often makes me **sneeze**.
sigh: She **sighed** with relief when she heard his plane had landed safely.
hiccough: Some people say that drinking out of the wrong side of a cup can help to stop you **hiccoughing**. (*Note:* pronunciation = /ˈhɪkʌpɪŋ/)
snore: She **snored** all night with her mouth wide open.

B Verbs connected with eating and the digestion

burp: He patted the baby's back to make it **burp** after its feed.
chew: My granny used to say you should **chew** every mouthful ten times.
rumble: It's embarrassing if your stomach **rumbles** during an interview.
swallow: Take a drink of water to help you **swallow** the pills.
suck: You're too old to **suck** your thumb!
lick: After having a meal, the cat **licked** herself clean.
bite: He always **bites** his nails when he's nervous.

C Verbs connected with the eyes and face

blink: She **blinked** several times to try and get the dust out of her eye.
wink: He **winked** at me across the room to try and make me laugh.
frown: Why are you **frowning**? What's the problem?
grin: She was so delighted with the present that she **grinned** from ear to ear.
blush: He **blushed** with embarrassment when she smiled at him.

D Verbs connected with the whole body

perspire/sweat: When it's hot you **sweat/perspire**.   [perspire is more formal]
tremble: My hands **tremble** when I've been drinking too much coffee.
shiver: Look at him! He's so cold that he's **shivering**!
shake: She laughed so much that her whole body **shook**.

The pronunciation of some of the words in this unit is unusual. The index will tell you how to pronounce them.

Exercises

72.1 Find the word to match the dictionary definitions given below.

Example: to draw the eyebrows together to express displeasure or puzzlement *to frown*

1 to go pink from embarrassment
2 to tremble especially from cold or fear
3 to hold something in the mouth and lick it, roll it about, squeeze it etc. with the tongue and teeth
4 to shut and open both eyes quickly
5 to deliberately shut and open one eye

72.2 Say what must be happening in each of the situations below.

Example: (Parent to child) Take your thumb out of your mouth! *The child is sucking its thumb.*

1 Listen to that! I can't sleep in the same room as him.
2 Am I boring you?
3 If you have a drink of water, it might stop!
4 I'd have a honey and lemon drink if I were you!
5 Are you hungry?
6 You shouldn't eat so much so quickly!

72.3 Which of the words on the opposite page do these pictures illustrate?

Example: 1 *blink*

72.4 Complete the puzzle. If you answer correctly, the central letters going downwards will form a word from the left-hand page.

1 a special kind of gum
2 a more formal word for sweating
3 what you need to do to a stamp
4 try to do this quickly with pills
5 smile broadly
6 James Bond liked to have his drinks .... not stirred.

72.5 Organise the words on the opposite page into one or more bubble networks. Add any other words that you wish to the networks.

73 What animals do

A Noises animals make

Cats **mew** when they're hungry, **purr** when they're happy and **caterwaul** when they're on the roof at midnight.

Dogs **bark**. They also **growl** when they're angry. Lions **roar**.

Sheep and goats **bleat**, horses **neigh** and pigs **grunt**. Cows **moo**.

Frogs **croak** and ducks **quack**. Cocks **crow**, hens **cluck** and owls **hoot**.

N.B. All these verbs are regular verbs.

B Movements animals make

Birds **fly** and fish **swim**.
Butterflies **flutter**.
Kangaroos **hop**.
Snakes **slither**.
Horses **trot** and **gallop**
   (**galloping** is faster
   than **trotting**).
Lambs **skip** in the spring.

N.B. **Fly** (flew, flown) and **swim** (swam, swum) are the only irregular verbs here.

C Babies animals have

Cats have **kittens** and **dogs** have **puppies**. Horses have **foals**. Sheep have **lambs**.
Cows have **calves**. Pigs have **piglets**. Bears, wolves and lions have cubs.
Ducks have **ducklings**. Hens lay eggs from which **chickens** hatch.
Tadpoles turn into **frogs**. Caterpillars turn into **butterflies**.

D People and animals

People are often compared to animals. The following adjectives can be used about people. A more formal translation is given.

catty or **bitchy**: malicious-tongued   **ratty**: bad-tempered
mousy: dull, uninteresting, shy, quiet   **dogged**: stubborn
sheepish: awkwardly self-conscious   **cocky**: arrogant

Exercises

73.1 Match the verb with the sound. The first example has been done.

1 hoot	meow
2 bleat	toowit toowoo
3 bark	oink
4 grunt	cockadoodledoo
5 mew	woof
6 crow	baa

73.2 Complete the following text, putting the appropriate missing verbs into the correct form.

It is not really all that peaceful out in the country. Yesterday I was woken at dawn when the cock started ....(1). The calves soon began ....(2) and this woke the dogs who ....(3) until the horses started ....(4). Lots of hens ....(5) right outside my window and so I got up. I tripped over the cat who was lying in the sun at the front door but she didn't even stop ....(6).

73.3 Which of the adjectives in D would you be pleased to be called?

73.4 Most of the sound verbs in A and all the movement verbs in B can also be used to describe sounds and movements made by humans. Mark the following statements true or false.

1 If someone growls at you, they are probably in a bad mood.
2 If someone croaks, they probably have a sore throat.
3 If someone hoots, they are probably very unhappy.
4 If someone is caterwauling, they are singing very sweetly.
5 If someone barks at you, they sound rather angry or abrupt.
6 If someone grunts when you ask something, they are showing a lot of interest in what you have said.

73.5 Illustrate the meaning of the words below by writing sentences (about people rather than animals).

Example: 1 skip   *The little girl loves skipping with her new rope.*

2 fly   3 swim   4 slither   5 hop   6 trot   7 gallop

73.6 Look at the following examples of notices and fill in the names of the appropriate young animal in each case. Which words help you decide?

1 New-born .... for sale. Pedigree spaniel.
2 Good home wanted for six .... All toms. Already house-trained. Part-Siamese. Very intelligent.
3 Come and see the brand-new polar bear .... at the zoo.
4 Hadley Farm open this weekend. All children will enjoy the chance to hold the baby .... and to stroke their soft wool.
5 Spend the weekend at Sun Park. Hundreds of new .... Just hatched but already able to swim happily behind their mums.

74 Idioms and fixed expressions – general

Idioms are fixed expressions with meanings that are usually not clear or obvious. The individual words often give you no help in deciding the meaning. The expression **to feel under the weather**, which means 'to feel unwell' is a typical idiom. The words do not tell us what it means, but the context usually helps.

A Tips for dealing with idioms

Think of idioms as being just like single words; always record the whole phrase in your notebook, along with information on grammar and collocation.

This tin-opener **has seen better days.**   [it is rather old and broken down; usually of things, always perfect tense form]

Idioms are usually rather informal and include an element of personal comment on the situation. They are sometimes humorous or ironic. As with any informal 'commenting' single word, be careful how you use them. Never use them just to sound 'fluent' or 'good at English'. In a formal situation with a person you do not know, don't say,

'How do you do, Mrs Watson. Do **take the weight off your feet.'**   [sit down].
Instead say 'Do sit down' or 'Have a seat'.

Idioms can be grouped in a variety of ways. Use whichever way you find most useful to help you remember them. Here are some possible types of grouping.

Grammatical

get the wrong end of the stick   [misunderstand] ⎫
pull a fast one   [trick/deceive somebody] ⎬ verb + object
poke your nose in(to)   [interfere] ⎭

be over the moon   [extremely happy/elated] ⎫
feel down in the dumps   [depressed/low] ⎬ verb + preposition phrase
be in the red   [have a negative bank balance] ⎭

By meaning e.g. idioms describing people's character/intellect
He's **as daft as a brush.**   [very stupid/silly]
He **takes the biscuit.**   [is the extreme / the worst of all]
You're **a pain in the neck.**   [a nuisance / difficult person]

By verb or other key word e.g. idioms with **make**
I don't see why you have to **make a meal out of** everything.
[exaggerate the importance of everything]
I think we should **make a move.** It's gone ten o'clock.   [go/leave]
Most politicians are **on the make.** I don't trust any of them.
[wanting money/power for oneself]

B Grammar of idioms

It is important when using idioms to know just how flexible their grammar is. Some are more fixed than others. For instance, **barking up the wrong tree** [be mistaken] is always used in continuous, not simple form, e.g. I think you're **barking up the wrong tree.**

A good dictionary may help but it is best to observe the grammar in real examples.

Note how Units 76–91 group idioms in different ways.

Exercises

74.1 Complete the idioms in these sentences with one of the key words given, as in the example. If you are not sure, try looking up the key word in a good dictionary.

clanger   shot   ocean   plate   block   handle   pie

1 All the promises these politicians make! It's just *pie* in the sky. (big promises that will never materialise)
2 The small amount of money donated is just a drop in the .... compared with the vast sum we need. (tiny contribution compared with what is needed)
3 You really dropped a .... when you criticised the Americans last night; that man opposite you was from New York! (said something inappropriate/embarrassing)
4 I can't do that job as well; I've got enough on my .... as it is. (have more than enough work)
5 When I told her she just flew off the .... and shouted at me. (lost her temper)
6 His father was a gambler too. He's a real chip off the old .... (just like one's parents/grandparents)
7 I wasn't really sure; I guessed it; it was just a .... in the dark. (a wild guess)

74.2 Use a good general dictionary or a dictionary of idioms to see if it can help you decide which version of these sentences is in the normal grammatical form for the idiom concerned, as in the example. Check the meaning too, if you are not sure.

Example: You **bark /** **are barking** up the wrong tree if you think I did it. (see B opposite)

1 Holland <u>is springing / springs</u> to mind as the best place to go for a cycling holiday; it's very flat.
2 That remark <u>is flying / flies</u> in the face of everything you've ever said before on the subject.
3 He was innocent after all. It <u>just goes / is just going</u> to show that you shouldn't believe what you read in the papers.
4 You <u>sit / 're sitting</u> pretty! Look at you, an easy job, a fantastic salary, a free car!
5 His attitude <u>is leaving / leaves</u> a lot to be desired. I do wish he would try to improve a little.

74.3 How would you organise this selection of idioms into different groups? Use some of the ways suggested on the opposite page, plus any other ways you can think of.

be in a fix   child's play   rough and ready   be up to it   hold your tongue
be out of sorts   hold your horses   a fool's errand   odds and ends
stay mum   give or take

74.4 Without using a dictionary, try to guess the meaning of these idioms from the context.

1 It's midnight. Time to <u>hit the sack</u>.
2 This is just <u>kid's stuff</u>. I want something challenging!
3 He was <u>down and out</u> for two years, but then he got a job and found a home for himself.

75 Everyday expressions

> Everyday spoken language is full of fixed expressions that are not necessarily difficult to understand (their meaning may be quite 'transparent') but which have a fixed form which does not change. These have to be learnt as whole expressions. These expressions are often hard to find in dictionaries, so listen out for them.

A Conversation-building expressions

These are some common expressions that help to modify or organise what we are saying. There are many more expressions like these. (See also Unit 100.)

expression		meaning/function
As I was saying, I haven't seen her for years.	→	takes the conversation back to an earlier point
As I/you say, we'll have to get there early to get a seat.	→	repeats and confirms something someone has already said
Talking of skiing, whatever happened to Bill Jakes?	→	starting a new topic but linking it to the present one
If you ask me, she's heading for trouble.	→	if you want my opinion (even if no-one has asked for it)
That reminds me, I haven't rung George yet.	→	something in the conversation reminds you of something important
Come to think of it, did he give me his number after all? I think he may have forgotten.	→	something in the conversation makes you realise there may be a problem/query about something

B Key words

Some everyday expressions can be grouped around key words. **This** and **that**, for example, occur in several expressions:

This is it. [this is an important point]

We talked about **this and that,** or **this, that and the other.** [various unimportant matters]

THIS/THAT

That's it. [that's the last thing, we've finished]

So, **that's that,** then. [that is agreed, settled, finalised]

C Common expressions for modifying statements

If the worst comes to the worst, we'll have to cancel the holiday. [if the situation gets very bad indeed]

If all else fails, we could fax them. [if nothing else succeeds]

What with one thing and another, I haven't had time to reply to her letter. [because of a lot of different circumstances]

When it comes to restaurants, this town's not that good. [in the matter of restaurants]

As far as I'm concerned, we can eat at any time. [as far as it affects me / from my point of view]

As luck would have it, she was out when we called. [as a result of bad luck]

Exercises

75.1 Complete the fixed expressions in these sentences, as far as possible without looking at the left-hand page.

1 Come ...., I don't remember giving her the key. I'd better ring her and check, just in case.

2 If you ...., the economy's going to get much worse before it gets any better.

3 .... holidays, have you got any plans for next year?

4 A: It's going to be expensive.
B: Yes, it'll be fun, and a great opportunity, but, as ...., it will be expensive.

5 That ...., I have a message for you from Sid.

6 As ...., before the postwoman interrupted us, we plan to extend the house next spring.

75.2 Which of the expressions with *this/that* opposite would be most suitable for the second parts of these mini-dialogues?

1 A: What were you and Lindsay talking about?
B: Oh, ...

2 A: How many more?
B: No more, actually, ...

3 A: The most important thing is that nobody's happy.
B: Yes, well, ...

4 A: Okay, I'll take our decisions to the committee.
B: Right, so ...., then. Thanks.

75.3 See if you can complete this network of everyday expressions with *now*, as with the *this/that* network opposite. Use a dictionary if necessary.

```
                    .................................................
                             [occasionally]
                                  |
                        ___ NOW ___
                       /           \
.................................       .................................
   [attract attention because           [immediately; also used
   you're going to say something]        to emphasise your point]
```

Use the expressions with *now* to rewrite these sentences.

1 Do you want me to do it straight away, or can it wait?

2 So, everybody, listen carefully. I have news for you.

3 I bump into her in town occasionally, but not that often.

75.4 Which expressions contain the following key words?

1 comes   2 luck   3 fails   4 worst   5 far   6 thing

Follow-up: Make a list of common expressions like the ones in this unit in your language. How do you say them in English?

76 Similes – as...as... / like...

As...as... similes are easy to understand. If you see the phrase **as dead as a doornail**, you don't need to know what a **doornail** is, simply that the whole phrase means 'totally dead'. But, remember, fixed similes are not 'neutral'; they are usually informal/colloquial and often humorous. So, use them with care, and keep them generally as part of your receptive vocabulary.

Creating a picture in your mind can often help you remember the simile:

as blind as a **bat**   as thin as a **rake**   as strong as an **ox**   as quiet as a **mouse**

Some can be remembered as pairs of opposites.

as **heavy** as **lead** ≠ as **light** as a **feather**   as **drunk** as a **lord** ≠ as **sober** as a **judge**
as **black** as **night** ≠ as **white** as **snow**

Some can be remembered by sound patterns.

As **brown** as a **berry**   as **good** as **gold**   as **cool** as a **cucumber**

Some other useful as...as... phrases.

The bed was **as hard as iron** and I couldn't sleep.
I'll give this plant some water. The soil's **as dry as a bone**.
He's **as mad as a hatter**. He crossed the Atlantic in a bathtub.
She told the teacher, **as bold as brass**, that his lessons were boring.
You'll have to speak up; he's **as deaf as a post**.
Don't worry. Using the computer's **as easy as falling off a log**.
She knew the answer **as quick as a flash**.
When I told him, his face went **as red as a beetroot**.

Sometimes the second part can change the meaning of the first.

The Princess's skin was **as white as snow**.   [beautifully white]
When he saw it, his face went **as white as a sheet**.   [pale with fear/horror]
The fish was bad and I was **as sick as a dog**.   [vomiting]
She ran off with my money; I felt **as sick as a parrot**.   [bad feeling of disillusionment/frustration]

B Like...

My plan **worked like a dream**, and the problem was soon solved.
Be careful the boss doesn't see you; she has **eyes like a hawk**.
No wonder he's fat. He **eats like a horse** and **drinks like a fish**.
Did you **sleep** well? Yes, thanks, **like a log**.
Sorry, I forgot to ring him again. I've got **a head like a sieve!**
The boss is **like a bear with a sore head** today.   [in a very bad temper]
She goes around **like a bull in a china shop**.   [behaving in a very clumsy, insensitive way]
Criticising the government in his presence is **like a red rag to a bull**.   [certain to make him very angry]

Exercises

76.1 Complete the as...as... similes.

1 Rose is as mad as a ....; you wouldn't believe the crazy things she does.
2 You're not eating enough; you're as thin as a ....
3 He never says a thing; he's as quiet as a ....
4 You'll have to shout; she's as deaf as a ....
5 I'm afraid I can't read this small print; I'm as blind as a .... without my glasses.

76.2 Different similes contain the same word. Fill the gap with the appropriate words.

1 I feel great now. I .... like a log.
2 No! It's as easy as .... off a log.
3 After eating that bad cheese I was as sick as a ....
4 I knew she had swindled me. I felt as sick as a ....
5 The old man's hair was as white as ....
6 Her face suddenly went as white as ....

76.3 Put the correct number in the right-hand boxes to complete the similes, as in the example. There are two that are not on the left-hand page. Try and guess them.

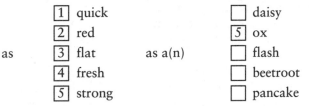

as
1	quick
2	red
3	flat
4	fresh
5	strong

as a(n)
☐	daisy
5	ox
☐	flash
☐	beetroot
☐	pancake

76.4 Simile word puzzle. Fill in the answers, as in the example.

Across
1 bold
2 mad
4 white
5 fresh
7 quiet
9 dry

Down
1 blind
2 iron
3 log
6 cold
8 cool
10 light

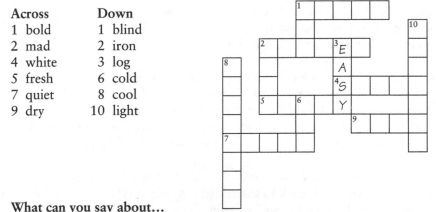

76.5 What can you say about...

1 a person who sees everything and never misses a thing?
2 a plan or course of action that works very well?
3 someone who eats and drinks a great deal?
4 someone with a very bad memory?

Tip: You can always make a simile using **as...as can be**, for example, I need a drink; I'm **as thirsty as can be!**

77 Binomials

Binomials are expressions (often idiomatic) where two words are joined by a conjunction (usually 'and'). The order of the words is usually fixed. It is best to use them only in informal situations, with one or two exceptions.

> **odds and ends**: small, unimportant things, e.g. Let's get the main things packed; we can do the **odds and ends** later.
>
> **give and take**: a spirit of compromise, e.g. Every relationship needs a bit of **give and take** to be successful.

A You can often tell something is a binomial because of the sound pattern.

Tears are **part and parcel** of growing up.　[part of / belong to]
The boss was **ranting and raving** at us.　[shouting / very angry]
The old cottage has gone to **rack and ruin**.　[ruined/decayed]
He's so **prim and proper** at work.　[rather formal and fussy]
The hotel was a bit **rough and ready**.　[poor standard]
She has to **wine and dine** important clients.　[entertain]

B Other times, the clue is that the words are near-synonyms.

You can **pick and choose**; it's up to you.　[have a wide choice]
My English is progressing in **leaps and bounds**.　[big jumps]
It's nice to have some **peace and quiet**.　[peace/calm]
The doctor recommended some **rest and recreation**.　[relaxation]
First and foremost, you must work hard.　[first / most importantly]

C Many grammar words combine to form binomials.

There are cafés **here and there**.　[scattered round]
We've had meetings **on and off**.　[occasionally]
I've been running **back and forth** all day.　[to and from somewhere]
To and fro can be used just like **back and forth**.
He is unemployed and **down and out**.　[without a home or money]
She's better now, and **out and about** again.　[going out]
She ran **up and down** the street.　[in both directions]

D Your language probably has many binomials. Make sure those which look similar in English have the same word order as your language. These four are very neutral binomials and can be used in formal or informal situations. Try translating them.

A **black and white** film, please.　　**Ladies and gentlemen**, your attention, please!
She ran **back and forth**.　　There was **hot and cold** water in every room.

E Binomials linked by words other than **and**.

You've got your sweater on **back to front**.　[the wrong way]
He won't help her; she'll have to **sink or swim**.　[survive or fail]
Slowly but surely, I realised the boat was sinking.　[gradually]
Sooner or later, you'll learn your lesson.　[some time/day]
She didn't want to be just friends; it had to be **all or nothing**.
Well I'm sorry, that's all I can offer you; **take it or leave it**.
It's about the same distance as from here to Dublin, **give or take** a few miles.　[perhaps a mile or two more, or a mile or two less]

Exercises

77.1 Here are some jumbled binomials (some are from the left-hand page and some are new). Using similarities in sound, join them with *and*. Then check opposite or in a dictionary that you have the word order right, and that you know the meaning.

prim   dine   high   ruin   rough   dry
rack   ready   proper   sound   safe   wine

Now use them to fill the gaps in these sentences.

1 I was left .... and ...., with no-one to help me.
2 The room's a bit .... and ...., but you're welcome to stay as long as you like.
3 I'm glad you're .... and .... after such a dangerous journey.
4 My hosts .... and .... me at the best restaurants.
5 Our old house in the country has just gone to .... and ....; nobody looks after it now.
6 The secretary is always so terribly .... and ....; the whole atmosphere always seems so very formal.

77.2 In the left-hand box below are the *first* words of some binomials. On the right are a selection of words, some of which you will need, and some you will not. Your task is to find a word on the right which can form a binomial with the left-hand word, as in the example *law and order*. Look for words that are either near-synonyms or antonyms (opposites) of the left-hand word.

(law)
now
hit
clean   and
pick
sick
leaps

money   tidy   drop
tired   soon   snow
pay   bounds   terrible
clocks   after   whisper
(order)   then   dogs
scratch   heart   choose
flowers   miss   chase

Now use them to make informal sentences by re-writing these.

1 There are lots of courses. You can make your own selection.
2 The flat looks all neat and spotless now for our visitors.
3 I have had enough of traffic jams. I'm going to start using the train.
4 Finding the right people was rather difficult; sometimes we succeeded, sometimes we failed.
5 My knowledge of English has progressed rapidly since I've been using this book.
6 The new Prime Minister promised that efficient policing would be the most important priority.
7 I've seen her occasionally, taking her dog for a walk.

77.3 These binomials do not have *and* in the middle. What do they have? Check opposite or in a dictionary if you are not sure.

1 Sooner .... later   3 Back .... front   5 Slowly .... surely
2 All .... nothing   4 Sink .... swim   6 Make .... break

78 Idioms describing people

Positive and negative qualities

positive	*negative*
She **has a heart of gold.** [very kind, generous]	She's **as hard as nails.** [no sympathy for others]
He's **as good as gold.** [generous, helpful, well-behaved used generally for children]	He's rather **a cold fish.** [distant, unfriendly]

Note also:

He's such **an awkward customer.**   [difficult person to deal with]
She's **a pain in the neck.** Nobody likes her.   [nuisance, difficult]
He **gets on everyone's nerves.**   [irritates everybody]

B ## People's 'fast' and 'slow' qualities

fast	*slow*
He's very **quick off the mark;** he always gets things before everybody else.	I was a bit **slow off the mark;** the job had been filled by the time I got the forms.
You've asked him to marry you! You're **a fast worker!** You only met him three weeks ago!	Come on! Hurry up! You're such **a slow-coach!**

C ## How people relate to the social norm

She's a bit of **an odd-ball;** very strange.   [peculiar, strange]
He's really **over the top.**   [very exaggerated in behaviour]
He's **round the bend,** if you ask me.   [absolutely crazy/mad]
My politics are very **middle-of-the-road.**   [very normal; no radical ideas; neither left- nor right-wing]

D ## Who's who in the class? Idioms for 'people in the classroom'

teacher's pet   Mary's **top of**   **a real know-all**   **a bit of a**   **a lazy-bones**
                        the class   **big-head**

The last three idioms are used of people outside of the class, too.

Exercises

78.1 Try to complete these idioms from memory if possible.

1 She does a lot of voluntary work; she has a heart...
2 Don't expect any sympathy from the boss; she's as hard...
3 I'm sure Gerry will help you; he's as good...
4 I was too late to get on that course; I was a bit slow...
5 You won't find him very friendly; he's rather a cold...
6 Tell him to hurry up! He's such a...

78.2 What do we call...

1 an irritating person who knows everything?
2 the person who is the teacher's favourite?
3 someone who thinks they are the best and says so?
4 the one who gets the best marks?
5 a person who is very lazy?

78.3 You can also learn idioms by associating them with a key word or words. For example, two idioms on the left-hand page had *gold* in them and two had *mark*. Which were they? Here is a work-fork based on *to have + head*. Use the expressions to finish the sentences below.

one's head screwed on   [be sensible]
a head for heights   [not suffer from vertigo]
to have — a head like a sieve   [bad memory; see Unit 76]
a good head for figures   [be good at maths]
one's head in the clouds   [unaware of reality]

1 I'd better write it in my notebook. I have...
2 Ask Martha to check those sums. She has...
3 Don't ask me to go up that tower. I'm afraid I don't...
4 She's very sensible and knows what she's doing. She...
5 He's quite out of touch with reality. He really...

Look out for other sets of idioms based on key words.

78.4 Mini-quiz. Which parts of your body might a difficult person (a) *get on* (b) *be a pain in*?

78.5 Which idioms do you think these drawings represent?

1   2   3

78.6 Try guessing from the context what the underlined idioms mean.

1 Don't get angry with him. <u>His heart's in the right place</u>.
2 Joe's <u>a bit of a square peg in a round hole</u> here. I think he should get a job which suits his character better.
3 A: Hey! I'm talking to you! B: Sorry, I <u>was miles away</u>.

79 Idioms describing feelings or mood

A Positive feelings, moods and states

Jo's **as happy as the day is long**. [extremely content]
Mary seems to be **on cloud nine** these days. [extremely pleased/happy]
Everyone seemed to be **in high spirits**. [lively, enjoying things]
She seems to be **keeping her chin up**. [happy despite bad things]

B Negative feelings, moods and states

He had **a face as long as a fiddle**. [looked very depressed/sad]
She certainly **looked down in the dumps**. [looked depressed/sad]
Gerry is **in a (black) mood**. [a bad mood/temper]
Mark was **like a bear with a sore head**. [extremely irritable] (See Unit 76.)

C Physical feelings and states

I could eat a horse! [very hungry]
I'm **feeling all in**. [exhausted]
You're looking **a bit under the weather**. [not very well / ill]
She looked, and felt, **on top form**. [in good physical condition]
I suddenly **felt as if my head was going round**. [dizzy]
I was almost **at death's door** last week! [very sick or ill]
Old Nora's **as fit as a fiddle**. [very fit indeed]

D Fear/fright

She was **scared stiff**. [very scared]
She **frightened the life out of him**. [frightened him a lot]
We were all **shaking in our shoes**. [trembling with fear]
The poor lad was **scared out of his wits**. [very scared indeed]
I **jumped out of my skin** when I heard the bang. [gave a big jump]

Remember: there is an element of **exaggeration** in these idioms; they make comments on the situation and lighten the tone of what you are saying. So use them only informally.

E

Horoscopes in English language newspapers and magazines are often a good place to find idioms about moods and states, since the horoscope usually tries to tell you how you are going to feel during the coming day/week/month. Look at these horoscopes and note the idioms in italics. Each one is given a literal paraphrase below the text. Collect more idioms from horoscopes if you can.

Capricorn (21.12–19.1)

*D*on't *get carried away* (1) by promises that won't be kept. *Keep a cool head* (2) and take everything as it comes. On the work front, things are looking better.

Taurus (21.4–20.5)

*S*omeone will say something that will *make you swell with pride* (3) and you may *feel on top of the world* (4) for a while, but the evening will not be so easy.

(1) be fooled   (2) stay calm   (3) feel very proud   (4) very happy indeed

Exercises

79.1 Here are some more idioms that can be grouped as expressing either *positive* or *negative* feelings. Try to group them using a dictionary if necessary.

to be over the moon   to feel/be a bit down
to feel/be as pleased as Punch   to feel/be browned off

79.2 Using the idioms from 79.1 and from A opposite, say how you would probably feel if...

1 you were told you had just won a vast sum of money. *I'd be over the moon!*
2 your boss said you had to do again a piece of work you'd already done three times.
3 you were told you'd got a very high mark in an exam.
4 you had a bad toothache and your neighbour was making a lot of noise late at night.
5 nothing seemed to have gone right for you that day.
6 someone you were secretly in love with told you they were in love with you.

79.3 Complete the idioms in these sentences.

1 Don't creep up behind me like that! You frightened the...
2 I don't need a doctor, I just feel a bit under...
3 As long as he has his car to work on, he's as happy...
4 Last year, when I won that medal, I really was on...
5 I wasn't expecting such a loud bang; I nearly jumped...
6 I've had nothing since lunch; I could...
7 I feel a bit down this week; last week I felt on top...

79.4 Spot idioms to do with feelings, moods and states in these horoscopes. Underline them, then check the meaning if necessary in a dictionary.

Scorpio (23.10–22.11)

ou may get itchy feet today, but be patient, this is not a good time to travel. Events at work will keep you on the edge of your seat for most of the day. Altogether an anxious time for Scorpians.

Leo (21.7–21.8)

ou'll be up in arms over something someone close to you says rather thoughtlessly today, but don't let it spoil things. You may be in two minds over an invitation, but think positively.

Now use the idioms to rewrite these sentences.

1 I can't decide about that job in Paris.
2 I've been in suspense all day. What's happened? Tell me!
3 Her son became restless to travel and went off to Uruguay.
4 Everyone protested loudly when they cancelled the outing.

79.5 Which idioms opposite include the words *head, wits, swell, black* and *carried*? Write a sentence using each one.

80 Idioms connected with problematic situations

A Problems and difficulties

idiom		literal phrase
to be in a **fix**	=	be in difficulty
to be in a **tight corner**	=	be in a situation that is hard to get out of
to be in a **muddle**	=	be confused/mixed up

(these three go together as all having **be + in + a**)

Reacting in situations

Three pairs of more or less opposite idioms.

to **take a back seat** [not do anything; let others act instead]	≠	to **take the bull by the horns** [act positively to face and attack the problem]
to **stir things up** [do/say things that make matters worse]	≠	to **pour oil on troubled waters** [do/say things that calm the situation down]
to **keep one's cards close to one's chest** [hold back information]	≠	to **lay one's cards on the table** [be very open, state exactly what your position is]

B Idioms related to situations based on get

This has to be done by next week; we must **get our act together** before it's too late. [organise ourselves to respond; informal]

We need a proper investigation to **get to the bottom of things**. [find the true explanation for the state of affairs]

It's quite difficult to **get** people **to sit up and take notice**. [make them pay attention]

I'm trying to **get a grasp of** what's happening; it's not easy. [find out / understand]

C Changes and stages in situations

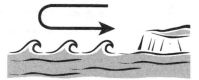

The tide has turned for us; better days are ahead.

We can **see light at the end of the tunnel** at last.

I'm afraid we've just **come to a dead end** with our plans.
I think I've **reached a turning-point** in my career.

D Some idioms connected with easing the situation

The government and the unions have **buried the hatchet** for the time being. [made peace / stopped fighting each other]

All that trouble last year was just **swept under the carpet** in the end. [ignored / deliberately forgotten, without solving it]

You should say sorry. **It would go a long way.** [would help a lot]

Exercises

80.1 When looking up idioms (or any type of words) in your dictionary, it is often a good idea to look at what is just before and just after the information you are looking for. In this way you can pick up some related words and/or expressions which you can record together.

For example, if you look up *take the bull by the horns* in a dictionary, you will probably also find these idioms:

(to be/act) like a bull in a china shop [be very clumsy]
(to talk) a load of bull [talk nonsense]

Look up these idioms using the words underlined as your key word and see what other idioms or useful phrases you can find around them in the dictionary.

1 let the <u>cat</u> out of the bag
2 be in a <u>fix</u>
3 to <u>pour</u> oil on troubled waters
4 to <u>stir</u> things up

80.2 Choose a suitable idiom from the opposite page to fill the gaps.

1 I think I'll just .... and let everyone else get on with sorting matters out.
2 No, please, don't say anything; you'll only ....
3 It's been a long, hard struggle, but I think at last we can see ....
4 The police are trying their best to get to ...., but it's a real mystery at the moment.
5 I'm sorry, I'm in ....; could you explain that again?
6 At last I've managed to get him to sit ....; he's done nothing at all for us so far.
7 I find it difficult to get a .... this global warming business, don't you?
8 I think we should take the bull .... and sort it out. I don't think it should be just swept ....

80.3 Here are some more idioms connected with situations. From the context, can you paraphrase their meaning, as in the example?

1 It's not working; we'll have to <u>go back to square one</u>. *go back to the beginning again*
2 The teachers want one thing, the students want the exact opposite. I'm sure we can find <u>a happy medium</u>.
3 We were <u>on tenterhooks</u> all night waiting for news from the hospital. They finally rang us at 6.30 a.m.
4 Poverty and crime <u>go hand in hand</u> in this part of town.
5 You've been in a lot of trouble lately; you'd better <u>toe the line</u> from now on.

80.4 What *questions* could be asked to get these answers?

1 Well, we've buried the hatchet for the moment, but I'm sure it's not for good.
2 Yes, it's been a real turning-point in my career.
3 Yes, I think it would go a long way. You know how sensitive he is, and how he appreciates little gestures.

81 Idioms connected with praise and criticism

A Idioms connected with praise

Saying people/things are better than the rest

Mary is **head and shoulders above** the rest of the girls. *or* She's **miles better** than the other girls.   [used usually of people]

When it comes to technology, Japan **is streets ahead** of most other countries.   [can be used of people or things]

When it comes to exam passes, St John's school usually **knocks spots off** the other schools.   [used of people or things]

That meal was just **out of this world**.   [outstanding/superb; usually used of things]

Saying people are good at something

Some expressions with idiomatic compound nouns, noun-phrases and compound adjectives.

She's **a dab-hand at** carpentry, just like her father.   [usually for manual skills]

She's a really **first-rate / top notch** administrator, the very best.

When it comes to grammar, she's **really on the ball**.   [knows a lot]

Bill **has a way with** foreign students. The other teachers envy him.   [good at establishing good relations / motivating them, etc.]

Marjorie really **has green fingers**; look at those flowers!   [good at gardening]

Let him do the talking; he's **got the gift of the gab**.   [good at talking]

B Idioms connected with criticism

Note: There are far more of these in common use than ones connected with praise!

You can group some according to form; for example, 's idioms include several connected with criticising people and things.

She thinks she's **the cat's whiskers / the bee's knees**.   [thinks she's wonderful]

He was dressed up like **a dog's dinner**   [over-dressed in a showy way]

When it comes to time-keeping, he's **the world's worst**.   [no-one is worse]

I'm sorry, this essay of yours is **a dog's breakfast**.   [a mess / very badly done]

This group could be learned in association with 'food' words.

When it comes to unreliability, he really **takes the biscuit**.   [is the epitome / most striking example of some negative quality] (See Unit 74.)

Mary **wants to have her cake and eat it**!   [wants everything without any contribution from her side]

I think he's just trying to **butter me up**.   [give false praise in order to get something]

A pay-rise and a company car! You **want jam on it**, you do!   [have totally unreasonable expectations/demands]

Note these idiomatic synonyms of the verb **to criticise**:

You shouldn't **run down** your own country when you're abroad.

Why do you always have to **pick holes** in everything I say?

Exercises

81.1 Using idioms from A opposite, rewrite these sentences without changing the basic meaning.

1 The hotel we were staying in was absolutely superb.
2 Joe is a long way above the other kids when it comes to doing hard sums.
3 This restaurant is much, much better than all the other restaurants in town.
4 You're a long way ahead of me in understanding all this new technology; I'm impressed.

81.2 Which idioms opposite might these pictures help you to remember?

1   2   3   4

81.3 Which of the expressions in 81.2 is most suitable for:

1 praising someone's knowledge/ability in their profession?
2 saying that something is a real mess?
3 saying someone has a very high opinion of themselves?
4 praising someone's gardening skills?

81.4 Express the *opposite* meaning to these sentences using idioms from the left-hand page.

Example: He's a third-rate athlete. *He's a first-rate (or top-notch) athlete.*

1 She was <u>dressed beautifully</u>, just right for the occasion.
2 Penny <u>has such an inferiority complex</u>.
3 She's <u>hopeless at</u> DIY; just look at those bookshelves she made.
4 He is <u>no good at talking to people</u> at all.
5 Mick <u>doesn't get on with</u> the secretaries; just look at how they react when he wants something done.
6 He wants a new office, a secretary and a new computer. But compared to what Geoff wants he <u>isn't expecting much</u>!
7 She said I was the best boss they'd ever had. It was obvious she was <u>praising me sincerely</u>. I wonder what she wants?
8 He often <u>says how wonderful</u> his school is.
9 She always <u>praises</u> everything I say.

81.5 Using a good general dictionary or a special dictionary of idioms, see what further idioms you can find that include the 'food' words listed below and which are used in contexts of praising or criticising people/things/actions. Make sentences with the expressions.

1 ham   2 tea   3 icing   4 nut   5 onion   6 cream

82 Idioms connected with using language

A Idioms connected with communication problems

They're **talking at cross-purposes.**

He's got **the wrong end of the stick.**

She **can't get a word in edgeways.**

I **can't make head or tail** of what he's saying.

B Good talk, bad talk

The boss always **talks down** to us.   [talks as if we were inferior]

My work-mates are always **talking behind my back.**   [saying negative things about me when I'm not there]

It was just **small talk,** nothing more, I promise.   [purely social talk, nothing serious]

Let's sit somewhere else; they always **talk shop** over lunch, and it bores me rigid.   [talk about work]

Hey! Your new friend's become a real **talking-point** among the staff! Did you know?   [subject that everyone wants to talk about]

It's gone too far this time. I shall have to **give him a talking to.**   [reproach/scold him]

C Talk in discussions, meetings, etc.

1 start the discussion
2 say exactly what I think
3 say it in few words
4 say things in a long, indirect way
5 finish the discussion
6 say stupid things
7 come to the important part of the matter
8 say intelligent, reasonable things

Exercises

82.1 **Look at these dialogues and comment on them, as in the example.**

Example: A: £98 for a meal! that's outrageous!
          B: Not the meal, you twit! The room!
          They seem to be talking at cross-purposes.

1   JOE: So that's what I'm going to do, take it all away.
    ANN: What about –
    JOE: And if they don't like it they can just go and do what they like.
    ANN: If she –
    JOE: Not that I have to consult them, anyway, I'm in charge round here.
    ANN: I wonder whether it –
    JOE: You see, I'm the kind of person who can take a hard decision when it's needed.

It seems that Ann can't get ....

2   MICK: I got very upset when you said I was childish.
    GRACE: I didn't, honestly! All I said was that you seemed to get on very well with the
            children. Honestly.
    MICK: Oh, I see. Oh, sorry.

It seems that Mick got the ....

3   DAN: So, area-wise the down-matching sales profile commitment would seem to
           be high-staked on double-par.
    REG: Eh? Could you say that again? You've got me there.

It seems that Reg can't make ....

4   MADGE: I don't expect someone with your intelligence to understand this document.
    ERIC: Thank you.

Madge seems to be talking ....

82.2 **What idioms opposite do these drawings represent?**

 the discussion

1

3

start

 talk

2

4   get to / come to

82.3 **Fill the gaps to complete the collocations.**

1   She is very direct and always .... her mind.
2   I get bored with small ....; let's get down to serious matters. I'm in
    love with you.
3   The boss gave me a real .... to after that stupid mistake I made. Still, I
    was in the wrong.
4   You're behind the times! Darren's girlfriend was *last* week's ....-point.

83 Idioms – miscellaneous

A Idioms connected with paying, buying and selling

He **bought a real pig in a poke** when he got that car.   [buy something without examining it properly first]

We'll probably have to **pay over the odds** for a hotel room during the week of the festival. [pay more than the usual rate]

He did £600 worth of damage to the car and his parents had to **foot the bill**.   [pay up, usually a large amount]

That restaurant was **a real rip-off**. *or* That taxi-driver really **ripped us off**.   [made us pay much too much; very informal]

If I were you I'd **drive a hard bargain**. She's desperate to buy a flat and wants yours. [ask a lot and resist lowering the price]

See also **nose** on the human body below.

B Idioms based on names of the parts of the body

I've got that song **on the brain**!
[just can't stop myself singing it]

He's **made quite a bit of headway** with his maths lately.
[make progress]

We **had to pay through the nose** for those tickets.
[pay a huge amount]

I hope you didn't mind me telling you. I just had to **get it off my chest**.
[tell something that's been bothering you a lot]

Oh, he's got a **finger in every pie**.
[is involved in many different things]

You've got to **hand it to** her; she's a great singer.
[acknowledge/admit]

C Idioms connected with daily routine

Come on! **Rise and shine!** We've got to leave! [a command to someone to get up, often said to someone who doesn't want to and at a very early hour]. There's no time for breakfast. We can **get a bite to eat** on the motorway [have a snack or meal]. I'll drive and you can **have a nap** in the back seat [a short sleep]. When we get there, there'll just be time to **freshen up** before the meeting. [wash and tidy oneself]. It's going to be a long day; I'll **be ready to crash out** about 8 o'clock, I should think [be very tired/ready to sleep almost anywhere]. Still, we can stay home the following evening and **put our feet up** [relax], and just **watch the box** [watch television].

Exercises

83.1 Look at these mini-dialogues and decide which idiom from the opposite page you could use to answer the questions.

1 A: I'll give you $85.
   B: No, $100 or nothing.
   A: Oh, come on. Look, $90, there.
   B: No, I said $100 and I mean $100.

What's B doing?

2 A: I'm president of the squash club, I'm on the teacher-parent committee and I run three youth clubs.
   B: Really?
   A: Yes, oh, and I'm on that working party at the Social Centre, and there's the Union...

What sort of person could A be described as?

3 A: 'Lady in red, la-da-da-di-da...'
   B: I wish you'd stop singing that blasted song!
   A: What? Oh, sorry... 'Lady in red, la-la ...'

What's A's problem?

4 A: Oh, no! You know that box of wine glasses I bought from that guy in the street? Half of them are cracked!
   B: Well, you should have looked at them first. It's your stupid fault.

What has A done?

83.2 Rewrite these sentences using an idiom instead of the underlined bits.

1 Can I tell you about a problem I have? I just have to <u>tell somebody</u>. It's been bothering me for a while now.
2 They charged us £100 for a tiny room without a bath. It was <u>just robbery</u>!
3 There'll just be time to <u>have a quick meal</u> before the show.
4 I <u>must admit</u>, Maria coped with the situation brilliantly.
5 I think I'll just go upstairs and <u>have a sleep for a while</u>, if nobody objects.
6 Well, I <u>was very tired and fell asleep</u> on the sofa at about two o'clock, and the party was still in full swing.

83.3 Can you think of a situation where you might...

1 have to get a bite to eat on the way?
2 have to pay over the odds for a hotel room?
3 find it hard to make any headway?
4 be willing to pay through the nose for tickets?

83.4 Which idioms do these drawings suggest?

1   2   3

Follow-up: Look up idioms under further parts of the body, for example, *tongue, heels, toe, back,* and make a note of examples.

84 Proverbs

Speakers tend to use proverbs to comment on a situation, often at the end of a true story someone has told, or in response to some event. As with all idiomatic expressions, they are useful and enjoyable to know and understand, but should be used with care.

A Warnings/advice/morals – do's and don'ts

proverb		paraphrase
Don't count your chickens before they're hatched.	⟶	Don't anticipate the future too much.
Don't put all your eggs in one basket.	⟶	Don't invest all your efforts. or attention in just one thing.
Never judge a book by its cover.	⟶	Don't judge people/things by their outward appearance.
Never look a gift horse in the mouth.	⟶	Never refuse good fortune when it is there in front of you.
Take care of the pence and the pounds will take care of themselves.	⟶	Take care of small sums of money and they will become large sums.

B Key elements

Proverbs can also be grouped by some key elements, for example, animals and birds.

When the **cat's** away, the **mice** will play. [people will take advantage of someone else's absence to behave more freely]

You can lead a **horse** to water but you can't make it drink. [you can try to persuade someone, but you can't force them]

One **swallow** doesn't make a summer. [one positive sign does not mean all will be well]

C Visualising

As with learning all vocabulary, visualising some element often helps.

There's no smoke without fire. [rumours are usually based on some degree of truth]

Too many cooks spoil the broth. [too many people interfering is a bad way of doing things]

People who live in glass houses shouldn't throw stones. [don't criticise others' faults if you suffer from them yourself]

Many hands make light work. [a lot of people helping makes a job easier]

Exercises

84.1 Find proverbs on the left-hand page which would be suitable for these situations.

Example: Someone says they have just been offered a free two-week holiday, but are hesitating whether to take up the offer. *Never look a gift-horse in the mouth.*

1 Someone thanks you and your friends for helping to load heavy boxes into a van.

2 Someone says they can't be bothered applying to different universities and will just apply to one.

3 Three different people have made different arrangements for the same meeting, and so everyone comes at different times and the result is total confusion.

84.2 Some proverbs are similar in meaning to one another. Which proverbs on the left go with which on the right, and what do they have in common in terms of meaning?

1 A bird in the hand is worth two in the bush.

Never judge a book by its cover.

2 Don't count your chickens before they are hatched.

Familiarity breeds contempt.

3 All that glitters is not gold.

Never look a gift-horse in the mouth.

4 Absence makes the heart grow fonder.

Don't cross your bridges before you come to them.

84.3 In spoken language, people often refer to proverbs by only saying half of them and leaving the rest for the listener to 'fill in'. Complete the proverbs in these dialogues.

1 A: 'Joel's always criticising people who are selfish, yet he's terribly selfish himself.
   B: Yes, well, people who live in glass houses...
   C: Exactly.

2 A: The people in the office have been playing computer games all day since the boss fell ill.
   B: Well, you know what they say: when the cat's away...
   A: Right, and they're certainly doing that.

3 A: I didn't believe those rumours about Nick and Gill, but apparently they are seeing each other.
   B: You shouldn't be so naive, you know what they say, no smoke..., eh?
   A: Mm, I suppose you're right.

4 A: Amazing, he's made a fortune from just one little shop!
   B: Well, I think it's a case of take care of the pence...
   A: Sure, he's always been very careful with his money.

Follow-up: Try translating some proverbs from your language, word for word into English, and then, if you can, ask a native speaker if they recognise any English proverb as having the same or similar meaning.

85 Expressions with do and make

A The next seven units deal with phrasal verbs and other expressions based on common verbs. Phrasal verbs are basic verbs which can combine with different prepositions (or particles) to make verbs with completely new – and often unguessable – meanings. Phrasal verbs are used more in speaking than in writing. There is almost always a more formal way of conveying the same idea. In this unit we look at phrasal verbs formed from **do** and **make**.

B Here are some of the most useful phrasal verbs based on **do** and **make**.

phrasal verb	meaning	example
do with	need, want	I could do with something to eat.
do without	manage without	We'll have to do without a holiday this year as money is so short.
do away with	abolish	Slavery was not done away with until last century.
do out of	prevent from having (by deceit)	He did me out of my rightful inheritance.
make for	move in the direction of	Let's make for the city centre and find a restaurant on the way.
make of	think (opinion)	What do you make of him?
make off	leave hurriedly	He made off as soon as he heard their car turn into the drive.
make up for	compensate for	The superb food at the hotel made up for the uncomfortable rooms.
make up to	be nice to in order to get s.t.	He made up to her until she agreed to help.

C Some phrasal verbs have a number of different meanings; **do up** can mean not only 'fasten' but also 'renovate' and 'put into a bundle'. Similarly, **make out** can mean 'claim', 'manage to see' and 'understand' as well as 'write' or 'complete'; **make up** can mean 'compose' or 'invent'; it can also mean 'constitute' or 'form', 'put cosmetics on', 'prepare by mixing together various ingredients' and 'make something more numerous or complete'.

D There are a lot of other common expressions based on **do** and **make**.

You **do**: the housework / some gardening / the washing-up / homework / your best / the shopping / the cooking / business with…, and so on.

You **make**: arrangements / an agreement / a suggestion / a decision / a cup of tea / war / an attempt / a phone call / the best of… / an effort / an excuse / a mistake / a bed / a profit / a loss / love / the most of / a noise / a good or bad impression / a success of… / a point of… / allowances for… / a gesture / a face / fun of… / a fuss of… / a go (a success) of…, and so on.

The more collocations with **do** and **make** you learn, the more you will get a 'feel' for the difference between the two verbs.

Exercises

85.1 Here are some different ways in which *do up*, *make up* and *make out* can be used. What is the meaning of the phrasal verb in each case?

1 Take this prescription to the chemist and she'll make it up for you.
2 Can you make out the little grey house on the shore?
3 A human being is made up of many, often conflicting, desires.
4 If you do up the newspapers, I'll take them to be recycled.
5 I find it impossible to make Jo out.
6 Let's advertise the talk in the hope of making up the numbers a bit.
7 He made out that he had never loved anyone else.
8 We're planning to do up our bathroom at the weekend.

85.2 Add the necessary prepositions or particles to complete this story.

Last weekend we decided to start doing ....(1) our bedroom. We agreed that we could do ....(2) the old fireplace in the corner. As we began to remove it from the wall we found some old pictures done ....(3) in a bundle behind a loose brick. At first we could not make ....(4) what was in the pictures but we wiped them clean and realised they all depicted the same young man. We spent an enjoyable evening making ....(5) stories to explain why the pictures had been hidden.

85.3 Correct the mistakes in the sentences below. Either the wrong preposition has been used or the word order is wrong.

1 This weekend we are planning to make the seaside for.
2 Vast amounts of money do not always make of happiness.
3 He makes up for anyone he thinks can help him.
4 Your shoelaces are untied. Do up them or you'll trip.
5 They like to make away that they have important connections.

85.4 Write word forks (see Unit 2) to help you learn the meanings of *make up, make out, do with* and *do up*.

85.5 Divide the expressions in D opposite into any groups which will help you to learn them.

85.6 Complete the following sentences using an appropriate expression from D.

1 Pacifist posters in the 1960s used to say 'MAKE LOVE NOT ....!'
2 It doesn't matter if you pass or not as long as you do ....
3 Though many companies are going bankrupt, ours made a huge ....
4 Mrs Thatcher said she could do .... Mr Gorbachev.
5 You must make .... the fact that he's only seven years old.
6 Dressing smartly for an interview helps you to make ....

85.7 Choose ten phrasal verbs and other expressions from the opposite page that you particularly want to learn and write a paragraph using them.

86 Expressions with bring and take

A Here are some common phrasal verbs with **bring**. Each is exemplified in a typical spoken sentence and a more formal equivalent is provided in brackets.

I was **brought up** in the country.   [raise]
Don't give up. I'm sure you'll **bring** it **off**.   [succeed]
Cold winds always **bring on** her cough.   [cause to start]
The strike **brought about** a change of government.   [cause to happen]
I hope they don't **bring back** capital punishment.   [re-introduce]
They promised to **bring down** taxes but have they?   [lower]
Inflation will **bring down** the government.   [destroy, remove from power]
Ford are **bringing out** an interesting new model in the spring.   [introduce]
Keep at it and you'll **bring** him **round** to your point of view.   [persuade]

B Here are some common phrasal verbs with **take**.

Doesn't he **take after** his father!   [resemble]
I wish I could **take back** what I said to her.   [withdraw]
I find it very hard to **take in** his lectures.   [absorb, understand]
She was completely **taken in** by him.   [deceive]
Sales have really **taken off** now.   [start to improve]
The plane **took off** two hours late.   [left the ground]
She's very good at **taking off** her teacher.   [imitate]
We'll have to **take on** more staff if we're to **take on** more work.   [employ; undertake]
She **took to** him at once.   [form an immediate liking for]
When did you **take up** golf?   [start (a hobby)]

C Here are some other common idioms with **bring** and **take**.

The new regulations will **be brought into force** in May...   [become law]
His research **brought** some very interesting facts **to light**.   [revealed]
Matters **were brought to a head** when Pat was sacked.   [reached a point where changes had to be made]
It's better that everything should be **brought into the open**.   [made public]
His new girlfriend has really **brought out the best in** him.   [been good for him]
Don't let him **take advantage of** you.   [unfairly use superiority]
After 20 years of marriage they **take** each other **for granted**.   [don't appreciate each other's qualities]
I **took it for granted** you'd come.   [assumed]
She immediately **took control of** the situation.   [started organising]
His words **took my breath away**.   [surprised]
She loves **taking care of** small children.   [looking after, caring for]
We **took part in** a demonstration last Saturday.   [participated]
The story **takes place** in Mexico.   [happens]
He doesn't seem to **take pride in** his work.   [draw satisfaction from]
Mother always **takes** everything **in her stride**.   [copes calmly]

Exercises

86.1 Complete these sentences with the appropriate preposition.

1 The new school reforms which plan to bring .... regular exams for young children are generally unpopular.
2 The long journey brought .... labour and the baby was born on the bus.
3 I think the strikes will bring .... some changes in management.
4 If anyone can bring it ...., he can.
5 He won't agree to it for me but she can always bring him ....
6 She brought .... six children all on her own.

86.2 The diagram below can be called a ripple diagram. Can you complete it?

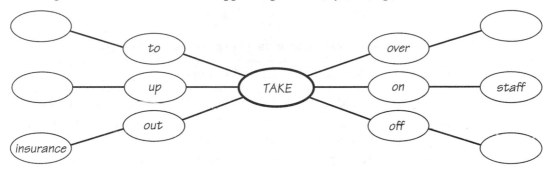

86.3 Reword these sentences using expressions from C opposite.

1 The story of the film happens in Casablanca during the war.
2 Today's newspaper has revealed some fascinating information about the Prime Minister.
3 The situation reached crisis point when the union called for a strike.
4 How does she always manage to be so calm about things?
5 The view from the place was astonishing.
6 He capitalised on her weakness at the time and she sold it to him.
7 The main function of a nurse is to look after the sick.
8 You shouldn't assume that anyone or anything will always be the same.

86.4 Reply to these questions using one of the phrasal verbs in A or B opposite.

1 What is the Conservative Party promising in its manifesto?
2 How did you like her?
3 What causes your rash?
4 Who does your little boy resemble?
5 Have you any special hobbies?
6 How's your new business doing?
7 What is a mimic?
8 Do you think you'll manage to persuade him to let you come?

86.5 Make up a ripple diagram like the one in 86.2, based on phrasal verbs with *bring*.

86.6 Which of the expressions in C mean the opposite of:

1 to keep quiet   3 to disregard   5 to be careless about
2 to look on   4 to drop an old law   6 to be subordinate to

87 Expressions with get

A Get seems to be used all the time in spoken English. It has the following basic meanings:
- receive, obtain or buy something, e.g. Please **get** me a newspaper when you're in town; I **got** a letter from John today; She **got** top marks in her exam.
- show a change in position – move or be moved, e.g. How are you **getting** home tonight?
- show a change in state – become or make, e.g. We are all **getting** older if not wiser.

B Get also has a number of other more specific meanings.
It's my turn to **get dinner** tonight.   [prepare a meal]
I don't **get** it. Why did he speak like that?   [understand]
His behaviour really **gets** me at times.   [annoy]

C The table below shows just some of the phrasal verbs based on **get**.

phrasal verb	meaning	example
get at	reach, find	I hope the enquiry will get at the truth.
get away with	do something wrong without being caught	The robbers got away with several thousand pounds.
get behind	fail to produce something at the right time	I've got terribly behind with my work.
get by	manage (financially)	We could never get by on my salary alone.
get down	depress	This weather is really getting me down.
get down to	begin to give serious attention to	It's time you got down to some work.
get on	manage	However will we get on without you?
get on	advance, develop	Jo is getting on very well at school now.
get out of	avoid a responsibility	I'll try and get out of my lesson tomorrow.
get over	recover from	She's getting over a bad attack of flu.
get round	spread	The rumour soon got round the whole village.
get through	come to a successful end	What a relief that she got through all her exams!
get through	use up all of	He got through his month's salary in just one weekend.
get up to	to do (especially something bad)	They're very quiet. I wonder what they're getting up to?

D Here are some other expressions based on **get**.
You seem to have **got out of bed on the wrong side** today.   [be in a bad mood]
The meeting **got off to a good/bad start** with JR's speech.   [started well/badly]
I'm organising a little **get-together**. I hope you can come.   [informal meeting/party]
When their relationship ended he **got rid of** everything that reminded him of her.   [threw away, destroyed]
I'm going to **get my own back** on her somehow.   [take my revenge]

Exercises

87.1 There are a lot of instances of *get* in this text. Replace them all with another way of conveying the same idea. Notice that by doing this you are changing the text from something very informal to something slightly more formal.

I don't often <u>get</u> interesting advertising circulars these days. However, quite an unusual one came this morning. It was headed 'Are you worried about <u>getting out of touch</u>?' And it went on, 'If so, <u>get</u> some of our special tablets today. Taking just one in the morning will help you <u>get on well</u> at work and at home. It will stop little problems from <u>getting you down</u> and will ensure that you <u>get</u> rich and successful with the minimum of effort on your behalf. Send just $25 today and you will <u>get</u> your tablets and your key to success within ten days.'

87.2 Fill in the blanks in the sentences below in the most appropriate way.

1 Although they had only told their parents about their engagement, the news soon got
.... the village.
2 She must have made a good impression last week because she has got ....
to the second round of interviews for the post.
3 I love watching TV cookery programmes but when they describe a recipe, it can be hard
to get .... all the details in time.
4 We get .... only because we live very economically.
5 What have you been getting .... since we last met?
6 Surely you haven't got .... all the biscuits already?

87.3 Match the situations in list A with the appropriate expressions in list B.

A 1 Someone has been very impolite to one of your friends.
   2 Someone is about to throw something away.
   3 Someone is being very bad-tempered.
   4 Someone has done something very unkind to you.
   5 A good friend is leaving.

B 1 I don't know how we'll get by without you!
   2 You wait! I'll get my own back on you one day!
   3 Don't get rid of that yet!
   4 You got out of bed on the wrong side this morning!
   5 Your rudeness really gets me!

87.4 Complete the following sentences in any appropriate way.

1 I should hate to get rid of...
2 The dinner got off to a bad start when...
3 I find it very hard to get down to...
4 I wish I could get out of...
5 I don't think she has got over...
6 ...is really getting me down.

87.5 There are a number of other common phrasal verbs and expressions based on *get* not listed on the opposite page. Write example sentences using any that you can think of.

88 Expressions with set and put

A Look at the examples of following phrasal verbs based on **set**.

You should **set aside** some money for a rainy day.   [reserve]
He tried to **set aside** his dislike of his daughter's fiancé.   [ignore (not think about)]
We should **set off** before dawn to get there on time.   [begin a journey]
The redundancies **set off** strikes throughout the area.   [cause]
The bank helps people wanting to **set up** business.   [establish]
He **set out** to climb Everest.   [begin work with a particular aim in mind]

B Here are some of the many phrasal verbs with **put**.

He **put** his own name **forward** to the committee.   [propose]
He's good at **putting** his ideas **across**.   [communicate to others]
Please **put away** all your toys at once.   [tidy]
He is always **putting** her **down**.   [make someone look small]
We had central heating **put in** last year.   [install]
I'm going to **put in** an application for that job.   [submit]
Every now and then she would **put in** a remark.   [interject]
They've **put off** making their decision for another week.   [postpone]
Her sniffing really **puts** me **off** my dinner.   [discourage]
The school is **putting** Hamlet **on** next year.   [present]
He's good at **putting on** all sorts of accents.   [pretend to have]
The fireman quickly **put out** the fire.   [extinguish]
Please don't let me **put** you **out**.   [inconvenience]
You're not allowed to **put up** posters here.   [fix]
I can **put** you **up** for the weekend.   [give accommodation to]
The government is sure to **put up** taxes soon.   [raise]
How do you **put up with** such rudeness?   [tolerate]

C Here are some more expressions with **set**.

He has **set his heart/sights on** becoming a ballet dancer.   [longs to become (an important aim/goal)]
They sat up till the small hours **setting the world to rights**.   [discussing important problems]
Did someone **set fire to** the house deliberately?   [put a match to]
The house was **set on fire** by a match thrown onto some old newspapers.   [ignited]
Di had never **set foot in** Italy before.   [been to]
Jill is very **set in her ways**.   [fixed in her habits]
Try to **set a good example**.   [be a good example for others]

D Notice also the following common expressions with **put**.

to put your foot down: to be firm about something
to put all your eggs in one basket: to risk all you have on a single venture
to put your mind to: to direct all your thoughts towards
to put two and two together: to draw an obvious conclusion
to put something in a nutshell: to state something accurately and in a few words only
to put someone's back up: to irritate someone
a put-up job: something arranged to give a false impression

Exercises

88.1 Put the following sentences into slightly more formal English by replacing the phrasal verbs with their formal equivalents.

1 They have recently set up a committee on teenage smoking.
2 We try to set aside some money for our holiday every week.
3 Set aside all your negative feelings and listen with an open mind.
4 If we hadn't set off so late, we would have arrived on time.
5 The government's unpopular proposals set off a wave of protests.

88.2 Write down three nouns which could follow each of the verbs. Remember that their meanings might be different depending on the noun which follows.

Example: put in money / a comment / a telephone system

1 put out	3 put off	5 put up	7 put away
2 put forward	4 put across	6 put on	8 put up with

88.3 Complete the responses to the following statements or questions using any appropriate phrasal verb from A or B opposite.

Example: He's always so rude. I wouldn't put up with it if I were you.

1 How should we publicise our play?
2 This room is in a terrible mess.
3 What time do we have to leave for the airport tomorrow?
4 Any chance of a bed on your floor this weekend?
5 Why have you suddenly lost interest in the project?
6 What is Geoff planning to do when he gets his business degree?

88.4 Using the expressions in C and D opposite, reword the following sentences without changing their meaning.

1 He never wants to do anything in a new or different way.
2 He's bound to draw the obvious conclusion if you keep on behaving like that.
3 Her aim is to become Prime Minister.
4 I find her terribly irritating.
5 It's sound business advice not to risk everything at once.
6 Please concentrate on the problem in hand.
7 She is determined to get a seat in Parliament.
8 She threw petrol on the rubbish and put a match to it.
9 She's very good at stating things succinctly.
10 The building started burning because of terrorist action.
11 This is the first time I've ever been to the southern hemisphere.
12 We spent most of our evenings discussing the problems of the world rather than studying.
13 You really should be firm with him or there'll be trouble later.
14 If the teacher doesn't behave properly, the children certainly won't.

88.5 Choose ten of the phrasal verbs and other expressions with *set* and *put* which you particularly want to learn and write them down in example sentences of your own.

89 Expressions with come and go

A Here are some phrasal verbs based on **come**.

Did the meeting you were planning ever **come off**?   [take place]
I don't think his jokes ever quite **come off**.   [succeed]
When do the exam results **come out**?   [be published, made public]
The mark on the carpet won't **come out**.   [be removed]
An important point **came up** at the meeting.   [was raised]
Please **come round** and see me sometime.   [pay an informal visit]
Nothing can **come between** him and football.   [separate; be a barrier between]
I **came across** a lovely old vase in that junk shop.   [found by chance]
How did you **come by** that bruise / that car?   [receive, obtain]

B Notice the large number of expressions with **come to** (usually with an idea of arriving at) and **come into** (often with an idea of starting). Where the meaning isn't obvious, help is given in brackets.

come to: an agreement / a conclusion / a standstill [stop] / an end / a decision / blows [to start fighting] / to terms with [acknowledge and accept psychologically] / one's senses [to become conscious after fainting or to become sensible after behaving foolishly]

come into: bloom / flower / contact / a fortune / money / a legacy / operation [start working] / sight / view / power [of a political party] / existence / fashion / use

C Here are some phrasal verbs based on **go**. Some have a number of different meanings.

Go on: What is **going on** next door? [happening]; They **went on** working despite the noise. [continued]; As the weeks **went on**, things improved. [passed]; You **go on**, we'll catch you up later. [go in advance]; The oven should **go on** at six. [start operating]; He's always **going on at** me about my hair. [complaining].

Go through: I wouldn't like to **go through** that again. [experience, endure]; Let's **go through** the plans once more. [check]; Unfortunately, the business deal we were hoping for did not **go through** in the end. [was not completed or approved]; He **went through** a fortune in one weekend. [spent, used]

Go for: He really **went for** her when she dared to criticise him. [attack]; He **goes for** older women. [is attracted by]; Which course have you decided to **go for**? [choose]

Those shoes don't **go with** that dress.   [suit, match]
The alarm **went off** when the burglars tried to open the door.   [rang]
He would never **go back on** his word.   [break a promise]

D Here are some expressions based on **go**.

Let me **have a go**!   [Let me have a turn or try!]
I hope they'll **make a go of** the business.   [make a success of]
He's been **on the go** all day and he's exhausted.   [very busy, on the move]
It **goes without saying** that we'll all support you.   [clear without being said]
Your work is good, **as far as it goes**.   [but is limited or insufficient]
The story goes that they were once very close friends.   [It is said that...]
I'm sure she'll **go far**.   [be very successful]
They **went to great lengths** to keep it a secret.   [took a lot of trouble]
The business has **gone bankrupt**.   [not got enough money to pay debts]

Exercises

89.1 Which of their several meanings do these underlined verbs have?

1 He <u>went on</u> composing music till his eighties.   *continued*
2 She was so suspicious that she used to <u>go through</u> his pockets every night.
3 The dog <u>went for</u> the postman.
4 The actor's interpretation of Hamlet was interesting but it didn't quite <u>come off</u>.
5 He has a new book <u>coming out</u> in June.
6 I wish you'd stop <u>going on</u> at me!
7 I was sure he'd <u>go for</u> a sports car.
8 I <u>went through</u> three pairs of tights this weekend.

89.2 Choose one of the expressions in B to complete each of the sentences.

1 I found it really hard to make up my mind but in the end I came ....
2 When his grandmother dies, he'll come ....
3 I love it in spring when my cherry tree comes ....
4 Halfway up the hill, the bus came ....
5 They say that long skirts are coming .... again.
6 The telephone first came .... over a hundred years ago.
7 They disagreed so strongly that I was afraid they'd come ....
8 As we rounded the corner the house came ....

89.3 Replace the underlined expressions with one of the expressions in D.

1 <u>I don't need to say</u> that we wish you all the best in the future.
2 They <u>took great pains</u> to avoid meeting each other.
3 I've been <u>moving around</u> all day and I'm longing for a shower now.
4 His school-teachers always said that he would <u>be a success in life</u>.
5 I don't think you'll be able to push the car on your own. Let me <u>try</u>.
6 The film is quite good <u>up to a point</u> but it doesn't tackle the problem deeply enough.

89.4 Which answer on the right fits each question on the left?

1 Why is she looking so miserable?   Any time after eight.
2 Did anything new come up at the meeting?   The firm went bankrupt.
3 When does your alarm clock usually go off?   A bit of a fight, I think.
4 What's the worst pain you've ever gone through?   From a doting aunt.
5 How did he come by so much money?   Seven thirty, normally.
6 When should I come round to your place?   Only Jack's proposal.
7 What's going on over there?   When I pulled a ligament.

89.5 Complete the following sentences in any appropriate way.

1 I'm sure they'll make a go of their new clothes boutique because...
2 The stain won't come out unless you...
3 Those shoes don't go with...
4 I never want to go through...
5 As the party went on...
6 It is not easy to come to terms with...
7 The interview committee came to the conclusion that...
8 I came across not only some old letters in the attic...

Expressions with look

A This diagram illustrates some of the most useful phrasal verbs formed with **look**. The meaning of the phrasal verb is given in brackets.

look
- **up to** — He has always **looked up to** his elder brother.   [respect]
- **into** — The police are **looking into** the case.   [investigate]
- **for** — Could you help me **look for** my keys, please?   [try to find]
- **back on** — I **look back on** my schooldays with great pleasure.   [recall]
- **up** — **Look** her town **up** in the atlas.   [find information in a book]
- **after** — She is very good at **looking after** her sister.   [take care of]
- **forward to** — I'm **looking forward to** starting work.   [expect with pleasure]
- **on** — **Look on** this day off as a reward for your hard work.   [consider]
- **out** — If you don't **look out** he'll take your job from you.   [take care]

B Here are a few more useful phrasal verbs based on **look**. All of them are illustrated below in a business context but they can also, of course, be used in other situations.

Please **look through** the proposal and let me know what you think.   [examine]
I've **looked over** your proposal but I still need to read the fine print.   [examined quickly]
Business is **looking up** at last.   [starting to improve]
When you go to New York, be sure to **look up** our representative there.   [find and visit]
We are **looking to** the Far East for an increase in sales.   [depending on]
The company seems to be **looking ahead** to a bright future.   [planning for the future]

C Here are some other useful expressions based on **look**.

Try to **look on the bright side of things**.   [be cheerful in spite of difficulties]
He's beginning to **look his age**.   [appear as old as he really is]
They're always **on the lookout for** new talent.   [searching for]
I **don't like the look of** those black clouds.   [what I see suggests trouble ahead]
There's going to be a heavy thunderstorm, **by the look(s) of it**.   [It appears probable. (This expression usually comes at the end of the sentence.)]
I know she's hiding something when she won't **look me in the eye**.   [look directly at someone without fear or guilt]
The officer **looked** the men **up and down** and then started to tell them what he thought of them in no uncertain terms.   [inspect closely in order to judge]
Everyone hates being made to **look small**.   [appear unimportant or silly]
She **looks down her nose at** anyone who is no good at sport.   [regards as unimportant or socially inferior]
It's **not much to look at** but it's comfortable.   [not attractive in appearance]
The office has been given **a new look** over the weekend.   [a fresh and more up-to-date appearance]
Look before you leap.   [Think before you act boldly.]

180   *English Vocabulary in Use*

Exercises

90.1 **What words do you need to complete the sentences below?**

1 I look .... that summer with some regrets.
2 He has a great respect for his colleagues but he doesn't really look .... his boss.
3 You're going to London? Do look .... my sister when you're there.
4 A government inquiry is looking .... the cause of the accident.
5 We are looking .... you to bring the company successfully out of the recession.
6 I'm sorry to hear you lost your job. I do hope that things will look .... for you soon.
7 Six nurses look .... the patients in this ward.

90.2 **Match the statements or questions on the left with the responses to them on the right. The first one has been done.**

1 Try to look on the bright side of things.   Why, what do you expect to happen?
2 Look out!   I thought it was time I had a new look.
3 Why don't you think she's honest?   You'd never think she was a grandmother.
4 She certainly doesn't look her age.   Why, what's the…
5 I don't like the look of the situation.   She'll be lucky at the moment.
6 She's on the lookout for a new job.   She never looks you in the eye.
7 What have you done to your hair?   It's rather hard in the circumstances.

90.3 **Complete the sentences below in any logical way.**

Example: I must look up *their number in the phone book.*

1 I'm really looking forward to…
2 It's wrong to look down on…
3 The book looks back on…
4 When I look ahead…
5 If you have time tonight, please look over…
6 Look us up when…

90.4 **Replace the more formal underlined expressions with one of the phrasal verbs or other expressions based on *look* from the opposite page.**

1 <u>He appears to be</u> in need of a good night's sleep.
2 The headteacher <u>inspected</u> the children and then nodded her approval.
3 No-one likes being made to <u>appear foolish</u>.
4 The garden isn't <u>very attractive</u> now but it's lovely in summer.
5 The expression on his face <u>seems rather ominous</u>.
6 Try to <u>remain optimistic</u> if you possibly can.

90.5 **Write three nouns that are likely to be found after each of the phrasal verbs below.**

1 look for   2 look after   3 look through   4 look to

91 Miscellaneous expressions

A The units which deal with phrasal verbs and other expressions present only a small number of the expressions that exist. There are many others based on both the basic verbs focused on in Units 84–90 and on a whole range of other verbs. This unit looks at some other verbs, giving examples of a few of the phrasal verbs and expressions connected with them.

B ## See

I must **see about/to** arrangements for the conference.   [deal with]
They've gone to **see** Jim **off** at the airport.   [go with someone about to set off on a journey]
It's easy to **see through** his behaviour.   [not be deceived by]
It's sometimes hard **to see the wood for the trees**.   [get a clear view of the whole of something because of distracting details]
Do you think you could **see your way to** lending me a fiver?   [feel it was possible to]
I must be **seeing** things.   [having hallucinations]

C ## Run

I **ran into** an old friend yesterday.   [met unexpectedly]
Her patience has **run out**.   [come to an end]
Let's **run over** the plans again.   [review]
The children have **run me off** my feet today.   [kept me so busy that I'm exhausted]
She **runs** the business while he looks after the children.   [manages / has overall responsibility for]
How often do the trains **run**?   [go]

D ## Turn

There was a very large **turnout** at the concert.   [number of people who came]
She **turned down** their offer of promotion.   [refused]
Who do you think **turned up** last night?   [made an appearance, often unexpectedly]
I'm going to **turn over a new leaf** this year.   [make a fresh start]
It's your turn to do the washing-up.   [It's your duty this time because I did it last time.]
He did me a **good turn**.   [a favour]

E ## Let

He has been **let down** so many times in the past.   [disappointed]
He won't **let us into** the secret.   [tell us]
I hope the rain **lets up** soon.   [becomes less strong]
Let go of the rope.   [stop holding]   Please **let me** be.   [stop bothering me]
She **let it slip** that she had been given a pay rise.   [mentioned accidentally or casually]

F ## Break

The car **broke down** again this morning.   [stopped working]
There isn't going to be a wedding – they have **broken off** their engagement.   [ended]
Burglars **broke into** our house while we were on holiday.   [forcibly entered]
I'm dreading **breaking the news to** him.   [telling him the news]
He has **broken her heart**.   [made her deeply unhappy]
The athlete **broke the record** for the 1000 metres.   [created a new record]

Exercises

91.1 Use the expressions on the opposite page to help you fill in the gaps in the text below. Use one word only in each gap.

Let's run ....(1) the plans for tomorrow's disco just once more. First, I must see ....(2) the food arrangements while you make sure that none of the equipment is likely to break ....(3). I don't imagine that many people will turn ....(4) until later but Nick and Jill have promised to come early to help us and I'm sure they won't let us ....(5) even though Jill let it ....(6) the other day that they are thinking of breaking ....(7) their engagement.

91.2 Rewrite the following using the words in brackets.

1 Why does she let herself be deceived by him? (see)
2 I met Jack by chance at the station yesterday. (run)
3 I cooked the dinner yesterday. It's up to you to do it today. (turn)
4 I thought I was hallucinating when I saw a monkey in the garden. (see)
5 I wish you'd stop bothering me. (let)
6 He told us in secret that they were planning to break into the house. (let)
7 An enormous crowd came to hear the Prime Minister speak. (turn)

91.3 Complete the sentences in an appropriate way.

1 If the snow doesn't let up soon...
2 A person who cannot see the wood for the trees does not make a good...
3 Halfway up the mountain he let go...
4 Although the turnout for the meeting was not large...
5 He felt terribly let down when...
6 She didn't turn up...
7 I'm afraid we've run out...
8 He asked if I could see my way...

91.4 Answer the questions below.

1 Have you ever turned down an offer or invitation that you later regretted?
2 Have you ever had problems because of something (a vehicle or a piece of equipment, perhaps) breaking down at an inconvenient time? What happened?
3 Who really runs the country, in your opinion?
4 Have you done anyone a good turn today? If so, what did you do?
5 Which record would you most like to break?
6 Do you think it is possible for someone's heart to be broken?
7 Have you ever resolved to turn over a new leaf? In what way(s)?
8 Have you any particular jobs that you must see to today? If so, what?
9 Has your home ever been broken into? What happened?

91.5 The expressions opposite are only some of many expressions using these five verbs. Can you think of two other phrasal verbs or other idiomatic expressions using each of the verbs? If you can't, try to find them in a dictionary.

92 Headline English

A

Headline writers try to catch the reader's eye by using as few words as possible. The language headlines use is, consequently, unusual in a number of ways.

- Grammar words like articles or auxiliary verbs are often left out, e.g. EARLY CUT FORECAST IN INTEREST RATES
- A simple form of the verb is used, e.g. QUEEN OPENS HOSPITAL TODAY
- The infinitive is used to express the fact that something is going to happen in the future, e.g. PRESIDENT TO VISIT MINE

B

Newspaper headlines use a lot of distinctive vocabulary. They prefer words that are usually shorter and generally sound more dramatic than ordinary English words. The words marked * can be used either as nouns or verbs.

newspaper word	meaning	newspaper word	meaning
aid *	help	key	essential, vital
axe *	cut, remove	link *	connection
back	support	move *	step towards a desired end
bar *	exclude, forbid	ordeal	painful experience
bid *	attempt	oust	push out
blast *	explosion	plea	request
blaze *	fire	pledge *	promise
boost *	incentive, encourage	ploy	clever activity
boss * } head* }	manager, director	poll *	election / public opinion survey
		probe *	investigation
clash *	dispute	quit	leave, resign
curb *	restraint, limit	riddle	mystery
cut *	reduction	strife	conflict
drama	tense situation	talks	discussions
drive *	campaign, effort	threat	danger
gems	jewels	vow *	promise
go-ahead	approval	wed	marry
hit	affect badly		

Newspaper headlines often use abbreviations, e.g. PM for Prime Minister, MP for Member of Parliament. (See Unit 98 for more abbreviations.)

C

Some newspapers also enjoy making jokes in their headlines. They do this by playing with words or punning, e.g. a wet open air concert in London by the opera singer Luciano Pavarotti was described as:

> **TORRENTIAL RAIN IN MOST ARIAS** ['most areas']

An announcement that a woman working at the Mars chocolate company had got an interesting new job was:

> **WOMAN FROM MARS TO BE FIRST BRITON IN SPACE**

(Note that the word 'Briton' is almost exclusively found in newspapers.)

Exercises

92.1 On the left there is a list of headlines. On the right there is a list of news topics. Match the headlines with the appropriate topic as in the example.

1 PM BACKS PEACE PLAN   marriage of famous actress
2 MP SPY DRAMA   royal jewels are stolen
3 SPACE PROBE FAILS   person who saw crime in danger
4 QUEEN'S GEMS RIDDLE   proposal to end war
5 STAR WEDS   satellite is not launched
6 KEY WITNESS DEATH THREAT   politician sells secrets to enemy

92.2 Explain what the following headlines mean in ordinary English.

Example: SHOP BLAZE 5 DEAD *Five people died in a fire in a shop.*

1 MOVE TO CREATE MORE JOBS
2 GO-AHEAD FOR WATER CURBS
3 WOMAN QUITS AFTER JOB ORDEAL
4 POLL PROBES SPENDING HABITS
5 BID TO OUST PM
6 PRINCE VOWS TO BACK FAMILY

92.3 The words marked * in the table opposite can be either nouns or verbs. Note that the meaning given is usually in the form of a noun. In the headlines below you have examples of words from the table used as verbs. Look at the underlined verbs and explain what they mean. You may need to use more than one word.

Example: PM TO CURB SPENDING *limit*

1 BOOK LINKS MI5 WITH KGB
2 CHANCELLOR CUTS INTEREST RATES
3 BOMB BLASTS CENTRAL LONDON
4 PM PLEDGES BACKING FOR EUROPE
5 PRESIDENT HEADS PEACE MOVES

92.4 Would you be interested in the stories under the following headlines? Why (not)?

Mortgages cut as bank rates fall again

New tennis clash

Price curbs boost exports

Teenage £4m fraud riddle

Women barred from jobs

Royal family quits

92.5 Look through some English language newspapers and find some examples of headlines illustrating the points made on the opposite page. Beside each headline make a note of what the accompanying story is about. Try to find some examples of amusing headlines.

93 US English

A

English in the USA differs considerably from British English. Pronunciation is the most striking difference but there are also a number of differences in vocabulary and spelling as well as slight differences in grammar. On the whole, British people are exposed to a lot of American English on TV, in films and so on and so they will usually understand most American vocabulary.

B

American spelling is usually simpler. For example, British English words ending in -**our** and -**re**, end in -**or** and -**er** in American English, e.g. colour/color, centre/center. There are differences in individual words too, e.g. British 'plough' becomes 'plow'. The American spelling usually tries to correspond more closely to pronunciation.

C

Here are some common US words with their British equivalents.

Travel and on the street *American English*	*British English*	In the home *American English*	*British English*
gasoline	petrol	antenna	aerial
truck	lorry	elevator	lift
baggage	luggage	eraser	rubber
blow-out	puncture	apartment	flat
sidewalk	pavement	closet	wardrobe
line	queue	drapes	curtains
vacation	holiday	faucet	tap
trunk (of car)	boot	kerosene	paraffin
hood (of car)	bonnet	Scotch tape	sellotape
cab	taxi	yard	garden
freeway	motorway	cookie	biscuit
round trip	return	candy	sweets
railway car	railway carriage	garbage	rubbish
engineer (on train)	engine driver	diaper	nappy
baby carriage	pram	panti-hose	tights

Note also: the fall = autumn   semester = term [semester is becoming common in Britain.]

D

Here are some words and phrases which can cause confusion when used by Brits and Americans talking together because they mean something different in each 'language'.

when they say:	*an American means what a Brit calls:*	*and a Brit means what an American calls:*
a bill	a (bank) note	a check (in a café)
the first floor	the ground floor	the second floor
pants	trousers	underpants
potato chips	potato crisps	french fries
purse	a handbag	a wallet
subway	an underground railway	an underpass
vest	a waistcoat	an undershirt
wash up	wash your hands	wash the dishes

Exercises

93.1 If you saw words spelt in the following way would you expect the writer in each case to be British or American? Why?

1 labor   2 centre   3 hospitalized   4 movie theater   5 favour   6 thru

93.2 What are (a) the American and (b) the British words for the following things?

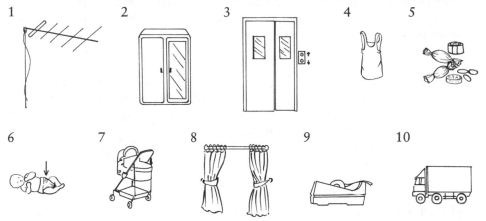

93.3 You are going on holiday to the States. Which of the words listed in B and C opposite do you think it would be most important for you to know? Which of the words would a person travelling with a baby might well need to know?

93.4 Translate the following into British English.

1 I had a blow-out.
2 Pass me the cookies.
3 It's in the closet.
4 Open the drapes.
5 We've run out of gas.
6 It's in the trunk.
7 One-way or round trip?
8 He left the faucet on.
9 We're leaving in the fall.
10 I hate waiting in line.

93.5 Can you avoid some of the most common confusions arising between British and American speakers? Try the following quiz.

1 Where would you take (a) an American visitor (b) a British visitor who said they wanted to wash up – the kitchen or the bathroom?
2 Would (a) an American (b) a Brit be expected to get something hot or something cold if they asked for some potato chips?
3 Which would surprise you more – an American or a British man telling you that he wanted to go and change his pants?
4 You have just come into an unknown office block. If (a) an American (b) a Brit says that the office you need is on the second floor, how many flights of stairs do you need to climb?
5 If (a) an American (b) a Brit asks for a bill, is he or she more likely to be in a bank or a café?

93.6 Do you know any other examples of American English? Make a list at an appropriate place in your vocabulary notebook or file.

94 Other Englishes

A US or American English (see Unit 93) is not the only special variety of English. Each area of the English-speaking world has developed its own special characteristics. This is usually mainly a matter of vocabulary and pronunciation. This unit just gives you a small taste of some of the different varieties of English by drawing your attention to vocabulary used in various English-speaking regions. All the words covered in this unit would be understood by educated native speakers of British English although they might not choose to use them themselves. They are all words which you may come across in your own reading, listening or viewing.

B Australian English is particularly interesting for its rich store of highly colloquial words and expressions. Australian colloquialisms often involve shortening a word. Sometimes the ending '-ie' or '-o' is then added, e.g. a **smoko** (from smoking), is a 'tea or coffee break' and a **milko** delivers the milk; **beaut**, short for 'beautiful' means 'great'. Because of the current popularity of Australian TV programmes and films, some of these words are now being used by British people too.

C Indian English, on the other hand, is characterised by sounding more formal than British English. It has retained in everyday usage words that are found more in the classics of nineteenth century literature than in contemporary TV programmes from London, e.g. The **bereaved** are **condoled** and the Prime Minister is **felicitated** on his or her birthday. An Indian might complain of a pain in his **bosom** (rather than his chest) and an Indian bandit is referred to as a **miscreant**.

D Scottish English uses a number of special dialect words. Some of the more common of these are worth learning.

aye: yes	**loch:** lake	**dreich:** dull
ben: mountain	**to mind:** to remember	**janitor:** caretaker
brae: bank (of river)	**bairn:** child	**lassie:** girl
dram: drink (usually whisky)	**bonny:** beautiful	**outwith:** outside
glen: valley	**burn:** stream	**wee:** small
kirk: church	**stay:** live	**ken:** know

E Black English is the term used to refer to the English which originated in the Caribbean islands and has now spread to many parts of the UK, Canada and the USA. Listed below are some words which are characteristic of Black English but are also now used in other varieties of English. Many are particularly associated with the music world.

dreadlocks: Rastafarian hairstyle	**beat:** exhausted
chick: girl	**dig:** understand
jam: improvise	**pad:** bed
rap: street-talk	**square:** dull

Exercises

94.1 What do you think these examples of Australian colloquialisms mean? They are all formed by abbreviating an English word which you probably know.

1 Where did you go when you were in <u>Oz</u>?
2 She wants to be a <u>journo</u> when she leaves <u>uni</u>.
3 We got terribly bitten by <u>mozzies</u> at yesterday's <u>barbie</u>.
4 He's planning to do a bit of farming <u>bizzo</u> while he's in the States.
5 What are you doing this <u>arvo</u>?
6 We decided to have a party as the <u>oldies</u> had gone away for the weekend.

94.2 The words on the left are more common in Indian English than British English. The words on the right are the equivalent words more frequently used in British English. Match the Indian word with its British English equivalent.

1 abscond ———————————————— catch (e.g. by police)
2 nab   man who annoys girls
3 bag (i.e. a seat in an election)   plimsolls, sneakers
4 Eve-teaser   underwear
5 the common man   flee
6 fleetfoots   people awaiting trial
7 undertrials   the general public
8 wearunders   capture/obtain

94.3 Below you have some statements made by a Scot. Answer the questions about them.

1 Mary had a bonny wee lassie last night.
   What happened to Mary yesterday?

2 They stay next to the kirk.
   What noise is likely to wake them on Sunday mornings?

3 It's a bit dreich today.
   Is it good weather for a picnic?

4 He's got a new job as janitor at the school.
   What kind of duties will he have?

5 Would you like a wee dram?
   If you say 'yes', what will you get?

6 'Are you coming, Jim?' 'Aye'.
   Is Jim coming or isn't he?

7 They have a wonderful view of the loch from their window.
   What can they see from the window?

94.4 Answer the following questions relating to Black English.

1 Would you be pleased to be called square?
2 What does hair that is in dreadlocks look like?
3 When might you feel dead beat?
4 If musicians have a jam session, what do they do?

95 Slang

A Slang is a particular kind of colloquial language. It refers to words and expressions which are extremely informal. Slang helps to make speech vivid, colourful and interesting but it can easily be used inappropriately. Although slang is mainly used in speech, it is also often found in the popular press.

B It can be risky for someone who is not a native speaker to use slang.

Firstly because some slang expressions may cause offence to some sections of the population. For example, most policemen are quite happy to be referred to as **coppers** but are offended by the term **pigs**. Similarly, you could probably use the word **sozzled** (meaning drunk) in front of anyone but using the words, **pissed** or **arseholed**, which also mean drunk, could upset some people.

Secondly, slang words date very quickly. Different generations, for instance, have used different slang expressions to say that something was 'wonderful'.

> pre-war: **top-hole**   1970s: **ace, cosmic**
> 1940s: **wizard**   1980s: **brill, wicked**
> 1960s: **fab, groovy**

It can be possible to work out a native speaker's age from the expressions which they use, as people tend to stick with the slang expressions of their youth.

To sum up, you may find it interesting to learn about slang and you may come across slang expressions (particularly when you are watching films or reading popular newspapers or novels) but you might be well advised to avoid using slang yourself.

C Here are some examples of some slang words and expressions which you may come across. The ones which are most likely to cause offence are underlined.

> **Expressions for money:** dough, bread, dosh, loot, brass, spondulicks
> **Expressions for the police:** <u>pigs</u>, fuzz, cop(per)s, bill
> **Expressions for drunk:** <u>pissed</u>, sozzled, <u>paralytic</u>, <u>legless</u>, <u>arseholed</u>
> **Expressions for a stupid person:** wally, prat, nerd, jerk, <u>dickhead</u>, plonker, <u>pillock</u>
> **Expressions for lavatory:** loo, lav, <u>bog</u>, john
> **Expressions for drink:** booze, plonk (wine), a snifter, a snort
> **Drug-related expressions:** a fix, dope, grass, high, stoned, snow (heroin)
> **Prison-related expressions:** nick (prison), nark (informer), screw (warder)

D Slang is often used by one particular group and is unintelligible to other people. Here are some examples from American truck-drivers using CB radio to talk to each other.

> **grandma lane:** slow lane   **five finger discount:** stolen goods   **super cola:** beer
> **doughnuts:** tyres   **anklebiters:** children   **affirmative:** yes
> **motion lotion:** fuel   **eyeballs:** headlights

Exercises

95.1 Replace the slang words which are underlined in the sentences below with more formal equivalents. If the meaning is not given opposite, then it should be possible to guess what it is. Notice that some of the words have a slang meaning which is different from their everyday meaning.

1 The newsreader on TV last night seemed to be <u>pissed</u> as he was reading the news.
2 He's quite a nice <u>bloke</u> really.
3 I've got a terrible <u>belly ache</u> – I think I'd better make an appointment with the <u>quack</u>.
4 Her dad was furious when he learnt he had to wear a <u>penguin suit</u> to the wedding.
5 Can you lend me some <u>dosh</u> till tomorrow?
6 I know there'll be plenty of <u>nosh</u> but do we need to take some <u>booze</u> to the party?
7 Have you got <u>wheels</u> or shall we call a taxi?
8 I'm dying for a <u>cuppa</u>. I haven't had one since breakfast.
9 Can I use your <u>loo</u>, please?
10 I was absolutely <u>gobsmacked</u> when she told me she was leaving.

95.2 Match the statements on the left with the responses to them on the right.

1 How was the party?   Let's take him home.
2 What does that guy over there do? Sure. I'll keep my eyes skinned.
3 He's getting legless.   He's in the nick.
4 Keep a lookout for the pigs.   It's in a drawer, over here.
5 Where's the dough?   He's a cop.
6 Where's her hubby?   Let's go for a run in the motor.
7 What'll we do tomorrow?   Wicked!

95.3 A particular well-known kind of slang is Cockney rhyming slang where an expression is used in place of something that it rhymes with.

Example: trouble and strife = wife   apples and pears = stairs

How would you translate the Cockney rhyming slang expressions in the sentences below?

1 Let's have a <u>butcher's</u> (short for <u>butcher's hook</u>) at your homework.
2 Just look at those <u>Gawd forbids</u> playing football!
3 It's on the <u>Cain and Abel</u> next to the phone.
4 What a set of <u>Hampstead Heath!</u>
5 She'll get him to the <u>lean and lurch</u> by hook or by crook.
6 Have you seen my <u>titfer</u>? (short for <u>tit for tat</u>)

95.4 Another common way of making slang words is by using short forms or loosely pronounced forms of ordinary words. Thus <u>fab</u> is a slang form of 'fabulous' and <u>hubby</u> is a slang form of 'husband'. Can you work out the meanings of the following underlined slang words?

1 He's my <u>fella</u>.   3 It was a <u>freebie</u>.   5 I took a <u>sickie</u>.
2 Let's have <u>brekkie</u>.   4 He's a <u>brickie</u>.   6 Let's have a <u>barbie</u>.

96 The language of notices

A Notices in English often use words and expressions that are rarely seen in other contexts. Look at the notices below with their 'translations' into more everyday English.

> **Do not alight from the bus whilst it is in motion**

1 Don't get off the bus while it's moving.

> **TRESPASSERS WILL BE PROSECUTED**

2 People who walk on this private land will be taken to court.

> **KINDLY REFRAIN FROM SMOKING IN THE AUDITORIUM**

3 Please don't smoke in the theatre/hall.

> **PENALTY FOR DROPPING LITTER – UP TO £100 FINE**

4 You can be taken to court and made to pay £100 for dropping rubbish.

> **Lunches now being served**

5 You can buy lunch here now.

> **NO ADMISSION TO UNACCOMPANIED MINORS**

6 Young people under 18 years old can only come in if they are with an adult.

> **FEEDING THE ANIMALS STRICTLY PROHIBITED**

7 You are not allowed to feed the animals.

> **No through road for motor vehicles**

8 There is no way out at the other end of this road for cars.

> **NO BILL-STICKING**

9 You mustn't put up any posters here.

> **Please place your purchases here**

10 Please put the things you are going to buy / have bought here.

> **This packet carries a government health warning**

11 What is in this packet is officially considered bad for your health.

> **Reduce speed now**

12 Start going more slowly now.

> **Pay and display**

13 Buy a ticket and put it in a place where it can easily be seen.

> **Cyclists dismount here**

14 Cyclist should get off their bikes here.

> **FISHING: PERMIT HOLDERS ONLY**

15 Only people with special cards giving them permission are allowed to fish here.

B You will find more examples of a specific kind of notice, road signs, in Unit 49.

Exercises

96.1 Where would you expect to see each of the notices on the opposite page?

Example: 1 *on a bus*

96.2 Match each of the words on the left with their more everyday translations from the list on the right.

1	to prosecute	a young person under the age of 18
2	a penalty	to get off a bicycle or a horse
3	a purchase	to bring a legal case against
4	a trespasser	not to do something
5	to refrain	to forbid something
6	to alight from	a means of transport
7	to prohibit	a punishment
8	an auditorium	something which has been or is to be bought
9	to dismount	to get off a means of public transport
10	a minor	large place where an audience sits
11	a vehicle	someone who goes on private land without permission

96.3 Explain the notices below. Where might you see each of these notices?

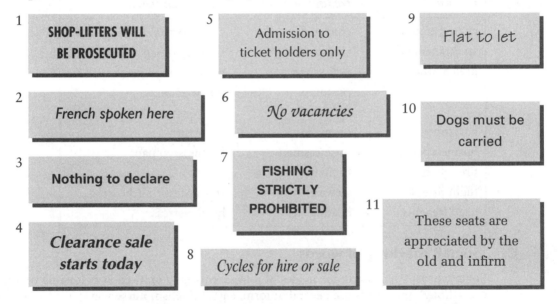

1 SHOP-LIFTERS WILL BE PROSECUTED

2 *French spoken here*

3 Nothing to declare

4 *Clearance sale starts today*

5 Admission to ticket holders only

6 *No vacancies*

7 FISHING STRICTLY PROHIBITED

8 *Cycles for hire or sale*

9 Flat to let

10 Dogs must be carried

11 These seats are appreciated by the old and infirm

96.4 What notice would a café-owner put up if they wanted to:

1 indicate that their café was now open for coffee?
2 let people know that the café staff can speak Spanish?
3 stop people from smoking in their café?
4 let people know that they can buy free-range eggs there too?
5 ask people not to fix notices onto their wall?
6 tell people that they could rent rooms there overnight?

96.5 If you are in or go to visit an English-speaking country, make a collection in your vocabulary book of any notices that you see.

97 Words and gender

In this unit we look at the problems of using words in a way that is not offensive to either gender. In English, a lot of words are marked as masculine or feminine by suffixes, but many other words have 'female' or 'male' associations and should be used carefully.

A Suffixes marking gender

-er(-or)/-ess: traditionally used to mark male (m) and female (f), e.g. actress (f) / actor (m); waitress (f) / waiter (m).

These two words are still often used in both forms, but forms such as **authoress, poetess, murderess** and **manageress** are considered old-fashioned. If you want to be neutral, you can use the -er/-or suffix for male or female.

Schoolmistress/master sound old-fashioned, use **teacher** instead; **air hostess** also sounds out of date, use **flight attendant** (neutral) or **stewardess**.

B -man, -woman and -person

Traditional social roles often meant that -**man** was used even for roles performed by women. Now many people prefer a neutral form for both sexes, if there is one available.

neutral	traditional male	traditional female
chair(person)	chairman	chairwoman
spokesperson	spokesman	spokeswoman
police officer	policeman	policewoman
—	postman	postwoman
—	fisherman	—
bartender	barman	barmaid
businessperson	businessman	businesswoman
firefighter	fireman	—
flight attendant	steward	stewardess / air hostess
head (teacher)	headmaster	headmistress

C 'Social' marking of words

Some words, particularly the names of jobs, are socially marked as belonging to one gender, even though the words are neutral in form, e.g. in English, **nurse** was considered so 'female' that if a man was a nurse, he was often referred to as a **male nurse**.

Just consider your own reaction to these words, and whether most people would tend to think of a man or a woman upon hearing them.

    barber   hairdresser   burglar   secretary   farmer   butcher

Note: **bachelor** and **spinster** can both have negative or undesirable associations. Use **unmarried** or **single (man/woman)** instead. Likewise, instead of **fiancé(e)**, you can use **partner**, especially for someone you live with as a couple but are not married to.

Many women nowadays prefer the title **Ms** /məz/, rather than **Miss** or **Mrs**.

Exercises

97.1 Look at this rather sexist advertisement for an airline. Change the wording to make it more neutral.

> ## Now! Eagle Airlines offers even more to the businessman who needs comfort.
>
> Let us fly you to your destination in first-class comfort, looked after by the best-trained air hostesses in the world. Any businessman knows that he must arrive fresh and ready for work no matter how long the journey. With Eagle Diplomat-Class you can do just that.
>
> And, what's more, your wife can travel with you on all intercontinental flights for only 25% of the normal fare! Your secretary can book you on any flights 24 hours a day on 0557-465769. All she has to do is lift the phone.

97.2 Here are some more names of jobs and occupations. Are they marked for gender either in the form of the word itself, or 'socially' marked as typically male or female? How are they translated into your language, by neutral or by gender-marked words?

1 conductor	4 typist	7 general	10 milkman
2 shepherd	5 station master	8 detective	11 tailor
3 cheerleader	6 dressmaker	9 monk	

97.3 These words include some that many people consider sexist. Put the words into appropriate pairs with their neutral alternatives.

cabin attendant   man-hours   unmanned   air hostess   unstaffed   spinster
human beings   single woman   mankind   person-hours

97.4 Change gender-marked words into neutral ones.

1 We shall have to elect a new chairman next month.
2 Several firemen and policemen were hurt in the riots.
3 A spokesman for the store said the manageress had decided to resign.
4 I wonder what time the postman comes every day.
5 I can't see a barman anywhere. Shall I press this bell and see if someone comes?
6 Her brother's a male nurse, and she's an authoress.

97.5 Make this letter more neutral.

> The Manager
> Frinstowe Engineering Ltd   22/11/92
>
> Dear Sir,
> I am a spinster aged 22 and am seeking employment. I saw your
> advertisement for part-time workers in *The Globe* last week.
> However, your 24-hour answering service seemed to be unmanned
> when I tried it. Could you please send me application forms
> by post? Thank you.
>
>   Yours sincerely,
>
>   Sally Hewings
>
>   Sally Hewings (Miss)

98 Abbreviations

A Some abbreviations are read as individual letters:

WHO (W-H-O) World Health Organisation		**IRA**	Irish Republican Army
PLO	Palestine Liberation Organisation	**UN**	United Nations
BBC	British Broadcasting Corporation	**PM**	Prime Minister
ANC	African National Congress	**MP**	Member of Parliament

In the following three cases, the name of each country and the name of its secret police are pronounced as individual letters/numbers.

CIA (USA)   MI5 (UK)   KGB (former USSR, now CIS)

Note: When these abbreviations are stressed words in the sentence, the stress falls on the <u>last</u> letter, e.g. She works for the CI<u>A</u>.   I heard it on the BB<u>C</u>.

B Some abbreviations are read as words; we call them **acronyms**.

NATO	/ˈneɪtəʊ/	North Atlantic Treaty Organisation
OPEC	/ˈəʊpek/	Organisation of Petroleum Exporting Countries
AIDS	/eɪdz/	Acquired Immune Deficiency Syndrome

Some acronyms have become so normal as words that people do not think of them as abbreviations any longer, and so they are not written all in capital letters.

laser   **radar**   **yuppy**   **Esso**

C Some abbreviations are only written forms; they are still pronounced as the full word.

Mr (Mister)   Dr (Doctor)   St (Saint or Street)

D Abbreviations are used in the organisation of language.

etc. /etˈsetrə/ and so on   [Latin: et cetera]
i.e. (I-E): that is to say   [Latin: id est]
PTO (P-T-O) please turn over
NB (N-B) please note   [Latin: nota bene]
RSVP (R-S-V-P) please reply   [French: répondez s'il vous plaît]
e.g. (E-G) for example   [Latin: exempli gratia]

E Clippings: some words are normally used in an abbreviated form in informal situations. (See also Unit 7.)

lab (laboratory)   **phone** (telephone)   **fridge** (refrigerator)
TV or **telly** (television)   **board** (blackboard)   **bike** (bicycle)   **case** (suitcase)
exam (examination)   **plane** (aeroplane)   **rep** (business representative)
ad/advert (advertisement)   **fax** (telefax)

F Some abbreviations you might see on a letter/fax/envelope.

c/o care of   [e.g. T. Smith, c/o J. Brown; the letter goes to J. Brown's address]
enc. enclosed   [e.g. enc. application form]
PS postscript   [extra message after the letter has been ended]
asap as soon as possible   [e.g. ring me asap]

Exercises

98.1 What things in these addresses are normally abbreviated? How is *Ms* pronounced in the second address?

1 Mister A. Carlton
Flat number 5
Hale Crescent
Borebridge

2 Ms P. Meldrum
care of T. Fox
6, Marl Avenue
Preston

3 N. Lowe and Company
7, Bridge Road
Freeminster
United Kingdom

98.2 Match these abbreviations with their meanings and then group them according to groups A to D opposite.

1 BSc   compact disc
2 FBI   for example
3 Fr   Federal Bureau of Investigation
4 ext.   personal identification number (usually on a bank card)
5 CD   United Nations Educational, Scientific and Cultural Organisation
6 asap   Bachelor of Science
7 PIN   extension
8 e.g.   Father (title for a priest)
9 Unesco   as soon as possible

98.3 'Translate' this note from the boss to a group of workers in an office, into full words.

> Memo from: Mr Braneless (MD)   To: All staff
> Date: 3/5/91   Ref: 04056/DC
> May I remind you that all new lab equipment should be
> registered with Stores & Supplies, Room 354 (ext 2683). NB:
> new items must be notified before 1700hrs on the last day of
> the month of purchase, i.e. within the current budgeting
> month. All a/c nos must be recorded.   *Braneless*

98.4 Explain 1–5 and match them with the contexts on the right.

1 Students and OAPs: £1.50   on an aerosol can
2 WC Gents   in a newspaper headline
3 US forces take 5,000 POWs   on a museum entrance
4 Ozone-friendly: CFC-free   on an airline timetable
5 Dep 1500   Arr 1742   on a door in a pub

98.5

Across	Down
3 Flying saucer	1 %
6 N, S, <u>E</u> or W?	2 Same as 13 across
8 Royal Navy	4 Refrigerators
9 Rest in Peace	5 Means 'or nearest offer'
10 Short for biological	7 Serious illness
11 Type of record	10 'Please note' backwards
12 &	14 Place for a short drink?
13 Means 'especially'	16 British Telecom
15 British car-plate	18 South East
17 American	
19 Famous film alien	
20 Short name for London Underground	

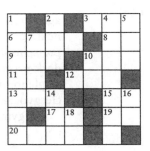

99 New words in English

No language stands still. New words and expressions are always being created, usually because something new is invented or sometimes just for fun. No government committee decides whether a new word is acceptable or not; if it is used frequently, and in a variety of contexts, it will find its way into the dictionary. Here are some of the words and expressions that have come into English since 1980.

B New science and technology

faxable: able to be sent by fax machine
junk fax: unsolicited material, such as adverts, sent by fax
tummytuck: a plastic surgery operation to remove fat from the stomach
sound bite: a brief excerpt from a speech or statement, broadcast on TV

C New sports and fashions

monoboarding: the sport of skiing downhill on a large single ski
snowsurfing: skiing downhill standing sideways on a large single ski
vogueing: a style of dancing to house music incorporating the movements and gestures of models displaying clothes

D Political and social trends

eco-friendly: not harming the environment
cardboard city: area occupied by cardboard boxes serving as homes for the homeless
teleworking: working from home communicating by computer and fax
advertocracy: pursuit of public policy by mass advertising campaigns
destatisation: withdrawal of the state from areas that were previously state-controlled as in the (former) Soviet bloc in the 80s and 90s
Gorbymania: extreme enthusiasm for the former Soviet President, Mikhail Gorbachev
newmannery: behaviour of the new man (gentle, caring, non-sexist)
couch potato: a lazy person who prefers watching TV to being active

E New words from other languages

fatwa: formal legal opinion delivered by an Islamic leader (Arabic)
karaoke: singing pop songs solo to recorded music in bars (Japanese)
glasnost: policy of openness or frankness (Russian)

F New forms or meanings for old words

ageism: prejudice against someone because of their age
nostalgise: to indulge in nostalgia
pre-schooler: a child not yet old enough for school
dark-green: holding radically green political beliefs
singlehood: the state of being single rather than married
clergyperson: a male or female member of the clergy (a typical development from clergyman. Compare: **chairperson**)

Exercises

99.1 Here are some more new words. Match them with their definitions. Which of the five categories opposite does each fit best in?

1 collectomania — a specially bred miniaturised form of vegetable
2 bio-house — a hypothetical miniaturised device capable of making its way through bodily passages and performing various tasks
3 bimbo — an irresistible urge to collect things
4 mini-vegetable — an indoor version of American football
5 arenaball — a house constructed solely from natural materials
6 microbot — a female of limited intelligence but high sex appeal

99.2 Choose which word from those defined opposite fits into the following sentences.

1 I always buy roll-on rather than aerosol deodorants ever since I learnt how much more .... they are.
2 .... was much more common in the West than the USSR just as Mrs Thatcher was probably more popular outside the UK.
3 Most of my married friends think there's a lot to be said for ....
4 I don't think I'd like to try .... It sounds too dangerous to me.
5 They think that in the next ten years more and more people will start .... It should certainly ease traffic in the rush hours.
6 The size of London's .... seems to grow every time I go there. It sometimes seems as if the country is going backwards.
7 He's such a .... His only activity is pressing the remote control.
8 Many politicians now try to ensure they write some effective .... into their speeches.

99.3 Many of the words on the opposite page will have a very short life. Pick out three that you think may be widely used still in ten years.

99.4 If you meet a new word it is often possible to work out its meaning from its context. Practise by explaining what the underlined words in the following sentences must mean.

1 I very much prefer restaurants where there is no microwavery.
2 They're building a new cineplex on the edge of the town so we should be able to choose from a variety of films on Saturday nights.
3 Upskiing, which uses small parachutes, is a rapidly developing sport in the USA.
4 World AIDS Day was inspired by the health globocrats of the World Health Organisation.
5 He is writing a thesis on humorology.
6 The boss is very much a hands-on manager who likes to be involved in all aspects of the company's work.
7 Many large shops now have their own store cards.
8 The post-war baby-boomers are now becoming grandparents.

100 Discourse markers

Discourse markers are small words and phrases whose job it is to organise, comment on or in some way frame what we are saying or writing. A common everyday example is the use of **well** in speech:

A: So you live in Boston? B: **Well**, near Boston.

Well here shows that the speaker is aware he/she is changing the direction of the conversation in some way (not giving the expected 'yes' answer). In other words, **well** is a comment on what is being said. Another example is how teachers use words like **right** and **okay** to organise what is happening in a classroom:

Teacher: **Right/okay**, let's have a look at exercise 3.

A

Common markers to organise different stages of talk (as in the teacher example).

Now, what shall we do next?   **So**, would you like to come to the table now, please?
Good, I'll ring you on Thursday, then.   **Well then**, what was it you wanted to talk about?
Now then, I want you to look at this picture. [said by someone in control of the conversation, e.g. a teacher]
Fine/Great, let's leave it at that, then, shall we?

B

In these mini-dialogues, the markers in bold *modify* or *comment* on what is being said.

A: It's cold, isn't it?
B: Yeah.
A: **Mind you**, it is November, so it's not surprising.
[an afterthought – however]

A: What's her number?
B: **Let me see**, I have it here somewhere...
[a hesitation – gaining time]

A: It's quite a problem...
B: **Listen/Look**, why don't you let me sort it out?
A: Would you? Thanks a lot.
[introducing a suggestion/point]

A: And he said he was go –
B: **Well**, that's typical!
A: **Hang on / Hold on**! Let me tell you what he said!
[preventing an interruption]

Here are some other similar markers.
I can't do that. **You see**, I'm only the secretary.   [explaining]
He was, **you know, sort of**... just standing there.   [hesitation]

C

Common markers in written English for organising a formal text.

First / Firstly / First of all, we must consider... }
Next, it is important to remember that... } for lists
Finally/Lastly, we should look at...   [NB *not* 'at last']
In summary, we can say that...   [summing up the main points]
In conclusion, I should like to say that...   [finishing the text]

D

Markers for explaining, rephrasing, etc., in speech and writing.

Memorising words requires reinforcement; **in other words / that is to say**, you have to study the same words over and over again.
Some words are hard to say, **for example / for instance**, 'crisps'.
She is, **as it were / so to speak**, living in a world of her own.
[make what you are saying sound less definite/precise]

Exercises

100.1 Underline all the discourse markers in this monologue. Not all of them are on the left-hand page.

'Well, where shall I start? It was last summer and we were just sitting in the garden, sort of doing nothing much. Anyway, I looked up and...see we have this kind of long wall at the end of the garden, and it's...like...a motorway for cats, for instance, that big fat black one you saw, well, that one considers it has a right of way over our vegetable patch, so...where was I? Yes, I was looking at that wall, you know, day-dreaming as usual, and all of a sudden there was this new cat I'd never seen before, or rather, it wasn't an ordinary cat at all...I mean, you'll never believe what it was...'

100.2 Here are some small dialogues where there are no markers used at all, which would be unusual in real informal talk. Add markers from A, B and D opposite and from exercise 1 above, where you think the speakers might use them.

1 A: Are you a football fan?
  B: I like it; I wouldn't say I was a fan.

2 A: I'll take care of these.
  B: That's everything.
  A: See you next week.
  B: That was a very useful meeting.

3 A: It was last Monday. I was coming home from work. I saw this ragged old man approaching me. I stopped him –
  B: Jim Dibble!
  A: Let me tell you what happened first.
  them off.

4 A: Which number is yours?
  B: (*pause*)...it's that one here, yes, this one.

5 A: He's looking exhausted.
  B: Yes, he is.
  A: He has an awful lot of responsibility, so it's hardly surprising.

6 A: What do you mean 'cold'?
  B: She's not friendly, very distant. Last week I gave her a jolly smile and she...scowled at me.
  A: What do you expect? I've seen the way you smile at people, it puts

100.3 Fill the gaps with markers often found in written texts. You may need some which are not on the left-hand page. The first letter of each phrase/word is given.

Crime and Punishment

F.............. .... (1), it is important to understand why people commit crimes, i.......
.... (2), what are the motives which make people do things they would never normally do? F.......... .... (3), a young man steals clothes from a shop; is it because he is unemployed? a drug addict? mentally disturbed? N.................... (4) it is essential to consider whether punishment makes any difference, or is it just, a ....
.... (5), a kind of revenge? L....................... (6), how can we help victims of crime?
I................ .... (7), how can we get to the roots of the problem, rather than just attacking the symptoms?

Follow-up: If you can, make a recording of a natural conversation between native speakers (get their permission, but don't say why you need it). What markers do they use?

Key

Many of your answers will depend on your own particular interests and needs. It is only possible for the key to suggest answers in some cases.

Unit 1

A   1 d   2 b   3 b   4 a

B   1 *Some possible answers:*
   a) a **chilly** day
   b) to **dissuade** someone from doing something
   c) a popular **king** / to crown a **king**
   d) **up to the ears** in work
   e) **independent** of someone / an **independent** country
   f) **get married** to someone

   2 a) scissors – only used in plural; if you want to count **scissors**, you have to say, for example, 'two pairs of **scissors**'.
   b) weather – uncountable
   c) teach, taught, taught; **teach** someone to do something; **teach** someone French.
   d) advice – uncountable; a piece of **advice**; verb = to advise (regular).
   e) lose, lost, lost
   f) trousers – only used in plural; if you want to count **trousers** you have to say, for example, 'three pairs of **trousers**'.

   3 a) The 'b' in **comb** is silent, as it is in **tomb** and **lamb** too.
   b) The final 'e' in **catastrophe** is pronounced as a syllable as it is in **apostrophe**. Catastrophe, has 4 syllables. (See Index for pronunciation)
   c) The stress is on the first syllable in **pho**tograph, and on the second syllable in pho**to**grapher; it is on the third syllable in photo**gra**phical. The 'rule' is that the stress in long words in English very frequently falls on the third syllable from the end of the word.

D   The picture is a good clue to help you understand **tortoise**. You may recognise the word **shell** in **shelled** (as in **egg shell**, for example). Similarly, your knowledge of **life** and **long** together with the context should enable you to work out what **lifespan** and **longevity** mean. The whole context of the sentence should help you to work out the meaning of **tended**. Some of the underlined words may be similar to words in your own language which can be another useful way of working out the meaning of a word you have not seen before.

E   Research into language learning can help you to prepare a sensible vocabulary learning plan. What you plan to do will, of course, depend very much on your own circumstances. You cannot realistically aim to learn as many new words a day if you are working a full day at something else as if you are doing a full-time English course. In general, however, 10 to 20 words a week is probably a reasonable aim.

It does not matter where you try to learn vocabulary but it seems to be better to do a little on a regular basis rather than a lot infrequently. Research also suggests that it is a good idea to revise your work on a very regular basis – once a week, perhaps, but do not revise only the words that you've learnt in that week. Look back over your work of the previous month(s).

Unit 2

A   1 *Possible words to add:* **purr, scratch, tomcat, tail** and **whiskers**

   2 a) **Child, tooth** and **ox** are all words with irregular plurals (**children, teeth, oxen**). You could add more examples, e.g. **mouse** (**mice**); **goose** (**geese**); **foot** (**feet**); **phenomenon** (**phenomena**).

b) **Cut, split** and **burst** are all irregular verbs whose three basic forms are identical to each other (i.e. **cut, cut, cut; split, split, split** and **burst, burst, burst**). You could add **put, hurt** and **set** to this group.

c) **Information, furniture** and **food** are all uncountable nouns – you could add **milk, money** and **work** to this group.

3 *Possible words and expressions to add:*
a) **pricey, underpriced, price tag** b) **to lend someone a hand, a handful; a handbag, underhand,** etc.

B 1 *Possible word tree for* **school:**

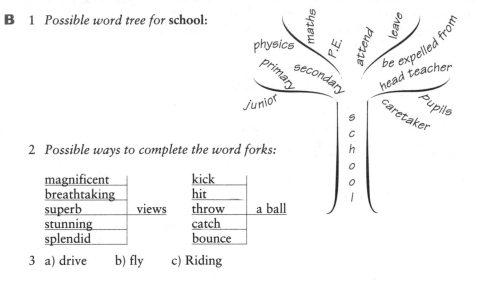

2 *Possible ways to complete the word forks:*

magnificent			kick		
breathtaking			hit		
superb	views		throw	a ball
stunning			catch		
splendid			bounce		

3 a) drive   b) fly   c) Riding

Unit 3

3.1   The list is probably connected to a lesson or lessons about time or a text about someone's relationship with time. A possible organisation might include bringing the **clock** words together in a word-map or bubble diagram (**clock, wristwatch, hands, minute-hand**); other words could then be added later (**hour-hand, face/dial, digital,** etc.)

Tell the time and What time do you make it? could form a separate list of 'time phrases', to which others could be added, e.g. **Have you got the time?, My watch is fast/slow,** etc. **Drowsy** and **wide awake** could be treated as antonyms, and some notes about the usage of **beneath** and **under** would be useful. The list could have information about word-class too.

3.2   **Theatre** seems the obvious word.

3.3   Other testing systems include re-entering any word you have difficulty remembering, so that it appears more than once in the notebook. Another useful discipline is to set yourself a small, fixed number of words to memorise each week, e.g. 20, and to tick them off in the book as you do them. You could also take out any ten words from your book and put them on individual slips of paper which you stick in prominent places around your room or house, e.g. on the fridge door, so that you are regularly looking at them.

3.4

noun	verb	adjective	person
production	produce	productive	producer
industry	industrialise	industrial	industrialist
export	export	export	exporter

Note the change in stress from <u>export</u> (noun) to ex<u>port</u> (verb); adjective: <u>export</u>, e.g. Our export figures have increased; person: ex<u>port</u>er.

Unit 4

4.1 *Suggested answers:*

1 style   situation   people   4 extremely   mainly   frequently
2 mean   be   know   5 of   by   for
3 informal   colloquial   suitable

4.2 Obviously your answers here depend on how you answered 4.1. If you chose the same words as we did, then your answers to 4.2 will be as follows:

style *C*   situation *C*   people *U* (Remember that it needs a plural verb.)
mean *T, R*   be *IT, IR*   know *T, IR*

4.3

verb	infinitive	-ing form	past participle
define	define	defining	defined
mean	mean	meaning	meant
write	write	writing	written

4.4

1 root – *form*   prefix – *in*   suffix – *al*
2 formal
3 casual e.g. of dress
4 form, formality, formless, deform, reform, reformation and so on.
5 a) an informal occasion
   b) We use a more informal kind of English when we speak than when we write.

4.5 syllable onomatopoeia register colloquial pejorative collocation comma semi-colon apostrophe (note that there are four syllables in **apostrophe**) hyphen exclamation mark question mark brackets inverted commas capitals

4.6 1 converse   2 lavatory   3 man   4 tolerate   5 violin

4.7 1 terrorist   2 skinny   3 wordy   4 mean   5 cunning   6 extravagant

4.8 *Some possible answers:*

countable *or* abstract noun; unfamiliar *or* polysyllabic word;
colloquial expression *or* colloquial language.

4.9 ( ) brackets   ? question mark   ' apostrophe
    ; semi-colon   – dash   - hyphen
    , comma   " " inverted commas

Unit 5

5.2 1 All the words are possible. Some people feel that **sofa** and **couch** are a bit 'lower class', and that **settee** is the so-called 'refined, middle-class' word. **Divan** could also be used, but its normal British English meaning is a kind of bed with a very thick base. It can also, less commonly, mean a kind of sofa with no back or arms.

2 **Luxury** most typically collocates with **yacht**, though **ketch** (a double-masted sailing ship) would also be possible. A **dinghy** is a very small, open boat, hardly suitable for going around the world. **Sailing boat** sounds just too general here, since it covers all types of boats with sails.

3 **Wellingtons** is the most likely word, since they are rubber boots designed to keep the water out. **Boots** are any kind of high-sided footwear. **Bootees** suggests a kind of ankle-length shoe, fairly lightweight, usually with fur inside for cold weather, often referring to what babies wear.

4 **Dinghy** would be a good word here (see 2 above), though **sailing boat** would also fit, as it's quite general.

5.3 1 3   2 1.1   3 4   4 1.1

5.4 1 education   2 passport   3 length   4 liberty   5 revision   6 brother

There is no key for Unit 6.

Unit 7

7.1 1 **kip** – to sleep / have a sleep
2 **a pal** – a friend; nowadays, **mate** is perhaps the most common informal word for 'friend' in British English
3 **a chap** – a man; **chap** does have associations of being a middle-class word and perhaps not used so much by young people
4 **cheerio** – goodbye; **bye** and **ta-ta** (pron: /tə tɑː/) are also common, **ta-ta** being the most informal
5 **swot** – study hard, e.g. for an exam; you can call someone a **swot** too
6 **ta** – thank you, or (slightly less formal) thanks
7 **brainy** – clever / intelligent; intelligent is the most formal.

7.2 *Suggested changes:*
JIM: Annie, can you lend me five **quid**?
ANNIE: What for?
JIM: Well, I've **got** to go and **see** my mum and dad, and my **bike's** not working, so I'll have to **take/get a taxi**.
ANNIE: Can't you **phone/ring/call** them and say you can't come?
JIM: Well, I could, except I want to go because they always have lots of food, and the **fridge** at our flat (or 'our place', which is a common way of talking about your house/flat) is empty, as usual.
ANNIE: Can't you **get the / go by tube**?
JIM: Erm…
ANNIE: Anyway, the answer's no.

For the sake of practice, we have created here a dialogue that probably has more of a concentration of informal words than would occur in reality. Don't forget the advice given at the beginning of the unit about using too much informal language.

7.3 1 A teenage boy would probably say a **date** (or '**Fancy going out?**'), not an **appointment** in this situation; **appointment** is for business contexts; too formal.
2 **Offspring**, if the parent used it, would be heard as humorous, certainly not the normal word for this situation; **children** or **kids** (informal) would be the normal words. **Offspring** would be suitable for legal contexts, religious language and serious history books/biographies; too formal.
3 As with 2, this would be heard as humorous/mock-serious. Most people would say 'I never drink' or 'I never touch alcohol' in this situation. **Alcoholic beverages** is very formal/legalistic and you might see it on, e.g. a notice prohibiting drinking in a particular place or the sale of drink at particular times; too formal.

4 Probably acceptable. People who work together or share an institutional context often develop a high degree of acceptable informality. Such is often the case in British universities and colleges. In such institutional settings, clippings and other short forms are widely used by everyone and operate as a sort of slang among the people involved, and are not heard as disrespectful.

5 The use of **ads** here sounds out of place compared with the formal tone of the rest of the letter ('Dear Sir/Madam... I should like to enquire... etc.'), so it is too informal. Over the phone, however, the same person might well say 'Could you tell me how much it'd cost to put an ad in your paper?' in order to create a friendly relationship with the person answering the call.

7.4 1 in motion   3 a) to regret   b) to purchase   c) to address
2 to alight   4 Hi! Bye!

7.5 *Suggested versions:*

1 Children shouldn't / are asked not to drop rubbish/litter in the play-area.
2 You can only get your expenses/money back if you've got / if you hand in receipts with the date on.

Unit 8

8.1 1 windscreen wiper(s)   5 payee
2 classical violinist   6 dishwasher (normally written as one word)
3 professional photographer   7 kidney donor
 (pron: pho<u>tog</u>rapher)   8 addressee
4 amateur actor

8.2 1 stapler   3 can-opener (or tin-opener)   5 coat-hanger
2 grinder   4 nail-clipper

8.4 1 a cooker – a thing (the stove on which you cook); the person who cooks is a **cook**.

2 a typewriter – a thing (machine for typing); the person is a **typist**.

3 a ticket-holder – person or thing; a person who has a ticket, e.g. for a concert, or a kind of wallet for holding tickets, e.g. a season ticket for the train/bus.

4 a record player – a thing (machine for playing records).

5 a cleaner – person or thing; person who cleans, e.g. in an office or other place of work; a substance or instrument for cleaning, e.g. 'this cleaner will get the grease off your oven'.

6 a smoker – person or thing; a person who smokes; a short name for a seat in the smoking area of a plane or train (or the whole smoking compartment on a train).

7 a drinker – person (someone who drinks alcohol, usually regularly or in large quantities).

8.5 1 forgivable   2 admission   3 laziness   4 productive   5 readable

8.7 1 neighbourhood – it is a place (an area); all the others refer to human relationships.

2 step-ladder – all the others means 'thing for doing x', e.g. hair-restorer restores your hair, a plant-holder holds a plant, etc.

3 compliment – all the others are verb + 'ment', e.g. appoint + ment. There is no verb 'compli'.

4 handful – all the others are adjectives; **handful** is a noun, meaning a pile of something about as big as you can hold in your hands, e.g. a handful of sand.

5 worship – all the others are kinds of human relationships; **Worship** refers to paying tribute to a God, or, figuratively, as a verb, to loving someone very very much, e.g. 'he worships his teacher'.

Unit 9

9.1
1 indiscreet 4 irrelevant 7 irresponsible 10 intolerant
2 insensitive 5 disobedient 8 ungrateful
3 unconvincing 6 inefficient 9 disloyal

9.2
1 unmarried 3 illiterate 5 impartial
2 inedible 4 unemployed 6 irreplaceable

9.3
1 unwrapping 3 disprove 5 to unload
2 disagree 4 unveiled 6 disconnected

9.4
1 microwave 3 multi-national 5 postgraduate
2 antibiotic 4 on auto-pilot 6 subway

9.5
1 mispronouncing 3 post-dated his cheque 5 rewrite it
2 are overworked but underpaid 4 her ex-husband

9.6 *Other examples:*

prefix	examples	prefix	examples
anti	anti-government antiseptic	over	overrun overcharge
auto	autocue automobile	post	post-colonial post-industrial
bi	bi-plane bi-focals	pro	pro-Iranian pro-nuclear
ex	ex-flatmate ex-partner	pseudo	pseudo-democracy pseudo-liberal
ex	express extort	re	rephrase redefine
micro	micro-chip microprocessor	semi	semi-literate semi-conscious
mis	misspell mislead	sub	sub-editor sub-human
mono	monorail monosyllable	under	underachieve underweight
multi	multi-cultural multi-faceted		

Unit 10

10.1 The stress is on the underlined syllable in each of the words in the table.

verb	person noun	adjective	abstract noun
con<u>vert</u>	<u>con</u>vert	con<u>vert</u>ed	con<u>ver</u>sion
pro<u>duce</u>	pro<u>du</u>cer	pro<u>duc</u>tive	pro<u>duc</u>tion, <u>pro</u>duce, <u>prod</u>uct, produc<u>tiv</u>ity
con<u>duct</u>	con<u>duc</u>tor	con<u>du</u>cive	<u>con</u>duct, con<u>duc</u>tion
im<u>press</u>	–	im<u>press</u>ive	im<u>press</u>ion
sup<u>port</u>	sup<u>por</u>ter	sup<u>por</u>tive	sup<u>port</u>
im<u>pose</u>	–	im<u>pos</u>ing	impo<u>si</u>tion

10.2
1 oppressive 3 advertisements 5 inspector(s) 7 to advertise
2 was deported 4 introduce 6 introductory 8 composed

10.3 1 It isn't easy to find synonyms for these words; the meaning is as follows: 'She spends a lot of time thinking about her own thoughts and feelings and so does he; he's quite shy and not very talkative.'

2 argue against   6 made public
3 training   7 hold down
4 hold back   8 put...into an appropriate form
5 work out

10.4 *Some possibilities:*

spect – circumspect behaviour; a retrospective exhibition; a fresh perspective.
vert – an extroverted person; inverted commas; to pervert the innocent.
port – a railway porter; reported speech; transportation costs.
duc, duct – to reduce taxes, to induce labour; a railway viaduct.
press – blood pressure; compressed air; an original expression.
pose, pone – to pose for a photograph; to suppose something to be true; to repose peacefully.

10.5 support – hold up   postpone – put off   oppose – go against   inspect – look at
reduce – cut down   deposit – put down   divert – turn away

Unit 11

11.1
1 affection   5 amusement   9 attentiveness   13 equality
2 excitement   6 grace   10 happiness   14 hope
3 kindness   7 originality   11 popularity   15 resentment
4 security   8 stupidity   12 weakness   16 wisdom

11.2 *Some possible answers:*

There are many more possibilities for the B suffixes but not many for the C ones.

B *-ment* (un)employment   entertainment   involvement   requirement
   -ion diversion   attraction   direction   rejection
   -ness awkwardness   foolishness   loveliness   madness
   -ity brutality   familiarity   productivity   superiority

C *-dom* dukedom   earldom
   -ship citizenship   chairmanship   sponsorship   championship
   -th growth   wealth   stealth
   -hood babyhood   nationhood

11.3
1 hostility or aggressiveness   5 replacement   9 sight
2 amazement   6 stardom   10 freedom
3 curiosity   7 reduction   11 rage
4 brotherhood   8 neighbourhood   12 prosperity

11.4

abstract noun	adjective	verb	adverb
contentment	content(ed)	to content	contentedly
argument	argumentative	to argue	arguably
emptiness	empty	to empty	emptily
intensity	intense	to intensify	intensely
satisfaction	satisfied, satisfactory	to satisfy	satisfactorily
sentiment	sentimental	to sentimentalise	sentimentally
strength	strong	to strengthen	strongly

11.5 1 Jealousy 2 Happiness 3 Hope 4 Love 5 permanence; beauty
('Coke' in question 2 means the fuel produced while taking gas from coal. A migraine is a very bad headache.)

11.6 How you answer this question is a matter of your own originality. Here are some 'real' quotations about these abstract nouns, however:

1 Freedom is an indivisible word. If we want to enjoy it, and to fight for it, we must be prepared to extend it to everyone.

2 Friendship is unnecessary, like philosophy, like art... It has no survival value; rather it is one of those things that gives value to survival.

3 Life is a foreign language; all men mispronounce it.

4 Four be the things I'd be better without:
Love, curiosity, freckles and doubt.

5 Where there is no imagination, there is no horror.

Unit 12

Note that when you are looking compound adjectives up in the dictionary, you may sometimes find the word listed under its second element rather than its first. Sometimes, in some dictionaries, the word will not be listed at all if the meaning is absolutely clear from an understanding of the two elements.

Notice that the descriptions of Tom and Melissa on the left-hand page are light-hearted and far-fetched! They are not examples of good style as such long lists of adjectives would be inappropriate in a normal composition.

12.1 *Some possible answers:*

1	brown	3	broad	5	British	7	hot
	bright-eyed		narrow-minded		ready-made		pig-headed
	wide		single		home		bald
2	fool	4	polo	6	tax	8	kind
	dust-proof		low-necked		problem-free		soft-hearted
	fire		high		care		hard

12.2 Here is one possible way of categorising the words. There will be many other ways of categorising them. What is important is not how you categorise them but the process of doing the exercise itself. The process should help you to learn the words.

Words connected with money: cut-price duty-free interest-free
Words connected with comfort, safety and convenience: air-conditioned drip-dry hand-made remote-controlled sugar-free bullet-proof
Words connected with time: last-minute long-standing off-peak part-time record-breaking time-consuming
Words often connected with travelling: long-distance second-class
Words often used to describe people: so-called world-famous
Odd man out: top-secret!

12.3 *Some examples:*

self-assured *P*   self-satisfied *N*   self-confident *P*   self-conscious *N*
self-seeking *N*   self-possessed *P*   self-indulgent *N*   self-employed *neutral*
self-evident *neutral*   self-sufficient *neutral*   self-willed *N*   self-effacing *N*

12.4 1 No, she's long-sighted.   4 No, they're flat-heeled/low-heeled.
2 No, he's hard-up (or badly-off).   5 No, it's hand-made.
3 No, he's badly-behaved.   6 No, in the north-west.

12.5 *Some possible answers:*

air-conditioned car/room
bullet-proof car/vest
cut-price clothes/sale
drip-dry shirt/sheets
duty-free perfume/cigarettes
hand-made clothes/chocolates
interest-free credit/loan
last-minute preparations/arrival
long-distance train/runner
long-standing arrangement/relationship

off-peak travel/viewing
part-time work/job
record-breaking performance/jump
remote-controlled TV/toy
second-class ticket/citizen
so-called expert/specialist
sugar-free diet/coca cola
time-consuming work/preparations
top-secret information/file
world-famous film star/novelist

12.6   1 up   2 on   3 back   4 off   5 of   6 out

Unit 13

13.1   Here are words which would fit appropriately into the networks suggested.

money	health	social problems
luxury goods	blood donor	race relations
book token	heart attack	human rights
credit card	contact lens	arms race
burglar alarm	birth control	brain drain
income tax	blood pressure	death penalty
mail order	hay fever	generation gap
pocket money	food poisoning	greenhouse effect
	junk food	welfare state
		air traffic control

13.2   Blood pressure and blood donor; air traffic control and birth control.

Here are some possible answers for this question. There are some other possibilities also. Check with a dictionary or a teacher if you are not sure whether your answers are correct or not.

1 record token
2 junk mail
3 sound bite
4 blood ties

5 teapot
6 mother country
7 inheritance tax
8 word-processing

9 level-crossing
10 footlights
11 food-processor
12 rat-race

13.3
1 pedestrian crossing
2 the greenhouse effect
3 hay fever

4 the arms race
5 air traffic control
6 contact lens

7 the death penalty
8 package holiday
9 handcuffs

13.4 *Suggested sentences:*

1 'I always like getting one of these so that I can choose the music I like myself.' (a record token)
2 'I get an enormous amount through the post these days.' (junk mail)
3 'They say these are thicker than water.' (blood ties)
4 'I can't understand how people find sport in killing.' (blood sports)
5 'He couldn't stand it any longer and went to be self-sufficient on a Scottish island.' (the rat-race)
6 'They had a huge amount to pay after their father died.' (inheritance tax)
7 'It is so much more efficient than using a typewriter.' (word-processing)

Unit 14

14.1 1 queue of traffic 3 attempt to conceal information 5 delay to traffic
2 burglaries 4 obstacle in the way of progress 6 escape

14.2 *Some possible answers:*

1 radioactive fallout 5 final output (or outcome)
2 nervous breakdown 6 sales outlets
3 computer printout 7 positive feedback
4 annual turnover 8 drastic cutbacks

14.3 1 takeover 3 walkout 5 BREAK-OUT 7 outbreak
2 shake-up 4 input 6 check-out 8 pin-ups

14.4 1 write 3 work; press 5 clear 7 turn
2 hand 4 write 6 hold 8 lie

14.5 1 **Outlook** means prospect whereas a **look-out** is a person watching out for an enemy or danger.

2 **Set-up** means organisation whereas **upset** means disturbance.

3 **Outlet** means place where something is released whereas **let-out** means way of escaping from a difficult situation.

4 **Outlay** means amount of money spent on something whereas **layout** means the way something is arranged, e.g. the **layout** of a page or a room.

Unit 15

15.2 *Possible answers:*
inventions network: saxophone biro braille
(**watt** might also fit here as might some of the clothes illustrated)

politics network: machiavellian boycott pamphlet

15.3 1 wellingtons (wellies); mackintosh (mac) 4 boycott
2 saxophone 5 cashmere or angora
3 bedlam

15.4 *Some possible answers:*

1 rowdy, terrible 3 large, wide-brimmed 5 black, lycra
2 political, free 4 dark-eyed, wild 6 red, chewed

15.5 1 suede boots/jacket 3 spartan furnishings/atmosphere
2 machiavellian policy/plan 4 tawdry goods/clothes

15.6 *Some possible endings for the sentences:*

1 ...to her every whim. 4 ...the Olympic Games.
2 ...the wind was getting cooler. 5 ...very hot to wear.
3 ...round the field.

15.7 1 A **herculean effort** is a major effort, one that demands a lot of strength and the word **herculean** comes from the name of the mythical Greek hero, Hercules, who was famed for his strength.

2 A **platonic friendship** is one between a man and a woman based on affection but with no sexual element (from the name of the Greek philosopher, Plato).

→

3 A **teddy bear**, the name given to the soft stuffed bear which is a popular child's toy, comes from Theodore Roosevelt, the American president. A hunter of bears, Roosevelt was once said to have saved a young bear cub. The story was illustrated by a cartoon in the Washington Post and the toy bears drew their name from the pet form of Theodore.

4 A **jersey**, meaning sweater or jumper, comes from the name of one of the Channel Islands, Jersey, well-known for its knitting.

5 **Caesarean section** is a surgical operation to remove a baby from its mother's womb. The name originates from the name of the Roman Emperor, Julius Caesar, who was reputedly born in this way.

6 **July**, the month, is also named after Julius Caesar.

7 **A bottle of champagne** is named after Champagne, the region of France where this particular type of sparkling wine is made.

8 An **atlas** or book of maps is named after the Greek mythological Titan, Atlas, who as a punishment for attempting to overthrow Zeus was condemned to support the world on his shoulders. One of the first atlases, that produced by Mercator in the late 16th Century, had a picture of Atlas on its cover.

9 Like many other plants – camellia, dahlia, freesia, begonia and so on – **magnolia** takes its name from a person. **Magnolia** comes from the French botanist, Pierre Magnol, who devised a system of classifying plants.

Unit 16

16.3   *Some words which fit most obviously into the networks suggested:*

food	politics	the arts	animals
yoghurt	embargo	avant-garde	mosquito
cuisine	junta	piano	poodle
gateau	guerrilla	soprano	dachshund
spaghetti	coup	ballerina	rottweiler
frankfurter	ombudsman	easel	mammoth
hamburger	perestroika	balalaika	lemming
marmalade			dodo
delicatessen			lasso
bistro			jackal
aubergine			
sauté			
sherbet			

16.4   *Other networks could include:*

clothes: anorak   yashmak   caftan   shawl
things in the house: futon   mattress   alcove   carafe   duvet   bidet   patio
sports and hobbies: origami   judo   karate   caravan   kayak   ski   slalom   yacht   easel
     waltz   casino   snorkel
geographical features: fjord   floe   tundra   steppe

16.5   1 right-wing coup   7 total embargo
2 prima ballerina   8 long-standing vendetta
3 strawberry yoghurt   9 noisy kindergarten
4 ice floe   10 cosy duvet
5 Chinese cuisine   11 all-night casino
6 long-sleeved caftan

16.6
1 practise karate
2 paddle a kayak
3 wear mufti
4 place an embargo
5 be a guerrilla
6 live in a cul de sac
7 attempt a coup
8 throw confetti
9 have a siesta
10 go on / take a cruise
11 take/have a sauna
12 attend/give/hold a seminar

16.7 macho man/behaviour/clothes; avant-garde art/design/furniture

Unit 17

17.2 *Some possible answers:*

gr: **grizzle** and **grudge**, both have rather unpleasant meanings – **grizzle** is to cry because of bad temper rather than pain or discomfort and **grudge** is to be unwilling to give or do something.

cl: **clap** or **clatter**, both represent quite sharp sounds – **clap** is to applaud with your hands and **clatter** is to make a long, continuous resounding noise like hard metallic things falling on a hard surface.

sp: **spatter** or **spill** both have an association with liquid or powder – **spatter** means to splash or scatter in drips, **spill** means to knock over something liquid.

wh: **whirl** and **whisk** both have associations with the movement of air – **whirl** means to move quickly round and round and **whisk** means move or sweep quickly through the air.

17.3
1 click
2 whirred
3 sizzling
4 clinked
5 crash
6 groaned
7 splashing
8 trickling

17.4
1 spit (spat, spat)
2 grumpy
3 spit (a spit is a long, thin metal spike on which meat is put for roasting)

17.5
1 splosh – colloquial form of splash
2 gargle – wash the throat with liquid kept moving by a stream of breath
3 rustle – make a gentle light sound like dry leaves in the wind or silk clothes moving
4 mumble – speak softly and indistinctly
5 creaks – make a sound like that of an unoiled door hinge
6 whacked – hit hard

17.6
1 a gash in someone's arm
2 a referee whistling
3 someone bashing something
4 someone spraying their hair
5 someone sprinkling sugar on a cake
6 water spurting out of the ground

17.7 schoolchildren giggle   fire crackles   the bell on a cat's collar tinkles
a bad-tempered person or dog growls   a bored child wriggles   a churchbell clangs
a steam train whistles   a prisoner's chain clanks   someone with asthma wheezes

Unit 18

18.1
1 They sang a psalm to honour the memory of the world-famous psychologist as she was laid to rest in the family tomb. (Note that although the 'r' in 'world' is not really pronounced, in Standard British English, it affects the way the word is pronounced.)
2 The psychiatrist was knifed in the knee as he was walking home.
3 He should have whistled as he fastened his sword to his belt. (Note that the 'h' in 'have' is not really pronounced when following an auxiliary verb as in this sentence and the next one.)
4 You could have left me half the Christmas cake on Wednesday.

18.2 The odd one out appears first.

1 worry /ʌ/   sorry, lorry /ɒ/   5 could /ʊ/   doubt, shout /aʊ/
2 word /ɜː/   sword, cord /ɔː/   6 plough /aʊ/   rough, tough /ʌ/
3 dome /əʊ/   come, some /ʌ/   7 wand /ɒ/   land, sand /æ/
4 plead /iː/   head, tread /e/   8 root /uː/   soot, foot /ʊ/

18.3 1 cup   2 allow   3 now   4 threw   5 off   6 go

18.4
1 <u>transfer</u>; trans<u>fer</u>ring   5 in<u>creased</u>; <u>decrease</u>
2 sus<u>pected</u>; <u>suspect</u>   6 <u>permit</u>; per<u>mits</u>
3 con<u>flicting</u>; <u>conflict</u>   7 <u>record</u>; re<u>cord</u>
4 <u>upset</u>; up<u>set</u>   8 <u>conduct</u>; con<u>ducting</u>

18.5
1 muscle   3 handkerchief   5 subtle   7 height
2 catastrophe   4 chemical   6 receipt   8 recipe

18.6
1 ph<u>o</u>t<u>o</u>graph, phot<u>o</u>graphy, phot<u>o</u>grapher, photo<u>gra</u>phically
2 <u>te</u>lephone, tel<u>e</u>ph<u>o</u>nist
3 zo<u>o</u>logy, zo<u>o</u>logist, zo<u>o</u>logical
4 <u>ari</u>thmetic, arith<u>me</u>tical, arith<u>me</u>tician
5 psy<u>cho</u>logy, psy<u>cho</u>logist, psycho<u>lo</u>gical
6 psy<u>chia</u>try, psychi<u>a</u>tric, psy<u>chia</u>trist

18.7 Keep this question in mind as you continue with your English studies. Whenever you come across a word whose pronunciation seems strange, write it down with its phonetic transcription too.

Unit 19

19.1
1 The girl I <u>live</u> (give) with knows a good pub with <u>live</u> (dive) music.
2 The main <u>house</u> (mouse) <u>houses</u> (rouse) a collection of rare stamps.
3 They <u>bathed</u> (path) the children after they had <u>bathed</u> (lathe) in the sea.
4 You <u>sow</u> (glow) the seeds while I feed the <u>sow</u>. (cow)
5 The violinist in the <u>bow</u> (flow) tie made a <u>bow</u>. (allow)
6 He's the <u>lead</u> (deed) singer in the group '<u>Lead</u> (head) piping'.
7 What a <u>row</u> (plough) from the last house in the <u>row</u>! (though)
8 Does he still suffer from his war <u>wound</u>? (mooned)
9 I <u>wound</u> (round) the rope around the tree to strengthen it against the gale.
10 It's quite hard to <u>wind</u> (find) in the sails in this <u>wind</u>. (tinned)

19.2
1 waste   3 pane   5 allowed   7 through; phase
2 sole   4 heir   6 practise   8 peel

19.3 *Possible answers:*

1 **They're** going to take **their** aunt to have dinner **there** this evening.
2 **It's** the first time the car has left **its** garage this year.
3 Let's **practise** with these grammar exercises first and then do some vocabulary **practice**.
4 It's **great** to see such a lovely fire burning in the **grate**.
5 Don't **whine** so much, just because the **wine's** finished.
6 He has **sought** a job of this **sort** for ages.
7 The archaeological **site** was a marvellous **sight** at sunset.
8 Let us **pray** that we may never be **prey** to evil thoughts.
9 Although she was a little **hoarse**, it did not put her off **horse** riding in the snow.
10 The beautiful sight of the moon's **rays** reflected in the lake did a great deal to **raise** her spirits.

Note: Most sentences in 'real' English avoid using homophones as they are confusing.

19.4   1   You're too young to smoke.
This is a play on words on the two meanings of **smoke** – to smoke a cigarette and a fire or chimney smokes (i.e give out smoke).

2   I think I'm going down with something.
This is a play on words on two meanings of **going down**. There is the literal meaning go down (descend) and then there is the expression, 'go down with an illness', which means be at the start of an attack of that illness.

3   Let's play draughts.
This is a play on words on the two meanings of **draughts**. One is the game played with round counters and a chess board and the other is a current of air as in 'There's a terrible draught coming from under the door'.

4   He wanted to draw the curtains.
This is a play on words on two meanings of **draw**. The first means make a picture and the second means pull.

5   Because it's full of dates.
This is a play on words on the two meanings of **dates**. One refers to 1066, 1892 and all that and the other to a sweet fruit coming from a kind of palm tree or to an evening spent together by two people (usually romantic).

6   A drum takes a lot of beating.
This is a play on words on two meanings of **beating**. A drummer beats a drum. There is also an expression, 'takes a lot of beating' which means 'is hard to improve on'.

7   Because it's got a tender behind.
This is a play on words on two meanings of two words – **tender** and **behind**. **Tender** can mean either susceptible to pain, or a wagon for fuel and water behind a steam locomotive. **Behind** is normally, of course, a preposition but it can also be an informal noun meaning 'bottom', as in the part of the body that a person sits on.

8   A nervous wreck.
A **wreck** is a boat or ship that, for example, hits a rock and sinks to the bottom of the sea. A **nervous wreck**, however, is an expression commonly used to describe someone who is extremely nervous.

Unit 20

20.1
1 Prior	3 By the time	5 Previously/Earlier	7 When/Once/After
2 Till then	4 While/When	6 As soon as	8 The moment/minute

Other possible sentences:

While she was in Paris, she missed home a lot.
She went to the theatre **after** she'd been to the Pompidou Centre.
While driving home from Glasgow, she saw a bad accident on the motorway.
Prior to going on to Glasgow, she was in Manchester.

20.2   *Possible answers:*

1   ... I usually dream a lot.
2   ... I usually feel guilty and go on a diet for a while.
3   ... look at the clock to see what time it is.
4   ... lived in the same house.
5   ... reading a story.
6   ... go back home and look for a job.
7   ... double-check that everything is booked.
8   ... upset and want to make it up as soon as possible.

Unit 21

21.1 1 **as long as / providing / provided that** are all okay; **on condition that** is fine too, and sounds a little stronger.

2 **In case of**; you can also say **In the event of**, which is often seen in notices and regulations.

3 **Unless**

4 Since this is legal/official language **on condition that** would be very suitable, or **providing / provided that**; **so long as** is also possible, but **as long as** sounds just a little too informal.

5 **Supposing** or **What if** (less tentative, more direct).

21.2 *Suggested sentences:*

1 You cannot enter unless you have an Entry Visa. *or* You may enter providing / provided that you have an Entry Visa.

2 You may go on to university as long as you get 70% or more in the exam. *or* Unless you get 70%, you cannot go on to university.

3 You can't come in unless you're over 18. *or* You may enter the club providing you are over 18.

4 Visitors may enter the mosque on condition that they remove their shoes. *or* You may go in as long as you take off your shoes.

21.3 1 No matter where she goes, she always takes that dog of hers.

2 If anyone rings, I don't want to speak to them, whoever it is.

3 Whatever I do, I always seem to do the wrong thing.

4 It'll probably have meat in it, no matter which dish you choose. They don't cater for non-meat eaters here.

5 However I do it, that recipe never seems to work.

21.4 *Some possible answers:*

1 For the authors of this book, who are teachers, the prerequisites are a degree and a teaching qualification.

2 Many people might move if they were offered a good job in another part of the country, or if a motorway was going to be built at the bottom of their garden!

3 In Britain, the normal entry requirements are A-level exam passes in relevant subjects. (A-levels are exams taken at 18 years old.)

4 For most people it would be a good idea to make the condition that the person should pay for any breakages, keep the place clean and perhaps pay coal/gas/oil/electricity and phone bills.

Unit 22

22.1 *Suggested answers:*

1 The announcement **provoked/generated** a strong attack from the opposition.

2 The new Act of Parliament has **brought about / led to** great changes in industry.

3 The train crash was **caused by / due to** a signalling fault.

4 A violent storm **caused** the wall to collapse. *or* **Owing to** a violent storm, the wall collapsed.

5 The food shortages **sparked off** riots in several cities.

6 The food shortages **stemmed from / arose out of** poor management of the economy.

22.2 1 The reason I didn't contact you was (because) I'd lost your phone number. *or* My reason for not contacting you was... (this is also acceptable, but sounds more formal).

2 I will not sign, on the grounds that this contract is illegal.

3 The aim of the new law the government passed was to control prices. *or* The government passed a new law with the aim of / with a view to controlling prices.

4 I wonder what her motives were in sending everyone flowers.

5 The high salary prompted her to apply for the job.

22.3 *Possible answers:*

1 There were awful blizzards, which caused the road to be blocked.
2 Owing to the fact that the performance was cancelled, everyone got a refund.
3 The service was terribly slow. Consequently, all the customers got angry.
4 We missed the last bus. As a result we had to walk home.

22.4 1 for   2 of   3 with; of   4 in   5 out of   6 with; to   7 given; to

Unit 23

23.1 *Suggested answers:*

1 I accept (or more formal: I acknowledge) that you weren't solely to blame, but you must take *some* responsibility. (**Accept** and **acknowledge** are most suitable here since the speaker is prepared to agree with one aspect but wants to go on to make another point to support his/her case.)
2 Okay, I admit I was wrong, you were right; he *is* a nice guy. (This seems to be a situation where somebody is accusing someone or trying to get them to say they were wrong. **Admit** is ideal in this case.)
3 The company acknowledges that you have suffered some delay, but we do not accept liability. (**Acknowledge** is perhaps best here; it is often used in formal, legalistic situations like this because it simply says 'We understand your message, but we do *not* necessarily accept any blame/responsibility'; **admit** might suggest the company *does* accept legal responsibility; **accept** is also possible though less formal.)
4 She accepted / conceded that we had done all we could, but she was still not content. (**Concede** usually suggests an argument or debate where people might 'give' small points to one another while still holding on to their basic position, and would seem to be a likely choice here; **concede** here suggests she did not really want to say it.)

23.2 *Possible answers:*

2 The house itself is rather small.
3 Jim: Isn't the *Plaza* rather expensive?
4 In most of the rest of Europe, the traffic drives on the right. (Ireland also drives on the left.)
5 I'm not at all hungry, thanks.

23.3

Across	Down
1 yawning	2 apart
3 world	4 divide
5 huge	6 gap
7 poles	

Possible comments using the phrases:

1 There's a great divide between those who believe in the nuclear deterrent, and those who believe in world disarmament.
2 There's a huge discrepancy between what she says and what she does.
3 Jim and Sandra are poles apart when it comes to believing in God.
4 There's a world of difference between being a student and being a teacher.

23.4 *Suggested answers:*

1 that's all well and good   3 for all that
2 After all   4 It's all very well

23.5 1 on the contrary (it's *not* true that I'm worried)
2 on the other hand (it *is* true that it's expensive)

Unit 24

24.1   *Suggested answers:*
1   Further to
2   In addition to / As well as / Apart from / Besides
3   etc. / and so on
4   in addition to / as well as / apart from / besides
5   Furthermore / Moreover / Likewise

Comments: In (2) and (4), the choice is quite wide, but, depending on which one she chooses for (2), the writer would probably then choose a different one, to avoid repeating herself, for (4).

In (5), if she wanted to use **what's more**, the writer would probably write it in full as **what is more**, so as not to sound too informal. However, **what's more / what is more** can often sound a little abrupt and argumentative (as if you're trying very hard to convince the reader) and might sound just a bit too strong here.

In (3), **etc.** is slightly more formal than **and so on**, and the writer may well wish to avoid sounding too informal.

In (5), **furthermore / moreover** add her previous experience on to the rest; **likewise** not only adds the information but suggests it is of quite equal value to the other experience she has mentioned. **Equally** would not be suitable here, as it is best used when arguing points (trying to convince someone of the equal value of a point added on to other points).

24.2   1   Physical labour can exhaust the body very quickly. Equally, excessive study can rapidly reduce mental powers.
2   My cousin turned up, along with some schoolmates of his.
3   As well as owning a big chemical factory, he runs a massive oil business in the USA. *or* He owns a big chemical factory as well as running a massive oil business in the USA.
4   She was my teacher and she was a good friend into the bargain.
5   In addition to being their scientific adviser, I also act as consultant to the Managing Director.

24.3   1   I work part-time as well as **being** a student, so I have a busy life.
2   Besides **having** a good job, my ambition is to meet someone nice to share my life with.
3   Alongside **my** many other responsibilities, I now have to be in charge of staff training.
4   In addition **to** a degree, *or* In addition **to having** a degree, she also has a diploma.
5   My father won't agree. **Likewise**, my mother's sure to find something to object to.
6   She is a good footballer and she's a good athlete **to boot.**
7   He said he'd have to first consider the organisation, then the system, then the finance **and so on and so forth.**

24.4   1   to boot   2   into the bargain   3   plus (+)   4   on top of (all) that

Unit 25

25.1   1 fact   2 issue   3 belief   4 problem   5 evaluation   6 view

25.2   1   issue (best here because it is something everyone is debating and disagreeing on; **question** and **problem** are also okay)
2   problem/matter; **crisis** if it is really serious.
3   question (**mystery** would also be possible)
4   topic
5   approach/response/solution/answer

25.3 1 Situation in Sahel worsening daily
2 Scientist rejects claims over fast food
3 Prime Minister sets out views on European union
4 New approach to cancer treatment
5 Solution to age-old mystery in Kenya
6 New argument over economic recession

Unit 26

26.1 1 no article   2 no article   3 an   4 no article   5 no article
6 no article; if you said **a film** here it would sound as if you mean one film, and then suddenly change your mind and decide to buy five rolls.
7 no article in both cases

26.2 *Uncountables:* clothing   information   advice   travel   work   baggage
Countables: garment   fact   tip   trip   job   case

26.3 *Some uncountable items you might put into your suitcase:*

soap   toothpaste   make-up   underwear   clothing   writing-paper   film   medicine

26.4 1 We had such terrible weather that we left the camp-site and got accommodation in town instead.
2 In the North of England, most houses are made of stone, but in the South, brick is more common.
3 I love antique furniture, but I would need advice from a specialist before I bought any. My knowledge in that area is very poor.
4 Her research is definitely making great progress these days. She has done a lot of original work recently.

26.5 *Possible answers:*

A soldier needs a lot of courage, determination, stamina, loyalty and a lot of training.

A nurse needs a lot of patience and goodwill. A bit of charm also helps, and a lot of commitment and training is needed.

A teacher needs great patience, a lot of energy, a bit of creativity, intelligence and some training.

An explorer needs a lot of stamina, courage and determination, as well as energy.

An actor needs a lot of creativity and talent, and some training.

An athlete needs great stamina and determination, and a lot of commitment.

A writer needs a lot of creativity, talent and a bit of intelligence.

A surgeon needs experience, patience and a lot of training.

A receptionist needs charm, goodwill, reliability and energy.

26.6 Could I have **some** vinegar?   Could I have **some** sellotape?
Could I have **a** duster?   Could I have **a** tea-bag?
Could I have **a** needle?   Could I have **some** polish?
Could I have **some** thread?

Unit 27

27.2
1 shears	6 binoculars
2 (weighing) scales	7 pincers/pliers (pliers are usually best for
3 scissors	electrical jobs, e.g. cutting wires/cables)
4 braces	8 handcuffs
5 tweezers	

27.3 knickers   trousers   tights   shorts   dungarees

27.4
1 pyjamas	3 acoustics	5 jodhpurs
2 proceeds	4 whereabouts	6 authorities; goods

27.5   1 trousers   2 billiards   3 scissors   4 dungarees

27.6 I decided that if I wanted to be a pop star I'd have to leave home and get **lodgings** in London. I finally got a room, but it was on the **outskirts** of the city. The owner didn't live on the **premises**, so I could make as much noise as I liked. The **acoustics** in the bathroom **were** fantastic, so I practised there. I made so much noise I almost shook the **foundations**! I went to the **headquarters** of the Musicians' Union, but a guy there said I just didn't have good enough **looks** to be famous. Oh well, never mind!

Unit 28

28.1
1. Yes, most people have a **cloth** somewhere in the kitchen to wipe the work surfaces and in case somebody spills something.
2. It is not likely that most people will have a **wood**. A **wood** is a rather big area of land covered with trees (a small forest).
3. Most people do not keep **iron** (the material) in their homes, but they may have some things made of **iron**, such as a frying pan.
4. A lot of people have a **fish** (or several **fish**) swimming around in a tank in their living room.
5. Most people have **pepper** (together with salt) in their kitchen or dining room.
6. Most homes have **glass** somewhere, usually in the windows.
7. Most people have **paper** somewhere, for writing letters and notes, or for wrapping parcels.
8. You would have a **tape** if you have a tape recorder or a video recorder, and you'd probably keep it near the machine.
9. Only people who consume alcohol would have **drink** in their house; they'd probably keep it in a cocktail cabinet or a cupboard.
10. A **rubber** is quite common. It is used for rubbing out writing done in pencil, and would be kept with pens and pencils.

28.2 *Suggested answers:*
1 Can I borrow an iron?	4 Can I borrow some paper?
2 Can I have some pepper?	5 Can I borrow a rubber?
3 Can I have a chocolate?	6 Can I have a glass?

28.3 *Possible answers:*
1. I rode over some glass. *or* There was glass in the road.
2. No, she's living in a home now.
3. Perhaps he should get a trade, become a carpenter or something.
4. Well, it had a lot of land with it.
5. It's a very famous work of art, a painting.
6. Well, look at the policy; that should tell you everything.

28.4 1 **Some sauce** here means bottled sauce, such as tomato ketchup. **A sauce** means a specially prepared sauce to go with a particular dish, e.g. a white sauce, a cheese sauce.

2 **Plant** means very heavy equipment, e.g. heavy machinery for building. **A plant** means a botanical plant for cultivation. **A plant** can also mean a factory or large installation, e.g. a nuclear power plant – a place where electricity is generated.

3 **Light** (uncountable) usually means light to see by, e.g. electric light or a torch. Used countably in the request 'Can I have / can you give me **a light**?' it usually refers to a match or lighter to light a cigarette or pipe.

Unit 29

29.1 1 swarms 2 shoal 3 gang 4 pack 5 team

29.2 1 swimmers 2 a book 3 a hospital 4 cats 5 pigs

29.3 1 a clump of fir-trees 5 a row of houses
2 a range of mountains 6 a heap of bed-linen
3 a gang of schoolkids 7 a herd of elephants
4 a swarm of midges

29.4 1 There's a stack of tables in the next room.
2 There's a crowd of people waiting outside.
3 The staff are very well-paid.
4 A flock of sheep had escaped from a field.
5 She gave me a set of six sherry glasses.
6 She gave me a bunch of beautiful roses *or* a beautiful bunch of roses.

29.5 a whole **host** of a **barrage** of a **string** of a **series** of

Unit 30

30.1 1 a stroke of luck 5 a flash of lightning
2 a shower of rain 6 a blade of grass
3 an article of clothing 7 an item of news
4 a lump of coal 8 a rumble of thunder

30.2 1 My mother gave me a piece of advice which I have always remembered.
2 Suddenly a gust of wind almost blew him off his feet.
3 We had a spell of terribly windy weather last winter.
4 Would you like another slice of toast?
5 He never does a stroke of work in the house.
6 Let's go into the garden – I need a breath of fresh air.
7 I can give you an important bit of information about that.
8 We could see a cloud of smoke hovering over the city from a long way away.
9 There is an interesting new piece of equipment in that catalogue.
10 I need to get some pieces of furniture for my flat.

30.3 1 emergency 2 health 3 disrepair 4 uncertainty 5 poverty

30.5 *Possible sentences:*

1 We moved over a month ago but we are still in a state of chaos.
2 The company has been going through a state of flux for some months now as two chairmen have died in rapid succession.
3 Everything seems to be in an impossible state of confusion at the moment but I'm sure it'll all be sorted out before the wedding.
4 It is not unusual for job candidates to get themselves into a terrible state of tension before a final interview.

Unit 31

31.1 1 Argentinian   Venezuelan   Costa Rican   Panamanian   Mexican   Peruvian (note the v)   Ecuadorian   Bolivian   Uruguayan   Paraguayan etc.

2 Ukrainian   Serbian   Croatian   Slovenian   Bulgarian   Rumanian   Albanian   Mongolian   Moldavian   Hungarian etc.

3 *Other groupings:* -i adjectives seem to be Middle Eastern or Muslim countries (except Israeli); three of the -ese adjectives are oriental.

31.2 *Possible answers:*

1 Mao-Tse Tung   3 Pope John Paul II   5 U2
2 Nelson or Winnie Mandela   4 Luciano Pavarotti

31.3 1 Panama → Panamanian /ˌpænəˈmeɪnɪən/   4 Jordan → Jordanian /dʒɔːˈdeɪnɪən/
2 Cyprus → Cypriot /ˈsɪprɪət/   5 Egypt → Egyptian /ɪˈdʒɪpʃən/
3 Ghana → Ghanaian /gɑːˈneɪən/   6 Fiji → Fijian /fɪˈdʒiːən/

31.4 1 Madonna to marry a **Frenchman**? Hollywood sensation! (Note how Frenchman is normally written as one word. French woman is usually two words.)
2 **Britons** have highest tax rate in EC
3 **Vietnamese** refugees leave Hong Kong camps
4 Police arrest **Dane** on smuggling charge
5 **Iraqi** delegation meets **Pakistani** President

31.5 1 Malays, Chinese (or various ethnic sub-types), and Indians (many are Tamils and Sikhs).
2 If we take Scandinavia as strictly the geographical peninsula, then Sweden and Norway are the only countries completely in Scandinavia. If we consider it more as a language family, then Denmark and Iceland can be added, and if as a cultural family, then Finland can be added too.
3 Approximate populations are China: 975,000,000; India: 638,000,000; USA: 218,000,000; Indonesia: 141,000,000; Brazil: 116,000,000. The former Soviet Union used to be third, with 260,000,000 (source: *The Times Atlas*)
4 A difficult question! However, most linguists seem to agree on around 5,000 mutually incomprehensible tongues. There are, of course, many many more dialects.
5 Kiribati is an independent country in the middle of the Pacific Ocean. It has only about 57,000 people.
6 Inuit is an Eskimo language, and its speakers may be found in Northern Canada.
7 Languages most widely spoken, in the following order, are Chinese, English, Spanish, Hindi, Arabic (source: *The Cambridge Encyclopedia of Language* CUP)

Unit 32

32.1 Some of these combinations form one solid word and some remain as two words.

1 thunderstorm   3 downpour   5 hailstones   7 gale warning
2 torrential rain   4 heatwave   6 snowdrift

32.2 1 slush   2 sleet   3 frost   4 blizzards   5 snowdrifts   6 thaws   7 melts

32.3 *Possible answers:*

1 There was a heatwave in July. *or* It was scorching/boiling (hot) last month.
2 It was terribly muggy and humid as we worked.
3 It's absolutely stifling today.
4 There was ice/snow/slush on the roads this morning.
5 We had terrible floods that winter.
6 There was a heavy blizzard that night.
7 Do you remember how mild it was that year?
8 There was a very bad drought that summer.
9 Suddenly there was a very strong gust of wind.
10 After the hurricane/gale, the damage was unbelievable.
11 There was a very dense fog that morning.

32.4 1 *bad*: too dry, a drought, or frost   *good*: mild weather just after rain
2 *bad*: cold weather or windy weather or wet weather
   good: warm, mild, or even cool (if it has been a terribly hot day) and preferably dry
3 *bad*: gales, high winds, hurricanes, storms, wet weather, mist/fog
   good: clear, sunny dry, breezy weather
4 *bad*: cold, wet and windy weather or humid, muggy weather   *good*: fine, dry, but not too hot
5 *bad*: wet, windy, snowy weather   *good*: dry, no wind, warm nights
6 *bad*: fog/mist, rain   *good*: clear, dry, sunny weather

Unit 33

33.1 *Suggested answers:*

1 ... the fair, bald guy. *or* straight/curly-haired man.
2 ... scruffy and untidy.
3 ... that slim, dark-haired woman over there.
4 ... unattractive, in fact. (You could also say he/she was 'rather plain' or 'rather ordinary', if you felt they were neither attractive nor unattractive. 'Ugly' is a very strong word indeed, and could be offensive.)
5 ... a teenager/ in her twenties. (Another useful word is 'she's only a youngster', for a person who is a teenager or who is still very young.)

33.2 1 The author who wrote this exercise is tall, with brown hair which is going grey; he's white, in his forties and thinks he's good looking! What about you?

33.3 stocky build   overweight   middle-aged   round-faced   good-looking
long-haired   long-legged (pronounced /'legɪd/)   well-dressed   mixed race
tanned complexion (tanned = brown from the sun)

33.4 *Suggested answers:*

Ian Prowse, height 6ft, thin-faced, dark, curly hair, fair skin.
Sandra King, height 5'4, dark, wavy hair, stocky build, round-faced.
Louise Fox, age 7, Asian, straight, dark hair.
Jake 'Dagger' Flagstone, 6ft, bald, with beard and moustache; muscular build.

Unit 34

34.1 *Opposites:*

1 clever – half-witted	3 rude – courteous	5 generous – tight-fisted
2 extroverted – introverted	4 cruel – kind-hearted	6 unsociable – gregarious

34.2

1 likes	3 likes	5 dislikes	7 dislikes
2 likes	4 dislikes	6 dislikes	8 likes

34.3

1 Di's very stingy.	5 Dick's quite assertive.
2 Molly's usually brusque.	6 I find Dave self-assured.
3 Liz's quite unprincipled.	7 Don't you think Jim's inquiring?
4 Sam can be assertive.	8 Jill is peculiar.

34.4

1 sociable	3 assertive	5 extravagant	7 sensitive
2 pessimistic	4 inquisitive	6 argumentative	

34.5 *Possible questions:*

1 thrifty – Do you always keep old pieces of string in case they come in handy (might be useful)?
2 blunt – If a friend asks you if you like her awful new dress, would you say 'No'?
3 sensible – If you won a lot of money, would you put it in the bank rather than spend it on a luxury you have always wanted?
4 intelligent – Can you give the next letter in this sequence S, M, T, W, T, F? (If you are not sure of the answer, think of the days of the week.)
5 even-tempered – If someone spills soup on some new clothes of yours, do you just sigh and say 'That's life'?
6 original – Do you never wear blue jeans?
7 obstinate – Do you become even more determined to do something, if people try to persuade you not to?

34.6 *Possible answers:*

1 self-confident – She's very-confident; speaking in public never bothers her at all.
  self-centred – I've never met anyone as self-centred as he is; he thinks the world revolves around him alone.
  self-indulgent – Buying a box of chocolates just for yourself is very self-indulgent.

2 bad-tempered – She's always bad-tempered first thing in the morning although she's very good-natured at other times.
  good-tempered – The dog is far too good-tempered to be much use as a watchdog.
  quick-tempered – She's very quick-tempered, she gets very angry at the slightest provocation.

3 narrow-minded – It's surprising how narrow-minded he is given the fact that he is so well-travelled.
  single-minded – He's totally single-minded; he never thinks of anything but work.
  open-minded – I'm sure she won't be shocked; she's far too open-minded.

Unit 35

35.1 1 This is Jack. He's my flatmate. *or* He and I are flatmates.
2 My grandad still writes to his old (*or* former) shipmates.
3 We were classmates in 1978, weren't we? *or* You were a classmate of mine…
4 She's not really a friend, she's just a workmate.

35.2 *Some possible answers:*

John Silver and Lorna Fitt were colleagues in 1984–5.
Josh Yates is Eve Cobb's ex-husband.
Eve Cobb is Josh Yates' ex-wife.
Eve Cobb used to be Bill Nash's flatmate.
Bill Nash and John Silver are colleagues.
Ada Brigg and Nora Costa were Olympic team-mates. (usually written with a hyphen because 'm' is written twice)
Ana Wood is Bill Nash's partner. (or vice-versa)
Nora Costa and Ada Brigg were classmates.
Bill Nash and Eve Cobb were flatmates.
Bill Nash is Eve Cobb's ex-flatmate. (or vice-versa)
Fred Parks and Ada Brigg were once acquaintances.

35.3 1 A teenage music fan might not see eye to eye with his/her parents, might worship or idolise a pop star, might dislike, but might (secretly!) respect a strict teacher, and probably likes or even loves his/her mates.

2 A secretary might like another secretary, might or might not get on well with them, might despise or hate their boss, or perhaps look up to him/her, and might fancy a very attractive workmate, because that person turns them on.

3 A 45-year-old may well dislike teenagers or look down on them, or fancy them if they are attractive; he/she might be repelled by their ex-husband/wife, or might still fancy them.

35.4 1 Jo and Phil don't see eye to eye. *or* … don't get on with each other.
2 I fell out with my parents.
3 We had a quarrel but now we've made it up.
4 Do you think Jim and Nora are having an affair?
5 I get on very well with my colleagues at work.
6 She should learn to respect her elders.
7 Jo's attractive, but her mate just turns me off completely.

Unit 36

36.1 1 a garden shed or a garage
2 a kitchen or dining-room drawer
3 a bathroom cabinet (dental floss is a kind of thread for cleaning between your teeth)
4 a wardrobe
5 a cupboard, or perhaps an attic
6 a kitchen or utility room
7 usually in every room
8 in front of one of the entrance doors (front or back)
9 in the kitchen, probably in a drawer
10 in the loft or in the cellar, or in a shed

36.2 1 attic or loft; in this picture it looks more like a loft, where things are stored.
2 landing
3 the hall
4 utility room
5 pantry or larder

36.3 1 cellar (or perhaps **basement,** though they normally have windows)
2 power point (or you can also say **socket)**
3 coaster
4 bin-liners
5 loft (attic is also possible)
6 shed/garage; terrace/patio (or **balcony;** or **verandah,** if it is covered)
7 landing
8 bungalow

36.5 *Suggested answers:*
1 You could use a grater (or a food-processor).
2 A dust-pan and brush (perhaps followed by a vacuum-cleaner).
3 A table-mat.
4 Use the remote-control.

Unit 37

37.1 *Suggested answers:*
1 My car broke down / wouldn't start.
2 Our washing machine broke down / stopped working.
3 Maybe the door-handle has come off, or something that was held on with a screw or screws.
4 Oh dear! I've cut my finger. It's bleeding.
5 The batteries have run down on my radio/walkman.
6 I seem to have mislaid my glasses / false teeth / slippers, etc.

37.2 1 break down – this means to 'fail mechanically'; **break** and **smash** both mean to break physically.
2 stain – means to 'leave a mark'; **run out** and **stop** can both refer to things failing to work, e.g. the clock has stopped; the batteries have run out.
3 leak – refers to liquids; **come off** and **chip** can both refer to small pieces falling off an object.
4 flood – refers to an excess of water; **cut** and **bruise** are both types of injury.

37.3 *Possible answers:*
1 Contact the bank / credit agency and get them to cancel it at once.
2 Apologise and offer to get them a new one.
3 Sew it back on again.
4 Get it repaired.
5 Put an ice-cube on it. (There are lots of remedies for this, including rubbing good butter on it!)
6 Put it right by moving the hands forward.

37.4 *Things that typically go together:*

	cake-tin	vase	elbow	clock	moped	sink
banged			✔			
cracked		✔				
broken down					✔	
dented	✔					
stopped				✔		
blocked						✔

37.5 1 ... overslept.
2 ... locked myself out.
3 ... mislaid her number.
4 ... broken down. (It could also be **jammed** which means mechanically stuck, e.g. by some broken film.)
5 ... fell and twisted my ankle / cut my leg/knee, etc.

Unit 38

38.1 1 Drought; if the plants and trees are **withered**, they are probably dying because they have no water, and since the earth is **cracked** (hard, with a pattern of deep lines over it), it suggests it is very dry.
2 Earthquake; a **tremor** is a trembling movement of the earth. Note how disasters of various kinds can **strike**, e.g. The hurricane **struck** the coastline at noon.
3 A violent storm or wind, a hurricane/typhoon/tornado; if you **board up** your house you cover the windows and doors with wooden boards to protect them.
4 War/a battle of some kind; **shells** and **mortars** are projectiles which cause explosions when they strike.
5 Probably a plane crash; people who witness such crashes often describe the explosion as a **fire-ball**, or **ball of fire**.
6 Probably a flood, since if your house is flooded, the natural thing to do is to go to the upper floor(s) or the roof to escape the water.

38.2

verb	noun: thing or idea	noun: person
explode	explosion	–
survive	survival	survivor
injure	injury	the injured
starve	starvation	the starving
erupt	eruption	–

38.3 1 getting worse (**spreads**)
2 becoming more serious/heading for a major disaster (a **time-bomb** ticks like a clock and eventually explodes)
3 a disaster was avoided (the bomb was **defused** – made safe)
4 disaster avoided (a **crash-landing** is an emergency landing when the pilot has no proper control over the plane, e.g. without wheels if the undercarriage fails to drop.)
5 getting better (the oil is **receding** – going away from where it was heading, for example, towards a beach)
6 disaster has occurred/is occurring (if you **heed** a warning, you take note, and do something; here the warning was ignored)

38.4 1 victims 2 refugees 3 casualties 4 survivors 5 dead; wounded

38.5 1 malaria 2 leprosy 3 cholera or typhoid 4 rabies 5 yellow fever

Unit 39

39.2 1 primary   5 further/higher
2 nursery   6 evening classes
3 grammar   7 grant
4 comprehensive   8 teacher-training college

39.3 1 I'm **taking/doing/sitting** an exam tomorrow.
2 I hear you **passed/did well in** your examination.
3 You can **study** a lot of different **subjects** / **take** a lot of different **courses** at this university.
4 I got some good **marks/grades** in my continuous assessment this term.
5 She's a **teacher** in a primary school. (Professors are only in universities and are very senior teachers.)
6 He gave an interesting 45-minute **lecture** on Goethe. (A **conference** is a meeting of people with the same interests, usually lasting several days.)
7 She got a **diploma** in personnel management. (Only universities can give degrees.)

39.4 *Possible questions:*
1 Do students in your country get a grant?
2 What's the difference between a university and a polytechnic in Britain?
3 What goes on at play-schools and nursery schools?
4 Why did you choose a teacher-training college instead of a university?
5 What's the school-leaving age in Britain now?
6 You look terribly tired. What've you been doing?
7 Do you get marks/credits/points for your exams?
8 Did you skip yesterday's lecture?

39.5 You could look up these things in an encyclopaedia, or else write to your American Embassy and ask them to send you information about education in the USA. Broadly speaking a **high school** is like a British secondary school, **college** means further education, a **sophomore** is a second-year college student and **graduate school** is where you study for further degrees, e.g. MA/MSc, after graduating for your first degree.

Unit 40

40.1 1 union official   2 executive manager   3 director   4 unskilled worker   5 administrator
6 safety officer (not the security officer – the person who makes sure everything is locked and secure, that there are no burglaries or other crimes, etc.)
7 supervisor   8 labourer   9 personnel officer   10 public relations officer

40.3 *Suggested answers:*
1 This person's been **made redundant**.
2 He/She's **taken early retirement**.
3 This is a person who **works shifts** / is **a shift-worker**.
4 She's **been promoted**.
5 I **got the sack** (*or* I **was fired**; *or* I **was dismissed** – more formal).
6 He/She works **nine-to-five**. *or* He/She **has a nine-to-five job**.
7 You're a **workaholic**.

40.4 1 teacher   4 actor/broadcaster/performer of some kind
2 surgeon   5 farmer
3 secretary/typist/clerk   6 tailor/dressmaker

40.5 1 profession   5 trade
2 a difficult one; it could be called a trade,   6 trade (though could be called a profession)
but many chefs may prefer to be thought   7 unskilled job
of as 'professionals'   8 same as 'dressmaker'
3 trade   9 unskilled job
4 profession   10 profession

40.6 1 get/have   2 living   3 work   4 offered   5 take...on

Unit 41

41.1 *Probable answers:*

1 bowls (the bowls have a weight on one side which gives them a bias as they roll)
2 hang-gliding ('at the top' = at the top of the hill from which the hang-glider is launched)
3 motor-racing
4 riding (most people get a very sore seat/legs when they first try it)
5 windsurfing (being able to stay upright on the water)
6 snooker/pool/billiards/darts, but could, of course, apply to a number of other sports too (golf, shooting, etc.) (Snooker, pool and billiards are similar games but have different rules.)

41.3 *Equipment:* 1 arrows   2 shuttlecock   3 ball   4 ball   5 dartboard
Clothing:

1 Archers usually wear special gloves, and probably a cap to shade their eyes.
2 Usually sweat-shirt and shorts or tennis-skirt, with tennis-style shoes, possibly sweat-bands too.
3 Hockey-players usually wear shorts or a short tennis-skirt, but also protective gloves, shin-pads and possibly a safety-helmet.
4 Baseball players often wear caps, plus protective clothing (special gloves, shin-pads, etc.).
5 No special clothes, since the game is usually played informally in pubs and clubs.

41.4 1 broken   2 beaten/defeated   3 win   4 take up   5 holds   6 scored

41.5 1 a long jumper   4 a discus/javelin thrower   7 a footballer or a football player
2 a jockey   5 a gymnast   8 a pole-vaulter
3 a racing driver   6 a hockey player

41.6 1 tennis, squash etc.
2 could be golf (golf-course) or horse-racing (racecourse)
3 usually boxing or wrestling
4 used for football, rugby and cricket
5 ice-skating
6 ten-pin bowling or skittles (a traditional British game similar to ten-pin but with only nine pins)
7 a track where you ski

Unit 42

42.1 *Probable answers:*

1 Sculpture (The verb **stand** is often associated with statues; it could also be architecture, if 'Peace' is interpreted as the name of a building or huge monument.)
2 Cinema (Animated films are often associated with Walt Disney, e.g. the Mickey Mouse cartoons, but are also a serious art form.)
3 Dance (**Movement** and **rhythm** are the clues.)
4 Poetry (**Rhyme** – having the same sounds at the ends of consecutive lines – is often thought of as a necessary quality of good poetry.)
5 Painting (Oil-based and water-based paints are the two most popular types of paint used by artists.)
6 Architecture (We talk of the **design** of a building.)
7 Drama texts/plays in written form.
8 Perhaps a novel, but it could be any book divided into chapters, e.g. an academic textbook.
9 A play at the theatre (Plays are divided into **acts** – major divisions, and **scenes** – smaller divisions.)

42.2
1 article (The arts relates to all the things in the network on the left-hand page.)
2 no article (the subject in general)
3 article (a particular performance)
4 article (the technique/creative requirements)
5 no article (modern poetry in general – all of it)
6 no article (the speaker is talking about drawing and painting)

42.3
1 What's the name of the **publisher** of that book you recommended? Was it Cambridge University Press? (An **editorial** is an article in a newspaper or magazine giving the opinions of the editor on matters of interest/concern.)

2 'I wandered lonely as a cloud' is my favourite **line** of English poetry. (A **verse** is a collection of lines separated from the next verse by a space.)

3 He's a very famous **sculptor**: he did that statue in the park, you know, the one with the soldiers. (**Sculpture** is the name of the art form; **sculptor** is the person who does it.)

4 Most of the (**short**) **stories** in this collection are only five or six pages long. They're great for reading on short journeys. (A **novel** is a long work (usually more than 100 pages). Here **short story** or just **story** is clearly what the speaker is referring to.)

5 There's an **exhibition** of **ceramics** at the museum next week. (**Exposition** is only used in very formal academic texts to talk about how an argument is presented. **Ceramics** as the name of the art form is always plural.)

6 The **sets** are excellent in that new production of *Macbeth*, so dark and mysterious. (**Scenery** is uncountable and refers to natural beauty in the landscape, e.g. 'There's some wonderful scenery on the west coast of Ireland'. The attempt to represent a place on a theatre stage is called the **set**.)

7 **What's on at** the Opera House next week? Anything interesting? (When we want to know what events are taking place, what a cinema is showing, etc., we use the question **what's on?** We also need a preposition for **opera house**; in this case, **at** is the best one.)

42.4 *Suitable questions:*
1 Was the play a success?
2 Would you like a ticket for the Beethoven tonight?
3 What's the architecture like in your home-town?
4 Was it a good production?
5 What are they showing at the Arts Cinema at the moment? **or** What's on at the cinema?

Follow-up:

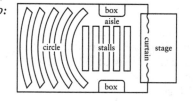

Unit 43

43.1 *Possible groupings:*

Found in salads: cucumber   green/red pepper   lettuce   radish
'Onion-family' vegetables: leek   shallot   garlic   onion
Grow underground: potato   carrot   turnip
Usually long-shaped: aubergine   courgette   sweetcorn

There are, of course, other possible groups too.

43.2 1 hot, spicy   3 salty   5 sugary, sickly   7 bland, tasteless
2 savoury   4 sour   6 bitter, strong

43.3 *starters:* pâté and toast   prawn cocktail   shrimps in garlic
main courses: chicken casserole   Irish stew   rump steak   grilled trout
desserts: coffee gateau   fresh fruit salad   sorbet   chocolate fudge cake

43.4 1 These chips are rather oily/greasy/fatty.   3 This meat is done to a turn.
2 This dish is overcooked.   4 This is just tasteless / very bland.

43.6 1 *Fish:* sardines   mackerel   hake   plaice   trout   cod   sole   whiting
Seafood: prawns   squid   oysters   mussels   crab   lobster
2 calf – veal   deer – venison   sheep – lamb (young animal), mutton (older animal)
pig – pork, ham, bacon

Unit 44

44.1 1 waterfall   4 peninsula   7 volcano   10 gorge
2 cliff   5 estuary   8 straits   11 summit or peak of a mountain
3 glacier   6 tributary   9 geyser   12 chain or mountains

44.2 Brazil is the fifth largest country in the world. In the north the densely forested basin of the River Amazon covers half the country. In the east the country is washed by the Atlantic. The highest mountain chain in South America, the Andes, does not lie in Brazil. Brazil's most famous city is Rio de Janeiro, the former capital. The capital of the Brazil of today is Brasilia.

44.3 1 Mount Kilimanjaro
2 The Volga
3 Venezuela (The Angel Falls)
4 New Zealand
5  A delta is at the mouth of a river where the river divides and flows into the sea in a number of different channels. The River Nile has one.

6 The Straits of Gibraltar are at the western entrance to the Mediterranean and the Cape of Good Hope is at the southern tip of Africa.

44.4 *Possible answers:*
1 Scotland   5 flatter   9 the Western Highlands
2 country   6 agriculture   10 Ben Nevis
3 the north of Britain   7 Scotland   11 Overfishing
4 mountainous   8 the Clyde   12 Scotland

44.5 1 sandy beach/shore   3 shallow brook/bay   5 turbulent river/sea
2 steep gorge/hill   4 rocky coast/mountain   6 dangerous cliff/current

44.6 *Some possible answers:*

Spray cans destroy the ozone layer.

Organic farming means that fewer chemicals pollute the land – and our bodies.

Unleaded petrol causes less air pollution than leaded petrol.

Recycling paper means that fewer trees need to be cut down.

Using bottle banks means that glass is re-used rather than thrown away. There is, thus, less wastage of resources.

Environmentalists are also in favour of using solar or wind power, of using as little plastic as possible (because it is not bio-degradable) and of planting new trees instead of simply increasing the amount of land given over to agriculture.

Unit 45

45.1
1 Cork is in the south of the Republic of Ireland.
2 It lies on an island between two channels of the River Lee.
3 It has a desperately complex one-way traffic system. Moreover, its buses are terribly crowded.
4 St Anne's Church was built on a site where another church stood previously. That church was destroyed during a siege of the city.
5 In the French Gothic style.
6 Probably not as they do not cater specifically for tourists.
7 The Crawford Gallery is worth visiting because it regularly puts on interesting exhibitions of modern art.
8 Well-off people live in fashionable residential areas overlooking the harbour while others live in suburbs on the edge of the city.

45.2 *Some possible answers, based on the city of Cambridge in England:*

Cambridge has the second oldest university in England (after Oxford). The main tourist area of the town lies in the town centre, around the university colleges.

King's College Chapel is in the Perpendicular style.

Most of the main hotels in the town are within walking distance of the centre.

The town centre tends to be terribly crowded on Saturdays.

A number of the colleges are built on the site of former monasteries or convents.

Cambridge has been called the intellectual centre of the world. I am not sure whether or not it still merits this description.

There are plenty of sports facilities catering for both young and old.

Those who enjoy boating must not miss the opportunity to go for a punt on the River Cam.

Most of the more picturesque colleges overlook the River Cam.

An interesting new Science Park has been built on the outskirts of the town.

The Fitzwilliam Museum is well worth visiting

Kettle's Yard regularly mounts quite varied exhibitions.

Railway enthusiasts do not have to travel far from Cambridge to find a working steam railway open to the public.

Everyone who visits Cambridge is sure to appreciate its character.

45.4

1	3	5
natural history	art	night
science	music	tennis
folk	community	social

2	4	6
leisure	basket ball	employment
shopping	squash	accommodation
city	royal	press

45.7 *Some possible answers:*

The most picturesque parts of Cambridge are beside the river.
Cambridge is one of England's most historic towns.
The town could hardly be called spacious as most of its streets are very narrow.
Some of the eighteenth century buildings are particularly elegant.
The most magnificent building in the town, in my opinion, is the Pepys Library.
The town is at its most atmospheric on the day of a student graduation.
Tourists often find Cambridge's narrow lanes very quaint.
Cambridge is very lively at night because so many young people live there.
The city centre is quite hectic at weekends.
When the university is on vacation the town can suddenly seem quite deserted.
The market is particularly bustling on Saturdays.
The shops are always very crowded in the weeks before Christmas.
The shopping centre always seems to be packed with people.
We are lucky in that nowhere in the town is filthy; everywhere is quite clean.
Some of the suburbs have become quite run-down in recent years.
The old buildings in Cambridge are generally not allowed to become shabby but are kept in good repair.

Unit 46

46.1
1 mammal
2 crocodile
3 poplar and birch are deciduous; the yew is evergreen
4 pollen
5 hedgehog, tortoise and bear
6 s/he loves me, s/he loves me not
7 cheetah
8 dove
9 rose, thistle, maple leaf and kiwi bird
10 breathing
11 An endangered species is any species which is in danger of dying out or becoming extinct, e.g. some breeds of tiger or whale.
12 The dinosaur is extinct; the emu is still in existence and the phoenix was a mythical creature not a real one.
13 snowdrop, daisy and lily of the valley; parrot, pigeon and seagull.
14 Your answer to this question depends, of course, on where you come from.

46.2 *Possible answers:*

prickly hedgehog   flowing mane   sweet-smelling petals   noble eagle
sturdy oak   graceful willow   wriggly worm   rough bark

46.3
1 roots
2 claws; trunk/bark
3 blossom/flower
4 thrive/grow
5 hoof
6 stalks
7 bud
8 thorns
9 twigs
10 bat; fish
11 bee; snail
12 harvested

Notice how people are compared to animals in sentences 10 and 11. This is quite common.

46.4 The words underlined below are worth learning. You can use them when talking about other animals too.

camel A <u>mammal</u> of the <u>family</u>, Camelidae, (2 <u>species</u>): the **Bactrian**, from cold deserts in Central Asia and <u>domesticated</u> elsewhere, and the **dromedary**; <u>eats</u> any vegetation; <u>drinks</u> salt water if necessary; closes slit-like <u>nostrils</u> to exclude sand; humps are stores of energy-rich <u>fats</u>. The two <u>species</u> may <u>interbreed</u>: the <u>offspring</u> has one hump; the <u>males</u> are usually <u>sterile</u> while the <u>females</u> are <u>fertile</u>.

46.5 The description of an elephant from the same encyclopaedia is given below. While it is unlikely that you would need or want to write anything quite so technical, look at it carefully and pick out any vocabulary from it that could also be useful for you to learn.

> **elephant** A large mammal of the family, Elephantidae; almost naked grey skin; massive forehead; small eyes; upper incisor teeth form 'tusks'; snout elongated as a muscular, grasping 'trunk'; ears large and movable (used to radiate heat). There are two living species. The **African elephant** is the largest living land animal, with three sub-species. The **Asian elephant** has four sub-species. The African is larger with larger ears, a triangular tip on the top and bottom of the trunk tip (not just on the top) and obvious tusks in the female.

If you chose to write about another animal, compare your description if possible with one in an English-language encyclopaedia. If not ask a teacher to correct your work.

Unit 47

47.1
1 heel; soles
2 laces
3 dressing-gown
4 slippers
5 belt
6 hem; buttons

47.2
1 pyjamas
2 jeans
3 shorts
4 pairs of pants
5 pair (of tights)
6 tights (*or* new ones)

47.3
1 silk evening blouse
2 cashmere sweater
3 leather boots
4 corduroy trousers
5 velvet ribbon
6 cotton T-shirt

47.4 *Possible answers:*

The man is wearing baggy corduroy trousers with a shabby sweater. The collar of a tartan shirt is visible. He has lace-up shoes and one of the laces is undone. He has a pair of mitts on and a flat cap.

The woman is wearing a round-neck close-fitting spotted long-sleeved blouse with plain cuffs and a knee-length striped skirt. She has high-heeled shoes on and is carrying a large handbag and some gloves.

47.5
1 fits
2 matches
3 suits

Unit 48

48.1
1 flu – headache, aching muscles, fever, cough, sneezing
2 pneumonia – dry cough, high fever, chest pain, rapid breathing
3 rheumatism – swollen, painful joints, stiffness, limited movement
4 chickenpox – rash starting on body, slightly raised temperature
5 mumps – swollen glands in front of ear, earache or pain on eating
6 an ulcer – burning pain in abdomen, pain or nausea after eating

48.2
1 For measuring temperature.
2 For weighing people.
3 For measuring people.
4 For doing operations.

48.3
1 c   2 g   3 e   4 a   5 b   6 f   7 h   8 d

48.4

noun	adjective	verb
breathlessness, breath	breathless	breathe
faint	faint	faint
shiver, shivering	shivery	shiver
dislocation	dislocated	dislocate
ache	aching	ache
treatment	–	treat
swelling	swollen	swell

48.5 *Possible answers:*

1 blisters
2 indigestion
3 lung cancer
4 bruises
5 a broken leg
6 sunburn
7 a rash
8 breathlessness
9 sickness
10 an itch
11 a cold
12 hypochondria

Unit 49

49.1

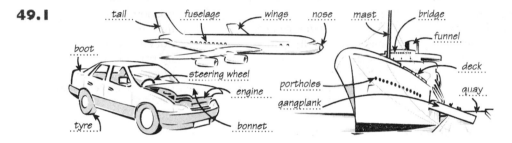

49.2 bonnet – part of car
balloon, glider – types of air transport
deck-chair – facilities used by ship's passenger
guard's van – part of train
mast, anchor, oar, rudder – part of boat (**rudder** can also be part of a plane)
petrol pump, dual carriageway – facilities used by road travellers
bus driver – person working in road transport
left luggage lockers – facilities used by rail or air travellers
check-in desk, control tower – facilities associated with air travel
canoe – type of boat

49.3
1 There are roadworks ahead.
2 There's a cross-roads ahead.
3 There may be low-flying aircraft overhead.
4 The road ahead has an uneven surface.
5 There is a crossing point for the elderly ahead.

49.4
1 flight
2 boot
3 bonnet
4 garage
5 mechanic
6 run out
7 check
8 departure lounge
9 delayed
10 train
11 ferry
12 deckchair
13 passengers
14 galleys

49.5

Type of transport	advantages	disadvantages
road	takes you door to door; easy with luggage	tiring for driver; slow for long distances
train	can enjoy scenery; can work on train	poor catering; frequent delays
sea	can move around; fresh sea air	slow; can feel seasick
air	quick; convenient	cramped; difficult to get to airports

Unit 50

50.1 *Possible advantages and disadvantages:*

place	advantage	disadvantage
camp-site	cheap	uncomfortable
self-catering flat	free to eat when you want	hard work
guest-house	meals cooked for you	not so free perhaps
youth hostel	cheap	no privacy
holiday camp	lots to do	noisy
time-share apartment	can be attractive accommodation	same place every year

50.3
1 They canoed in the Dordogne last year.
2 Have you ever windsurfed?
3 I love sailing.
4 He spends too much time going fishing.
5 It's quite expensive to go shopping in Rome.
6 I enjoy going cycling at weekends.

50.4 *Possible answers:*

1 Can I book a double room with a cot, please?
2 Could I have a call at 6 a.m., please?
3 The television in my room isn't working. Could you send someone up, please?
4 Am I too late to get something to eat?
5 Can I have breakfast in my room, please?
6 Is service included?

50.5

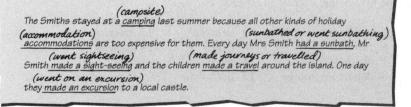

The Smiths stayed at a <u>camping</u> *(campsite)* last summer because all other kinds of holiday <u>accommodations</u> *(accommodation)* are too expensive for them. Every day Mrs Smith <u>had a sunbath</u> *(sunbathed or went sunbathing)*, Mr Smith <u>made a sight-seeing</u> *(went sightseeing)* and the children <u>made a travel</u> *(made journeys or travelled)* around the island. One day they <u>made an excursion</u> *(went on an excursion)* to a local castle.

Unit 51

51.1
1 1, 3, 5, 7
2 2, 4, 6, 8
3 1, 2, 3, 5
4 10.6 (ten point six)
5 ⅜ (three eighths)
6 *e* equals *m c* squared; it is Einstein's relativity equation in which *e* = energy, *m* = mass and *c* = the speed of light.
7 two pi r; this is the formula for the circumference of a circle when r = the radius of the circle. π is the mathematical symbol for 3.14159...

51.2
1 Two per cent of the British population owned ninety per cent of the country's wealth in nineteen ninety two.
2 Nought degrees Centigrade equals thirty-two degrees Fahrenheit.
3 Sixty-two point three per cent of adults have false teeth.
4 Two thirds plus one quarter times four squared, equals fourteen and two thirds.
5 Two million, seven hundred and sixty nine thousand, four hundred and twenty five people live here.

51.3   square   circular   rectangular   oval   triangular   pentagonal   octagonal
spherical   cubic   spiral   pyramidal

51.4
1 forty six point six per cent
2 thirty three billion, nine hundred and twenty three thousand, three hundred and ten million kilometres
3 nine hundred and seventy nine metres
4 one thousand eight hundred and ninety two cups
5 one hundred and seventy three metres or five hundred and sixty eight feet high
6 twenty three thousand two hundred and fifty umbrellas; nineteen eighty seven to nineteen eighty eight
7 seven hundred and thirty three telephones per thousand population
8 nought point four square kilometres

51.5

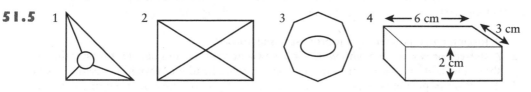

Unit 52

52.1

science	scientist
chemistry	chemist
physics	physicist
zoology	zoologist
genetics	geneticist
information technology	information technologist
cybernetics	cyberneticist
civil engineering	civil engineer

Note: a **physician** is a doctor. Check in the index for the pronunciation of these words as they are frequently mispronounced.

52.2
1 video recorder – a machine which records and plays back sound and pictures
2 photocopier – a machine which makes copies of documents
3 fax machine – a machine which makes copies of documents and sends them down telephone lines to another place
4 tape recorder – a machine which records and plays back sound
5 modem – a piece of equipment allowing you to send information from one computer down telephone lines to another computer
6 camcorder – a camera which records moving pictures and sound
7 robot – a machine which acts like a person
8 word-processor – a kind of sophisticated typewriter using a computer
9 food-processor – a machine for chopping up, slicing, mashing, blending, etc.

52.3 *Some possible definitions:*
1 **VDU** stands for **visual display unit** and it is the part of the computer which includes the screen or monitor, on which you look at your work as you do it.
2 A **stapler** is a useful piece of office equipment which allows you to join two or more pieces of paper together by bending a small bit of wire, called a staple, through the pages which you want to connect.
3 A **cordless iron** is an iron which gets its power from a base unit on which it stands when not in use. It is not connected to the base unit by a flex and so can be used freely and easily.
4 An **alarm clock** is useful for waking you up in the morning.
5 A **hole punch** is a useful piece of office equipment which allows you to make holes in sheets of paper so that they can then be inserted into a file.

52.4
1 discovery   3 rotation   5 patent   7 dissection   9 combination
2 invention   4 conclusion   6 analysis   8 experiment

52.6 *Time* and *Newsweek* often have articles on general scientific interest as does the newspaper, *The Times*.

Unit 53

53.1
1 detective story/film   3 sports programme   5 current affairs programme
2 documentary   4 game show   6 drama

53.3
1 A **foreign correspondent** is a journalist based abroad.
2 A **sub-editor** is someone who works in a newspaper office and decides on how the pages should be laid out, how stories need to be cut, what headlines should be used and so on.
3 A **continuity person** is responsible for seeing that the continuity between one scene and another in a film is correct – for making sure that people do not suddenly wear different earrings, for example.
4 An **editor** is the person responsible for the production of a newspaper or magazine.
5 A **librarian** is a person who works in a place which lends books.
6 A **bookseller** is someone who owns or works in a shop which sells books.
7 A **publisher** is a person or company responsible for having a book printed and organising its sale.
8 A **columnist** is a journalist who writes a regular column or feature for a newspaper/magazine.
9 A **camera operator** is the person who operates a camera filming a TV programme or a film.
10 A **critic** is a person who writes reviews of books, films or theatre plays.

53.4
1 buttons; remote control   3 pick up / receive   5 comics
2 broadcasts/programmes   4 camcorder

Unit 54

54.1   1 independence   2 bye-election   3 running   4 elected   5 policy   6 statesman

54.2   1 chambers   3 constituency   5 Prime Minister
2 MPs (Members of Parliament)   4 majority   6 election

54.3

abstract noun	person-noun	verb	adjective
revolution	revolutionary	revolutionise	revolutionary
representation	representative	represent	representative
election	elector	elect	elective
dictatorship	dictator	dictate	dictatorial
presidency	president	preside	presidential

54.4   1 UK   Sweden   Belgium
2 Iceland
8 Member of Parliament; Prime Minister; United Nations; European Union; North Atlantic Treaty Organisation; Organisation of Petroleum Exporting Countries
(You will find more work on abbreviations in Unit 98.)

Unit 55

55.1   1 robbed; stole   2 was stolen   3 are robbed   4 was robbed

55.2

crime	criminal	verb	definition
terrorism	terrorist	terrorise, commit acts of terrorism (the verb to terrorise is used more generally than in the criminal sense, e.g. The wild dogs terrorised the neighbourhood.)	using violence for political ends
blackmail	blackmailer	blackmail	threatening to make a dark secret public in order to get money
drug-trafficking	drug-trafficker	to traffic in drugs, to peddle drugs, to deal in drugs	buying and selling drugs
forgery	forger	forge	to try to pass off a copy as the real thing
assault	attacker, assailant	assault	physical attack on another person
pickpocketing	pickpocket	pickpocket	stealing from someone's pocket or handbag
mugging	mugger	mug	attacking someone, often on the street, generally to get money

55.3   1 was convicted   2 defended   3 sentenced   4 be released   5 was acquitted

Possible groupings:

Crimes: theft hi-jacking smuggling bribery drunken driving rape
Punishments: prison flogging death penalty probation community service fine
People connected with the law: witness detective traffic warden lawyer judge
members of a jury

Unit 56

56.1 1 Japan – yen; Australia – dollar; India – rupee; Russia – rouble.
2 It is any currency which is reliable and stable.
3 American Express and Visa.
4 Alcohol and tobacco.
5 Rents from property; winnings from gambling; interest from investments.
6 It is an index used for calculating the value of shares on the Stock Exchange in New York. The FT (or Footsie) Index in London and the Nikkei in Japan.
7 An ancient Greek vase in perfect condition is priceless and an old biro that doesn't work is valueless.

56.2 1 interest – money chargeable on a loan
2 mortgage – a loan to purchase property
3 an overdrawn account – a bank account with minus money in it
4 savings account – an account that is used mainly for keeping money
5 current account – an account that cheques are drawn on for day-to-day use
6 pension – money paid to people after a certain age
7 disability allowance – money paid to people with a handicap
8 child benefit – money paid towards the cost of raising a family
9 grant – money given by the government for education, welfare, etc.

56.3 The only two headlines that most people would be pleased to see are 'Interest rates down' and 'VAT to be reduced'.

56.4 1 inheritance tax   2 loan   3 black   4 rebate   5 refund

Unit 57

57.1 *Suggested answers:*

1 That's a vast amount of money to be wasted like that!
2 That's a considerable number of people.
3 It seems it'll be about average again this year, then.
4 At least that's only a small amount of money.
5 You've wasted a huge amount of time.

57.2 *small:* miniscule minute meagre insignificant
large: gigantic overwhelming excessive sizeable

1 minute/miniscule   4 sizeable
2 overwhelming/excessive/gigantic 5 excessive
3 a(n) excessive/gigantic

57.3 1 a lot of (this gives a rather negative feel; **lots of** would sound too positive)
2 plenty of / lots of (a positive quantity)
3 much / a lot
4 a good / great deal of / a lot of
5 Many / A lot of (**Many** and **much** *are* sometimes used in affirmatives, but they do have a somewhat formal feel about them used in that way; the general rule of thumb is not to use **much** and **many** in simple affirmatives.)

57.4 *Possible answers:*

1 quite shocked / extremely anxious
2 slightly anxious / a bit surprised
3 rather/quite/totally confused
4 quite surprised
5 a bit / rather sad
6 absolutely/utterly/completely exhausted / extremely tired

57.5 *Possible sentences:*

1 There are dozens of empty jam-jars in this cupboard. What shall I do with them?
2 He's got heaps of money; he can pay for himself.
3 There's tons of rubbish in the garden; it'll take us months to clear it all.
4 I only ever take a tiny drop of milk in my tea, thank you.

Unit 58

58.1 1 period   2 age (era could also be used)   3 era   4 time   5 spell

58.2 *Possible answers:*

1 I've told you time and time again not to leave that fridge door open!
2 Hello! Nice to see you! You're just in time for tea/coffee!
3 By the time you get this card, I'll probably already be at your house.
4 I'd rather talk to you one at a time, if you don't mind.
5 Could you use the old photocopier for the time being? The new one's being repaired.
6 It can get extremely cold at times in…
7 I'll do my best to get there on time.

58.3 *Possible answers:*

1 …takes about three hours.
2 …run/last for about half an hour each side.
3 …lasted me three winters.
4 …went on for ages.
5 …have elapsed/passed since then, but people still remember that day.
6 …pass quickly.
7 …take your time.

58.4 1 Yes, she's permanent now.   4 Yes, I believe it's eternal.
2 Yes, absolutely timeless.   5 It's a temporary measure.
3 Well, provisionally.

Unit 59

59.1 1 …them shortened?   3 …a short cut.   5 …widened it /…'ve widened it.
2 …extremely tall.   4 …height.   6 …heighten the feeling.

59.2 1 a width of the pool   3 a very narrow range of goods   5 shallow water
2 to lengthen   4 a long-distance call   6 faraway/distant places

59.3 1 it's much bigger now.   3 to give us more room.   5 you should broaden it.
2 it's a lengthy business.   4 there's a wide range.   6 for miles along the river.

59.4 1 at; of   2 in   3 from (or possibly at)   4 from; to

59.5 1 spread   2 expanded/grew; contracted   3 shrunk   4 stretches   5 grown

Unit 60

60.1
1 ...was obliged/forced to close down / had to close down / had no choice/alternative but to close down.
2 ...it's optional.
3 ...have to / 'll have to pay a deposit.
4 ...no choice/alternative, otherwise we'll go/be bankrupt.
5 ...must / ought to / should take it to the cleaners.
6 ...forced him to hand it over.
7 ...mandatory (or perhaps **obligatory**) for dangerous driving.
8 ...compulsory/obligatory in all secondary schools.
9 ...needn't have bought us a present / didn't have to buy us a present / shouldn't have bought us a present.
10 ... exempt from military service / not obliged to do military service.

60.2 *Possible answers:*

2 Most people usually suffer from a lack of time or of money.
3 Filling out a tax return is obligatory once a year in many countries.
4 Most people feel they are in need of more time and money, and millions of people in the world are in need of food and a decent home.
5 Death is certainly inevitable for all of us.
6 If you are an adult you probably no longer have to go to school or wear nappies!
7 When I was at school, sport, maths, English and French were compulsory.

60.3 *Suggested answers:*

	highly	*quite*	*very*	*absolutely*
possible	✗	✔	✔	✗
impossible	✗	✔	✗	✔
probable	✔	✔	✔	✗
(un)likely	✔	✔	✔	✗
inevitable	✗	✗	✗	✔
certain	✗	✔	✗	✔

60.4 *Suggested answers:*

1 A videophone in every home is quite possible by 2025.
2 Rain in the Amazon forest within eight days is highly likely!
3 A human being living to 250 is absolutely impossible.
4 We'll all be dead by 2250: absolutely inevitable.
5 A flying saucer in Hong Kong is highly unlikely.
6 An opportunity to meet the US President is highly unlikely for most people but quite possible for some.
7 A third world war? Very possible if we continue to build nuclear weapons.

Unit 61

61.1
1 **racket** would be an ideal word here
2 **sound**, since it is obviously pleasant
3 **noises** if you mean different sounds, but **noise** is also possible here if you interpret 'some' to mean not a plural number, but *one* sound of 'a certain, unidentifiable type', e.g. 'Some animal must have come into the garden last night; look at these footprints.' (it's not clear what sort of animal)
4 **din** or **racket**; **din** is often used for discordant music
5 **noise** is the only word in the group that can be used uncountably (without *a*)

Suggested words:

1 hiss   2 clatter *or* crash   3 rustle   4 thud   5 bang   6 roar   7 rumble

61.3

verb/noun	typical source(s) of the sound
hum	an electrical appliance when switched on, e.g. computer, freezer, record player
rattle	small stones in a tin being shaken
bleep	the alarm on a battery-driven clock
screech	a car's tyres when the brakes are applied very suddenly or when the car drives off with extremely high acceleration
chime	an old-fashioned pendulum clock or a big public clock on a building when they are sounding the hour or quarter-hour

61.4   1 It was a police officer holding a flashlamp.   3 Then it died, leaving us in complete darkness.
2 I'd never seen such a beautiful bracelet.   4 It was clearly time to get up and move out.

61.5   1 a   2 c   3 b

Unit 62

62.1   *Suggested questions:*

1 Do you rent this house?
2 Could I possibly borrow your camera? / Would you lend me your camera?
3 Which room have I been allocated?
4 Does the school provide exercise books and things?
5 Would you like to contribute to our collection for the disabled?
6 What sort of property do you have / live in / own?
7 Is it possible to hire a room for a meeting?

62.2   1 The millionaire donated a swimming pool to the school.
2 The Director was allocated the best parking-place.
3 My mother's cousin left me £5,000 in her will.
4 A farmer nearby provided us with logs for the fire.
5 When I retired they presented me with a camcorder.
6 The restaurant catered for vegetarians.

62.3   1 handed down   2 give out   3 let go of   4 gave...away   5 hand over

62.4   1 your wallet/handbag/money   4 hand-out/tests
2 jewellery/furniture   5 an antique / a set of books
3 a book / a picture of someone

62.5
1 properties	4 tenants	7 borrowed	10 belongings/possessions
2 loans	5 owner/proprietor	8 properties	
3 landlords	6 estate	9 possessions	

Unit 63

63.1 *Possible first sentences:*

1 That big tree was swaying back and forth in the wind.
2 The cruise-liner is leaving tomorrow.
3 The most famous river in France is the Seine.
4 A cat ran out in front of the car.
5 A train was derailed near London yesterday.

63.2

1 a person dancing; a person who is drunk trying to walk may sway from side to side; a boat or a bus can also sway from side to side.
2 an insect crawls; a baby does too before it can walk; there is a fast over-arm swimming style called 'crawl'.
3 anything moving extremely fast, e.g. a bird or animal can shoot by, a plane can shoot overhead, a fish can shoot through the water.
4 a bird's or butterfly's wings; a piece of washing on the line in the wind; a person's eyelashes; a curtain in the wind.
5 anything moving slowly on water, e.g. a boat, a piece of wood; a person can drift through life (moving without any sense of purpose or direction); your thoughts can drift to something or someone (it happens unintentionally).

63.3 1 rate 2 pace 3 velocity 4 speed

63.4 *Possible answers:*

	usage	grammar
quick	something that takes a short time, e.g. quick snack; quick loo visit	adjective only; can be used with 'to', e.g. she was quick to respond
rapid	more formal; used for things like 'rapid economic growth'; 'rapid increase/decline'	adjective only
swift	more restricted generally; used for things like 'swift-flowing stream'; swift response/decision/ reaction	adjective only; can be used with 'in', e.g. 'He was swift in pointing out how wrong I was.'

63.5 *Possible situations:*

1 If you are very late for something.
2 If you *want* to be late for something, e.g. something unpleasant.
3 If you aren't in a hurry. You can also say this about your studies, if you are not going either particularly fast or slow.
4 If you were hiding from someone, e.g. under a bed or behind a door.
5 If you really don't want to meet them or talk to them, or don't want them to see you.

63.6

1 A **slowcoach** is a person who does everything too slowly, who takes an unacceptably long time to do things.
2 A **streaker** is someone who takes off all their clothes in a public place and runs naked in front of everyone.
3 A **plodder** is a person who sticks at a task and completes it slowly and usually with great effort and difficulty, no matter how long it takes.
4 A **stirrer** is a person who deliberately 'stirs up' or causes trouble between people by saying things that set them against one another.

Unit 64

64.1 *Suggested answers:*

1 glossy	4 prickly	7 jagged	10 gnarled
2 downy/fluffy	5 rough/coarse	8 coarse	
3 slippery	6 fluffy	9 polished/smooth	

Things you might find in your house:

1 a pair of silk stockings; the metal surface of a hi-fi or television
2 a heavy-duty carpet; a garden path
3 a highly-varnished table-top; a mirror; a brass object
4 a cat or dog; a pet rabbit; a fur coat
5 bed-linen; the surface of a table

64.2
1 This is about average for a baby.
2 A 20-stone person is a huge, probably very overweight person.
3 8 ounces is half a pound, i.e. 227 grams. It's enough for many people; is it enough for you?
4 The person writing this weighs 11st 7lb.

64.3 *Possible answers:*

1 a big cat such as a panther or leopard
2 a fish; an eel
3 a hedgehog; a porcupine
4 a bear; a panda
5 a baby chick or duckling; the new-born of many animals

64.4

```
P             SHADY        D         S         C           D
O             U            E         H         O           A
OUNCE         L            N         VIVID     A           Z
N             L      SPARSE          N         ROUGH       Z
D             E            E         Y         S           GLARE
                                               E           E
```

Possible pair-puzzles:

```
   H                H       VY        L
CUMBERSOME          (EA)              I
   A                L       D         G
   V                            FEATHER
   Y                                  T
```

Unit 65

65.1
1 reached/secured 3 reach/attain/achieve 5 realise/fulfill 7 come
2 fulfilled 4 attain/realise/fulfill 6 reach/achieve

65.2

verb	noun	adjective	adverb
realise	realisation	realisable	–
–	difficulty	difficult	–
target	target	targeted	–
–	ambition	ambitious	ambitiously
fail	failure	failed	–
trouble	trouble	troubling troublesome troubled	–

Comments:

targeted is used in sentences such as 'The government has decided to give the extra funds to targeted groups in society.' (specifically chosen)

difficult has no adverb in English; we say 'We did it **with difficulty**'.

troubling: We have seen some very **troubling** developments recently. (worrying)

troublesome: They are a **troublesome** group of students. (cause trouble)

troubled: I've been feeling rather **troubled** lately about my daughter. (worried with problems)

unfailingly: 'failingly' doesn't exist, but unfailingly does, e.g. She is unfailingly honest; you can trust her completely.

failed: They have made three failed attempts to save the company.

65.3
1 I find **it** very difficult to understand English idioms.
2 She succeeded **in rising** to the top in her profession.
3 Do you ever have any trouble **using** this photocopier? I always seem to.
4 I've **managed** to work quite hard this last month. (**accomplish** usually has a direct object, e.g 'I've accomplished a lot this month.')
5 I'm amazed that you can cope **with** all the work they give you.

65.4 *Possible answers:*

2 I'd get it seen to / repaired.
3 It would probably fold eventually.
4 The marker(s) might take the overall performance into account and ignore the one bad result.
5 Perhaps try again, or abandon it.
6 Perhaps give up, or ask for help and advice from my teacher.

65.5 *Possible answers:*

1 Someone is finding their housework / family responsibilities impossible to manage.
2 Perhaps someone who invested £5,000 and lost it all.
3 It could be about a business someone started, or about a project, or something they were building!
4 Talking about someone's success, e.g. in getting a job / in sport; **pull it off** means to succeed, to win, when it is difficult or people are not expecting you to succeed.

Unit 66

66.1

> 2 bottles/cartons of milk
> 4 cans of coke
> a tin of condensed milk
> a packet/box of chocolate biscuits
> a packet of cigarettes
> a large box of matches
> a jar of honey
> 6 packets of crisps

66.2
1 tub, pot
2 barrel, bottles, sack (of potatoes)
3 cans, bottles, barrels, packs, crates, cases
4 *any of these:* bottle/carton (of milk), jug (of milk), mug (of tea), packet (of cornflakes), jar (of marmalade), glass (of milk), bowl (of sugar, for cornflakes)
5 sack (or perhaps a bag)
6 bag and basket
7 (a) 200 (b) 20

66.3
1 a jar of peanut butter
2 a packet of washing powder
3 a carton of cream
4 a tube of skin cream
5 a tin of sardines
6 a tin of tomatoes
7 a bag of apples
8 a box of tissues
9 a packet of butter
10 a pack of 12 cans of beer
11 a bottle of washing-up liquid

66.4
1 chocolate/tool/match
2 wine/milk/water
3 carrier/shopping/mail
4 milk/cream/water
5 wine whisky hour
6 flower/tea/coffee

Unit 67

67.1
1 I have strong views on marriage.
2 Most people believe in life after death.
3 I was in favour of the proposed changes.
4 What does she think of the new teacher?
5 This is absurd from our point of view.
6 He's quite wrong in my opinion.
7 Well, that's just silly, to my mind.

67.2 *Possible answers:*

1 eccentric
2 firm/strong
3 moderate/middle-of-the-road
4 fanatical/obsessive
5 conservative/traditional

67.3
1 I've always doubted that ghosts exist.
2 I have always held that people should rely on themselves more.
3 Claudia maintains that the teacher has been unfair to her.
4 I was convinced (that) I had been in that room before.
5 He feels we should have tried again.

Unit 68

68.1

adjective	abstract noun	adjective	abstract noun
furious	fury	frustrated	frustration
anxious	anxiety	cheerful	cheerfulness
grateful	gratitude	enthusiastic	enthusiasm
ecstatic	ecstasy	apprehensive	apprehension
inspired	inspiration	excited	excitement

68.2

1 confused 3 frustrated 5 enthusiastic 7 fed-up 9 thrilled
2 depressed 4 discontented 6 cross 8 upset

68.3 *Possible answers:*

1 I felt anxious until we heard the results of my mother's medical tests.
2 I felt slightly apprehensive before my first trip to China.
3 I was very grateful to him for lending me his car.
4 I was in a terrible rage when I heard about the unkind things the teacher had said to my best friend.
5 I was miserable for days when I broke up with my boyfriend.
6 I was so inspired by the book, *The Story of San Michele*, that I decided I would become a doctor too.
7 I was initially very enthusiastic about skating but I soon lost interest.

68.4

1 exciting 2 inspired 3 depressing 4 frustrating 5 confused

68.5

1 I'm hot 2 I'm thirsty 3 I'm cross 4 I'm cold 5 I'm hungry 6 I'm tired

Unit 69

69.1

verb	noun	adjective	adverb
–	passion	passionate	passionately
tempt	temptation	tempting	temptingly
attract	attraction	attractive	attractively
appeal	appeal	appealing	appealingly
disgust	disgust	disgusting	disgustingly
hate	hatred	hateful	hatefully
repel	repulsion	repulsive/ repellent	repulsively
–	affection	affectionate	affectionately
adore	adoration	adoring	adoringly

69.2

1 women 2 birds 3 spiders 4 steal 5 pain 6 the future

69.3

1 I can't stand jazz.
2 Beer revolts me.
3 I'm not really keen on tea.
4 His art appeals to me.
5 She has totally captivated him.
6 Would you like a pizza tonight?
7 She is keen on rowing and golf.
8 I'm not looking forward to the exam.

69.4

1 b 2 a 3 b 4 a 5 a

69.5   *Suggested answers:*
1 I like all fruit and I adore curry but I can't stand tripe.
2 the holidays
3 language
4 Their eyes, probably.
5 I enjoy meeting people from all over the world.
6 A chocolate ice-cream.
7 Arrogance and a negative attitude to life.
8 Losing my health.
9 I rather fancy going to the theatre.

Unit 70

70.1   *Possible answers:*

| 1 confessed | 3 shrieked | 5 stammered/stuttered | 7 complained |
| 2 boasted | 4 threatened | 6 begged | 8 urged |

70.2
1 He confessed to breaking the vase (*or* that he had broken...).
2 The little boy boasted of being the cleverest person in the class (*or* that he was...).
3 She shrieked that there was a mouse over there.
4 She threatened to stop my pocket money if I did not behave.
5 He stammered/stuttered that he had done it.
6 He begged me to help him.
7 She complained that the hotel was filthy.
8 He urged Jim to try harder.

70.3

adverb	adjective	noun	adverb	adjective	noun
angrily	angry	anger	cheerfully	cheerful	cheerfulness
furiously	furious	fury	gratefully	grateful	gratitude
bitterly	bitter	bitterness	anxiously	anxious	anxiety
miserably	miserable	misery			

70.4

| 1 a threat | 3 an objection | 5 insistent |
| 2 a complaint | 4 a beggar | 6 argumentative |

70.5
1 urged/begged   3 threatened
2 a) to   b) on   c) about/of   4 all except **urge** and **beg**

5 complain – grumble; maintain – declare; confess – admit; urge – encourage; beg – plead; grumble – moan.

70.6   *Possible answers:*
1 'We can easily break into the bank,' she said **boldly**.
2 'Thank you so much,' he said **gratefully**.
3 'I wish you'd get a move on,' he said **impatiently**.
4 'I love you so much,' she said **passionately**.
5 'I'll do it if you really want me to,' he said **reluctantly**.
6 'I don't know anyone here,' she said **shyly**.
7 'Of course, I believe you,' he said **sincerely**.

Unit 71

71.1 *Some possible answers:*

1 That smells wonderful.
2 Your hair looks great.
3 It sounds brilliant.
4 This tastes delicious.

5 I feel great.
6 That sounds fantastic.
7 You look upset. What's the matter?
8 He smells disgusting.

71.2 1 witness   2 peer   3 observe   4 glance   5 stare

71.3
1 witnessed   3 grasped   5 stroked   7 grabbed/snatched
2 gazed/stared   4 press   6 observed   8 glanced

71.4 1 bitter   2 sweet   3 hot   4 sour   5 spicy   6 salty

71.5 1 snatch/grab   2 finger   3 handle   4 paw

71.6 *Possible answers:*

1 aromatic   3 evil-smelling   5 sweet-smelling
2 smelly   4 fragrant   6 scented

71.7 1 UFOs   2 telepathy   3 ghosts   4 intuition   5 déjà-vu   6 premonition

71.8 *Possible answers:*

1 *sight:* I climbed up to the top of a mountain and was above the level of some low clouds. I could not see the ground but could see the tops of half a dozen other mountains rising out of the clouds.
2 *hearing:* I heard my newborn baby crying for the first time.
3 *taste:* I tasted some wonderful soup after a long day's walking in the hills.
4 *smell:* I shall always remember smelling the sea after a long time away from it.
5 *touch:* I love the feel of fur against my skin.
6 *sixth sense:* I have often had the experience of not having written to an old friend for a long time and then our letters to each other suddenly cross in the post.

Unit 72

72.1 1 blush   2 shiver   3 chew   4 blink   5 wink

72.2
1 Someone is snoring.   4 Someone is coughing and/or sneezing.
2 Someone is yawning.   5 Someone's stomach is rumbling.
3 Someone is hiccoughing.   6 Someone has burped.

72.3
1 blink   3 frown   5 sigh   7 snore   9 yawn
2 blush   4 grin   6 sneeze   8 wink

72.4 1 chewing   2 perspiring   3 lick   4 swallow   5 grin   6 shaken
The central word is **hiccough**.

72.5 It is possible to draw bubble networks in any way that seems logical to you and that helps you to learn. You could group together words associated with **illness – sneeze, cough, shiver** and so on, or you could organise your networks around **parts of the body** – you could put **yawn, lick, bite**, etc. around the word **mouth**. Words that might be added to the networks include **hug, sip** and **stare**.

Unit 73

73.1 1 toowit toowoo 3 woof 5 meow
2 baa 4 oink 6 cockadoodledoo

73.2 1 crowing 2 mooing 3 barked 4 neighing 5 were clucking 6 purring

73.3 You would probably be unhappy to be called any of the adjectives in D except perhaps **dogged**.

73.4 1 *true*
2 *true*
3 *false* – **hoot**, when used about people, is normally followed by the phrase 'with laughter'.
4 *false* – if singing is called **caterwauling**, it must be very discordant and unpleasant to the ear.
5 *true*
6 *false* – **grunting** at someone suggests a lack of interest in that person.

73.5 *Possible sentences:*
2 As soon as she heard the phone, she flew across the room to answer it.
3 I learnt to swim when I was about seven years old.
4 The hillside was covered in loose stones and the walkers slithered uncertainly down the slope.
5 He hopped across the room to avoid putting any weight on his painful ankle.
6 The little children happily trotted off to school.
7 I'll have to gallop through my work if I'm going to get it done on time.

73.6 1 puppy or puppies (a spaniel is a kind of dog)
2 kittens (a **tom** is a male cat and a **Siamese** is a kind of cat)
3 cub(s) (polar bears like all other bears have cubs)
4 lambs (**wool** comes from sheep)
5 ducklings (the verb **hatched** makes it clear that the sentence is talking about a creature coming from an egg, and **swim** makes it clear that a water-bird is being described, rather than a hen, for example.)

Unit 74

74.1 1 pie 2 ocean 3 clanger 4 plate 5 handle 6 block 7 shot

74.2 1 springs to mind 3 just goes to show 5 leaves a lot to be desired
2 flies in the face of 4 're sitting pretty

74.3 *Possible groupings:*

be in a fix (be in trouble/have a serious problem), **be up to it** (be capable of something), **be out of sorts** (be unwell) all have in common the verb **be**, but also the fact that they are followed by prepositional phrases.

child's play (very easy) and **a fool's errand** (a wasted/pointless journey to get something) are both **'s** idioms. (See Unit 81 for more of these.)

hold your tongue (be silent), **hold your horses** (wait before acting/speaking) both of course contain **hold**, but **hold your tongue** could also go with **stay mum** (be silent) because they are very close in meaning. The difference is that **hold your tongue** is often used in aggressive commands, e.g. Hold your tongue, you! (shut up!).

rough and ready (basic / lacking in comfort), **odds and ends** (small items difficult to group along with others), **give or take** (as in 'It'll cost £700, give or take £50', meaning between £650 and £750 pounds approximately) are all **binomials** (phrases joined by **and, but, or**; see Unit 77).

74.4　1　go to bed
　　　　　2　a stronger, more informal version of **child's play**, i.e. simple, too easy for me.
　　　　　3　clearly means more than just 'unemployed', as he didn't have a home; it means totally without money or property, living and sleeping on the streets.

Unit 75

75.1　1　to think of it　　3　Talking of　　5　reminds me
　　　　　2　ask me　　　　　4　you say　　　　6　I was saying

75.2　1　this and that *or* this, that and the other　　2　that's it　　3　this is it　　4　that's that

75.3

now and then or every now and then
(occasionally)

now then!　　　　　　　　　　　　　　　　here and now / right now
[attract attention because　　　　　　　　[immediately; also used
you're going to say something]　　　　　　to emphasise your point]

　　　　　1　Do you want me to do it here and now, or can it wait?
　　　　　2　Now then, everybody, listen carefully. I have news for you.
　　　　　3　I bump into her in town (every) now and then, but not that often.

75.4　1　When it comes to...　　　　4　If the worst comes to the worst...
　　　　　2　As luck would have it...　　5　As far as I'm concerned...
　　　　　3　If all else fails...　　　　　6　What with one thing and another...

Unit 76

76.1　1　hatter　　2　rake　　3　mouse　　4　post　　5　bat

76.2　1　slept　　2　falling　　3　dog　　4　parrot　　5　snow　　6　a sheet

76.3　1　as quick as a flash　　3　as flat as a pancake　　5　as strong as an ox
　　　　　2　as red as a beetroot　　4　as fresh as a daisy

76.4　**Across**
　　　　　1　brass　　2　hatter　　4　sheet　　5　daisy　　7　mouse　　9　bone

　　　　　Down
　　　　　1　bat　　2　hard　　3　easy　　6　ice　　8　cucumber　　10　feather

76.5　1　He/She has eyes like a hawk.　　　　3　She/He eats like a horse.
　　　　　2　Our plan went like a dream.　　　　4　He/She has a head like a sieve.

Unit 77

77.1　1　high and dry　　3　safe and sound　　5　rack and ruin
　　　　　2　rough and ready　　4　wined and dined　　6　prim and proper

77.2 law and order   now and then   hit and miss   clean and tidy
pick and choose   sick and tired   leaps and bounds

Suggested sentences:

1 There are lots of courses. You can pick and choose.
2 The flat looks all clean and tidy now for our visitors.
3 I'm sick and tired of traffic jams. I'm going to start using the train.
4 Finding the right people was rather difficult; sometimes it was hit and miss.
5 My knowledge of English has progressed in leaps and bounds since I've been using this book.
6 The new Prime Minister promised that law and order would be the most important priority.
7 I've seen her now and then, taking her dog for a walk.

77.3   1 or   2 or   3 to   4 or   5 but   6 or

Unit 78

78.1   1 ... of gold   3 ... as gold   5 ... fish
2 ... as nails   4 ... off the mark   6 ... slow-coach

78.2   1 a know-all   4 top of the class
2 the teacher's pet   5 a lazy-bones (or you could say this person is **bone-idle**)
3 a big-head

78.3   *Idioms with gold:* to be as good as gold / to have a heart of gold
Idioms with mark: to be quick/slow off the mark

1 ... a head like a sieve.   4 ... has her head screwed on.
2 ... a good head for figures.   5 ... has his head in the clouds.
3 ... have a head for heights.

Another example of a key-word family might be **eye**:

He only has eyes for Mary. (he never looks at other girls)
He has eyes in the back of his head. / He has eyes like a hawk. (said of someone who never misses anything, especially when people are doing something wrong)
She has an eye for antiques. (she is good at spotting them)
Look up **eye** in a good dictionary and see how many more idioms there are using the word.

78.4   a) your nerves (always with possessive, my, our, John's, etc.)   b) the neck (always used with **the**)

78.5   1 an odd-ball   2 middle-of-the-road   3 over the top

78.6   1 If you say that someone's **heart's in the right place**, you mean they have good intentions and want to do good things, but have actually done something wrong/stupid/irritating without intending to.

2 If a person is **a bit of a square peg in a round hole**, we mean they do not fit in naturally, they are out of place in the situation they find themselves in.

3 If you say **I was miles away**, you mean you were not concentrating on what was happening or what someone was saying, and were thinking about something else.

Unit 79

79.1   *positive:*   to be over the moon   to feel/be as pleased as Punch
negative: to feel/be a bit down   to feel/be browned off

79.2 *Possible answers:*

2 Probably quite browned off, or even in a (black) mood.
3 Over the moon, as pleased as Punch, on cloud nine.
4 Probably like a bear with a sore head *and* in a (black) mood!
5 Down in the dumps, a bit down, browned off.
6 On cloud nine, over the moon.

79.3
1 ... life out of me.	5 ... out of my skin.
2 ... the weather.	6 ... eat a horse.
3 ... as the day is long.	7 ... form. (You could also say **on top of the world**.)
4 ... cloud nine.	

79.4 *Scorpio:*

get itchy feet – get a desire to be travelling or moving around.
(to be) on the edge of your seat – to be impatient, excited, in suspense, waiting for something to happen.

Leo:

to be up in arms – to be very angry and protesting loudly.
to be in two minds – unable to decide or make your mind up about something.

1 I'm in two minds about that job in Paris.
2 I've been on the edge of my seat all day. What's happened? Tell me!
3 Her son got itchy feet and went off to Uruguay.
4 Everyone was up in arms when they cancelled the outing.

79.5
1 felt as if my **head** was going round	4 to be in a **black** mood
2 was scared out of his **wits**	5 get **carried** away
3 **swell** with pride	

Example sentences:

1 So many people surrounded me all wanting to ask me questions. I felt as if my head was going round.
2 That programme about nuclear weapons scared me out of my wits.
3 Seeing her in the graduation procession made her parents swell with pride.
4 Careful! The boss is in a black mood today.
5 I know I shouldn't have listened to his lies, but I got carried away by his charming personality.

Unit 80

80.1 You might find the following idioms and expressions, depending on your dictionary:

1 let the **cat** out of the bag
  to think you are the **cat's** whiskers (think you're wonderful)
  fight like **cat** and dog (fight furiously)
  there's not enough room to swing a **cat** (very little room / cramped conditions)

2 be in a **fix**
  get a **fix** on your position (find out exactly where you are)
  something is **fixed** in your mind/brain (you remember it clearly)
  you **fix** somebody up with something (provide them with something)

3 **pour** oil on troubled waters
  pour cold water on an idea / a plan (criticise something so that people don't want to do it any more)
  pour your heart out to somebody (tell them all your troubles)
  it's **pouring** with rain (raining very heavily)

4 **stir** things up
   cause a **stir** (cause great excitement or anger among everyone)
   stir yourself (move yourself, get up, get moving)
   stir-fry (vegetables, meat, etc. fried very quickly on a fierce heat)

80.2 1 take a back seat   5 a muddle
       2 stir things up   6 up and take notice
       3 light at the end of the tunnel 7 grasp of
       4 the bottom of things   8 by the horns; under the carpet

80.3 1 go back to the beginning again
       2 a compromise
       3 in great suspense
       4 are found together and in the same place and connected to one another
       5 behave yourself / follow the rules

80.4 *Possible questions:*
       1 Are you still quarrelling all the time with Mabel?
       2 Has the new job been a success?
       3 Should I ring Maurice? Or send him a little gift, perhaps?

Unit 81

81.1 *Suggested rewrites:*
       1 The hotel we were staying in was out of this world.
       2 Joe is head and shoulders above the other kids when it comes to doing hard sums.
       3 This restaurant knocks spots off all the other restaurants in town.
       4 You're streets ahead of me in understanding all this new technology; I'm impressed.

81.2 1 to think you are the cat's whiskers   3 a dog's breakfast
       2 to have green fingers   4 to be on the ball

81.3 1 – 4   2 – 3   3 – 1   4 – 2

81.4 *Suggested answers:*
       1 She was dressed up **like a dog's dinner**.
       2 Penny thinks she's **the cat's whiskers/the bee's knees**. (these two are synonyms)
       3 She's a **dab-hand** at DIY; just look at those bookshelves she made.
       4 He has **the gift of the gab**.
       5 Mick **has a way with** the secretaries; just look at how they react when he wants something done.
       6 He wants a new office, a secretary and a new computer. But compared to what Geoff wants, he **wants jam on it!**
       7 She said I was the best boss they'd ever had. It was obvious she was **buttering me up**. I wonder what she wants?
       8 He often **runs down** his school.
       9 She always **picks holes** in everything I say.

81.5 1 There is a verb **to ham it up**, which can be used to criticise an actor's performance if it is overdone and grossly exaggerated; we can call such an actor **a ham actor.**

2 If you don't like something or somebody you can say it/he/she **just isn't my cup of tea**, which means you do not feel attracted to it or to the person.

3 If you say something **is the icing on the cake** you are praising it as something extra good on something that is already good. 'Flying first class was wonderful, and being met at the other end by a limousine really was the icing on the cake.'

4 If you call a person **a real nutcase**, you mean they are mad/crazy.

5 If you say someone **knows his/her onions**, you are praising their knowledge of a particular subject.

6 If you say a group of people really **are the cream**, you are saying they are the best possible representatives of a larger group. If they are the absolute best, you can say they are **the cream of the cream.**

Unit 82

82.1 *Suggested answers:*

1 It seems that Ann can't get a word in edgeways.
2 It seems that Mick got the wrong end of the stick.
3 It seems that Reg can't make head nor tail of what Dan is saying.
4 Madge seems to be talking down to Eric.

82.2 1 wrap up the discussion   2 talk rubbish   3 start the ball rolling   4 come/get to the point

82.3 1 speaks   2 talk   3 talking   4 talking

Unit 83

83.1 1 B is **driving a hard bargain.**
2 A could be described as someone who **has a finger in every pie.**
3 A seems to **have** the song 'Lady in Red' **on the brain.**
4 A seems to have **bought a pig in a poke.**

83.2 1 Can I tell you about a problem I have? I just have to **get it off my chest.** It's been bothering me for a while now.
2 They charged us £100 for a tiny room without a bath. It was **a real rip-off!** *or* They really **ripped us off!**
3 There'll just be time to **have a bite to eat** before the show.
4 **I've got to hand it to her,** Maria coped with the situation brilliantly. *or* **I've got to hand it to Maria,** she coped with... etc.
5 I think I'll just go upstairs and **have a nap**, if nobody objects.
6 Well, I **crashed out** on the sofa at about two o'clock, and the party was still in full swing.

83.3 *Possible answers:*

1 You might have to get a bite to eat on the way if you had to set off on a journey and didn't really have time to eat before leaving, or couldn't get anything before leaving, perhaps because it was too early.

2 Typically, hotels charge over the odds during festival weeks or if there is an important event on, for example, the Olympic Games. In short, any time when demand is very high.

3 Some people find it hard to make any headway in learning languages, but if you have got this far with this book, you don't have that problem!

4 You might be willing to pay through the nose if it is a performer you like very much and/or a once-in-a-lifetime opportunity to see that person.

83.4   1 foot the bill   2 put your feet up   3 watch the box

Follow-up:

to have a word/name on the tip of your tongue: 'Oh dear, her name's on the tip of my tongue! What is it? Laura? Lona? Laurel? Something like that, anyway.'

to hold one's tongue: 'I'm going to hold my tongue. The last time I said anything it only caused trouble, so this time, I'll say nothing.'

to be head over heels for someone / head over heels in love with someone: 'Jim's absolutely head over heels for that new girl. He talks about her all day long and blushes every time her name's mentioned.'

to toe the line: 'The boss gave him a very hard time yesterday about his lazy attitude and all the absences he's had. He warned him he might lose his job. He's going to have to toe the line from now on.'

to tip-toe / to walk on tip-toes: 'We'll have to tip-toe past the children's bedroom. I don't want to wake them up.'

to get someone's back up: 'Sally won't get any sympathy from her workmates, in fact, quite the opposite, she seems to get everybody's back up with her selfish attitude.'

Unit 84

84.1   1 Many hands make light work.   3 Too many cooks spoil the broth.
           2 Don't put all your eggs in one basket.

84.2   1 Never look a gift-horse in the mouth. (Both proverbs advise you to take advantage of good fortune when you have it in front of you.)
           2 Don't cross your bridges before you come to them. (Both proverbs warn you not to anticipate future events.)
           3 Never judge a book by its cover. (Both proverbs warn against trusting the external or superficial features of something.)
           4 Familiarity breeds contempt. (**Absence makes the heart grow fonder** says that if you cannot be with someone or something you will love them/it more. **Familiarity breeds contempt** says that being with someone/something too much makes you hate them.)

84.3   1 People who live in glasshouses shouldn't throw stones.
           2 When the cat's away, the mice will play.
           3 There's no smoke without fire.
           4 Take care of the pence and the pounds will take care of themselves.

Unit 85

85.1   1 prepare by mixing ingredients
           2 manage to see
           3 constitute (**make up** with this meaning is usually used in the passive)
           4 put into bundles
           5 understand (with this meaning **make out** is usually combined with 'can' or 'could' and 'not' or 'never')
           6 making something more numerous or complete
           7 claimed (**make out** implies that what is being claimed may well not be true)
           8 renovate

85.2   1 up   2 without   3 up   4 out   5 up

85.3
1 ... make for the seaside.
2 ... make for happiness.
3 ... makes up to anyone...
4 Do them up...
5 ... make out...

85.4 *Possible word forks:*

make up	a story
	her face
	an excuse
	the prescription
	the sum to £50

make out	a cheque
	a case for her pardon
	some figures in the distance
	the outline of the coast
	a shopping list

do with	a cup of tea
	a cold drink
	some help
	some advice
	something to eat

do up	the bedroom
	your buttons
	her dress
	the house
	your coat

85.5 *Possible answers:*

Work: do the housework / some gardening / the washing-up / some shopping / the cooking / business with; make a bed / a profit/loss / a cup of tea

Trying, succeeding and failing: do your best; make an attempt / an effort / a mistake / the most of / a success of / a go of / a good/bad impression / a point of / allowances for.

Things you say: make arrangements / an agreement / a phone call / a suggestion / a decision / an excuse / fun of / a fuss of

Physical things: make war / love / a noise / a gesture / a face

85.6
1 WAR
2 your best
3 profit
4 business with
5 allowances for
6 a good impression

Unit 86

86.1   1 about/back   2 on   3 about   4 off   5 round   6 up

86.2 *Here is one way of completing the diagram:*

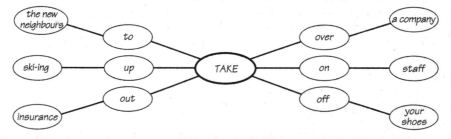

86.3
1 The story of the film takes place in Casablanca during the war.
2 Today's newspaper has brought to light some fascinating information about the Prime Minister.
3 The situation was brought to a head when the union called for a strike.
4 How does she always manage to take things in her stride?
5 The view from the place took my breath away.
6 He took advantage of her weakness at the time and she sold it to him.
7 The main function of a nurse is to take care of the sick.
8 You shouldn't take anyone or anything for granted.

86.4 *Possible answers:*

1 To bring down taxes, among other things.
2 I took to her at once.
3 It seems to be brought on by strong sunlight.
4 He really takes after his father.
5 I've taken up hang-gliding recently.
6 It really seems to have taken off now.
7 A person who takes off other people.
8 I'll bring him round somehow.

86.5 *Possible answer:*

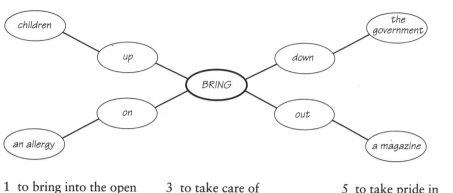

86.6

1 to bring into the open
2 to take part in
3 to take care of
4 to bring a law into force
5 to take pride in
6 to take control of

Unit 87

87.1 I don't often **receive** interesting advertising circulars these days. However, quite an unusual one came this morning. It was headed; 'Are you worried about **losing touch**?' And it went on, 'If so, **purchase** some of our special tablets today. Taking just one in the morning will help you **succeed** at work and at home. It will stop little problems from **depressing you** and will ensure that you **become** rich and successful with the minimum of effort on your behalf. Send just $25 today and you will **receive** your tablets and your key to success within ten days.'

87.2 1 round 2 through 3 down 4 by 5 up to 6 through

87.3 A1 – B5 A2 – B3 A3 – B4 A4 – B2 A5 – B1

87.4 *Possible answers:*

1 … my old teddy bear.
2 … Jack spilt tomato soup on Jill's dress.
3 … study in weather like this.
4 … going to the meeting.
5 … her father's death yet.
6 Living in such a small place…

87.5 *Some example sentences:*

She was the first to **get off** the plane. (disembark from)
I don't understand what you are **getting at.** (trying to say)
They are due to **get back** at six. (return)
You **get ahead** in that company only if you are related to the boss. (succeed, are promoted)
Get lost! (colloquial) (Go away, stop bothering me!)

Unit 88

88.1

1 They have recently established a committee on teenage smoking.
2 We try to reserve some money for our holiday every week.
3 Ignore all your negative feelings and listen with an open mind.
4 If we hadn't left home so late, we would have arrived on time.
5 The government's unpopular proposals caused a wave of protests.

88.2
1 put out a bonfire / your host / the rubbish
2 put forward an idea / a proposal / a suggestion
3 put off a football match / an appointment / customers
4 put across your feelings/ideas/opinions
5 put up an umbrella / prices / a picture
6 put on a concert / a limp / clothes
7 put away papers/books/files
8 put up with someone's behaviour / bad manners / temper

88.3 *Some possible answers:*
1 Let's put up some posters.
2 I haven't had time to put things away yet.
3 We'd better set out/off at 7 a.m.
4 Yes, of course, I can put you up.
5 The likely cost of it all has put me off.
6 He is hoping to set up a travel business of his own.

88.4 *Possible answers:*
1 He is very set in his ways.
2 He's bound to put two and two together if you keep on behaving like that.
3 She has set her sights on becoming Prime Minister.
4 She really puts my back up.
5 It's sound business advice not to put all your eggs in one basket.
6 Please put your mind to the problem in hand.
7 She has set her heart on getting a seat in Parliament.
8 She threw petrol on the rubbish and set fire to it.
9 She's very good at putting things in a nutshell.
10 The building was set on fire by terrorist action.
11 This is the first time I've ever set foot in the southern hemisphere.
12 We spent most of our evenings setting the world to rights rather than studying.
13 You really should put your foot down (with him) or there'll be trouble later.
14 If the teacher doesn't set a good example, the children certainly won't behave properly.

Unit 89

89.1
| 1 continued | 3 attacked | 5 being published | 7 choose |
| 2 check | 4 succeed | 6 complaining | 8 used |

89.2
1 ...to a decision.
2 ...into a fortune / money / a legacy.
3 ...into bloom.
4 ...to a standstill.
5 ...into fashion...
6 ...into operation/existence...
7 ...to blows.
8 ...into view/sight.

89.3
| 1 It goes without saying | 3 on the go | 5 have a go |
| 2 went to great lengths | 4 go far | 6 as far as it goes |

89.4
1 The firm went bankrupt.
2 Only Jack's proposal.
3 Seven thirty, normally.
4 When I pulled a ligament.
5 From a doting aunt.
6 Any time after eight.
7 A bit of a fight, I think.

89.5 *Possible answers:*
1 ...their horoscope was very favourable.
2 ...put salt on it at once.
3 ...that skirt.
4 ...such a terrible experience again.
5 ...it began to get quite noisy.
6 ...having a boss who is younger than you.
7 ...Jack should be offered the job.
8 ...but also a box full of diaries.

Unit 90

90.1 1 back on   2 up to   3 up   4 into   5 to   6 up   7 after

90.2 1 It's rather hard in the circumstances.
2 Why, what's the...
3 She never looks you in the eye.
4 You'd never think she was a grandmother.
5 Why, what do you expect to happen?
6 She'll be lucky at the moment.
7 I thought it was time I had a new look.

90.3 1 ...the party.
2 ...anyone less fortunate than yourself.
3 ...the time the author spent in India.
4 ...I feel rather apprehensive.
5 ...the proposals made at the end of the report.
6 ...you next come to this country.

90.4 1 By the looks of him, he's...   4 much to look at
2 looked...up and down   5 I don't like the look of
3 look small   6 look on the bright side of things

90.5 1 look for your glasses / your purse / a new job / trouble / the meaning of life / love
2 look after a baby / a house / pets / yourself / number one (i.e. yourself in a selfish way, to the exclusion of others)
3 look through a report / a document / a magazine / the window
4 look to your parents / a friend / the boss

Unit 91

91.1 1 over   2 to   3 down   4 up   5 down   6 slip   7 off

91.2 1 Why doesn't she see through him?
2 I ran into Jack at the station yesterday.
3 I cooked the dinner yesterday. It's your turn (to do it) today.
4 I thought I was seeing things when I saw a monkey in the garden.
5 I wish you'd let me be.
6 He let us into the secret that they were planning to break into the house.
7 An enormous crowd turned out to hear the Prime Minister speak.

91.3 *Possible answers:*

1 ...the village will be cut off.
2 ...manager.
3 ...of the rope and fell into a crevasse.
4 ...those who came were very enthusiastic.
5 ...she refused to help him.
6 ...until the party was nearly over.
7 ...of sugar.
8 ...to letting him sleep on my floor.

91.4 *Some possible answers:*

1 I very much regret turning down an opportunity to work in Greece.
2 A train I was on once broke down making me terribly late for an important interview.
3 Big business runs the country as much as government, in my opinion.
4 I did an old lady a good turn when I helped her to get on the bus.
5 I'd like to break a ski-jumping record.
6 I'm sure it is possible for someone's heart to be broken.
7 Every New Year I resolve to turn over a new leaf – I decide to reply to all my letters promptly and to be generally much more organised.
8 I have to see to some shopping today.
9 My own home has never been broken into but a friend's house was once when I was staying with her.

91.5 *Here are two possibilities for each of the verbs in the unit:*

see
His parents have promised to see him through university.
It's hard to find your way round this building – I'll see you out.

run
Our dog was run over by a car.
She ran up an enormous bill at the dressmaker's.

turn
Please turn down your walkman – I can't concentrate.
I'm very tired. I'm going to turn in soon.

let
Let sleeping dogs lie.
This skirt is too tight – I'll have to let it out.

break
I'm broke – can you lend me five pounds for a few days?
Breaking in new shoes can be a painful experience.

Unit 92

92.1
1 proposal to end war
2 politician sells secrets to enemy
3 satellite is not launched
4 royal jewels are stolen
5 marriage of famous actress
6 person who saw crime in danger

92.2 *Suggested answers:*
1 Steps are being taken with the aim of providing more work for people.
2 Approval has been given to a plan to place restrictions on people's use of water.
3 A woman resigned from her job after undergoing some kind of unpleasant experience there.
4 A public opinion survey has looked into how people spend their money.
5 An attempt has been made to remove the Prime Minister from his/her position.
6 The Prince has promised to give support to his family.

92.3
1 makes a connection between
2 reduces
3 explodes in
4 promises
5 leads / is a major figure in

92.5 Make sure that you note down not only the headline but also a brief indication of what the story was about so that the headline makes sense when you revise your work later.

Unit 93

93.1
1 American; a Brit would write **labour**.
2 Brit; an American would write **center**.
3 American; a Brit would be much less likely to use a word of this type, probably preferring a phrase like 'taken into hospital'. If s/he did, s/he would probably spell it **hospitalised**; however, the ending **ize** instead of **ise** is becoming much more common in British English these days.
4 American; a Brit would spell it **theatre** (and would call it **cinema**.)
5 Brit; an American would write **favor**.
6 American, writing in an informal context; a Brit would write **through**.

93.2 *The pictures represent*

	for a Brit:	*for an American:*
1	TV aerial	TV antenna
2	wardrobe	closet
3	lift	elevator
4	vest	undershirt
5	sweets	candy
6	nappy	diaper
7	pram	baby carriage
8	curtains	drapes
9	sellotape	Scotch tape
10	lorry	truck

93.4
1 I had a puncture.
2 Pass me the biscuits.
3 It's in the wardrobe.
4 Open the curtains.
5 We've run out of petrol.
6 It's in the boot.
7 Single or return?
8 He left the tap on.
9 We're leaving in the autumn.
10 I hate standing in a queue.

93.5
1 You'd take the American to the bathroom and the Brit to the kitchen.
2 Cold for the American but hot for the Brit.
3 The Brit, because people do not usually talk about needing to change their underwear although you might well express the desire to change outer clothes.
4 One flight for the American but two for the Brit.
5 An American would be in a bank and a Brit in a café.

93.6 There are many other words you could add. Some might be: US eggplant (GB aubergine); US trashcan (GB rubbish bin); US German Shepherd (dog) (GB Alsatian).

Unit 94

94.1
1 Australia
2 journalist; university
3 mosquitoes; barbecue
4 business
5 afternoon
6 adults/parents

94.2
1 flee
2 catch (e.g. by police)
3 capture/obtain
4 man who annoys girls
5 the general public
6 plimsolls, sneakers
7 people awaiting trial
8 underwear

94.3
1 She gave birth to a baby girl.
2 Church-bells.
3 No, it isn't, it's too dreary.
4 Looking after the school buildings.
5 A glass of whisky (in theory, a small one).
6 Yes, he is.
7 A lake.

94.4
1 Probably not.
2 It is in lots of small very tight plaits.
3 When you have been working or exercising very hard, for instance.
4 They improvise. In other words, they just play whatever comes into their heads, they don't follow any music score.

Unit 95

95.1
1 drunk
2 man
3 stomach ache; doctor (note the colloquial or slang use of **belly** to mean **stomach** and **quack** to mean **doctor**)
4 dinner jacket
5 money
6 food; drink
7 a car
8 cup of tea
9 toilet
10 amazed

95.2
1 Wicked!
2 He's a cop.
3 Let's take him home.
4 Sure. I'll keep my eyes skinned.
5 It's in a drawer, over here.
6 He's in the nick.
7 Let's go for a run in the motor.

95.3
1 look
2 kids
3 table
4 teeth
5 church (by hook or by crook means by any method, fair or unfair)
6 hat

95.4
1 fellow (boyfriend)
2 breakfast
3 something given away free
4 bricklayer
5 a day off work claiming to be sick
6 barbecue

Unit 96

96.1
1 on a bus
2 in the country
3 in a theatre
4 in the street
5 outside a café
6 outside a cinema
7 at the zoo
8 at the beginning of a road
9 on a wall
10 at a supermarket check-out
11 on a packet of cigarettes
12 on a motorway
13 at the entrance to a car park
14 on a cycle path
15 on a river bank

96.2
1 to bring a legal case against
2 a punishment
3 something which has been or is to be bought
4 someone who goes on private land without permission
5 not to do something
6 to get off a means of public transport (bus, train)
7 to forbid something
8 large place where an audience sits
9 to get off a bicycle or a horse
10 a young person under the age of 18
11 a means of transport

96.3
1 You would see this notice in a shop and it lets people know that people who take things from the shop without paying will be taken to court.
2 You would see this in a shop and it lets people know that the staff there speak French as well as English.
3 You would see this at Customs and it lets people know that this is the way to go if they do not have any goods to pay duty on.
4 You would see this in a shop window and it tells people that things are going to be sold off cheaply because the shop wants to get rid of its stock, perhaps because the shop is about to close down.
5 You would see this outside an exhibition or a dance or concert hall perhaps and it lets people know that they need a ticket to get in.
6 You would see this in the window of a hotel or bed and breakfast and it tells people that there are no free rooms there.

7   You would see this on a river bank and it tells people that fishing is not allowed.

8   You would see this notice outside a bicycle shop and it tells people that they can either hire or buy bicycles there.

9   You would see this outside a block of flats and it tells people that one flat is vacant for renting.

10 You would see this notice at the end of an escalator and it tells people that if they have a dog with them, they must carry it.

11 You would see this notice on public transport, a bus or an underground train, and it asks passengers to leave these seats for people who are elderly or find it difficult to move easily.

96.4 1 Coffee now being served.
2 Spanish spoken here.
3 Kindly/Please refrain from smoking *or* Smoking (strictly) prohibited.
4 Free-range eggs for sale.
5 No bill-sticking.
6 Rooms to let.

Unit 97

97.1 *Suggested re-wording:*

> **Now! Eagle Airlines offers even more to the business traveller who needs comfort.**
>
> Let us fly you to your destination in first-class comfort, looked after by the best-trained cabin attendants (or cabin staff) in the world. Any business person knows that they must arrive fresh and ready for work no matter how long the journey. With Eagle Diplomat-Class you can do just that. And, what's more, your partner/spouse can travel with you on all intercontinental flights for only 25% of the normal fare! Your secretary can book you on any flights 24 hours a day on 0557-465769. All he or she has to do is lift the phone.

97.2 1 **conductor** is marked on the word (-or); **conductress** used to be common but is less so now
2 **shepherd** is socially marked as male, though **shepherdess** used to be common also
3 **cheerleader** is socially marked as a female role
4 **typist** is socially marked as female
5 **station master** is marked on the word (-er); there never were any '**station mistresses**', and nowadays they are called **station manager** in the UK, regardless of sex
6 **dressmaker** is marked on the word as male, but socially marked as female
7 **general** is socially marked as male
8 **detective** is socially marked as male
9 **monk** is linguistically marked as male (female = **nun**)
10 **milkman** is marked on the word as male; **milkwoman** is quite common in the UK
11 **tailor** is linguistically and socially marked as male

97.3 mankind – human beings   spinster – single woman   unmanned – unstaffed
air hostess – cabin attendant   man-hours – person-hours

97.4 1 …a new chair/chairperson…
2 Several fire-fighters and police officers were…
3 A spokesperson for the store said the manager had…
4 I wonder what time the post comes… (recently someone referred to **the postie** on a BBC programme, but, at the time of writing, this form has not become established)
5 I can't see the bartender anywhere…
6 Her brother's a nurse, and she's an author / a writer.

```
        The Manager
        Frinstowe Engineering Ltd
        22/11/92

        Dear Sir or Madam,
        I am aged 22, single, and am seeking employment. I saw
        your advertisement for part-time workers in The Globe
        last week. However, your 24-hour answering service seemed
        to be unstaffed when I tried it. Could you please send
        me application forms by post? Thank you.
              Yours sincerely,


              Sally Hewings (Ms)
```

Note: In real life, the first sentence of this letter would be unnecessary. (However, the word 'single' is more neutral than 'spinster'.) Also, if Sally puts (Ms) at the end, she does not have to say she is female; it is obvious.

Unit 98

98.1

1 **Mr** A. Carlton	2 **Ms** /məz/ P. Meldrum	3 N. Lowe **& Co.**
Flat **no.** 5	c/o T. Fox	7, Bridge **Rd.**
Hale **Cresc.**	6, Marl **Ave.**	Freeminster
Borebridge	Preston	**UK**

Note: **Flat** could be abbreviated to **F.**, though this is not so common. **United Kingdom** is abbreviated, but **Great Britain** is not normally abbreviated in addresses. **Ms** is unusual in that English words do not normally like to have a stressed /ə/ vowel. For this reason, many people say /mɪz/.

98.2
1 Bachelor of Science   (A)
2 Federal Bureau of Investigation   (A)
3 Father (could also be 'French' or 'Franc')   (C)
4 extension (telephone)   (C)
5 compact disc   (A)
6 as soon as possible   (A)
7 personal identification number   (B)
8 for example   (C/D)
9 United Nations Educational, Scientific and Cultural Organisation   (B)

98.3
Memorandum from Mister Braneless (Managing Director)
To: All staff
Date: The third of May, 1991 Reference: 04056/DC

May I remind you that all new laboratory equipment should be registered with Stores and Supplies, Room 354 (extension 2683). Please note: new items must be notified before five o'clock in the afternoon on the last day of the month of purchase, that is, within the current budgeting month. All account numbers must be recorded.

98.4   1 OAPs – British English for 'Old age pensioners': retired people or senior citizens; on a museum entrance.
   2 WC – 'water closet': a lavatory; **Gents** – gentlemen; on a door in a pub.
   3 US – United States of America; **POWs** – prisoners of war; newspaper headline.
   4 CFC – Chloro-fluoro-carbons: nasty chemicals sometimes found in sprays, which can damage the ozone layer; on an aerosol can.
   5 **Dep** – depart; **Arr** – arrive; on an airline timetable.

98.5   **Across**
   3 UFO (pron. U-F-O) (Unidentified flying object of any kind)
   6 EAST (N = north; S = south; W = west)
   8 RN (Common abbreviation for the Navy in Great Britain)
   9 RIP (usually put on gravestones or in newspaper announcements of deaths)
   10 BIO (as in 'bio-degradable plastic')
   11 CD (compact disc)
   12 AND
   13 ESP (this can also mean 'English for Special Purposes' or 'extra-sensory perception', a power some people say they have to see ghosts and spirits of the dead, or to see the future)
   15 GB (each country has an abbreviation for car-plates when travelling in another country. What is your country's abbreviation?)
   17 US (United States)
   19 ET (Extra-terrestrial – a loveable creature from another planet in the film called 'ET')
   20 TUBE

   Down
   1 PERCENT
   2 See 13 across
   4 FRIDGES
   5 ONO (used in advertisements: eg 'Bicycle for sale: £25 o.n.o.' This means perhaps £23 or £24 would be accepted if nobody else offers £25.)
   7 AIDS
   10 BN (Please note = NB)
   14 PUB (**pub** is a short form of 'public house')
   16 BT (seen on phone boxes in Britain. The abbreviated name of the British Telecommunications company)
   18 SE (NW = north-west, SW = south-west, NE = north-east)

Unit 99

99.1   1 an irresistible urge to collect things
   2 a house constructed solely from natural materials
   3 a female of limited intelligence but high sex appeal
   4 a specially bred miniaturised form of vegetable
   5 an indoor version of American football
   6 a hypothetical miniaturised device capable of making its way through bodily passages and performing various tasks

These words can be classified as follows, relating to the sections on the left-hand page:

   1 collectomania (F)   3 bimbo (D)   5 arenaball (C)
   2 bio-house (D)   4 mini-vegetable (B)   6 microbot (B)

99.2   1 ozone-/eco-friendly   5 teleworking
   2 Gorbymania   6 cardboard city
   3 singlehood   7 couch potato
   4 monoboarding (*or* snow-surfing)   8 sound-bites

99.3 There are many possible answers to this question and it is, of course hard to predict which words will stand the test of time. I would suggest **faxable, teleworking** and **singlehood** as they express concepts that are already useful and are likely to remain so, whereas **vogueing** and **Gorbymania** are likely to go out-of-date quickly.

99.4
1 cooking by microwave oven
2 a building which houses a number of different cinemas
3 skiing uphill
4 high-ranking, powerful members of international organisations
5 the study of humour
6 practically active
7 credit cards for use in a particular shop
8 babies born at a time when the birth-rate was particularly high

Unit 100

100.1

'Well, where shall I start? It was last summer and we were just sitting in the garden, sort of doing nothing much. Anyway, I looked up and…see we have this kind of long wall at the end of the garden, and it's…like…a motorway for cats, for instance, that big fat black one you saw, well, that one considers it has a right of way over our vegetable patch, so…where was I? Yes, I was looking at that wall, you know, day-dreaming as usual, and all of a sudden there was this new cat I'd never seen before, or rather, it wasn't an ordinary cat at all…I mean, you'll never believe what it was…'

Comments:

Where/How shall I start/begin? This is a very common marker at the beginning of a story or monologue while the speaker is composing his/her thoughts.

Anyway is probably the most common marker in spoken story-telling to divide up the story into its different stages (introduction/main plot/resolution, etc.)

See is often used in informal talk instead of **you see**, when someone is clarifying or explaining something.

Like is often used when the speaker hesitates, or to make something less precise, a little more vague.

Where was I? is used when we want to come back to the main subject we were talking about after an interruption or diversion into another point or topic.

Yes is often used when we resume what we were talking about; it does not have to be an answer to a question from someone. **No** is also used in exactly the same way and could have been used here instead of **yes**.

Or rather is used when you change to a different word or a better/more accurate way of saying what you want to say.

I mean is used when you want to explain something or expand or illustrate what you are saying.

This extract is typical of the number of markers found in everyday informal talk. The speaker is not a 'lazy' or 'bad' speaker; everyone uses markers, even if they are not conscious of it or do not want to admit it! Informal conversation *without* markers sounds rather odd and strained, and a little too formal.

100.2 *Possible answers:*

1 A: Are you a football fan?
   B: **Well**, I like it; I wouldn't say I was a fan.

2 A: I'll take care of these.
   B: **Right**, that's everything.
   A: **Fine, so** see you next week.
   B: **Good**. That was a very useful meeting.

3 A: It was last Monday I was coming home from work. I saw this ragged old man approaching me. **Anyway**, I stopped him...
   B: Jim Dibble!
   A: **Hang on!** Let me tell you what happened first.

4 A: Which number is yours?
   B: **Let me see...** it's that one here, yes, this one.

5 A: He's looking exhausted.
   B: Yes, he is.
   A: **Mind you**, he has an awful lot of responsibility, so it's hardly surprising.

6 A: What do you mean 'cold'?
   B: **Well**, she's not friendly, very distant, **so to speak**. Last week I gave her a jolly smile and she... **like**...scowled at me. the way you smile at people,
   A: **Well** what do you expect? **Look**, I've seen the way you smile at people it **sort of** puts them off.

100.3

1 First of all
2 in other words
3 For example / For instance
4 Next
5 as it were / so to speak
6 Lastly
7 In summary (**In conclusion** would not be suitable here, since it just means 'this is the end of the text', whereas this sentence provides a summing up of the arguments in the text.)

Follow-up:

If it is difficult or impossible for you to get hold of tape-recordings of natural conversation, you can find transcripts in D. Crystal and D. Davy's *Advanced Conversational English* (London: Longman, 1975), where you will find a wide range of markers in actual use.

Phonetic symbols

Vowel sounds

Symbol	Examples		
/iː/	sleep	me	
/i/	happy	recipe	
/ɪ/	pin	dinner	
/ʊ/	foot	could	pull
/uː/	do	shoe	through
/e/	red	head	said
/ə/	arrive	father	colour
/ɜː/	turn	bird	work
/ɔː/	sort	thought	walk
/æ/	cat	black	
/ʌ/	sun	enough	wonder
/ɒ/	got	watch	sock
/ɑː/	part	heart	laugh
/eɪ/	name	late	aim
/aɪ/	my	idea	time
/ɔɪ/	boy	noise	
/eə/	pair	where	bear
/ɪə/	hear	beer	
/əʊ/	go	home	show
/aʊ/	out	cow	
/ʊə/	pure	fewer	

Consonant sounds

Symbol	Examples		
/p/	put		
/b/	book		
/t/	take		
/d/	dog		
/k/	car	kick	
/g/	go	guarantee	
/tʃ/	catch	church	
/dʒ/	age	lounge	
/f/	for	cough	
/v/	love	vehicle	
/θ/	thick	path	
/ð/	this	mother	
/s/	since	rice	
/z/	zoo	houses	
/ʃ/	shop	sugar	machine
/ʒ/	pleasure	usual	vision
/h/	hear	hotel	
/m/	make		
/n/	name	now	
/ŋ/	bring		
/l/	look	while	
/r/	road		
/j/	young		
/w/	wear		

Index

by(e)-election 54
by-pass 14

cab 93
cabbage /'kæbɪdʒ/ 43
cabin 49
cabin attendant 97
cabinet /'kæbɪnət/ 54
Caesarean /sə'zeərɪən/ 15
café /'kæfeɪ/ 45
caftan /'kæftæn/ 16
Cain and Abel 95
cake 28, 30 (~-tin) 37
calf /kɑːf/ 43, 73
call /kɔːl/ 7
calm /kɑːm/ 11, 18
camcorder /'kæmkɔːdə/ 52, 53
camel /'kæməl/ 46
camera operator 53
camp-site 50
can 66 (~ opener) 8
Canadian 31
cancer /'kænsə/ 48
candidate /'kændɪdeɪt/ 54
candy 93
canoe /kə'nuː/ (-noist) 41, 49
canter /'kæntə/ 15
cap /kæp/ 41
cape /keɪp/ 44
capital 44 (~ punishment) 86
captain /'kæptɪn/ 49
captivate 69
car hire/park/rental 45, 62
carafe /kə'ræf/ 16
caravan /'kærəvæn/ 2,16
card(s) 18, 66
cardboard city 99
cardigan /'kɑːdɪgən/ 15, 47
care for 69, 86
career /kə'rɪə/ 39
carefree /'keəfri/ 12
carelessness 11
caring /'keərɪŋ/ 69
carpenter 40
carrier bag 66
carrot 43
carton /'kɑːtən/ 30, 66
cartoon /kɑː'tuːn/ 53
case /keɪs/ 26, 55, 66, 98
cash /kæʃ/ 56
cashmere /'kæʃmɪə/ 15
casino /kə'siːnəʊ/ 16
casserole /'kæsərəʊl/ 43
cast 29, 42
cast-off 12
castle /'kɑːsəl/ /'kæsəl/ 18
casual /'kæʒʊəl/ 5

casualty /'kæʒʊəlti/ 38
(the) cat's whiskers 80, 81
(let the) cat out of the bag 80
Catalan 31
catastrophe /kə'tæstrəfi/ 1, 18
cater /'keɪtə/ 45, 62
caterpillar /'kætəpɪlə/ 73
caterwaul /kætəwɔːl/ 73
cathedral /kə'θiːdrəl/ 45
cattle /'kætəl/ 49
catty /kæti/ 73
cauliflower /'kɒlɪflaʊə/ 43
cause /kɔːz/ 22, 86, 88
    (~a stir) 80
caused by 33
CD /siːdiː/ (~ player) 52, 98
cease /siːs/ 3
celery /'seləri/ 43
cellar /'selə/ 36, 66
cellist /'tʃelɪst/ 8
censor /'sensə/ 53
centralise 8
ceramic /sə'ræmɪk/ 42
cereal /siːrɪəl/ 66
certain 60
chain 44
chair (person/man/woman) 97
chairmanship 11
chalk /tʃɔːk/ 18, 40
chamber /'tʃeɪmbə/ 54
champagne /ʃæmpeɪn/ 15
championship
    /'tʃæmpɪənʃɪp/ 11
chance 11, 60
change 47, 49, 87
chaos /'keɪɒs/ 30
chap /tʃæp/ 3, 7
chapter 42
charge /tʃɑːdʒ/ 55
charity 11
charm /tʃɑːm/ 26, 45
chat (~ show) 4, 53
chauffeur /'ʃəʊfə/ 16, 49
chauvinist /'ʃəʊvənɪst/ 15
check 89, 93
check-in 49
check-out 14
checked /tʃekt/ 47
cheerful (~ness) (~ly) 12, 68,
    70
cheerio /'tʃiːrɪəʊ/ 7
cheerleader 97
chef /ʃef/ 40
chemical /'kemɪkəl/ 52
chemist (~ry) 52
cheque /tʃek/ 56
chest (~ pain) 48

chew /tʃuː/ 72
chic /ʃiːk/ 47, 94
chicken 73
chickenpox 48
child benefit 56
child's play 74
child-minder 40
childhood 8, 11
Chilean /'tʃɪlɪən/ 31
chilli /'tʃɪli/ 71
chilly /'tʃɪli/ 1, 32
chime /tʃaɪm/ 61
china /'tʃaɪnə/ 66
Chinese 31
chip 37
    (a ~ off the old block) 74
chives /tʃaɪvz/ 43
chocolate(s) /'tʃɒklət/ 28, 30,
    66
choice /tʃɔɪs/ 60
cholera /'kɒlərə/ 38
chubby /'tʃʌbi/ 33
cigarettes 66
cinema /'sɪnəmə/ 42
cineplex /sɪnɪpleks/ 99
cinnamon /'sɪnəmən/ 43
cipher /'saɪfə/ 16
circle /'sɜːkəl/ (-cular) 2, 51
circumference
    /sə'kʌmfərəns/ 51
circumspect /'sɜːkəmspekt/ 10
circumstance
    /'sɜːkəmstæns/ 21
citizen /'sɪtɪzən/ 45 (~ship) 11
citizens' advice bureau, 45
City Hall 45
civil engineering /'sɪvəl/ 52
civil servant 40
civil war 38
claim /kleɪm/ 25, 85
clang /klæŋ/ 17, 61
clank /klæŋk/ 17
clap 17, 30
clash /klæʃ/ 17, 92
classical 42, 45
Classics 27
classmate 35
clatter /'klætə/ 17, 61
claw /klɔː/ 46
clean and tidy 77
cleaner 8, 40
clear-out 14
clearance sale 96
clergyperson
    /'klɜːdʒɪpɜːsən/ 99
clerk /klɑːk/ 40
clever 7, 34

court /kɔːt/ 41, 44, 55
cove /kəʊv/ 44
cover-up 14
crab 43, 46
crack /kræk/ 37, 38
crack-down 14
crackle /'krækəl/ 17
crafty /'krɑːfti/ /'kræfti/ 34
crash /kræʃ/ 17, 61
crash out 83
crash-landing 38
crate /kreɪt/ 66
crawl /krɔːl/ 63
crayfish /'kreɪfɪʃ/ 43
creak /kriːk/ 17
cream 18, 66
(the) cream (of the cream) 81
creativity 26
creche /kreʃ/ 16
(on/in) credit 56
credit card 13, 56
crew /kruː/ 29, 49
crew-cut 33
cricket 41
crime /kraɪm/ (-minal) 55
crisis /'kraɪsɪs/ 25
crisps 71
critic 53
croak /krəʊk/ 73
Croatian /krəʊ'eɪʃən/ 31
crocodile /'krɒkədaɪl/ 46
crop(s) 44, 46
cross 68
crosroads 49
cross-purposes, talk at 82
crossly 70
crossword 53
crow /krəʊ/ 73
crowd /kraʊd/ (~ed) 29, 45
cruel /'kruːəl/ 34
cruise /kruːz/ 16
cryogenics /kraɪə'dʒenɪks/ 52
cube /kjuːb/ 51
cucumber 43
cue /kjuː/ 41
cuff /kʌf/ 47
cuisine /kwɪ'ziːn/ 16
cul de sac 16
cumbersome /'kʌmbəsəm/ 64
cunning /kʌnɪŋ/ 4, 34
cup of tea 81, 85
cupid /'kjuːpɪd/ 18
cuppa /'kʌpə/ 95
curb /kɜːb/ 92
curiosity 11
curl /kɜːl/ (~y) 5, 33
curly-haired 12

currency /'kʌrənsi/ 26, 56
current /'kʌrənt/ 44
current affairs 53
curry /'kʌri/ 43, 71
curt /kɜːt/ 34
curtains /kɜːtənz/ 93
customs /'kʌstəmz/ 49, 56
cut 2, 18, 37, 53, 92
cut-out 12
cut-price 12
cutback 14
cutlery /'kʌtləri/ 36
cybernetics /saɪbə'netɪks/ 52
cycle route 49
cyclist /'saɪklɪst/ 41
Cypriot /'sɪprɪət/ 31

(a) dab-hand 81
(a) dog's breakfast/dinner 81
dachshund /'dæʃənd/ 16
dad 7
daft 34 (as ~ as a brush) 74
damage /'dæmɪdʒ/ 38
damp 32
dance 42 (~ hall) 45
Dane /deɪn/ (-nish) 31
dark-skinned 33
darling 69
darts 27, 41
Darwinist 67
dash /dæʃ/ 4, 17
data-processing 13
date /deɪt/ 7, 19
dawdle /dɔːdəl/ 63
dazzle /'dæzəl/ 64
(as) dead as a doornail 76
dead end, come to a 80
(as) deaf as a post 76
deafening /'defənɪŋ/ 71
deal /diːl/ 91
dear (~est) 69
death penalty 13, 55
debt (-or) /det/ 8, 18
decade /'dekeɪd/ 58
deceive 86 /dɪ'siːv/
deciduous /də'sɪdjʊəs/ 46
decimal /'desɪməl/ 51
decision /dɪ'sɪʒən/ 85, 89
deck (~ chair) 49
decrease /dɪ'kriːs/ /'diːkriːs/ 11, 18
dedicated 67
deduce /dɪ'dʒuːs/ 10
deep (~en) 59
deer /'dɪə/ 43
defeat /dɪ'fiːt/ 41
defend 55

define /dɪ'faɪn/ 3
defuse /dɪ'fjuːz/ 38
degree /dɪ'griː/ 39, 51
déjà-vu /deɪʒɑː 'vuː/ 71
delay /dɪ'leɪ/ 49
delicatessen /delɪkə'tesən/ 16
delicious /dɪ'lɪʃəs/ 8
delighted /dɪ'laɪtɪd/ 68
delta 44
democracy /dɪ'mɒkrəsi/ 54
denim /'denɪm/ 15, 47
dense (-sity) 64
dent 37
dental floss 36
dentist 40
department 54
department store 45
departure lounge 49
depend 90
deport (~ation) (~ee) 10
depose /dɪ'pəʊz/ 10
deposit 7, 56
depress /dɪ'pres/ 10, 87
depressed (-sing) 48, 68
depth /depθ/ 11, 59
descendant /dɪ'sendənt/ 46
desert /'dezət/ 18, 46
desert island 49
deserted /dɪ'zɜːtɪd/ 45
design /dɪ'zaɪn/ 42 (~er) 40
desire /dɪ'zaɪə/ 69
desperately 70
despise /dɪ'spaɪz/ 35
dessert /dɪ'zɜːt/ 43
destatisation
    /diːsteɪtaɪ'zeɪʃən/ 99
destroy /dɪ'strɔɪ/ 57, 87
destruction 44
detached /dɪ'tætʃt/ 36
detective 55, 97 (~ story) 53
determination 26
determined 3, 34
detest 69
develop 87
devoted 69
diagnosis /daɪəg'nəʊsɪs/ 48
diagonal /daɪ'ægənəl/ 51
dialect /'daɪəlekt/ 31
diameter /daɪ'æmɪtə/ 51
diaper /'daɪpə/ 93
diarrhoea /daɪə'rɪə/ 48
dickhead /'dɪked/ 95
dictate (-tator) (-tatorial) 54
dictatorship 54
die /daɪ/ 48
difficult (~y) 25, 65
dig 94

fine /faɪn/ 55, 96, 100
finger 71 (a ~ in every pie) 83
Finn 31
fir tree 29, 46
fire /fɪə/ 40
fire-ball 38
fire-proof 12
firefighter 40, 97
fireman /'fɪəmən/ 97
firm 67
first (~ly) 100
first-born 12
first-class 12
first-hand 12
first-rate 81
first and foremost 77
first impression 33
first of all 100
fish /fɪʃ/ 28, 46
fish finger 43
fisherman 97
fishing 44 (~-boat) 49
fit 30, 47 (as ~ as a fiddle) 79
five finger discount 95
fix, *expressions with*
  80, 88, 95
(in a) fix 74, 80
fjord /'fiːjɔːd/ 16
flash /flæʃ/ 30, 52, 61
flat 7, 93, 98
  (as ~ as a pancake) 76
flat-footed 12
flatmate /'flætmeɪt/ 35
flaw /flɔː/ 52
fleetfoots /'fliːtfʊts/ 94
Flemish /'flemɪʃ/ 31
flew /fluː/ 19
flexi-time /'fleksitaɪm/ 40
flexible /'fleksibəl/ (-bility) 8
flicker /'flɪkə/ 61
flight /flaɪt/ 49
flock 29
floe /fləʊ/ 16, 19
flogging /'flɒgɪŋ/ 55
flood /flʌd/ 32, 37, 38
floppy disc / flɒpi/ 52
flour /'flaʊə/ 26
flow /fləʊ/ 19, 63
flower /'flaʊə/ 46, 66, 89
  (~y) 47
flowing /'fləʊwɪŋ/ 46
flu /fluː/ 19, 48
fluent /'fluːənt/ 3
flutter /'flʌtə/ 63, 73
flux /flʌks/ 30
fly 49, 73
fly in the face of 74

fly off the handle 74
flying saucer 71
foal /fəʊl/ 73
foe /fəʊ/ 5
fog (~gy) 32
fold /fəʊld/ 65
following 20
fond /fɒnd/ 69
food 2, 26, 66
food poisoning 13
food processor 36, 52
  (-sing) 13
fool-proof 12
(a) fool's errand 74
foolish /'fuːlɪʃ/ 34 (~ness) 11
foot the bill 83
foot 2, 44
football player/pitch/match 41,
  45, 88
footballer 41
footlights 13
footpath 44
Footsie /'fʊtsi/ 56
for 67
for all that 23
for example/instance 100
for the time being 58
force /fɔːs/ 60
forceps /fɔːseps/ 40
forehead /fɔːhed/ 46
foreign correspondent 53
forest /'fɒrɪst/ (~ed) 44
forge /fɔːdʒ/ (~r) (~ry) 55
forgetful (~ness) 8, 12
forgivable /fə'gɪvəbəl/ 8
form 85
format 53
formation 52
formerly /'fɔːməli/ 20
formula /'fɔːmjələ/ 51
fortitude /'fɔːtɪtjuːd/ 11
fortune /'fɔːtjuːn/ 89
foundations /faʊn'deɪʃənz/ 27
fraction /'frækʃən/ 51
fragrant /'freɪgrənt/ 71
frank 34
frankfurter 16
fraternity /frə'tɜːnɪti/ 11
freckle /'frekəl/ 11, 33
freebie /'friːbiː/ 95
freedom 11, 54 (~-fighter) 4
freeway /'friːweɪ/ 93
freezing 68
freight train /freɪt/ 49
French /frentʃ/ 31, 98
french fries 93
(as) fresh as a daisy 76

freshen up 83
fridge /frɪdʒ/ 7, 98
friend /frend/ 7, 18, 35
  (~ship) 8, 11
frighten the life out of sb 79
frog 46, 73
frost 32
frown /fraʊn/ 72
fruit (~ salad/ juice) 43, 66
frustrated /frʌs'treɪtɪd/
  (-ting) (-tion) 68
fry /fraɪ/ 43
fudge cake 43
fuel /fjʊəl/ 95
fulfil /fʊl'fɪl/
  (~ling) (~ment) 65
full of oneself 34
full stop 4
function /'fʌŋkʃən/ 52
funnel /'fʌnəl/ 49
furious /'fjuːrɪəs/ 8, 68, 70
furniture /'fɜːnɪtʃə/ 2, 3, 26, 30
furry /'fɜːri/ 64
further /'fɜːðə/ 39
further to/furthermore 24
fury /'fjuːri/ 11, 68, 70
fuselage /'fjuːzəlɑːʒ/ 49
fuss 85
futon /'fuːtɒn/ 16
fuzz /fʌz/ 95

gale /geɪl/ (~ warning) 32
gallery 45, 49
gallop /'gæləp/ 73
game show 53
gang 29
gangplank 49
gap
garage /'gærɑːdʒ/
  /'gærɪdʒ/ 49, 93
garden 66, 93 (~ing) 85
  (~ centre) 45
gargle /'gɑːgəl/ 17
garlic /'gɑːlɪk/ 43
garment 26
gas 26
gash /gæʃ/ 17
gasoline /'gæsəliːn/ 93
gateau /'gætəʊ/ 16, 43
gauze /gɔːz/ 15
Gawd forbids
  /gɔːd fə'bɪdz/ 95
gaze /geɪz/ 71
gears /'gɪəz/ 49
gems /dʒems/ 92
general 97
generate /'dʒenəreɪt/ 22

in summary 100
in the event of 21
in the meantime 20
incisor /ɪnˈsaɪzə/ 46
income /ˈɪŋkʌm/ 9 (~tax) 13
inconvenient /ɪŋkənˈviːnɪənt/
  (-nce) 9, 88
increase /ˈɪŋkriːs/ /ɪŋˈkriːs/ 18
independence 54
index 56
Indian 31, 94
indigestion /ɪndɪˈdʒestʃən/ 48
indiscreet /ɪndɪsˈkriːt/ 9
induce /ɪnˈdʒuːs/ (-ction) 10
industrial (~ise) (~ist) 3, 8, 10
  (~ estate) 45
industry 3
inedible /ɪnˈedɪbəl/ 9
inefficient /ɪnɪˈfɪʃənt/ 9
inevitable /ɪnˈevɪtəbəl/ 60
infinitive 4
infirm 96
informal 4
information 2, 26, 30
  (~ technology) 52
informer 95
inheritance tax 13, 56
injection /ɪnˈdʒekʃən/ 48
injure /ˈɪndʒə/ (-ry) 38
innocent /ˈɪnəsənt/ 34
input 14
inquiring /ɪŋˈkwaɪərɪŋ/ 34
inquisitive /ɪŋˈkwɪzɪtɪv/
  (~ness) 11, 34
insensitive 9
insert /ˈɪnsɜːt/ /ɪnˈsɜːt/ 9, 52
insignificant
  /ɪnsɪgˈnɪfɪkənt/ 57
insist (~ent) 70
inspect (~ion) (~or) 10, 90

inspired /ɪnˈspaɪəd/ (-ration)
  (-ring) 68
install /ɪnˈstɔːl/ 88
instant coffee 66
institution /ɪnstɪˈtʃuːʃən/ 54
instruct /ɪnˈstrʌkt/ 88
insult /ˈɪnsʌlt/ /ɪnˈsʌlt/ 18
insurance /ɪnˈʃɔːrəns/ 48
intellectual /ɪntəˈlektʃʊəl/ 67
intelligent 7, 12, 34 (-nce) 26
intense (~ly) (-sify) (-sity) 11
intention /ɪnˈtenʃən/ 11
interbreed /ɪntəˈbriːd/ 46
interest (~-free) 12, 56
interesting 18, 68
interject /ɪntəˈdʒekt/ 88

internal 9
intestines /ɪnˈtestɪnz/ 2
into the bargain 24
intolerant /ɪnˈtɒlərənt/ 9
intransitive /ɪnˈtrænsətɪv/ 4
introduce (~r) 10, 86
introduction (-tory) 10
introspective
  /ɪntrəˈspektɪv/ 10
introverted
  /ˈɪntrəvɜːtɪd/ 10, 34
intuition /ɪntʃuːˈɪʃən/ 71
Inuit /ˈɪnjuɪt/ 31
invent (~ion) 52, 85
inverted 10
inverted commas 4
invest (~ment) 11, 56
investigate 55, 90 (-tion) 26
involvement 8, 11
Iranian /ɪˈreɪnɪən/ 31
Iraqi /ɪˈræki/ 31
Irish /ˈaɪrɪʃ/ 31 (~ stew) 43
iron /ˈaɪən/ (~ing-board) 28,
  36, 52
irregular /ɪˈregjʊlə/ 4
irrelevant 9
irreplaceable /ɪrəˈpleɪsəbəl/ 9
irresponsible 9
irreversible 9
Israeli /ɪzˈreɪli/ 31
issue /ˈɪʃuː/ 25
itchy feet /ɪtʃiˈfiːt/ 79
it's all very well 23
Italian 31
itch /ɪtʃ/ 48
item /ˈaɪtəm/ 30

jackal /ˈdʒækəl/ 16
jacuzzi /dʒəˈkuːzi/ 52
jagged /ˈdʒægɪd/ 64
jail /dʒeɪəl/ 55
jam 37, 66, 94 (~ on it) 81
janitor /ˈdʒænɪtə/ 94
Japanese 31
jar /dʒɑː/ 66
javelin /ˈdʒævlɪn/ 41
jealous /ˈdʒeləs/ (~y) 11, 34
jeans /dʒiːnz/ 27, 47
jerk /dʒɜːk/ 95
jersey 15
jet 49
jewellery /ˈdʒuːəlri/ 66
job 26
job centre 45
jockey /ˈdʒɒki/ 41
jodhpurs /ˈdʒɒdpəz/ 27
jog /ˈdʒɒg/ 41

john 95
joints /dʒɔɪnts/ 48
Jordanian /dʒɔːˈdeɪnɪən/ 31
journal /ˈdʒɜːnəl/ 53
journalism (-list) 8, 53
journo /ˈdʒɜːnəʊ/ 94
joystick /ˈdʒɔɪstɪk/ 49
judge /dʒʌdʒ/ 55
judgement /ˈdʒʌdʒmənt/ 25
judo 16 /ˈdʒuːdəʊ/
jug /dʒʌg/ 66
juice 66
July 15
jump out of one's skin 79
junior /ˈdʒuːnɪə/ 35
junk food/ mail 13
junta /ˈdʒʊntə/ 16
jury /ˈdʒʊəri/ 55
just as 20
justice /ˈdʒʌstɪs/ 11

kangaroo /kæŋɡəˈruː/ 73
karaoke /kæriˈəʊki/ 99
karate /kəˈrɑːti/ 16
kayak /ˈkaɪæk/ 16
keen 69, 80
keep a cool head 79
keep one's chin up 79
keep s.b. on the edge of their
  seat 79
ken 94
kerosene /ˈkerəsiːn/ 93
ketch /ketʃ/ 5
ketchup /ˈketʃʌp/ 43
key 25, 92
keyboard 52
kick 2
kick off 82
kid 7, 95 (~'s stuff) 74
kidnap /ˈkɪdnæp/ (~per)
  (~ping) 55
kidney(s) /ˈkɪdniːz/ (~ donor) 2,
  8, 43
kind of 100
kind (~ness) (~-hearted) 2, 8,
  11, 12, 43
kindergarten /ˈkɪndəɡɑːtən/ 16
king (~ly) (~dom) 1, 11
kinship /ˈkɪnʃɪp/ 8
kiosk /ˈkiːɒsk/ 16
kip 7
Kiribati /kɪrɪˈbɑːti/ 31
kirk /kɜːk/ 94
kitten /ˈkɪtən/ 2, 73
kiwi bird/fruit /ˈkiːwiː/ 43, 46
kleptomaniac
  /kleptəˈmeɪnɪæk/ 69

pincers /'pɪnsəz/ 27
pine /paɪn/ 46
pineapple 71
pissed /pɪst/ 95
piste /piːst/ 41
place /pleɪs/ 7, 19
plaice /pleɪs/ 19, 43
plain /pleɪn/ 33, 44, 47
plane /pleɪn/ 29, 98
plant 28, 46 (~ holder) 8
planting 44
plaster 48
plastic 26, 66
platonic /plə'tɒnɪk/ 15
play 29
plea /pliː/ 55, 92
(as) pleased as Punch 79
pledge /pledʒ/ 92
plenty (of) 45, 57
pliers /'plaɪəz/ 27
plod (~der) 63
plonk (~er) 95
plough /plaʊ/ 18, 40
ploy /plɔɪ/ 92
plug /plʌg/ 36
plum /plʌm/ 43
plumber /'plʌmə/ 40
plump /plʌmp/ 33
plus 24, 51
pneumatic /njʊ'mætɪk/ 18
pneumonia /njʊ'məʊnɪə/ 48
pocket money 13
poetry /'pəʊətri/ 42 (-tess) 97
point 25, 41, 51, 85
point of view 67
poke one's nose in (to) 74
polar bear 73
pole-vault (~er) 41
poles apart 23
police 95 (~man/woman/
    officer) 40, 97 (~ station) 45
policy /'pɒlɪsi/ 28, 54
polish /'pɒlɪʃ/ 26 (~ed) 6
politics /'pɒlətɪks/ (-tician)
    (-tical) /pə'lɪtɪkəl/
    (political party/issue) 54
polka-dotted /'pəʊlkədɒtɪd/ 47
poll /pəʊl/ 92
pollen /'pɒlən/ 46
pollution /pə'luːʃən/ 8, 44, 45
polo-necked /pəʊlə'nekt/ 12
polytechnic /pɒlɪ'teknɪk/ 39
pond 44
poodle /'puːdəl/ 16
pool /puːl/ 41
poplar /'pɒplə/ 46

popular /'pɒpjələ/ (~ity) 11,
    51
population 44
porch /pɔːtʃ/ 36
pork chop 43
port 49
port-hole 49
porter 10, 49
portion /'pɔːʃən/ 43
pose /pəʊz/ 10
position /pə'zɪʃən/ 25
possessions /pə'zeʃənz/ 62
possible (-bility) 60
post- 9
postie /'pəʊsti/ 97
postman/postwoman 66, 97
postpone /pə'spəʊn/ 10, 88
postwar 9
pot 66
potato 28, 43
    (~ chips/crisps) 93
pottery 66
pound /paʊnd/ 64
pour /pɔː/ 18
pour cold water on 80
pour down 32
pour oil on troubled waters 80
pour one's heart out to s.b. 80
pouring with rain 80
poverty /'pɒvəti/ 30
power 89 (~ cut) 37
    (~ point) 36
practice (-tise) /'præktɪs/ 19
pram /præm/ 93
prat 95
prawn /prɔːn/ (~ cocktail) 43
pray /preɪ/ 19
pre-schooler 99
prefix /'priːfɪks/ 4
pregnant 48
prejudiced /'predʒədɪst/ 45
premises /'premɪsɪz/ 27
prepare 85, 87
preposition 4
prerequisite /priː'rekwɪzɪt/ 21
preschool 39
prescribe /prə'skraɪb/ 48
present /'prezənt/ /prə'zent/
    18, 62, 88
preside /prə'zaɪd/ 54
president /'prezɪdənt/ (~ial)
    (-dency) 54
press 52, 53, 71
press agency 45
press-up 14
pressure /'preʃə/ 10
pretend 88

previously 20
prey /preɪ/ 19
price (~less) (~y) (~ tag) 2, 56,
    88
prickly /'prɪkli/ 46, 64
pride /praɪd/ 11
priest /priːst/ 40
priesthood /'priːsthʊd/ 8
prim and proper 77
primary 39
Prime Minister 54
prime number 51
principle /'prɪnsəpəl/ 11
print 53
printer 52
printout /'prɪntaʊt/ 14
prior to 20
prison 55, 95
pro-government 9
pro- 9
probable (-bly) 60
probation /prə'beɪʃən/ 55
probe /prəʊb/ 92
problem 25 (~-free) 12
proceeds /'prəʊsiːdz/ 27
produce /prə'dʒuːs/ /'prɒdʒuːs/
    (~r) 3, 10
product /'prɒdʌkt/
    (~ion) (~tive) (~tivity) 3, 10,
    11
professor 39
profit 56, 85
programme 53
progress 18, 26
prohibited /prə'hɪbɪtɪd/ 96
projector /prə'dʒektə/ 8, 40
promote /prə'məʊt/ 40
prompt /prɒmpt/ 22
pronoun /'prəʊnaʊn/ 4
proof 55
property 62
propose /prə'pəʊz/ (-sal) 88
proprietor /prə'praɪətə/ 62
prosecute /'prɒsəkjuːt/ 96
prospect 10
prosperity 11
protest /'prəʊtest/ /prə'test/ 18
proudly /'praʊdli/ 70
provide 62
provided/providing (that) 21
provisional /prə'vɪʒənəl/ 58
provoke (~d) 22
prudence /'pruːdəns/ 11
psalm /sɑːm/ 18
pseudo- /'sjuːdəʊ/ /'suːdəʊ/ 9
pseudonym /'sjuːdənɪm/
    /'suːdənɪm/ 18

psychiatry /saɪˈkaɪətri/ (-tric) (-trist) 18
psychic /ˈsaɪkɪk/ 18
psychology /saɪˈkɒlədʒi/ (-gical) (-gist) 18
pub (~lic house) 98
public relations officer 40
publish /ˈpʌblɪʃ/ (~er) (~ing) 42, 53, 89
pudding /ˈpʊdɪŋ/ 43
puddle /ˈpʌdəl/ 44
puff /pʌf/ 30
pull /pʊl/ 52
pull a fast one 74
pull it off 65
punctuation /pʌŋtʃuˈeɪʃən/ 4
puncture /ˈpʌŋtʃə/ 93
punish /ˈpʌnɪʃ/ (~ment) 55
puppy 73
purchase /ˈpɜːtʃəs/ 7, 56, 96
purify /ˈpjʊrɪfaɪ/ 8
purpose /ˈpɜːpəs/ 22
purr /pɜː/ 2, 73
purse /pɜːs/ 93
purser /ˈpɜːsə/ 49
pushy /ˈpʊʃi/ 34
put, *expressions with* 2, 3,18, 82, 88
pyjamas /pəˈdʒɑːməz/ 27, 47
pyramid /ˈpɪrəmɪd/ 51

quack /kwæk/ 73
quaint /kweɪnt/ 45
quarrelsome /ˈkwɒrəlsəm/ 34
quay /kiː/ 49
question /kwestʃən/ 25, 48 (~ mark) 3
queue /kjuː/ 93
quick 63 (as ~ as a flash) 76
quick off the mark 78
quick-tempered 34
quick-witted 12
quid /kwɪd/ 7
quiet /kwaɪət/ 71 (as ~ as a mouse) 76
quit /kwɪt/ 92
quite /kwaɪt/ 57, 60, 69
quite the opposite 23
quiz /kwɪz/ 53

rabies /reɪbiːz/ 38
race /reɪs/ 33 (~ relations) 13
racecourse /ˈreɪskɔːs/ 41
racing driver 41
rack and ruin 77
racket /ˈrækɪt/ 41, 61
radar /ˈreɪdɑː/ 98

radical /ˈrædɪkəl/ 67
radio station 45
radish /ˈrædɪʃ/ 43
radius /ˈreɪdiəs/ 51
rage /reɪdʒ/ 11, 68
rail /reɪl/ 49
railway car/carriage 45, 93
rain 19, 30 (~y) 32 (~forest) 44 (~water) 66
raise /reɪz/ 19, 86, 88
rake /reɪk/ 36
range /reɪndʒ/ 29
rant and rave 77
rap /ræp/ 94
rape /reɪp/ 55
rapid /ˈræpɪd/ 63
rash /ræʃ/ 48
raspberry /ˈræzbəri/ 43
rat-race /ˈræt reɪs/ 13
rate /reɪt/ 63
rate of exchange 56
rather /ˈrɑːðə/ 57
rattle /ˈrætəl/ 61
ratty /ˈræti/ 73
rave reviews 42
ray(s) /reɪz/ 19, 61
razor /ˈreɪzə/ 27
re-introduce 86
reach /riːtʃ/ 65, 80, 87
react /riˈækt/ 18, 52
reaction /riˈækʃən/ 25
readable /ˈriːdəbəl/ 8
readiness /ˈredɪnəs/ 8
ready-made 12
realise /ˈrɪəlaɪz/ (-sable) (-sation) 65
really 57
reason 11, 22
rebate /ˈriːbeɪt/ 56
recall /rɪˈkɔːl/ 90
recede /rəˈsiːd/ 38 (-ding) 33
receipt /rəˈsiːt/ 18, 56
receive /rəˈsiːv/ 18, 53, 87, 89
receptacle /rəˈseptɪkəl/ 66
receptionist 26, 40
recipe /ˈresɪpi/ 18
reckon /ˈrekən/ 67
recognition /rekəgˈnɪʃən/ 11
recognizable /rekəgˈnaɪzəbəl/ 8
record /ˈrekɔːd/ /rɪˈkɔːd/ 18, 91
record player/token 8, 13
record-breaking 12
recover /rəˈkʌvə/ 87
rectangle /ˈrektæŋgəl/ 51
recycled paper 44

(in the) red 56, 74
(as) red as a beetroot 76
(a) red rag to a bull 76
red-haired 12, 33
reddish /ˈredɪʃ/ 8
redefine 9
reduce /rɪˈdjuːs/ 10, 96
reduction 11, 56
redundant /rɪˈdʌndənt/ 40
reed /riːd/ 19
referendum /refəˈrendəm/ 54
refrain /rəˈfreɪn/ 96
refugee /refjuːˈdʒiː/ 38
refund /ˈriːfʌnd/ 56
refusal /rəˈfjuːzəl/ 8, 40
regal /ˈriːgəl/ 1
regional /ˈriːdʒənəl/ 31
register /ˈredʒɪstə/ 4
registry office 45
regret /rəˈgret/ 7
regular 4
reimburse /riːɪmˈbɜːs/ 7
rein /reɪn/ 18, 19
reinforce /riːɪnˈfɔːs/ 18
reject /rɪˈdʒekt/ /ˈriːdʒekt/ (~ion) 11, 18
relationship 11
relaxed /rəˈlækst/ 12, 34 (-xing) 2
release /rəˈliːs/ 55
relevant 9
reliability 26
reliable /rəˈlaɪəbəl/ 34
religious /rəˈlɪdʒəs/ 67
reluctantly 70
remote control 36, 53 (~led) 12
renovate /ˈrenəveɪt/ 85
rent 62
rep 98
repel /rɪˈpel/ 35, 69
repellent /rɪˈpelənt/ 69
rephrase /ˈriːfreɪz/ 9
replace 9 (~ment) 8, 11
report 10, 53, 90
reported speech 10
repose 10
representation (-tative) 54
repress 10
reprint 18
reptile /ˈreptaɪl/ 1, 46
republic 54
repulsion (-sive) 69
request /rɪˈkwest/ 7
requirement /rɪˈkwaɪəmənt/ 11, 21

research /'riːsɜːtʃ/ 26
  (~ worker) 40
resemble /rɪ'zembəl/ 86
resentful/resentment 11
reserve /rɪ'zɜːv/ 88
residence /'rezɪdəns/ 7
residential /rezɪ'denʃəl/ 45
resit /riːˈsɪt/ 39
resolution /rezə'luːʃən/ 25
respect /rɪ'spekt/ 10, 90
response 25
responsible 9
rest and recreation 77
restaurant-car 49
result /rɪ'zʌlt/ 22
retirement /rɪ'taɪəmənt/ 11
retract 86
retrospective
  /retrə'spektɪv/ 10
return /rɪ'tɜːn/ 87, 93
retype 9
reveal 86
revenge /rɪ'vendʒ/ 87
reverse /rɪ'vɜːs/ 23
revert /rɪ'vɜːt/ 10
review /rɪ'vjuː/ 2, 53, 91
revision 5
revolt /rɪ'vɒlt/ 69
revolution (~ary) (~ise) 54
rewind 9
reword 4
rewrite 9
rheumatism /'ruːmətɪzəm/ 48
rhyme /raɪm/ 42
ribbon /'rɪbən/ 47
rice /raɪs/ 26, 43
riddle /'rɪdəl/ 92
ride 2
ridge /rɪdʒ/ 44
riding 41
right /raɪt/ 19, 100
right-angled 51
right-wing 67
ring 7, 41
rink /rɪŋk/ 41
rip somebody off 83
rip-off /'rɪpɒf/ 56, 83
rise and shine 83
rite /raɪt/ 19
river 44
road 44, 61, 73 (~ works) 13,
  49
roast /rəust/ 43
rob 55
robot /'rəubɒt/ 52
rock 42 (~ y) 44
rod 41

romance /rə'mæns/ 35
room 50
root 4, 46
rosemary /'rəuzməri/ 35
rosy-cheeked 12
rotate /rəu'teɪt/ 52
rotation, 52
rotten /'rɒtən/ 71
rottweiler /'rɒtvaɪlə/ 16
rough /rʌf/ 18, 19, 46, 64
rough and ready 74, 77
round the bend 78
round trip 93
round-faced 33
round-neck 47
route /ruːt/ 18
row /rəu/ /rau/ 19, 29
rowing-boat /'rəuɪŋ/ 49
royal /'rɔɪəl/ 1, 45
rub /rʌb/ 48
rubber /'rʌbə/ 28, 93
rubbish /'rʌbɪʃ/ 66, 88, 93
  (~ bin) 93
rudder /'rʌdə/ 49
rude /ruːd/ 34
ruff /rʌf/ 19
rugby /'rʌgbi/ 41
ruined /'ruːɪnd/ 57
Rumanian 31
rumble /'rʌmbəl/ 30, 61, 72
rump steak 43
run, expressions with
  49, 54, 58, 63, 81, 91
run out 37, 49, 91
run-down 12, 45
runway 49
rural /'ruːrəl/ 3
rushing 63
Russian 31
rustle /'rʌsəl/ 17, 61

sack 66 (get the ~) 40
sadistic /sə'dɪstɪk/ 34
sadly 70
sadness 8
safe and sound 77
safety helmet /'seɪfti/ 41
safety officer 40
sail /seɪl/ 19, 49, 63
  (~ling boat) 5
sailor 8, 49
salad dressing 43
salary /'sæləri/ 56
sales assistant 40
salmon /'sæmən/ 18, 43
salt (~y) 28, 43, 71
salt water 46

sand 18, 66 (~y) 44
sardine(s) 29, 43
satellite dish /'sætəlaɪt/ 53
satin /'sætɪn/ 15
satisfaction (-torily) (-tory) 11
satisfy (-fied) 11
sauce /sɔːs/ 28
sauna /'sɔːnə/ 16
sauté /'səuteɪ/ 16
savings account 56
savoury /'seɪvəri/ 43
saxophone /'sæksəfəun/ 15
scales /skeɪlz/ 27, 46, 48
scalpel /'skælpəl/ 40, 48
scandal 53
Scandanavia 31
scarcity /'skeəsɪti/ 8
scared out of one's wits 79
scared stiff 79
scene /siːn/ 19, 42, 53
scenery /'siːnəri/ 42
scent /sent/ 19 (~ed) 71
school /skuːl/ 2, 39, 45
  (~kid) 29
schoolmaster/schoolmistress
  97
science /saɪəns/ 18, 52
scientist 40
scissors /'sɪzəz/ 1, 13, 27
scorching /'skɔːtʃɪŋ/ 32
score /skɔː/ 41
Scotch tape 93
Scottish 94
scratch /skrætʃ/ 2
scream /skriːm/ 70
screech /skriːtʃ/ 61
screw /skruː/ 95
screwdriver /'skruːdraɪvə/ 2
script /skrɪpt/ 40
scruffy /'skrʌfi/ 33, 47
sculptor /'skʌlptə/
  (-ture) /'skʌlptʃə/ 42
sea 44, 49
seafood 43
seagull /'siːgʌl/ 46
seal /siːl/ 46, 90
season /'siːzən/ 43
second-class 12
secondary /'sekəndri/ 39
secretary /'sekrətri/ 40, 97
secure /sə'kjuə/ 11, 65
security /sə'kjurɪti/ 11
  (~ officer) 40
see, expressions with
  35, 71, 91, 100
seen better days 74
seething /'siːðɪŋ/ 68

self- 12
self-assured 12, 34
self-catering 50
self-centred 12, 34
self-confident 12, 34
self-employed 2, 6
self-important 34
self-indulgent 12, 34
sellotape /'seləteɪp/ 26, 93
semester /sə'mestə/ 93
semi- 9, 36
semi-colon /semi'kəʊlɒn/ 4
seminar /'semɪnɑː/ 16
sender 8
senior 35
sensation 53
sense 11
sensible 34
sensitive 9, 34 (-vity) 11
sent 19
sentence 4, 55
sentiment (~al) (~alise) (~ally) 11, 45
Serbian 31
serial /'siːrɪəl/ 53
series /'siːriːz/ 27, 53
serve 50
service 50 (~ station) 49
set, expressions with 1, 2, 29, 42, 55, 88
set-up 14
setback 14
settee 5
settle 32
shabby /'ʃæbi/ 45
shade /ʃeɪd/ 1, 28, 64
shake 72
shake-up 14
shake in one's shoes 79
shallot /ʃə'lɒt/ 43
shallow /'ʃæləʊ/ 44, 59
shape /ʃeɪp/ 51
shares /ʃeəz/ 56
shark /ʃɑːk/ 46
shawl /ʃɔːl/ 16
shears /ʃɪəz/ 27
shed 36
sheep 29, 43, 73
sheepish 73
shell 38 (~ed) 1
shepherd /'ʃepəd/ 97
shepherdess /ʃepə'des/ 97
sherbet /'ʃɜːbət/ 16
shift-work /'ʃɪftwɜːk/ 40
shin-pads 41
shine /ʃaɪn/ 61 (-ny) 64
shipmate 35

shiver /'ʃɪvə/ 72 (~y) 48
shoal /'ʃəʊl/ 29
shock 11
shocking-pink 12
shoe horn 13
shook /ʃʊk/ 38
shoot /ʃuːt/ 2, 41, 53
shop-lifter (~lifting) 55, 96
shopping 66, 85 (~ centre) 45 (-per) 8
shore /ʃɔː/ 44
short (~en) 59 (~age) 60
short cut 59
short story 42
short-sighted 12
shorts 27, 41, 47
(a) shot in the dark 74
shout /ʃaʊt/ 18, 70
show /ʃəʊ/ 42, 53
show, it all goes to 74
shower /'ʃaʊə/ 30, 32, 50
shrewd /ʃruːd/ 4, 34
shriek /ʃriːk/ 70
shrimp /ʃrɪmp/ 43
shrink /ʃrɪŋk/ 59
shuttlecock /'ʃʌtəlkɒk/ 41
shyly /'ʃaɪli/ 70
Siamese 73
sick and tired 68, 77
sick 48 (~ leave) 40
(as) sick as a dog/parrot 76
sickie /'sɪki/ 95
sickly 43
sidewalk /'saɪdwɔːk/ 93
siesta /si:'estə/ 16
sigh /saɪ/ 72
sight /saɪt/ 11, 19, 71, 89
sight-seeing 2, 50
signal-box 49
Sikhs /siːks/ 31
silent 71
silk /sɪlk/ 26, 47 (~y) 64
silly 34
simple /'sɪmpəl/ 34
since then 20
sincere /sɪn'sɪə/ 34 (~ly) 70
singer 8, 29
single 50, 97
single-handed 2
single-minded 12, 34
singlehood 99
sink 37
sink or swim 77
sit 39
sitcom /'sɪtkɒm/ 53
site /saɪt/ 19, 45
sitting pretty 74

situation /sɪtjʊ'eɪʃən/ 25
sixth sense 71
sizeable /'saɪzəbəl/ 57
sizzle /'sɪzəl/ 17
skating rink 45
ski /skiː/ 16, 41, 50
skilled worker 40
skin cream 66
skinny /skɪni/ 4
skip 39, 73
skipper 49
skittles /'skɪtəlz/ 41
slalom /'slɑːləm/ 16
slang /slæŋ/ 4, 95
sleek /sliːk/ 64
sleep like a log 76
sleeping-car 49
sleet 32
sleeve 47
slice /slaɪs/ 30
slim 4, 33
slim-hipped 12
slipper(s) 27, 47
slippery 64
slither /'slɪðə/ 73
sloth /sləʊθ/ 11
slow 37
slow lane 95
slow off the mark 78
slowcoach 63, 78
slowly but surely 77
slum /slʌm/ 45
slush /slʌʃ/ 23
sly /slaɪ/ 34
small ads 53
small talk 82
smart /smɑːt/ 33, 34, 47
smash /smæʃ/ 37
smell (~y) 11, 71
smog /smɒg/ 32
smoke /sməʊk/ 30
smoker 8
smoko /'sməʊkəʊ/ 94
smooth /smuːð/ 64
smuggle /'smʌgəl/ (~r) (-ling) 55
snack 43
snail /sneɪl/ 46
snake /sneɪk/ 73
snatch /snætʃ/ 71
sneeze 72
snifter /'snɪftə/ 95
snobbish /'snɒbɪʃ/ 12
snooker /'snuːkə/ 41
snore /snɔː/ 72
snorkel /'snɔːkəl/ 16
snort 95

Proverbs & Sayings

Abbreviations

wearunders /'weərʌndəz/ 94
weather 1, 19, 26, 30
    (~ forecast) 53
wed 92
wee /wiː/ 94
weigh /weɪ/ 19, 48, 64 (~ty) 64
weird /wɪəd/ 34
welfare state 13
well (then) 100
well-behaved 12
well-built 33
well-dressed 12, 33, 47
well-off 12
well worth a... 45
wellingtons /'welɪŋtənz/
    (wellies) 5, 15, 27
whacked /wækt/ 17
what if 21
what with one thing and
    another 75
what's more 24
what's on? 42
wheels /wiːlz/ 95
wheeze /wiːz/ 17
when it comes to... 75
where was I? 100
whereabouts /'weərəbaʊts/ 27
wherever /weə'revə/ 21
whether 19
whichever 21
while 20
whine /waɪn/ 19
whip /wɪp/ 17
whirl /wɜːl/ 17
whirr /wɜː/ 17
whisk /wɪsk/ 17
whiskers /'wɪskəz/ 2, 46
whisper /'wɪspə/ 70
whistle /'wɪsəl/ 17, 18
(as) white as snow / a sheet 76
whiting /'waɪtɪŋ/ 43
whizz /wɪz/ 17
whoever /huː'evə/ 21
wicked /'wɪkɪd/ 95
wide (~n) 59
wide-eyed 12
width /wɪdθ/ 11, 59
wife-to-be 35
willow /'wɪləʊ/ 46
wind 19, 30, 32
window cleaner 40
windscreen (~ wiper) 8, 13
windsurfing 41, 50
wine 19, 66 (~ and dine) 77
wings /wɪŋz/ 46, 49
wink /wɪŋk/ 72
wisdom 11

wishbone /'wɪʃbəʊn/ 6
wishful thinking 6
with a view to / the aim of 22
withdraw /wɪð'drɔː/ 56
wither /'wɪðə/ 38
within walking distance, 45
with-it 47
witness 55, 71
wizard /'wɪzəd/ 95
wolf /wʊlf/ 29
womanhood 11
won /wʌn/ 41
womb /wuːm/ 18
wood 26, 28, 44, 66
    (can't see the ~ for the
    trees) 91
woof /wʊf/ 73
wool /wʊl/ (~len) 26, 47
word (~y) 3, 18
word-processing (-sor) 13, 52
work 18, 26, 28, 29, 30, 37,
    40 (~s) 42
workaholic /wɜːkə'hɒlɪk/ 40
worker 8
workmate 35
workout /'wɜːkaʊt/ 14
work like a dream 76
world of difference 23
(the) world's worst 81
world-famous 12, 18
worm /wɜːm/ 46
worn out 12, 68
worried /'wʌrid/ 57, 68, 70
worship /'wɜːʃɪp/ 8, 35, 69
worth /wɜːθ/ 45, 56
wound /wuːnd/ /waʊnd/ 19, 38
wrap up the discussion
    /ræp/ 82
wreck /rek/ 19, 49
wrestling /'reslɪŋ/ 41
wriggle /'rɪgəl/ (-gly) 17, 46
wrinkle /'rɪŋkəl/ 33
wrist /rɪst/ 48
writer /'raɪtə/ 8, 26, 97
write-off /'raɪtɒf/ 14
write-up /'raɪtʌp/ 14
wrong /rɒŋ/ 50, 57
    (get the ~ end of the stick)
    74, 82

yacht /jɒt/ 5, 16, 49, 93
yashmak /'jæʃmæk/ 16
yawn /jɔːn/ 72 (~ing gap) 23
yearn /jɜːn/ 69
yellow fever 38
Yemeni /'jeməni/ 31
yes 95, 100

yew /juː/ 46
yoghurt /'jɒgət/ 16, 66
you know/see 100
youngster /'jʌŋstə/ 33
youth club 45
youth hostel 13, 29, 45, 50
yuppy /'jʌpi/ 98

zinc /zɪŋk/ 66
zip 47
zoology /zuː'ɒlədʒi/ (-gist)
    (-gical) 18, 52, 71
zucchini /zʊ'kiːni/ 43

that is to say 100
that reminds me 75
that's all well and good 23
that's it/that 75
thaw /θɔː/ 32
theatre /ˈθɪətə/ 3, 42, 45
theft /θeft/ 55
then 20
thermal spring 44
thermometer /θəˈmɒmɪtə/ 48
thick /θɪk/ 64
thin 64 (~-faced) 33 (~-lipped)
  12 (as ~ as a rake 76
thinker 67
third /θɜːd/ 51
thirsty /ˈθɜːsti/ 68
thirtyish /ˈθɜːtiɪʃ/ 8
this and that 75
this is it 75
this, that and the other 75
thistle /ˈθɪsəl/ 46
thorn /θɔːn/ 46
though /ðəʊ/ 18
thought /θɔːt/ 11
thread /θred/ 26, 92
threaten /ˈθretən/ 70
three-dimensional 51
thrifty /ˈθrɪfti/ 4, 34
thrilled /θrɪld/ (-ling) 68
thrive /θraɪv/ 46
through /θruː/ 18, 19
through road 96
throughout /θruːˈaʊt/ 20
throw /θrəʊ/ 2
throw away 87
thud /θʌd/ 61
thunder 30 (~storm) 32
thyme /taɪm/ 43
ticket collector/holder/office 8,
  49
(the) tide has turned 80
tidy /ˈtaɪdi/ 88
tight(s) /taɪt(s)/ 27, 47, 93
(in a) tight corner 80
tight-fisted 34
tight-fitting 12
till then 20
timber /ˈtɪmbə/ 26
time, *expressions with* 58
time and time again 58
(the) time (that) 20
time bomb 38
time-consuming 12
time share 36, 50
timeless /ˈtaɪmləs/ 58
tin 66 (~ opener) 8, 13
tinkle /ˈtɪŋkəl/ 17

tiny /ˈtaɪni/ 57
tip 26
(on the) tip of one's tongue 83
tippex /ˈtɪpeks/ 40
tiptoe /ˈtɪptəʊ/ 83
tire /ˈtaɪə/ 19 (~d) 48, 57, 68
tissues /ˈtɪʃuːz/ 66
titfer /ˈtɪtfə/ 95
to and fro 77
to boot 24
to my mind 67
to the touch 64
toe 19
toe the line 80, 83
tolerant 9
tolerate 4, 88
tom 73
tomb /tuːm/ 18
tomcat 2
tongs /tɒŋz/ 27
tons of 57
toowit toowoo
  /təˈwɪt təˈwuː/ 73
tool /tuːl/ (~ box) 66
tooth /tuːθ/ 2 (~ paste) 26, 30,
  66
top 51
top-hole 95
top-secret 12
top of the class 78
(on) top form 79
(on) top of (all) that 24
(on) top of the world 79
topic /ˈtɒpɪk/ 25
topnotch /tɒpˈnɒtʃ/ 81
tore /tɔː/ 63
torrential rain 32
tortoise /ˈtɔːtəs/ 1, 46
totally 57
touch /tʌtʃ/ 11, 71
tough /tʌf/ 18
tour /tɔː/ 50
touring /ˈtɔːrɪŋ/ 2
tow /təʊ/ 19
town council 54
Town Hall 45
toy /tɔɪ/ 66
tracksuit 27
tractor /ˈtræktə/ 40
trade 28
traditional (~ist) 67
traffic (~ jam/lights/system/
  warden) 13, 27, 45, 55
trafficking /ˈtræfɪkɪŋ/ 55
tragedy /ˈtrædʒədi/ 38
training 26
tram 49

transfer
  /trænsˈfɜː/ /ˈtrænsfɜː/ 18
transitive 3
transport /ˈtrænspɔːt/ /trænˈspɔːt/
  (~ation) 10, 18, 30, 49
transpose /trænsˈpəʊz/ 10
trashcan /ˈtræʃkæn/ 93
travel 26, 50, 63
trawler /ˈtrɔːlə/ 49
tread /tred/ 18
treatment 48
tree 46
tremble /ˈtrembəl/ 72
tremor /ˈtremə/ 38
trendy /ˈtrendi/ 47
trespasser /ˈtrespəsə/ 96
trial /ˈtraɪəl/ 55
triangle /ˈtraɪæŋgəl/ 2, 51
triangular /traɪˈæŋgjələ/ 51
tributary /ˈtrɪbjətri/ 44
trickle /ˈtrɪkəl/ 17
trip 26
trot 73
trouble (~some) (-ling) 65, 90
trouble and strife 95
trousers 1, 27, 47, 93
trout /traʊt/ 43
truck 93
trunk 46, 93
trunks 27
trustworthy /ˈtrʌstwɜːði/ 34
try 55
try on 47
tsar /sɑː/ /tsɑː/ 16
T-shirt 47
tub /tʌb/ 66
tube /tʃuːb/ 7, 30, 66
tulip /ˈtʃuːlɪp/ 16
tumble dryer 36
tummytuck /ˈtʌmɪtʌk/ 99
tundra /ˈtʌndrə/ 16
tungsten /ˈtʌŋstən/ 16
turbulent /ˈtɜːbjələnt/ 44
Turkish 31
turn, *expressions with* 35, 91
turn-out 14
turning point 80
turnip 43
turnout 91
turnover 14
tusk 46
tutor /ˈtʃuːtə/ 39
TV (set) 50, 53, 98
tweed /twiːd/ 15
tweezers /ˈtwiːzəz/ 27
twig /twɪg/ 46
twinkle /ˈtwɪŋkəl/ 61